# ACHIEVING REGULATORY EXCELLENCE

# ACHIEVING
# **REGULATORY**
# EXCELLENCE

CARY COGLIANESE

EDITOR

*3/17*

*Katie —*
*Your talent and dedication have*
*contributed greatly to Reg Blog's success.*
*With many thanks and all best wishes!*

BROOKINGS INSTITUTION PRESS
*Washington, D.C.*

*Library of Congress Cataloging-in-Publication data*

Names: Coglianese, Cary, editor.
Title: Achieving regulatory excellence / Cary Coglianese, editor.
Description: Washington, D.C. : Brookings Institution Press, [2017] | Includes index.
Identifiers: LCCN 2016030034 (print) | LCCN 2016042988 (ebook) | ISBN 9780815728429 (cloth : alk. paper) | ISBN 9780815728436 (epub) | ISBN 9780815728443 (pdf)
Subjects: LCSH: Delegated legislation. | Administrative procedure.
Classification: LCC K3178 .A24 2017 (print) | LCC K3178 (ebook) | DDC 348/.025—dc23
LC record available at https://lccn.loc.gov/2016030034

9 8 7 6 5 4 3 2 1

Typeset in Baskerville

Composition by Westchester Publishing Services

To Orville G. Cope III
(1932–2016)

# Contents

# Foreword

**THROUGHOUT MOST OF MY** tenure in public service, I had been of the view that the primary role for regulatory activity is to serve a protective function. That is, regulators are to invoke the authority of the state to compel people and businesses to align their behavior with broader public interest considerations and manage societal risk. This conventional idea, that regulators assume a risk management role in society, continues to prevail, and it deservedly plays an important role and holds credence among the general public.

As I embarked on my journey as the CEO and president of one of the largest subnational energy regulators—the Alberta Energy Regulator (AER)—my team and I realized that regulation has a broader societal purpose. At its core, regulation is a human phenomenon. For this reason, regulators should not confine themselves merely to advancing their statutory objectives. We hold a moral and ethical obligation to initiate bold and courageous action to improve the human condition. John Braithwaite eloquently points out in chapter 2 of this book that excellent regulators incessantly probe for "strategic macro-opportunities to create public value, potentially by transforming an entire industry, even an entire economy." In other words, he continues, "risk management goes to the basics of regulation; seizing opportunities for transformation goes to the heart of regulatory excellence."

Braithwaite's words bear considerable weight at a timely moment in our evolution as an energy regulator in Alberta. As the international community commits to redefining a sustainable energy future in a carbon-constrained world, energy regulators like the AER are primed to play a critical role on this transformational journey. The level of vision, innovation, collaboration, and expertise required to meet such an ambitious goal will require energy regulators to elevate their organizational capabilities to a new level of strategic and operational excellence.

In my interactions with regulatory peers in Canada and abroad, I have observed that most regulators are confronted with similar twenty-first-century challenges that impede transformative change. First, most must navigate through "diffuse power structures" nested in complex policy systems to advance their strategic objectives. Building networks of trusted relationships with stakeholders, government ministries, and indigenous groups is an essential condition for regulators everywhere to leverage the diverse influence and knowledge required to sustain transformational momentum.

Second, regulators face mounting pressure from the private sector to be more agile and responsive to changes in technological and market conditions, and to simplify cumbersome regulatory procedures that impose unnecessary costs and impede innovation. Regulators have a tendency to respond to this pressure by taking a gradualist approach to reform that focuses on discrete, process-oriented problems that yield incremental changes, rather than pursuing transformative agendas that yield substantive and enduring societal benefits.

Third, regulators must respond to the tragic human and environmental consequences resulting from catastrophic failures. As Cary Coglianese has pointed out in another of his books, *Regulatory Breakdown*, major accidents and other calamitous events have the tendency to cast "grave doubts" over entire regulatory systems, leading to public outrage and the erosion of public confidence. In turn, regulators fall prey to the political fallout that typically ensues after such catastrophic events, ultimately reversing the momentum needed for positive transformational change.

Fourth, even in the absence of catastrophic failures, regulators contend with a growing, systemic trend of eroding public satisfaction with government—and with an increasing skepticism about the regulator's ability to avoid capture from corporate interests and to make unbiased decisions that are in the public interest. Citizens have grown increasingly cynical about the role and efficacy of governmental institutions and their ability to influence corporate behavior in positive ways. Furthermore, rapid advancements in social media and access to information expand the arena for emotionally charged policy discourse framed by hardened positions on either side of the ideological divide. Consequently, regulators need to devote a growing share of finite organizational resources to expanding their stakeholder engagement and communication efforts in response to increasing demands for greater democratic legitimacy and inclusiveness. Compounding these challenges is the fact that regulators often operate in some degree of isolation from the political organs of government to maintain their independence and impartial role as arbiters of competing societal interests. This sense of *isolation* results in a relative paucity of trusted peers that regulators can rely on to offer timely and unbiased advice.

Despite the best intentions of regulators to address these challenges, they persist and continue to confound even the most sophisticated regulatory agencies. Early on in my time at the AER, it became abundantly clear that we needed to place more emphasis on creating an ethos and culture of regulatory excellence that placed regulators in a favorable position to overcome the contemporary challenges of the twenty-first century. We were convinced that the AER needed to embark on this journey with the support and contribution of Alberta's stakeholder community and indigenous peoples. A cross-representation of societal values and interests was critical to producing a framework for action that would gain universal credibility and public consent. Furthermore, we recognized the importance of coalescing regulatory practitioners, environmental organizations, academics, and others to create a framework to guide the AER that would be both operationally practical and applicable to a broad suite of regulatory domains.

We were fortunate to retain the services of Cary Coglianese and his team from the Penn Program on Regulation as an independent, third-party convener. Professor Coglianese's team exceeded our expectations by capturing the spirit of regulatory excellence and seizing the opportunity, as Coglianese puts it in chapter 1 of this book, to "articulate bigger visions" by exploring ways to "innovate thinking about regulation" that go well beyond established frameworks.

The insightful chapters that fill this book are a reflection of not only our own journey at the AER to build a framework for regulatory excellence, but also a journey that many regulators around the world are pursuing as well. At a foundational level, the work assembled in this book exemplifies the best thinking in the world about regulation, and it tests the boundaries of what regulation is and what it can be. What we have learned from our overall work on the project with the Penn Program on Regulation is that the core attributes of regulatory excellence—empathic engagement, utmost integrity, and stellar competence—are the *means* to place regulators on a path toward building their capabilities, strengthening their resiliency, and improving their performance in order to overcome the challenges that too often deter them from achieving their full potential.

The central theme running through the chapters in this book—its core strategy for achieving regulatory excellence—is relatively simple to understand, however challenging it might be at times to implement in practice. Put simply, regulators need to

1. relentlessly focus on delivering publicly valuable outcomes that resonate with society's interests;

2. devise and execute actions to deliver those outcomes;

3. cultivate and embed a culture of excellence in the character of the regulator;

4. build and maintain public trust and relationships that give regulators the credibility to operate confidently with poise and stature;

5. measure, evaluate, and report on progress and adjust as necessary;

6. celebrate successes and yet equally confront failures with humility, honesty, and a resolute commitment to improve;

7. treat integrity as an inviolable and sacred principle; and

8. create avenues to engage empathically with all affected stakeholders in ways that complement statutory rights and procedures.

Over the past few decades, considerable attention has been placed on improving the quality of regulation and the performance of regulators around the world. The desire to move toward regulatory reform and performance improvement has been enshrined in national and global initiatives such as Canada's "smart regulation" movement and the Organization of Economic Cooperation and Development's principles for "quality regulation." The ideas about regulatory excellence that flow from the chapters of this book thus add richly to a growing body of knowledge on regulatory policy. But more significantly, the ideas from the global group of contributors to this volume combine with the work conducted in Alberta during 2015 by Professor Coglianese and the Penn Program on Regulation to produce a framework for regulatory excellence that contains a unique quality: it reflects the values and preferences of citizens, businesses, and indigenous groups that live, work, play, and invest within a major energy-producing jurisdiction. For this reason, the framework that has emerged from the larger project, of which this book is just a part, at its core embodies a deeply human story—the instinctive desire for people to collectively accomplish great things.

All of us desire to leave a positive legacy in the world in which we live. Regulators want this too. As Jim Collins points out in his book *Good to Great and the Social Sectors*, "A great organization is one that delivers superior performance and makes a distinctive impact over a long period of time." I am confident that by living out the ideas reflected in this book regulatory leaders will be well positioned to build "great organizations" that have the potential to create transformative and exceptionally positive impacts for citizens, communities, and entire economic sectors.

At the AER, our journey in the larger process of which this book is a part has become a permanent chapter in our institutional history. But we are looking forward, too. Formulating a strategy that embodies the core attributes of regulatory excellence is all about *building the future*. One of the most immediate and exciting ways the AER is moving forward is by creating the International Center of Regulatory Excellence (ICORE) to help us and others shape the future of global energy regulation by building our capabilities, strengthening our competencies, and improving our performance. In doing so, we will seize the opportunity to use the lessons we have learned, not for the narrow pursuit of excellence for its own sake but for the collective purpose of improving the human condition.

> *Jim Ellis*
> PRESIDENT AND CHIEF EXECUTIVE OFFICER
> ALBERTA ENERGY REGULATOR
> CALGARY, ALBERTA

# 1

# The Challenge of Regulatory Excellence

## CARY COGLIANESE

**IN HIS BESTSELLING BOOK, *BETTER*,** physician Atul Gawande explains why medical professionals must strive to achieve excellence: quite simply, he says, because "lives are on the line." Gawande also notes that doctors "face daunting expectations" in situations where the appropriate "steps are often uncertain" and with technical knowledge both "vast and incomplete." Doctors are nevertheless "expected to act with swiftness and consistency" and to "work humanely, with gentleness and concern."[1]

Gawande could just as well have been writing about regulators. Few government professionals today work as vitally as regulators do on the front lines of human welfare. Around the world, regulators are playing key roles in high-stakes efforts to protect their societies from widespread harms associated with economic activity and technological change, all while simultaneously promoting, or at least not unduly impeding, economic growth and development. Not only do regulators work with many lives very much on the line, but they also face daunting societal expectations, with vast and uncertain challenges that call for swift, consistent action as well as humane, empathic interaction with the public and the businesses they oversee. They are confronted as well with the need to integrate and achieve multiple objectives in a manner consistent with democratic principles and the best available scientific knowledge.

Excellence has long been a human aspiration, in every field of endeavor. Ancient Greek philosophers called it *arête*: "virtue" or, in what is thought the better translation, "excellence."[2] For the ancient Greeks, excellence was the key to human fulfillment, a vital aspiration for citizens and rulers alike. Today, *arête* has assumed a much different and narrower meaning, as mountaineers now use this term to refer to the knife's edge of a mountain ridge. Yet that meaning actually captures well the challenge regulators face in striving to achieve excellence. Like the mountain climber traversing an *arête*, the regulator seeking excellence also has to navigate carefully along a narrow path, facing criticism for regulating both too harshly and too laxly, where one false step could produce serious adverse consequences.

Regulators working in all domains of economic and social policy continue to confront long-standing problems, such as controlling monopolistic pricing, reducing threats to public health, avoiding environmental damage, and preventing financial calamities. They now face new regulatory demands too, whether in response to rapidly changing and ever more complex financial instruments, the emergence of the sharing economy, or the potential hazards of synthetic biology and other innovations. In the face of both new and old risks associated with different forms of economic activity, regulators must routinely make difficult judgment calls in the face of the conflicting demands that society places on them. Society wants the benefits of risky economic activity, but not the costs. In addition, with the rise of social media and expanding access to information on the Internet, the social and political climate within which regulators conduct their work has changed, sometimes dramatically. While most regulatory officials previously labored outside the public glare, many such officials today, in offices that no one had previously heard of, find themselves embroiled in highly visible policy conflicts—or at least they know that they are being watched more closely by a demanding public as well as by industry, nongovernmental organizations, legislators, and courts.

Confronted with public pressures and competing demands, regulatory officials need a lodestar for defining high-quality regulatory performance, and they need sound guidance about how to improve their organizations' performance. They need to know in what direction to aim and how to determine whether they are making progress. These needs motivate this book. Its contributors are internationally renowned scholars working in the fields of management, law, economics, criminology, sociology, political science, and risk analysis. They have been asked to place themselves in the shoes of the leaders of regulatory organizations and to explicate what it would entail for those organizations to achieve excellence, or at least to be the best regulators they can be. In other words, *what makes a regulator excellent?*

The open-ended nature of this question has presented each contributor with a significant intellectual challenge.[3] Scholars and policy analysts normally ask well-defined, incremental questions, gradually gaining analytical precision, and building slow but steady momentum in advancing knowledge. This approach is both a laudable and a valuable feature of the scientific and policy analytic enterprise. But scholars and practitioners also benefit from creative reflection and efforts to articulate bigger visions.[4] This book takes the latter approach and seeks to expand, synthesize, and innovate thinking about regulation, with the aim of giving its readers—government officials, practitioners, scholars, and informed citizens—much-needed insight about what it means (and what it takes) for a regulator to excel.

The intellectual challenge the contributors confront in this volume is more than theoretical. The ideas they develop hold vital practical significance. Thoughtful, in-depth consideration of regulatory excellence is long overdue and will likely continue to be needed for decades to come. This book clarifies what regulatory excellence means, and it offers general guidance for those regulators who undertake the climb toward its summit. In today's complex, globalizing economy, we should hope that regulators everywhere will join in such a journey.

## WHAT REGULATORS DO

A "regulator" can refer to an individual employee or official, such as an individual inspector or the head of a regulatory body. But "regulator" can also refer to public or governmental *institutions.* This book focuses on regulators as public institutions established to solve problems by implementing and enforcing laws or policies, among other tactics, in order to steer the behavior of individuals and organizations. Examples of regulatory institutions abound in all countries, at both the national and subnational level of governments: the Alberta Energy Regulator, the Australian Competition and Consumer Commission, the Autorité des Marchés Financiers (or the French Financial Markets Authority), the U.K. Civil Aviation Authority, and the U.S. Food and Drug Administration, to name just a few.

The ways that these regulators seek to solve problems vary, but by definition they tend to involve the application or enforcement of *regulation.* A regulation is typically understood as a *rule* backed up by *consequences.*[5] To implement a regulation, regulators often issue permits or approvals upon an applicant's demonstration that the criteria specified in the applicable rules have been satisfied. For example, the U.S. Food and Drug Administration approves new drugs upon finding them to be safe and effective. Regulators also inspect and monitor the behavior of the individuals and entities subject to governmental rules, and they check to ensure that the outputs of that private behavior comply with the rules. The U.K. Drinking Water Inspectorate, for instance, both monitors drinking water quality in England and Wales and inspects water suppliers for compliance with mandated protocols. When regulators find that rules have not been followed, they may take a variety of actions to respond, from affirmatively helping the noncompliant entities come into compliance to punitively taking enforcement actions and imposing fines.

But regulators are not only rule appliers and rule enforcers. They also take a variety of other actions—from educating to subsidizing to adjudicating disputes, all in an effort to solve the problems they have a responsibility to address. The U.S. Environmental Protection Agency, for example, devotes considerable effort to public education and has created dozens of voluntary programs designed to encourage businesses to improve their environmental performance in ways that go beyond mere compliance with regulations. In addition, regulators gather information and produce research. They engage with different segments of the public, interacting not only with the regulated industry and other government officials but also with a myriad of individuals and organizations interested in or affected by the work they do.

Through their many different types of actions, regulators seek to respond to immense societal challenges. The specific problems any regulatory institution aims to solve will depend on the mandate it has been given by political leaders, with different regulators tasked with solving different types of problems. That is why there are different fields of regulation and different regulatory institutions associated with virtually every sphere of the economy: aviation safety regulation, banking regulation, consumer product regulation, drug regulation, environmental and energy regulation, food safety regulation, and so forth.

Although regulatory problems come in many varieties associated with nearly every part of life, the major justifications for regulation are classically grouped into three categories that fall under the concept of *market failure* and its three main types:[6]

- *Concentrated power.* Markets fail either when competition does not exist or when it breaks down. If left unchecked, monopolies can generate higher prices or reductions in service and access. Regulators that protect competition by combating price fixing and market dominance, or that regulate prices and services of natural monopolies like public utilities, are often referred to as "economic regulators." Institutions that regulate the prices of water, electricity, and natural gas are often justified as a response to the problem of concentrated market power.

- *Externalities.* Markets work best when the prices of goods and services reflect their full costs and benefits. But some market activities have spillovers; that is, their costs (or benefits) are borne (or enjoyed) by third parties who are not involved in transactions for the relevant goods or services. Environmental pollution is a classic example of a negative externality, as the costs of pollution are imposed on community members who are not compensated by market transactions with the entity creating the pollution. If negative externalities are left unaddressed, the goods and services associated with the externalities will be overproduced; firms will invest too little in methods for reducing those externalities.

- *Information asymmetries.* Markets also depend on the parties to economic transactions having full information about what they are contracting over. But in many situations, one party to an economic transaction lacks access to relevant information. A patient who buys medication, for example, seldom knows as much as a pharmaceutical company does about the medication's effectiveness and its side effects. Some regulators mandate disclosure to close the information gap.

Regulators also address many other kinds of problems, even if those problems do not fit neatly within the three types of market failure. For example, regulatory scholars increasingly call attention to cognitive biases that prevent people from behaving in ways that serve their best interests, which may justify certain kinds of regulatory interventions.[7] In addition, regulators have been set up to protect civil rights, promote equity, and combat discrimination—all ways of advancing values selected by democratic legislatures but that are less easily justified by an appeal to the concept of market failure. Often a regulatory institution will be charged with solving a combination of several different types of problems at once.

Different regulators tackle different problems and oversee different industries, and their place in a system of government, such as their degree of separation from the legislature can also differ.[8] Some are headed by a single director, while others are headed by a multimember body. Some rely on funding from the legislature through normal governmental appropriations, while others are funded through fees collected from industry. Most regulators can set their own standards, norms, and directives to fill in gaps or provide clarity to laws created by legislatures or other policymaking bodies, but the nature and degree of regulators' rulemaking authority can vary from one regulatory domain to the next.

Variation in the design of regulatory institutions and in the problems they are charged with addressing means that no single, simple formula for success can apply across the board to all regulators. Indeed, even in the same jurisdiction and policy domain, regulators frequently confront a need to balance or choose among multiple or competing objectives, making any simple recipe for success elusive. And yet, despite regulators' varied mandates and institutional structures, regulators around the world still share some features that make it reasonable to think of them collectively and to consider their shared challenge of achieving excellence.

## COMMON FEATURES OF REGULATORS

Across the world's democracies, regulators share at least four commonalities: (1) a delegated mission; (2) tremendous discretion combined with public accountability for the use of that discretion; (3) complex, dynamic problems; and (4) a typically diverse set of regulated firms with interests at odds (at least to some degree) with those of the regulator. These four common features offer important implications for achieving regulatory excellence.

Mission. No matter what industries or types of problems regulators address, regulators everywhere must solve problems in a way that delivers public value, such as by solving market failures. Each regulator's mission will be defined largely by its legislative mandate. In pursuing this mandate, the regulator has an overarching responsibility to act in ways compatible with the overall good of society.

Discretion with Accountability. All regulators possess discretion. The day-to-day responsibility of implementing and enforcing laws brings with it a degree of discretion over the regulator's priorities, including what aspects of a problem to focus on or what rule violations to target or overlook. In democracies, regulators are also accountable for how they use their discretion. Accountability runs through to other governmental authorities, including the legislature, as well as to the regulated industry, rights holders, community interests, and ultimately the broader public.

Complex, Dynamic Problems. Regulators tend to face some of the most difficult challenges in society—ones that often present value tradeoffs. These problems frequently involve complex technological operations, social interactions, and new technologies—the very sorts of problems about which there exists a great deal of uncertainty. Accident avoidance, for example, is a common regulatory objective, but the sources of accidents can be both legion and interactive, making it difficult to foresee every pathway that might lead to accidents in systems with highly complex interactions of many moving parts. Regulatory problems are almost by definition problems that markets cannot solve. They also are often the problems that legislatures cannot solve either, whether for lack of expertise or lack of will. After all, if legislatures could solve all problems on their own, societies would not need regulators. Sometimes the only way legislatures can act is to build political coalitions based on broad or even unrealistic principles, such as principles that combine mutually contradictory or at least competing objectives into a single but ambiguous regulatory "mission."[9] When this happens, legislators are in effect telling regulators to surf the crest of a treacherous wave, but then leaving it up to the regulator to figure out how to stand up on the surfboard and do all the balancing and adjusting needed to stay afloat.

**Regulated Entities.** Success for regulators—unlike success in many other fields of endeavor, such as eminence in the arts or sciences—depends to a large extent on the choices and actions of others, namely, regulated entities. Those regulated entities, usually businesses, have at least five important characteristics that affect the work of the regulator. First, regulated entities can be highly diverse, comprising both individuals and organizations. The U.S. Securities and Exchange Commission, for example, regulates both individual stock brokers and large multinational corporations that issue stock. Second, many regulated businesses are themselves large complex organizations that often use advanced technologies as part of their industrial operations (such as nuclear reactors, to pick one example). The regulator is, in an important sense, a "metamanager" of regulated organizations: managing their managers. Third, many regulated firms operate in a competitive market environment and, as a result, are constantly innovating with new technologies, operations, and products. This dynamism presents challenges for regulatory overseers, who must strive to remain current. Fourth, regulated firms are themselves institutions that produce social value. Regulated businesses are employers in their communities and produce valued goods and services that make life possible and worthwhile. Although their private interests are not always fully aligned with the public interest—hence market failures—regulated firms' conduct is seldom banned outright, unlike criminal behavior, which is enforced by police officers. Normal business activities, whether automobile manufacturing, electricity transmission, or air transportation services, are *regulated*, not treated as something like narcotics trafficking, which is banned altogether. Finally, regulated firms are made up of thinking, strategic managers. The world-class violinist does not have to worry about her violin actively moving its strings to avoid her fingers or the bow. Regulatory enforcement officials, in contrast, find themselves engaged in a dynamic, strategic interaction with those upon whom their success depends. The imperfect alignment of regulated firms' private interests with the regulator's and public's interests gives firms reason to act strategically, complying with the letter but not the spirit of the law—or even trying to evade detection altogether.

The combination of the four common features of regulators makes the attainment of regulatory excellence different from, and often much more difficult than, excellence in other domains. To an extent greater than most other professions or endeavors, a regulator's performance is ultimately affected by those who reside outside the regulatory institution itself. It is dependent on a diverse and dynamic collection of other individuals and entities: not just regulated entities, but also legislatures and elected officials, regulatory beneficiaries and their representatives, advocacy groups, and other interested segments of the public.[10] These diverse actors will seldom share the same goals, and minority opinions and groups will exist that merit consideration. The dependence of the regulator on these other actors should be plain to see, as the political metrics of any specific regulator's success will depend on those other actors' goals (however conflicting they may be), while its attainment of success against those metrics will crucially depend on choices made by those within the regulated industry. The entities within that industry will themselves often vary greatly in size and capacity (large vs. small, firms vs. individuals) as well as in their willingness to cooperate (responsible compliers vs. recalcitrant laggards).[11]

Furthermore, regulators must often operate under changing conditions. Regulated firms are not static; in a competitive business environment they face constant pressure to innovate. Scientific knowledge changes with time, with a full understanding of a new technology's risks often lagging well behind technological change itself. Disruptive technologies emerge that upset well-established and well-understood economic patterns. For example, once wide-spread distributed energy production becomes possible with advances in solar and battery technology, the role for electric utility regulators will be dramatically altered. Public preferences can also shift over time, as can electoral and legislative coalitions, even if laws themselves are not amended.

All of these factors—dependency, diversity, and dynamism—combine to make excellence for regulators very different from excellence in other professional domains. They do not make regulatory excellence unattainable, but they do make the task of regulation daunting and can make it hard sometimes even to know when excellence has been achieved.

### HOW REGULATORS ARE LIKE PARENTS

It may help to see that a regulator's challenge is not unlike that of a parent's. This similarity exists for many of the reasons just discussed, entirely separate from any debate over paternalism and the proper role of the state in limiting individual liberty. I raise the analogy here not to enter such a policy debate but to point out that, in whatever sphere within which regulators operate, their success, like that of parents, is in an irreducible sense out of their hands. For each, success is *dependent* on others. Even parents who are by all accounts excellent (caring, nurturing, and wise) can have a child who turns out to be self-centered, rude, needy, or indolent. Likewise, examples abound of highly successful, self-actualizing individuals who had parents who were, if not abusive, at least neglectful and decidedly subpar.

In addition, as parents with more than one child can attest, different children—even twins—have different personalities and different needs. They are *diverse*. The best way to guide one child's growth may not work as well for another child, even within the same family. Although fairness may require a degree of horizontal equity, parenting still requires recognizing children's differences and showing a willingness to adjust to meet each child's needs. Obviously children are *dynamic* too, in that they change as they grow. How a parent treats a three-year-old will not be the best way to treat that same child at the age of ten, twenty, or thirty.

Regulators and parents have another thing in common: they only partially determine outcomes. In other words, as important as they can be in shaping behavior, whether of regulated firms or children, respectively, each is not the only important force affecting behavior. Children's behavior, and their ultimate success in life, will be shaped by more than just their parents. Nature (genetic predispositions or other ingrained qualities, such as personality) and environmental influences (teachers, peers, and the larger culture) matter. Similarly, much more than just the regulator's behavior influences the behavior of regulated individuals and organizations. Regulated firms have their own version of "nature"—their organizational culture and other internal factors.[12] They also respond to a variety of external factors in addition to regulation, including customer and community pressures. It is sometimes said that a regulated firm operates under more than just a regulatory license; it must comply with an economic license and a social license too.[13]

Recognizing the myriad nonregulatory factors that affect outcomes for a regulator leads to two implications for regulatory excellence. First, to be successful, regulators will often need to adapt their strategies to account for differences in these other economic and social factors. Regulators will likely need to vary their levels of inspections, for example, during different stages of the economic cycle, perhaps inspecting more frequently during times of economic distress. On the other hand, regulators may need to inspect less frequently those firms that are located in denser social networks where others—proxy "inspectors," such as unions, business competitors, or community groups—are keeping watch.[14]

Second, even when they take economic and social factors into account, regulators and those who evaluate them should recognize that they will not always be able to control completely regulated firms' behavior or its resulting outcomes. Internal, economic, and social factors will always matter, and to the extent that they overwhelm or counteract factors under the control of the regulator, even the best regulators will not be able to prevent all problematic behavior or eliminate all undesirable outcomes.

In the end, regulatory excellence is not the same as perfection. Even though managers of excellent regulatory organizations will undoubtedly seek perfection, the reality is that even within the best organizations mistakes sometimes happen, some of which might be tragic and catastrophic. No regulator can guarantee that, among the many employees and managers within the firms in a regulated industry, no one will ever make a mistake. Nor can regulators guarantee that no one on their own staffs will make mistakes. And they should not claim to. After all, sometimes mistakes provide valuable opportunities for knowledge generation.

Regulating is itself a risky business, with risks from acting as well as risks from not acting. A regulatory organization with an extreme culture oriented around the avoidance of all mistakes would mistakenly delay acting at all. Too much risk aversion on the part of a regulator will be no more conducive to regulatory excellence than too much risk taking.

### THREE FACES OF REGULATORY EXCELLENCE

In considering what makes a regulator excellent, different contributors to this volume view a regulatory organization from three vantage points, focusing at different times on its organizational *traits*, its *actions*, and the *outcomes* it achieves. In this respect, the contributors are not unlike other analysts and professionals who work for or interact with regulators. The three perspectives on a regulatory organization constitute three faces of regulatory excellence. Each is vital. Indeed, Adam Finkel argues in chapter 11 that regulatory excellence requires an alignment of all three faces so that they reinforce each other.[15] Keeping the three faces of regulatory excellence in mind will help in understanding the various visions and prescriptions found throughout the chapters in this book.

When excellence is conceived in terms of the *traits* of a regulator, the focus is not on specific actions or outcomes but rather on a general "state" of the regulator—a standing set of tendencies, values, and resources on which the organization has to draw or a posture that it generally holds in conducting its day-to-day operations and affecting outcomes in the world. Adjectives such as "strong," "well funded," "adequately staffed," "credible," "honest," and "legitimate" can be used to describe the regulator's traits as an organization.

Another way to think of excellence lies in the type of *actions* a regulator takes, whether in issuing rules, inspecting facilities, prosecuting violators, or undertaking other day-to-day work. Adjectives sometimes used to describe a regulator's actions include "vigilant," "serious," "reasonable," "evidence-based," and so forth. Excellent actions may also be described in terms of specific types of best practices—for example, "an excellent regulator targets the worst risks," "an excellent regulator uses flexible regulatory instruments," "an excellent regulator adopts a problem-solving rather than a punitive approach to enforcement," and so forth.

Ultimately, the traits of a regulator, as well as its actions, should lead to publicly valued *outcomes*, such as reduced safety risks or improved market efficiencies. After all, that is what makes people want to define excellence in terms of certain traits and actions, because they think those traits and actions are connected to excellent outcomes. A regulator possessing the trait of strength, for example, is thought to be more likely to achieve protective outcomes. A regulator who acts by using flexible regulatory instruments is expected to achieve more cost-effective or efficient outcomes.[16]

Desirable regulatory outcomes often define regulatory success. Sometimes these outcomes are substantive ones, which can be characterized by criteria such as *effectiveness* (solving a problem or achieving a desired outcome), *cost-effectiveness* (achieving a specific level of a desired outcome—namely, a reduction in the problem—at a low cost), *efficiency* (balancing problem reduction with other concerns, such as costs, so as to achieve an optimal level of reduction in the problem), and *equity* (resulting in a fair distribution of the costs and benefits of regulatory action, either across segments of society or over time). In addition, process-oriented outcomes often matter too, such as *legitimacy*, *credibility*, and *trustworthiness*. Some of these process-oriented adjectives are the same as ones used to describe general traits of a regulatory organization, but they can also describe the outcomes of specific processes. For example, an evaluator might ask whether a regulator's public hearings leave members of the public feeling that they were listened to and respected, and hence that the process resulted in a sense of legitimacy held by those affected.

Traits, actions, and outcomes all have a close bearing on each other. Traits can help reinforce certain kinds of actions, while consistency in actions over time can help determine traits. Both traits and actions, in turn, should affect outcomes. Given how all three faces interact, it is clear that the challenge of regulatory excellence is multifaceted. To create and sustain excellence, regulatory leaders must build and maintain an organization that fosters the kinds of regulatory and operational actions that lead consistently to superior performance. This means that a regulator's leaders must give at least as much attention to how they manage their organizations as to what kinds of regulatory policies they adopt and what types of enforcement strategies they follow. These leaders must work to define a clear mission to their organizations, ensure that they possess adequate financial and human resources, and maintain a culture that values the public interest over expediency or the primary advancement of industry's interests.

When it comes to their actions, regulators must proceed intelligently and follow, whenever possible, evidence-based practices. Among the important actions an excellent regulator takes are smart priority setting, sound problem solving, and empathic public engagement. Some actions will expressly aim at

achieving *substantive* outcomes by changing the behavior of regulated entities. These actions will involve the design of regulatory instruments, choosing
appropriately from among traditional "command-and-control" approaches
as well as more flexible forms of performance-, market-, management-, or
information-based approaches. They will also include decisions about how to
target enforcement resources, how to conduct inspections or other oversight,
and what types of consequences (penalties or rewards) to deploy for the desired compliance or deterrence objectives.

Other actions will expressly aim at procedural or process outcomes. Given
how much a regulator's success is dependent on others, the ways that a regulator interacts with industry, with concerned members of the public, and with
other governmental entities will prove instrumental to its attainment of excellence. All things being equal, the more opportunities for engagement the
better, and earlier opportunities will almost always be better than later ones.
Those who are interested in regulatory decisions should have opportunities
both to learn about what the regulator is planning to do and to provide
input. The regulator should not just "talk at" the public, but should strive to
listen carefully to all those who have information and perspectives to contribute, without bias toward one set of interests over another. Listening, of
course, is not the same as agreeing. Every interest group should not (and probably cannot) be made equally satisfied with a regulatory decision. But regulators should still be respectful and empathic to all, especially to those adversely
affected by its decisions. In particular, regulators should provide the public
with clear, transparent reasons for their decisions.

## REGULATORY EXCELLENCE AS "PEOPLE EXCELLENCE"

Regulation is widely associated with technical expertise. After all, the issues
regulators confront are highly complex and demand in-depth knowledge of
science, engineering, technology, economics, and more. To achieve excellence,
regulators must obtain detailed mastery of the technical aspects of their work
and the operations of the industries they oversee. Even if they cannot match
industry entirely in technical research and development, they must ensure they
have the in-house capability to assess the actions and associated risks of industry operations sufficiently to be able to oversee the industry.

Yet as vital as it is for a regulator to possess adequate technical skill and
knowledge, such expertise is only one necessary component of regulatory excellence. By itself, it is not sufficient. To move from good regulation to excellent regulation, the regulator also needs to master the people side of regulation.[17]
Regulation, at its core, is relational. It is motivational. It is fundamentally about

affecting people's behavior. The regulator is seldom *directly* fixing problems; rather, it is working with and through members of the public to identify problems that need to be prevented or redressed, and then working with and through the people in the businesses it regulates to shape, steer, and change their behavior and to motivate them to prevent and redress problems. Moreover, the problems regulators seek to redress are ones that affect other people, outside of the industry, who take great interest in the work of the regulator, who want to know what it is doing about those problems, and who want to have a voice in the regulatory process. The regulator also undertakes its work in a setting that involves other people interested in that work who serve in other governmental institutions, whether as elected or appointed officials, judges, or auditors. The regulator, finally, is itself an organization filled with people who need to be managed, motivated, and led effectively because what each employee does reflects on the regulator and affects its performance.

It should be apparent by now that regulators seeking to achieve regulatory excellence need to focus on "people excellence." In part that means, of course, that the people serving in regulatory organizations need to be technically knowledgeable and highly competent. But these organizations also need to possess and sustain an internal culture that fosters and reinforces humility, openness, empathy, and a steadfast commitment to public service on the part of all the people who serve in the regulator's name—and who serve on behalf of the public to which the regulator is accountable. Only if the people working in a regulatory authority are committed to doing their utmost to deliver public value, and to learning and improving in their ability to deliver that value through respectful engagement with others, can a regulator hope to achieve true excellence.[18]

### THE TRAIL AHEAD: DEFINING, SEEKING, AND ASSESSING REGULATORY EXCELLENCE

For regulatory professionals around the world, the trail ahead will never be an easy one. This book offers inspiration and guidance for improving the practice and performance of regulation. Its purpose is to inform public officials as well as members of the public, students of regulation as well as scholars of public management. It is intended to spark reflection as well as to impart practical guidance and insight. Its lessons are, of course, necessarily general ones about leadership and management in a regulatory context; this is not a "how-to" manual covering the myriad specific techniques and concrete knowledge that regulators working in particular fields need to master. Rather, it offers meaningful but intentionally "big picture" perspectives on regulatory leadership applicable to virtually any regulatory domain anywhere in the world, as useful for those at a national banking authority as at a local zoning board. Many of the ideas presented here have already found a receptive audience among leaders in fields as varied as public education and public utility regulation.

The remaining chapters in this book are organized into three sections, each demarcating three main challenges that any regulator confronts on its path to the summit of excellence: understanding what it is that *defines* excellence for a regulator, then knowing what steps to take to *seek* excellence, and finally being able to *assess* how much progress it has made. All three of these challenges—defining, seeking, and assessing—are related to each other and cannot be separated entirely, but the emphases provided in the chapters that follow do offer the reader thoughtful expert advice about what regulatory excellence entails, how to achieve it, and how to know how well a regulator is doing. Written by authors from different disciplines, countries, and substantive specialties in regulation, these chapters offer a variety of views—many of them compatible with one another, but also some with differing emphases—concerning each of the three challenges of regulatory excellence.

In the first section, the contributors advance broad, often ambitious, visions for defining regulatory excellence. In chapter 2, John Braithwaite emphasizes the importance of excellent regulators making transformational impacts on industry and even throughout society in ways that create significant public value. He cautions against focusing too much on the quality of the rules on the books, and instead urges that excellent regulators are those who assume responsibility for and end up solving society's most important problems. In a similar spirit, Wendy Wagner argues in chapter 3 that excellent regulators follow President Theodore Roosevelt's advice to keep their "eyes on the stars" (that is, prioritize the advancement of the public interest) while also keeping their "feet on the ground" (maintaining expert, accessible, and fair decision processes). Wagner emphasizes that the best regulators meet a series of vital process benchmarks that ensure that regulatory decisionmaking exhibits robust public engagement, well-reasoned decisions, and sound information-gathering strategies. Kathryn Harrison, in chapter 4, goes further to argue that process virtues, such as procedural fairness, transparency, and honesty, are the "fundamental underpinnings" of regulatory excellence in democratic societies. For Harrison, robust and fair democratic engagement provides not the exclusive measure of regulatory excellence, but one that technical experts within regulatory authorities too often overlook at their peril. In chapter 5, John Graham and Paul Noe urge regulators to go beyond a focus on fair process and ensure that in the end they actually achieve outcomes that significantly advance the well-being and overall welfare of citizens. Graham and Noe acknowledge that procedural fairness is a necessary condition for excellent regulation, but say that getting the substance right and ultimately promoting individual well-being throughout society is what determines whether excellence has been achieved. Ted Gayer, in chapter 6, argues that the best regulators show humility and even some degree of restraint before making substantive decisions, making sure to be guided by thoughtful consideration of scientific evidence and proceeding with the recognition that ill-considered regulation can cause its own kinds of harms. He offers suggestions for regulators to improve their capacity for rigorously assessing the quality of the evidence available to them when they make their decisions. Whether those decisions involve setting standards or targeting firms for inspection, regulators must assess and manage risks, which leads Bridget Hutter, in chapter 7, to argue that excellent risk-based regulation requires, in addition to sound technical and scientific analysis, careful consideration of a wide range of social, economic, and political values related to risks. She calls attention to the widening of the regulator's decisionmaking environment in today's interconnected world. In chapter 8, Robert Baldwin uses the concept of lucidity, which he defines as a clarity of approach in delivering on the essential tasks of regulation, to argue that the excellent regulator is defined by how attuned it is to its setting, how intelligent it is in knowing what it needs to achieve, and how dynamically it responds to changes in its environment.

With these definitional insights about regulatory excellence established, the chapters in this book's second section provide guidance for how a regulator should go about seeking to achieve excellence. Drawing on practices in the business world as well as on his experience leading a regulatory agency with combined economic and social regulatory responsibilities, Daniel Esty in chapter 9 outlines key strategies for achieving regulatory excellence, including a clear vision, thorough analysis, and willingness to innovate. Shelley Metzenbaum and Gaurav Vasisht in chapter 10 distill the essential ingredients for regulatory success down to a well-defined mission, adequate funding, sound information, and thoughtful judgment in selecting tools to solve regulatory problems. In chapter 11, Adam Finkel steps back and, after reconsidering the many underlying virtues of an excellent regulator, argues that regulatory excellence depends both on an alignment in a regulator's traits, actions, and outcomes and on finding the "sweet spot" on a spectrum of virtues that compete with each other. Neil Gunningham, in chapter 12, tackles what it takes for regulators to achieve excellence in their compliance and deterrence strategies, arguing that while common wisdom has implored regulators to select a single strategy, the best regulators deploy different strategies that they combine in varying ways, depending on the context. In chapter 13, David Vogel provides a focused consideration of three case studies of successful regulation, finding that the excellent regulatory officials in these cases worked to maintain public confidence, strove for continuous learn-ing, and interacted constructively with regulated industry. David Levi-Faur builds on regulators' need for learning in chapter 14, where he proposes that regulatory excellence requires regulators to draw on diverse forms of exper-tise, including knowledge of history and political science. In chapter 15, Howard Kunreuther and I consider how another societal risk management tool—insurance—provides a model for regulation as well as opportunities for building effective public-private partnerships that can contribute to regula-tory excellence. In chapter 16, Angus Corbett wraps up the advice for regula-tors who seek excellence by arguing that successful regulators will adopt a systems orientation, using their resources to find and exploit leverage points to influence systemic change in ways that achieve public goals.

The book's final section turns to the challenge of assessing regulatory ex-cellence. The kind of learning and continuous improvement that contributors emphasize as an inherent component of regulatory excellence demands that regulators regularly and systematically take stock of their progress. It is not enough to try to achieve excellence; especially in a fast-changing world, regu-lators need continually to assess their performance and adapt as needed. Toward this end, Donald Moynihan, in chapter 17, offers regulators a set of practical but research-based performance measurement principles to use as they measure their progress along the path toward excellence. Among other things, Moynihan cautions against making too strong a connection between measures of performance and incentives for regulatory employees. In the fi-nal chapter, chapter 18, I distinguish the measurement systems needed for a regulator to become excellent from measurement systems that purport to gauge whether a regulator is excellent, arguing that systems of the former kind (measurement *for* excellence) are more important than those of the lat-ter (measurement *of* excellence). This closing chapter serves as a reminder of this book's underlying premise, namely that regulators can do better by paying more attention to learning how what they are currently doing is advancing public policy goals, hindering them, or neither. Only by under-standing better what works and what does not, and then by taking steps to adjust their practices accordingly, can regulators meet the challenge of regu-latory excellence.

## CONCLUSION

The roles that regulators perform are vital to society, but the work they do is hard work. Just regulating well is demanding and difficult. Achieving excel-lence requires more. It requires full, consistent, and superlative mastery of all the technical, analytic, and social tasks involved in the enterprise of regulating. Not only do today's regulators oversee complex technologies and business practices during the course of their work, but they also operate in complex social, economic, and political systems where their success is ultimately defined and shaped by their interactions with others, including, in the end, regulated entities. Moreover, regulators do not operate in a static environment. Regulatory excellence requires listening attentively to changing public concerns. It requires constantly learning on the job. It also requires boldness and visionary leadership. The excellent regulator cannot stay in one place, content to have mastered the past or the present. The world changes, its problems change, its science and technologies change, its economic conditions change, and ultimately its social fabric can change too. In such a world, regulatory excellence demands forward momentum. It is not a static achievement.

**NOTES**

*Acknowledgments*: For helpful comments on this chapter, I am grateful to Bill Finan and Adam Finkel and the two anonymous reviewers of the book manuscript.

1. Atul Gawande, *Better: A Surgeon's Notes on Performance* (New York: Picador, 2008), p. 4.

2. Will Durant, *The Story of Philosophy: The Lives and Opinions of the World's Greatest Philosophers* (New York: Simon and Schuster, 1991).

3. This challenge was not eliminated for those contributors who have held high-level positions in the past within government agencies (for example, Braithwaite, Esty, Finkel, Graham, Metzenbaum, Noe, and Vasisht). Regulatory practitioners are too often focused solely on the weeds, each within their individual policy silos, while "regulatory excellence" calls for at least some thinking closer to the level of the Platonic ideal.

4. On professional self-reflection, see Donald A. Schön, *The Reflective Practitioner: How Professionals Think in Action* (New York: Basic Books, 1984).

5. Cary Coglianese, *Measuring Regulatory Performance: Evaluating the Impact of Regulation and Regulatory Policy* (Paris: OECD, 2012) (www.oecd.org/gov /regulatory-policy/1_coglianese%20web.pdf). See generally Frederick Schauer, *The Force of Law* (Harvard University Press, 2015).

6. For a discussion of market failure as a justification for regulatory intervention, see W. Kip Viscusi, John M. Vernon, and Joseph E. Harrington Jr., *Economics of Regulation and Antitrust*, 4th ed. (MIT Press, 2005); Office of Management and Budget, Circular A-4: Regulatory Analysis (September 17, 2003) (www.whitehouse .gov/omb/circulars_a004_a-4/). The concept of market failure provides an analytical and policy justification for regulation; it does not necessarily provide a historical or political economy account of why a particular set of economic activities actually came to be regulated.

7. Richard H. Thaler and Cass R. Sunstein, *Nudge: Improving Decisions about Health, Wealth, and Happiness* (New York: Penguin, 2008); Alberto Alemanno and Anne-Lise Sibony, eds., *Nudge and the Law: A European Perspective* (Oxford, U.K.: Hart, 2015).

8. See, for example, Kirti Datla and Richard L. Revesz, "Deconstructing Independent Agencies (and Executive Agencies)," *Cornell Law Review* 98 (2013): 769.

9. At the limit of contradictory demands, regulatory organizations have sometimes been charged with the dual tasks of regulating an industry while also fostering its growth and profitability. Sometimes such a dual mandate is given to the same entity (such as the former U.S. Atomic Energy Commission), while at other times it falls to several offices or divisions within the same larger organization (such as the U.S. Department of Agriculture).

10. Commentators agree that a regulatory body is only one institutional entity within a larger governmental and societal system. Sanford V. Berg, *Best Practices in Regulating State-Owned and Municipal Water Utilities* (Santiago: United Nations Economic Commission for Latin America and the Caribbean, 2013), p. 12; United Nations Economic Commission for Europe, *Risk Management in Regulatory Frameworks: Towards a Better Management of Risks* (Geneva: UNECE, 2012); Ashley C. Brown and others, *Handbook for Evaluating Infrastructure Regulatory Systems* (Washington: World Bank, 2006), p. 17 (http://siteresources.worldbank.org/EXTENERGY/Resources/336805-1156971270190/HandbookForEvaluatingInfrastructureRegulation062706.pdf).

11. Eugene Bardach and Robert Kagan, *Going by the Book: The Problem of Regulatory Unreasonableness* (Temple University Press, 1982); Neil Gunningham, Robert A. Kagan, and Dorothy Thornton, *Shades of Green: Business, Regulation, and Environment* (Stanford University Press, 2003).

12. Jennifer Nash and Cary Coglianese, "Constructing the License to Operate: Internal Factors and Their Influence on Corporate Environmental Decisions," *Law & Policy* 30 (2008): 73–107 (http://ssrn.com/abstract=1085058).

13. Gunningham, Kagan, and Thornton, *Shades of Green*; Dorothy Thornton, Robert A. Kagan, and Neil Gunningham, "When Social Norms and Pressures Are Not Enough: Environmental Performance in the Trucking Industry," *Law & Society Review* 43 (2009): 405–36 (http://dx.doi.org/10.1111/j.1540-5893.2009.00377.x); Neil Gunningham, Robert A. Kagan, and Dorothy Thornton, "Social License and Environmental Protection: Why Businesses Go Beyond Compliance," *Law & Social Inquiry* 29 (2004): 307–41 (http://dx.doi.org/10.1111/j.1747-4469.2004.tb00338.x).

14. On the value of proxy inspectors, see generally Ian Ayres and John Braithwaite, *Responsive Regulation: Transcending the Deregulation Debate* (Oxford University Press, 1992).

15. A regulator can only truly be said to be responsive (a trait) if it makes major policy decisions by soliciting public input (an action) and members of the public actually believe that the regulator is trying to listen (an outcome).

16. Cary Coglianese and Lori S. Bennear, "Flexible Approaches to Environmental Regulation," in Michael Kraft and Sheldon Kamieniecki, eds., *The Oxford Handbook of U.S. Environmental Policy* (Oxford University Press, 2012).

17. Deirdre Hutton, "The Role of Stakeholder Relationships in Regulatory Excellence," *RegBlog,* July 27, 2015, www.regblog.org/2015/07/27/hutton-regulatory -excellence/.

18. On the meaning of public value and its primacy for governmental organizations, see Mark Moore, *Creating Public Value: Strategic Management in Government* (Harvard University Press, 1997); Mark Moore, *Recognizing Public Value* (Harvard University Press, 2013).

# PART I

# Defining Regulatory Excellence

# 2

## Responsive Excellence

### JOHN BRAITHWAITE

**BEING A RESPONSIVE REGULATOR** means being responsive to the regulated community and its community of stakeholders (such as consumers of a regulated product or service). More fundamentally it means being responsive to the entire environment in which the regulator swims. Contemporary debates excessively narrow that definition to responsiveness to the regulator's risk environment.[1] Risk responsiveness is important. For a regulator aspiring to achieve excellence, however, responsiveness to opportunities is more important than responsiveness to risk. The excellent regulator scans for cases that offer strategic macro-opportunities to create public value, potentially by transforming an entire industry, even an entire economy, or a crucial aspect of freedom in a society. Put another way, risk management goes to the basics of regulation; seizing opportunities for transformation goes to the heart of regulatory excellence.

### BOTTOM-OF-THE-CLASS REGULATION

Consider the U.S. Federal Bureau of Investigation (FBI). In the theoretical terms of responsive regulation, the FBI is a regulator because its mission is to steer the flow of events. Its history is decidedly not as a best-in-class regulator. One reason is that under J. Edgar Hoover it overreached in its quest to grasp opportunities for a transformative impact. It investigated the sex lives of presidents, Hollywood stars, and civil rights campaigners, for example. Why this was a regulatory overreach is clear. These were not activities that pursued the principles embodied in the FBI's legal mandate. Worse, they were activities that threatened freedom and increased domination. According to responsive regulatory theory (and republican political theory),[2] the overarching test of regulatory excellence is whether the regulator increases freedom and reduces domination in the world. Put another way, J. Edgar Hoover is the archetypal evil regulator because he sought to be transformative by abusing arbitrary power.

Fast-forward to the twenty-first century. America has an FBI so chastened by the transformative excesses of Hoover that it constrains itself within a narrow criminal law enforcement mandate rather than the pursuit of national security, which is its legal mandate. So when an FBI agent does his job by reporting that trainee pilots had asked to be taught how to fly a plane but not how to land it, his supervisors respond in terms of the narrow ethos,[3] as they did when another FBI agent warned about Osama bin Laden sending students to the United States for flight lessons.[4] Sure, these activities raised suspicions, but where was the collar? The FBI's priority was to focus on its backlog of more serious criminal files where it had good prospects of putting the criminal in prison for a long time. Or as Condoleezza Rice put it: "The FBI treated the internal terrorism problem as a law enforcement matter. . . . Prevention was secondary to punishing terrorists after they were caught committing a crime."[5]

The FBI in 2001 had its opportunity to honor its legal mandate by putting American history on a better path in the twenty-first century. The "war on terror" that ensued was causally implicated in the difficulties of managing the second major geopolitical crisis of the twenty-first century, the global financial crisis. The war on terror caused the strongest surge yet in the growth of regulatory capitalism. There was a heavy fiscal burden from building the U.S. Department of Homeland Security and other surveillance bureaucracies. For foreigners, doing business with Americans became much more painful, from big regulatory aggravations, like a visa regime in which light-touch government was equivalent to treason, to small ones, like endless shoe removal on each leg of a long journey by plane. So international travelers began to minimize trips to the United States. That was great for carbon emissions, bad for the U.S. economy. It was good for the higher education exports from the Australian university system as international students shifted their enrollments to Australian universities, but at the expense of the export of U.S. higher education services. These regulatory impacts were of course not the main challenge for the U.S. economy. The big item was the trillion-dollar U.S. military bill for the war-on-terror campaigns in Afghanistan and Iraq. This fiscal hit was smaller for European allies in Afghanistan and Iraq, but ultimately more consequential for the world economy because the subsequent debt crisis was deeper in Europe. As a result of the FBI's 9/11 regulatory failure, the U.S. economy and its tax base were ill-prepared for the next big crisis.

With the global financial crisis, as with 9/11, street-level agents again did their job. In 2004, the FBI, to its credit, reported publicly that it had detected an epidemic of home loan mortgage fraud. It could hardly fail to notice such a disturbing tsunami of little frauds. In 2006, the Federal Financial Crimes Enforcement Network (FinCEN) reported a 1,411 percent increase in mortgage-related suspicious activity between 1997 and 2005, 66 percent of which involved material misrepresentation or false documents. Then another 44 percent increase was reported between 2005 and 2006. In 2007, BasePoint Analytics analyzed 3 million loans, concluding that 70 percent of early payment defaults had fraudulent misrepresentations on their original loan applications.[6] Because they were many little frauds, FBI leaders saw them as lower priority matters than other files in their in-trays that might deliver longer prison sentences.

The FBI missed the opportunity to see the big picture created by this large pattern of little frauds. Mortgages were being sliced and diced, securitized by Wall Street, and sold off to naïve European banks, which managed to cripple their economies with the bad debts. Their naïveté is hard to fathom, but the bonus culture of traders who were false fiduciaries for shareholders may have contributed, and perhaps managers wanted to be "state of the art" but were embarrassed to confess that they did not understand the complex derivatives they were trading. Revered former Federal Reserve chair Alan Greenspan characterized his regulatory error as assuming that banks would be competent to rationally assess such risks to their solvency. Packaged bundles of petty frauds enabled financial institutions to make large profits by risk shifting in some cases through major frauds ratcheted upward by the bonus culture of Wall Street.

So the FBI missed the opportunity to save its country from its second major crisis of the twenty-first century. American banks were finding housing loan fraud attractive because derivatives crafted for them by Wall Street changed the paradigm from risk management to risk shifting to other banks, sometimes far away. Yes, there were many other, perhaps more fundamental, root causes of the global financial crisis. Most of these are still present in the world economy, however. The business of crisis prevention involves all regulatory players seizing opportunities to eliminate those they can tackle before all those risks come together in another perfect storm. From 2004, aggressive criminal enforcement action, or the threat of it, was needed against the banks that had the highest percentages of fraudulent loans. The FBI showed no criminal justice system leadership to that end.

America should want an FBI that shuns the abuse of arbitrary power but takes opportunities to transform American national security for the better within the framework of the legally encoded regulatory principles that guide its work. When it prioritizes the narrowed regulatory imagination of locking up the best collars, it fails its citizens.

## TRANSFORMING THE REGULATORY STORYBOOK

How does one go about transforming the regulatory imagination so that regulators cultivate reflective professionalism about the opportunities they should seize? How do regulators develop an over-the-horizon imagination about how to transform their regulatory environments to deliver public value in line with the principles in their enabling statutes?[7] A starting point is Clifford Shearing and Richard Ericson's insight that regulatory culture is not a rulebook but a storybook.[8] Sure, regulatory organizations have thick volumes of rules and procedures they are expected to follow. So do universities. But just as street-level academics rarely read them and do not know their content, the same is true of street-level bureaucrats like police officers and regulatory inspectors. What adept professors and police officers know are stories about how this or that kind of organizational challenge gets managed. If you want to change how a street-level bureaucracy behaves, you cannot achieve that by changing its rulebook.[9] You must change its storybook. You must change the stories inspectors swap in the lunchroom about how excellent inspection practice has made a difference.

In an FBI that had been a better custodian of a safe and economically strong America, there would be stories about how an agent in Florida stood up to his supervisors and sent the message right up the line that the trainee pilots were likely planning something that would threaten the country, and then persuaded those supervisors to take action to prevent a major terrorist triumph. The stories would tell of the agent who said that a massive new micro-pattern of street-level mortgage fraud could not make sense unless it connected up to some dangerous new macro-strategy of finance capitalists.

Regulatory cultures obsessively wedded to a procedures manual or to risk analytics kill off transformative storytelling. Responsive regulatory organizations need to honor the principles laid down in their enabling statutes; but they are not rule-bound automatons. In an ideal world, legal principles that inform a regulatory storybook will transcend unresponsive regulatory rulebooks. Regulatory excellence eschews timidity. Excellent regulators are entrepreneurial risk takers in the cause of creating public value. The regulator sees itself as having a respected role in the separation of powers. Its statute should empower it to be semi-autonomous of executive government, a credible part of a fabric of checks and balances. It checks, and it is checked by, other semi-autonomous separated powers; it balances and it is balanced. Who wants a central bank hemmed in by detailed rules about when and how it can adjust the money supply, about when and how it can seize the opportunity to encourage a well-managed bank to take over a group of teetering banks that pose a systemic risk? Who wants a nuclear regulator like the one the United States had at the time of Three Mile Island,[10] one that cultivates an industry compliance culture of rule-following automatons rather than a culture of diagnosticians who transform safety systems responsively, based on systemic wisdom about safety management systems?[11]

How do we evaluate whether a regulator is excellent in these terms? We evaluate it by the best stories of transformation the regulator can offer up. Can it recount how it saved countless lives from domination by terror or from the fallout of a nuclear meltdown? Can it tell inspiring stories of how it seized opportunities to expand the realms of freedom that citizens enjoy? If it cannot, it may be time to change the top management team, transform staff induction and in-service training, remove the constraints its procedures manuals impose, or inspire an opportunity-seizing transformative mentality by redrafting the principles in the agency's legislative mandate.

## STORIES FROM THE AUSTRALIAN STREET

The Australian Competition and Consumer Commission (ACCC) is in various ways an example of an excellent regulator. It is an agency that in U.S. terms combines the functions of the Federal Trade Commission, the Antitrust Division of the Justice Department, and the Consumer Product Safety Commission; it has also embraced some functions in domains such as telecommunications regulation, financial regulation affecting consumers, and state regulation of certain prices. This is a broader brief than that given to U.S. regulators, but of course in a much smaller economy. The ACCC (originally named the Trade Practices Commission) has had a succession of outstanding chairs, deputy chairs, and top management staff who were in the business of creating a more competitive Australian economy in which consumers were not exploited. It has had a good number of unimaginative leaders as well, and in its history has taken steps backward as well as forward.[12]

The ACCC storybook is rich. The two stories I choose here to illustrate why, on balance, the ACCC should be seen as a regulator that has achieved formidable excellence are not necessarily the most dramatic or compelling ones. They are simply stories of industry transformation that I am familiar with because I had some inside involvement.

## *The Aboriginal Insurance Scandal*

In the early 1990s, widespread frauds were detected by the ACCC (then the Trade Practices Commission) involving major insurance companies, which were systematically ripping off consumers through misrepresentations about policies that in some cases were totally useless. The worst abuses occurred in twenty-two remote Aboriginal communities, and these were tackled first. In an effort to restore the integrity of the regulatory process, top management from insurance companies visited these communities and for days on end met with the victims, the local Aboriginal Community Council, the regulators, and local officials of the Department of Social Security about the deduction of useless policy premiums from welfare checks. Some of the insurance executives went back to the city deeply ashamed of what their company had done.

Back in Canberra, meetings were held about follow-up regulatory reforms with insurance regulators and industry associations and even with the prime minister, who was shocked by the exploitation of disadvantaged consumers. The restorative dialogue led to the adoption of numerous remedies. Colonial Mutual Life (CML) voluntarily compensated two thousand policyholders and also funded an Aboriginal Consumer Education Fund to prevent future abuses. It conducted an internal investigation to discover failings in the company's compliance program and to identify the officers responsible for the crimes. A press conference was then called to publicly reveal the scope of the problem. No one recognized quite how enormous it was until a police union realized that its own members were being defrauded through the practices of another company (in this case there were 300,000 victims). This case, against the AMP insurance company, which was Australia's largest corporation at the time, led to more robust law enforcement. Police victims were outstanding witnesses who could account very precisely for the misrepresentations made to them.

After the CML self-investigation, eighty officers and agents of CML were dismissed, including some senior managers and one large corporate agent, Tri-Global. CML also put in place new internal compliance policies. The Department of Social Security changed some of its procedures relating to welfare checks and there were also regulatory and self-regulatory changes to the licensing of agents and changes to the law.[13] This problem solving was accomplished without going to court (except for a couple of individuals who refused to cooperate with the restorative justice process).

As a commissioner, I was on the wrong side of the debate on the first case. I argued initially that the conduct was so serious that formal criminal charges should be brought. What would have happened had the commission prosecuted this case criminally? At best, the company would have been fined a fraction of what it ultimately paid out, and perhaps there would have been a handful of follow-up civil claims by victims. At worst, illiterate Aboriginal witnesses who had not kept a copy of their policy would have been humiliated and discredited by uptown lawyers, the case lost, and no further cases in this sequence of insurance frauds taken. Worse still, the case might have sat in the in-tray of the director of public prosecutions. A bad feature of Australian regulatory design (unlike that of many U.S. regulatory institutions, which have their own criminal enforcement units) is that regulators settle for civil enforcement because persuading the director of public prosecutions to fight legal battles in complex corporate cases is too difficult.

The industrywide pattern of fraudulent practices might never have been uncovered had the criminal referral approach I advocated been followed. Its revelation was only accomplished by engaging many locally knowledgeable actors in a more conversational process in which Aboriginal victims and their representatives sat in a circle with the insurers' top management. From that engagement there was a dawning of disgrace among the insurers' top management for the conduct of their organizations. The CEOs' sense of shame, communicated through apologies at press conferences convened by the regulator, catalyzed a transformation in the compliance culture and the ethical culture of an important industry. More generally, while the ACCC has not been the principal financial regulator in Australia, the catalytic role it has played across the decades has helped build a culture of somewhat greater prudence in the finance sector than exists in many other countries. The culture of Australian finance continues to have deep ethical flaws, but its comparatively greater prudence has helped Australia avoid banking bailouts and bankruptcies in this century and steered the economy through the 2008–2012 period of financial crisis with no recession and the highest growth rate of developed economies.

## Passive Smoking

Robert McComas was chairman of the Trade Practices Commission (now the ACCC) from 1985 to 1987. Although many see his actions as setting back the commission, he was a distinguished legal practitioner, and his positive contribution was to tighten the legal rigor of the commission's deliberations. Before he was appointed chair, he was a director of Australia's largest tobacco company, and after his term ended he became chairman of the board of that same company. He made an error of judgment that made his minister, the attorney general, and the deputy prime minister determined not to reappoint him. This is not so much a story of his error as it is of the strengths of the regulatory culture and the regulatory community in which the commission was embedded.

McComas negotiated a remedial advertisement with the Tobacco Institute
that was a statutory breach similar to the initial advertisement complained
about by Action Against Smoking and Health, a nongovernmental organization. The initial Tobacco Institute advertisement claimed that passive
smoking was not proven to be a danger to health. The Australian Federation
of Consumer Organizations (AFCO) appealed the commission's remedial advertisement for persisting with claims about the safety of passive smoking that
were false and misleading.[14] The federal court hearing the appeal found the
advertisement that had been approved by the regulator to be in breach of its
own statute because the evidence was clear that passive smoking *was* a danger
to health. It was the first time anywhere that a court had made this finding. As
soon as it did, risk managers across the globe started to advise restaurants,
workplaces, discos, and even sports arenas to prohibit smoking for fear of passive smoking suits. Such suits commenced quickly in Australia, citing that
federal court decision, and then spread globally. Surprisingly, even in the open
air of baseball stadiums throughout North America, after new passive smoking laws were enacted, consumer self-enforcement through raised eyebrows
quickly achieved 100 percent compliance with these bans.[15] It is hard to think
of a case of responsive tripartism in Australian regulatory enforcement that
could have saved more lives. It was a case where the potency of regulated
self-regulation came from the consumer movement, but also from within the
commission itself, from staff who asserted sympathies with the consumer
movement view (which they saw as the rule-of-law view) against their chair.

Robin Brown, the young CEO of AFCO, played a courageous hand in
supporting litigation which, had it failed, would have bankrupted the consumer movement through an order to pay the tobacco industry's costs. Brown
was well networked with commission insiders.[16] At that time, the ethos of the
commission and the government was infused with a philosophy of tripartism,
which values the full engagement of public interest groups in the regulatory
process.[17] The commission was an independent statutory authority run by regulatory professionals but balanced by representatives from business and consumer backgrounds and expertise. At that time I was the only commissioner
with a background in consumer expertise and engagement by civil society, and
only part-time; there had been, and is again, more than one part-time or full-
time commissioner with a consumer background, and indeed for two decades
there was a tradition of a deputy chair with a consumer background.

Brown's view was that McComas had cut a deal for a remedial advertisement with the tobacco industry in a "smoke-filled room." (McComas was formidable as a smoker, as well as a tobacco industry crony!) Especially in light of
his background with that industry, Brown's view was that a meeting of the
Tobacco Institute with the chair to negotiate the text of a controversial remedial

advertisement should not have occurred in the absence of the consumer-oriented commissioner also in the room. That was my view as well, and I confronted the chair with the view that the matter should have gone to a meeting of the full commission. Other staff also dissented robustly to the chair. The level of angst within the commission over both these procedural concerns and the fear that the chair had approved a remedial advertisement that was in breach of his commission's own statute hit the front page of the *Canberra Times*. Public airing of this contestation of the decision delivered to Brown the confidence of his nervous board to risk AFCO's financial future on the case.

Some years following the AFCO victory in court, Brent Fisse initiated a meeting at Australian National University's University House to discuss crafting statutory provisions for enforceable undertakings that were susceptible to public checks and balances ratified or modified by a court to replace the kind of deals in "smoke-filled rooms" exemplified by the initial passive smoking decision. This meeting had been preceded by years of advocacy of the need for such provisions, both by Brent Fisse and by many ACCC insiders. So again, this was an example of the larger regulatory community being responsive as a network, even as the government of the day was unmoved to legislate for many years. Some of the best regulatory minds from the bureaucracy, the ACCC, and the academy were in attendance at the meeting at University House that day. Today, most of Australia's important regulatory agencies have incorporated into their statutes the enforceable undertaking provisions discussed at that meeting.

The journey toward more meaningful metaregulation in Australia continues to take steps backward and forward.[18] "Regulatory capture" would be the best way to characterize a great many enforceable undertakings that have been negotiated in Australia. At the same time, the enforceable undertaking laws created following the University House meeting were a creative and powerful option in the hands of the entrepreneurially excellent regulator, a "soft option" in the hands of the captured regulator, and simply a different intermediate option in the middle of the regulatory pyramid for others. Yet the strengths of Australian metaregulation are encapsulated by this story of greater engagement of the street level of regulatory bureaucracies, greater publicness, and potent third-party contestation and engagement with metaregulation than can usually be seen with U.S. prosecutors negotiating deferred prosecutions or corporate integrity agreements.

## NURTURING TRANSFORMATIVE EXCELLENCE

Through the lens of these stories of transformative responsiveness, what attributes can be discerned to distinguish the truly excellent regulator?

- Excellent regulators are those with the most impressive stories about the opportunities their staffs have seized to advance their statutory objectives.

- These stories reveal that the *risk management* orientation of the agency is complemented by an *opportunity* orientation for advancing its statutory objectives.

- The stories reveal a culture of leadership from below in seizing innovative opportunities to advance the agency's objectives.

- The stories reveal innovative networking, outside-in rather than inside-out regulatory design, to advance the regulator's statutory objectives.[19]

- Excellent regulators seize opportunities to transform ethical cultures and cultures of compliance, engaging the kind of self-enforcement that the American public executes against passive smoking in open-air sports stadiums.

How should regulators measure and improve their performance in these terms? According to the view of excellence articulated here, key performance indicators (KPIs) and risk-reduction metrics can be highly dangerous things. They have a place but must be kept in their place. In a May 2015 Australian Senate committee hearing on human rights abuses in immigration detention centers for asylum seekers who arrive in Australian waters on boats, a senator asked if it was true that women were being sexually assaulted by staff when they walked to the washroom, as had been widely alleged? The private operator of the detention center replied that he did not know whether this was the case, but what was important to say in reply was that his company had consistently met all the KPIs for the detention center set by the government! Of course there was no KPI about making it safe for women to walk to the washroom.

KPIs risk the more measurable driving out the more important. If that contractor and its regulator had had a storytelling culture, the regulatory culture they share would be abuzz with dialogue about what its biggest problems were. This would allow them to do well at Malcolm Sparrow's regulatory craft, to "pick important problems and fix them."[20] The output would be a story about how well problems were fixed and what wider learnings were applied as a result. This is Eugene Bardach and Bob Kagan's old story of the virtues of "diagnostic inspectorates."[21]

The best regulators tell the best stories about how they pick the most important problems from an ever-changing regulatory landscape, how they diagnose them, fix them, and apply wider lessons from the experience. Strategically selected single cases can acquire the profile to ripple out widely, as illustrated by an advertisement in an Australian newspaper that catalyzed bans on passive smoking in the northern hemisphere. Excellent regulators have a record of plucking twenty dollar bills from the sidewalk that others walk past. Who could have seen in 2001 the huge opportunities to make America safer and stronger by responding to suspicious flight training and minor mortgage frauds? Who could have foreseen the opportunity an Australian environmental regulator had in 2009 to respond to an oil spill caused by Halliburton's cementing of a drilling rig that spilled oil into the Timor Sea for seventy-four days? The answer is that an excellent regulator might have foreseen an opportunity that could have prevented the Deepwater Horizon spill for eighty-six days in the Gulf of Mexico a year later.[22] The transformative response that was missed would have required Halliburton, as part of the Australian regulatory settlement, to retain engineering consultants to report on what the company had done to initiate remedies for this problem on the dozens of rigs it had cemented around the world in a defective fashion. Excellence is about over-the-horizon vision and seizing such strategic opportunities.

A limitation of the transformative vision may be that it expects a regulator or an observer of regulation to foresee more than is possible. On the positive side, a regulatory decision on passive smoking in Australia made Americans attending sporting events safer; on the negative side, a regulatory response to an Australian oil spill missed an opportunity to prevent an American spill. We do, however, expect public health officials and street-level physicians to distinguish one-off treatments for patients from responses that might identify a new virus and contain its spread. In fact, it is a core competency of health professionals to improve their ability to distinguish routine one-off treatments from opportunities to prevent an urban contagion or a global epidemic. My hypothesis is that this could and should also become part of our imaginary of regulatory excellence.

In addition, the globalization of disease has moved health professionalism toward a cosmopolitan imaginary of transformation. This means health professionals in all countries are on the lookout for opportunities to transform global food and medicine in positive ways, and to disrupt global epidemics. A cosmopolitan regulatory imagination was what was lacking in Australia's response to the Timor Sea oil rig catastrophe. The regulators felt no responsibility beyond their national horizon. Both a transformative imagination and a cosmopolitan regulatory imagination are virtues regulatory communities can cultivate just as well as health professionals, although also with many false positives and false negatives in their judgments about transformation. Social movement actors—like the consumer movement and Action Against Smoking and Health in the passive smoking case—are the yeast in the dough of regulatory cosmopolitanism. Social movement actors can be critical friends of regulators who relish the role of firing the imagination in their quest for transformational opportunities.

We want environmental regulators who foster transformative technologies and collaborations to make energy renewable, regulators who transform the stewardship of a powerful industry to benefit disadvantaged consumers, regulators who transform the lives of children previously afflicted with cancer caused by passive smoking. Methodologically, excellent regulators tell transformative stories that social scientists would call causal process tracing.[23] They are stories of a sequence of regulatory dialogues, diagnoses, and networked regulatory responses that credibly account for a transformation that enhances safety, justice, and a better future for our children.

## NOTES

*Acknowledgments*: The author thanks Robin Brown, Cary Coglianese, Brent Fisse, David Levi-Faur, and Hank Spier for helpful comments.

1. See, for example, Anthony Saunders, Marcia Millon Cornett, and Patricia Anne McGraw, *Financial Institutions Management: A Risk Management Approach*, vol. 8 (New York: McGraw-Hill/Irwin, 2006); Sidney A. Shapiro and Robert L. Glicksman, *Risk Regulation at Risk: Restoring a Pragmatic Approach* (Stanford University Press, 2002).

2. Philip Pettit, *Republicanism* (Oxford University Press, 1997).

3. The 9/11 Commission, *9/11 Commission Report* (New York: Norton, 2004).

4. Condoleezza Rice, *No Higher Honor: A Memoir of My Years in Washington* (New York: Broadway Paperbacks, 2011), p. 68.

5. Ibid.

6. See Tomson H. Nguyen and Henry N. Pontell, "Mortgage Origination Fraud and the Global Economic Crisis," *Criminology & Public Policy* 9, no. 3 (2010): 591–612; William K. Black, "Bill Moyers Journal," April 3, 2009, www.pbs.org/moyers/journal/04032009/transcript1.html.

7. Mark Moore, *Creating Public Value: Strategic Management in Government* (Harvard University Press, 1995).

8. Clifford Shearing and Richard Ericson, "Culture as Figurative Action," *British Journal of Sociology* 42 (1991): 481–506.

9. Michael Lipsky, *Street-Level Bureaucracy* (New York: Russell Sage, 2010).

10. After the partial meltdown at the Three Mile Island nuclear plant in 1979, U.S. nuclear safety regulation became more responsive and effective. SCRAMS (automatic shutdowns for safety reasons) today in the U.S. industry run at less than one-tenth their rate before the time of Three Mile Island. For a diagnosis of the nuclear regulatory pathologies before the disaster and improvement after, see Joseph V.

Rees, *Hostages of Each Other: The Transformation of Nuclear Safety since Three Mile Island* (University of Chicago Press, 1994).

11. Cary Coglianese and David Lazer, "Management-Based Regulation: Prescribing Private Management to Achieve Public Goals," *Law & Society Review* 37 (2003): 691–730.

12. There is a huge literature on what its critics see as its backward steps at every stage of its history, starting with the first few years; see George Venturini, *Malpractice: The Administration of the Murphy Trade Practices Act* (Sydney: Non Mollare, 1980). For a recent distinguished contribution, see Caron Beaton-Wells and Brent Fisse, *Australian Cartel Regulation: Law, Policy and Practice in an International Context* (Cambridge University Press, 2011).

13. Brent Fisse and John Braithwaite, *Corporations, Crime and Accountability* (Cambridge University Press, 1993), p. 235.

14. A declaration of interest is due here: I served in the early to mid-1980s as both CEO and chair of the Australian Federation of Consumer Organizations.

15. Robert A. Kagan and Jerome H. Skolnick, "Banning Smoking: Compliance without Enforcement," in *Smoking Policy*, edited by R. Rabin and S. Sugarman (Oxford University Press, 1993).

16. As Brown's predecessor as CEO of AFCO, I was one of those insiders, though far from the most important one. After holding that position, I served for ten years as a part-time commissioner of the Trade Practices Commission (now known as the ACCC).

17. Ian Ayres and John Braithwaite, "Tripartism: Regulatory Capture and Empowerment," *Law & Social Inquiry* 16 (1991): 435–96.

18. For a classic discussion of metaregulation, see Christine Parker, *The Open Corporation* (Cambridge University Press, 2002).

19. Inside-out design means the regulator designs a regulatory strategy and says to stakeholders: "Here are the new requirements." Outside-in design means regulators say to stakeholders: "We think this is a problem. Do you agree, and if so, how do you think we should respond to it?" See John Braithwaite, *Markets in Vice, Markets in Virtue* (Oxford University Press, 2005).

20. Malcolm K. Sparrow, *The Regulatory Craft: Controlling Risks, Solving Problems, and Managing Compliance* (Brookings Institution Press, 2000).

21. Eugene Bardach and Robert A. Kagan, *Going by the Book: The Problem of Regulatory Unreasonableness* (Temple University Press, 1982).

22. See the discussion of this story in John Braithwaite, "Flipping Markets to Virtue with Qui Tam and Restorative Justice," *Accounting, Organizations and Society* 38 (2013): 458–68.

23. See Andrew Bennett, "Process Tracing and Causal Inference," in *Rethinking Social Enquiry*, edited by H. Brady and D. Collier (Lanham, Md.: Rowman and Littlefield, 2010) (http://philsci-archive.pitt.edu/8872/); Andrew Bennett and Jeffrey T. Checkel, *Process Tracing: From Philosophical Roots to Best Practices,* Simons Papers in Security and Development 21/2012 (Simon Fraser University, 2012).

# 3

# Regulating by the Stars

## WENDY WAGNER

**THERE IS AN OLD** cliché that there are two things you never want to see made: laws and sausages. And although laws and regulations differ in their institutional means of production, the sausage-making analogy may be even more apt for decisionmaking by regulatory authorities. After all, the whole regulatory process is built on a conglomeration of potentially unsavory inputs. For example, in order to arrive at a decision, regulators must summarize and streamline information, solicit input from all relevant parties, respond to prods from elected officials, and ultimately produce a rule that—like the legislative process that created it—is inevitably more compromise and ad hoc politicking than synoptic decisionmaking.

However, precisely because of this sausage-making quality, reformers have sought to clean up the regulatory process over the past two decades by imposing numerous external checks on the quality of the agency outputs. These oversight requirements include output assessments such as benefit-cost analyses of significant rules, assessments of the effect of rules on small businesses, limiting agencies' information requests issued to private parties, and dozens of other requirements.[1] A variety of generic quantitative output measures—such as the number of rules or the number of pages of rules—have also been deployed in an effort to ensure that the quality of the agency's rules are palatable to a democratic system.

Yet when regulatory excellence, and not just regulatory serviceability, is the end goal, numerous experts in decisionmaking theory insist that, rather than adding new analytical criteria or output measures, the best way to make

36

progress is to focus on just a few core values or objectives.[2] Identifying a single or several "principal" objectives or "simple goals" helps keep a decision process on track and moving in a productive direction.[3] Performance and other outcome measures for a regulatory decision, if helpful, can then be calibrated directly to these value-focused goals. Indeed, without this calibration, output metrics run the risk of serving more as distractions from or obstacles to excellence rather than means for regulatory advancement.[4]

In putting these all-important end goals of the administrative process together, it is U.S. president Theodore Roosevelt's adage to "keep your eyes on the stars, and your feet on the ground" that supplies the central directive.[5] The best regulators possess an unwavering commitment to the overarching goal of advancing the public interest at every turn in the regulatory journey (the "stars"). This focus on advancing the public interest also brings out the best in regulatory creativity, entrepreneurship, and inventiveness.

But these accomplishments must also be grounded in a participation- and information-rich record supporting the decision. Indeed, precisely because a regulatory agency serves as a nation's bottom-up analyst to complement a legislature's top-down perspective, the integrity of the processes that the agencies use to do their important work becomes a vital ingredient in regulatory excellence. The excellent regulator actively seeks input from and engages all affected parties to the decision, including groups and communities that may lack the resources or expertise to participate on their own. By the same token, a regulator who is merely passive with respect to understanding and engaging the interests of affected groups equates to a bad regulator. Simply imposing quantitative models, such as benefit-cost analysis, at the end of a decision, without remediating or even taking note of a deficient record of public engagement, only adds insult to injury.

In modern times, it has also become clear that an excellent regulator must go beyond Roosevelt's adage and ensure an ability to move forward despite the morass of regulatory procedures and requirements. In other words, excellent regulators must keep their eyes on the stars, their feet on the ground, and make sure that those feet can move through the logistical quagmires of contemporary governmental bureaucracy.

## REGULATORS: FINDING THEIR INSTITUTIONAL PLACE

Excellent regulators operate in hotly contested political environments where legitimacy and accountability are up for grabs. While this chapter is no place to attempt to cover the ground identifying the normative place for regulatory agencies in government, it is difficult to discuss the qualities of excellent regulators without first at least mapping regulators' general institutional role.

As an institutional matter, agencies must retain some independence from the electoral process while remaining responsive and ultimately deferential to elected officials.[6] By combining staff expertise with a deliberative approach to policy analysis, regulators offer a different perspective on and line of engagement with policymaking.[7] This perspective offers an important dimension to the democratic machinery that otherwise might be driven by the urgent demands of well-financed interest groups and the crisis-of-the-day.

The regulator generates this distinctive voice in the democratic dialogue by implementing bottom-up (as opposed to top-down) techniques of analysis and then subjecting that analysis to diverse scrutiny. In ensuring this comprehensive, bottom-up assessment, an excellent regulator will identify the different sets of interests affected by a decision and ensure that they are actively engaged in the process. Doing so may entail not only soliciting information but also providing education and outreach, including for those who might not have the expertise or resources to participate.[8] If this outreach proves impracticable, the excellent regulator will find a way to ensure that the interests of thinly financed groups are otherwise vigorously represented by appointed advocates or others. The regulator must also scour the literature to ensure that no important options or facts are left out.

In a second step that consists of weighing this body of evidence and views, the regulator must adopt a deliberative decisionmaking process that continues to engage the public, affected groups, and experts in a rigorous and balanced way. Parties with greater resources are not allowed to dominate the proceedings or overwhelm the record.[9] In following this analytic-deliberative process, the regulator fulfills an "integrative function" that serves to "blend demands from past democratic coalitions with those from current democratic coalitions to produce a policy output at a consistent level."[10] Maintaining a clear separation between the regulator and elected officials is also vital to protecting the integrity of the regulatory voice in democratic decisionmaking.

However, it is easy to imagine how this agency independence is vulnerable to being co-opted or manipulated. Well-heeled special interests and political actors might rig an illusion of independent analysis that is, in fact, beholden to their views. In anticipation of this appropriation, the regulator must also establish formal ways to protect against these subterranean intrusions. For example, an excellent regulator might treat interest-group participation that occurs outside of the normal process for public comment to be an ex parte contact, which must be recorded in the administrative record available to the public. In protecting regulatory independence by creating rigorous deliberative records and providing reasons, excellent regulators resist serving as handmaidens to politicians.

To fulfill this essential institutional role of providing a rigorous, bottom-up analysis of the issues, an excellent regulatory leader is relentless in gaining a comprehensive understanding of the issues, identifying creative and plausible alternatives, selecting the best choice among all available options, and explaining how, exactly, he or she accomplishes this work as part of a democratically vibrant process. Regulatory excellence thus requires both a sound decision and a thorough and accurate record that supports the decision.[11] Indeed, if a benefit-cost assessment or other performance metric ignores this foundational role of a complete record of affected viewpoints and experts, or takes for granted that it will occur, the results will be suspect and potentially worthless. Excellent decisions require not only excellent decisionmaking models but also an assurance that the model's inputs are complete and represent all significant viewpoints.

Roosevelt's adage resonates loudly in this type of value-focused orientation. By keeping their eyes on the stars, excellent regulators ensure that their analysis and goals advance the public interest. By remaining grounded, excellent regulators also ensure that they have mastered the available information and evidence and used it as a foundation for policymaking. Political officials can trump their regulatory choices, but only after excellent regulators have established a rigorous, grounded record in a way that speaks truth to power.

These qualities of regulatory excellence should not minimize the more generic qualities of excellence that run through all managerial positions. The heads of regulatory bodies are managers, so all the qualities of an excellent manager are also apropos for an excellent regulator, including, but not limited to, the ability to lead and inspire a large staff; the ability to mentor and nurture talent; the ability to stand behind controversial decisions but remain strategic and alert to roadblocks; relentlessness in surmounting obstacles; and perseverance and integrity.[12] However, since these qualities of excellence are well-traveled ground in managerial studies, they are not discussed in this essay despite their ultimate importance in excellent regulation.

## EYES ON THE STARS: ADVANCING THE PUBLIC INTEREST

Since regulators act on behalf of the public at large, the lodestar for all regulatory decisions and processes is to ensure that the public is deriving the maximum net benefit. Much like James Madison's ideal statesman, the excellent regulator will "refine and enlarge the public views" in order to "best discern the true interest of their country."[13] And in locating this maximum benefit, assurance of a robust inventory of all interests, facts, and options is essential.

Yet advancing the public interest—while seemingly uncontroversial as an end goal—is especially difficult in the high-stakes, highly technical world of regulation. Consequently, truly excellent regulators must ensure that their policies are informed by all affected parties, that the public is not only solicited but engaged, and that the resulting decisions are justified. The quality of the work of excellent regulators derives in large part from the participatory and empirical integrity of their processes. Each of these steps is discussed in greater detail in the following sections.

### *Identifying All Interests and Public Considerations*

An excellent regulator must identify each of the significant interested parties affected by a decision and ensure that they are engaged or, at the very least, represented in the decision process. For example, in a rule setting toxic air pollution standards, the public interest includes, at the very least, the general diffuse public that is affected in some way by the toxin at issue, communities living close to the major sources of the pollutants, future generations (if some effects, like the accumulation of toxins, are irreversible), as well as the regulated industry. Accordingly, the excellent regulator is fully committed to developing a complete record for the decision process that ensures this broad constellation of significant perspectives are weighed against each other in a rigorous way.

Unfortunately, in the United States, this seemingly obvious quality of excellent regulation—namely that the regulator is ever-vigilant in locating and accounting for all affected interests—is largely lost and may even be discouraged in regulatory practice today.[14] U.S. administrative processes instead situate the regulator as a passive recipient of public input. The quasi-market model for participation holds regulators legally accountable only when they ignore written comments by individuals or groups during a discrete "comment period."[15] If affected groups or clearly at-risk interests do not formally weigh in during this window, their concerns can be legally ignored. Furthermore, if the agency *does* take the concerns of affected groups into account despite their absence from the rule-making record, they may find themselves in hot water with groups that submitted comments formally: if the two interests are competing, siding with the unexpressed complaint over the formal complaint (even if the interests of the former outweigh the interests of the latter) is grounds for a lawsuit. In other words, rather than weighing options and interests, the agency has an incentive to reward the squeaky wheels, who not coincidentally tend to be the most well-financed groups.

Exacerbating this passive design of administrative process is the fact that, while some regulatory decisions attract the full range of affected parties like moths to a light, in numerous instances the interests most affected—particularly underrepresented communities and future generations—are dormant and at risk of being passed over. In the leading theories of regulatory participation, now several decades old, both James Q. Wilson and William Gormley modeled the likelihood of inadequate engagement by the diffuse public on many regulatory issues that directly and significantly affect their interests.[16]

The Wilson and Gormley models, shown in table 3-1, are supported by empirical research that reveals that even the narrowest conception of public interest is absent from the deliberations in about half the rules in federal health and environmental regulatory programs in the United States.[17] Those living in polluted areas, for example, rarely provide comments or articulate their interests. And even their self-appointed public interest representatives are able to weigh in on only about half the rules and are badly outnumbered when they do submit comments. For example, in one set of rules—air toxicity standards—the public interest nonprofits were not only absent from half the rules, but when they did engage were vastly overpowered by industry in the number of comments filed (14 to 1).[18] Moreover, they were essentially absent from all extensive discussions leading up to the proposed rule that occurred between the agency and industry; in that category, for every eighty-seven communications the agency logged with industry, nonprofit groups logged in less than one communication.[19] Given these findings, one does not need a particularly nuanced theory of public interest to conclude that the engagement and agency pressures are lopsided in ways that lead to significant gaps in the consideration of all affected interests.

In light of this combined theory and experience, an excellent regulator must find ways to adjust and compensate for the inevitable lack of civic engagement, particularly by poor communities, future generations, and the diffuse public—the beneficiaries of much of the regulatory state. Ensuring rigorous engagement by all affected groups may be best accomplished by subsidizing participation of underrepresented groups. For example, the goal of comprehensive and meaningful engagement by all significantly affected groups necessitates that their concerns be logged into the record with meaningful, detailed comments that can be litigated later, in the event they are ignored by the agency. This work requires time and expertise, and thus some financial support or other subsidization may be necessary to enable thinly financed interests to participate in decisions that affect them. The resulting record will ultimately inform the agency and constrain even excellent regulators from drifting too far from the overarching national interest.

**TABLE 3-1. Models of Regulatory Politics**

*Model A: James Q. Wilson*

Costs

|  | Concentrated | Dispersed |
|---|---|---|
| **Concentrated** (Benefits) | **Interest group politics** Fights over specific kinds of regulation (for example, railroad freight rate regulation or telecommunications, or wage bargaining in public sector). Both sides can easily mobilize. | **Client politics** The only case in which Mancur Olson's collective action should work (for example, import restrictions, lobbying for tax breaks, lobbying for targeted funds). |
| **Dispersed** (Benefits) | **Entrepreneurial politics** Class-action suits against concentrated interests might be an example. So too might be restricting tobacco sales and tax cuts in general. | **Majoritarian politics** Pure appeals to public goods (for example, public smoking bans). |

*Source:* Adapted from James Q. Wilson, *The Politics of Regulation* (New York: Basic Books, 1980), p. 367.

*Model B: William Gormley*

Complexity

|  | Low | High |
|---|---|---|
| **High** (Salience) | Hearing room politics | Operating room politics |
| **Low** (Salience) | Street-level politics | Board room politics |

*Source:* William T. Gormley Jr., "Regulatory Issue Networks in a Federal System," *Polity* 18 (1986): 607.

Because the system works in this problematic way, which ignores the underrepresentation of affected groups, the excellent regulatory agency must make a point to identify and engage significant, underrepresented interests at the very beginning of the policymaking exercise as well as in the middle and at the end. For example, in the development of a proposed rule, the excellent regulator finds a way to ensure that affected but thinly financed groups weigh in on the development of regulatory proposals. Ideally, their influence will be equivalent to the influence of other significant groups, like industry, and not ignored by virtue of their limited resources. Creating this balance in influencing the agency's development of regulatory proposals might even require a limit on participation, at least during the informal policy development stages to ensure that the weight given in the decision reflects the merits and is not skewed by the weight of the submissions themselves.

If representatives of at least some of these diffuse groups cannot be found in the existing nonprofit community or grassroots organizations, then the excellent regulator will create ombudsmen or other external experts to advocate for their interests in their absence. This representation will obviously be incomplete, but in such matters perfection should not be the enemy of progress. It is far better to have some presence than none at all.

The point at which these various forms of supplemental representation become necessary requires further specification, although in cases where some important groups are routinely underrepresented relative to others, the excellent regulator will develop processes that automatically assume that added representation is needed and intervene only to eliminate subsidized advocates where their representation is duplicative.

In some policy settings, of course, mapping and engaging the full range of affected parties will take care of itself. Particularly in cases of especially controversial or salient issues, all of the significant interests may engage full-throttle, making the life of the excellent regulator much easier. In these instances, the excellent regulator need only ensure that he or she adequately considers and balances the interests at stake (as discussed later), rather than also ensuring they are represented in the first place.

Finally, the excellent regulator will identify ways in which various policy options might have consequences for future generations that are irreversible. Public health and environmental issues in particular involve potentially irretrievable losses. And yet counting on existing groups and representatives to account for these future concerns is unrealistic, particularly if one considers the added collective action problems entailed in representation. Hence a rigorous assessment of the adverse consequences that could flow to future generations is vital to an excellent regulator; without such an inventory, these costs are at risk of being neglected entirely.

### Engage the Public in the Journey

Since a regulator must make decisions that affect large segments of society, the regulator should engage the public in the journey. It is not enough for the choices to be made with the public interest in mind; the agency's work must also engage and inform society.

At a bare minimum, regulators must ensure that the most important factors and bases for their decision (as well as the decision itself) are shared openly and accessibly within the wider community. For example, in complex, science-intensive rules governing air toxins, the purpose of regulation is to minimize exposure to air toxins in industrial corridors. Since communities living in these corridors are the primary beneficiaries, an excellent regulator will educate the community as to the evidence and options to ensure they are able to engage in the deliberations in a meaningful way. Limited time and resources constrain what is possible for even the most excellent regulators, but, with their eyes on the stars, these regulators appreciate that each step in their decisionmaking processes presents an opportunity for education and outreach.

It is worth noting again that the dominant trend appears not to be toward excellence in outreach and education but in the opposite direction. Because regulators, at least in the United States, are subject to lawsuits, and because meaningful engagement of all affected interests is neither a requirement nor an implicit incentive in the design of the process, regulators tend to write rules in ways that are difficult for even the most expert audience to decipher.[20] Gaps in the evidentiary record are too often understated. And assumptions and other judgments made in order to reach a solution may be difficult for third parties to identify and understand. The end result, then, is a rulemaking process that can become more alienating than illuminating for the affected parties. The excellent regulator must consequently resist the impulse to follow the path of least resistance; education and outreach are central to the excellent regulator's mission.

### Explain the Final Decision in Light of the Diverse Interests Affected

Once the diverse interests of the public have been engaged and represented (including that most widely ignored group, future generations), excellent regulators must provide cogent and accessible explanations for their choices in the record and defend those choices to the best of their ability. In this way, the public interest is advanced through good-faith efforts at maximizing public benefits and minimizing inequities, inefficiencies, and long-term damage.[21] The public-advancing values thus serve to prioritize the concerns and issues that are most important and simplify the issues that need to be analyzed.[22]

Rather than engaging in a full synoptic analysis—an approach that Charles Lindblom and others maintain is both unrealistic and impossible—the excellent regulator compares a full range of policy alternatives with regard to their impact on diverse groups in the hope of finding a policy that best advances the welfare of all. Options are qualitatively evaluated by comparing the pros and cons of various alternatives from a public-based perspective.[23] Such an analysis is not content with a net showing of good relative to harm but forces the regulator to create and consider competing options that inevitably involve apples-and-oranges comparisons and may require dynamic adjustments. Selecting the best options stems from the fit of those alternatives with the diverse interests affected by the decision.

Because of the imbalance in resources and engagement, moreover, the excellent regulator adopts default assumptions that err on the side of the diffuse public and future generations.[24] These defaults are sensible both because the public is the primary beneficiary of regulation and because their interests are inevitably underrepresented as a result of free-rider problems. And while there is no formal method for balancing diverse views, excellent regulators explain the underlying comparisons as best they can to improve both the rigor and the comprehensiveness of the analysis. Blind spots in the consideration of important interests and future concerns are also identified more easily as a result of the regulators' candid explanations. Advancing the public interest thus becomes a good-faith effort to identify important issues and select the option that best balances competing concerns rather than a mechanical calculation that obscures the messy tradeoffs.[25]

When confronted with factual or empirical uncertainties, the excellent regulator also adopts policies that encourage the production of new information from those best able to produce it. Penalty-default rules thus apply in regulatory policy; when some parties enjoy superior access to information, the excellent regulator will ensure that the rules extract this information and encourage additional research and knowledge accumulation from these more sophisticated parties.[26]

Finally, the excellent regulator stays on this celestial course even in difficult times and in the face of challenging circumstances. Lawsuits, motions for reconsideration, political pressures brought from elected officials, and other battles can cause less committed regulators to drift, sometimes quite far, from their overarching public goal. Excellent regulators will not only resist being driven by these forces, but they will make extra efforts to embrace and advance the public interest and to take up the cause of process reform voluntarily, despite the impediments and disincentives. Only in the most exceptional cases will regulators be forced to abandon their public interest outcomes. However, when they do have to forgo the public good, the excellent regulator is vigilant about pointing out both the shortfall and the institutional incentives that contributed to their defeat in order to prevent a recurrence.

**FEET ON THE GROUND**

Regulatory agencies are considered to be the grounded, expert analysts in most government systems, and it is therefore critical that they employ exemplary deliberative processes that are informed, accessible, and equitable. If agencies do not have their feet on the ground, even the most ingenious and public-advancing policies will lack democratic legitimacy.

## A Commitment to Professionalism and Expertise

Excellent regulators will develop decision processes that build on and engage the top experts in the field to ensure that the information used in regulatory decisions is as rigorous as possible. Science-intensive rules, for example, should meet or even exceed the standards for scientific reliability set in the scholarly community. This expert engagement should also help to highlight the political nature of decisions, choices, and issues that do not rely on empirical knowledge.

The U.S. Environmental Protection Agency's (EPA) revised process for setting national ambient air-quality standards illustrates this type of excellent, empirically grounded approach.[27] The process is broken into four distinct analytical stages—scoping, literature search, modeling, and policy implications—and at each stage the public is provided with at least one opportunity to comment.[28] EPA also draws on the larger expert community by tasking them to write attributed literature reviews so that their own contributions are acknowledged and rewarded. Finally, EPA solicits iterative peer review at each step of the process and responds, on the record, to the comments it receives. Indeed, it is common for EPA to run its drafts through peer reviewers several times in order to ensure that its decisionmaking is as grounded as possible. Through this vigorous vetting, EPA's process becomes heavily mediated by the views of the operative expert community. Excellent regulatory processes, particularly for scientific and technical decisions, are thus marked by a commitment to organized, vigorous skepticism from a broad and diverse group of experts and affected parties. Indeed, the regulatory process could not be complete without this meaningful organized skepticism.

But EPA's analytical processes do more than just solicit expert feedback and ensure that that feedback is incorporated into agency choices; they also help to isolate the work of the staff from the work of political appointees. That is, while the EPA's political staff and sister agencies help set the agenda by framing the questions that arise from the existing scientific evidence, it is the EPA's technical staff who summarize the current literature and develop multiple models for each decision the agency could make.[29] The technical staff is also firewalled from political pressure during the literature review and model development: political officials can offer comments, but only on the record. Finally, after that work is done and the reports are reviewed by scientific experts and the public, then the political process can click in and select models and choices that advance the political officials' view of the best resolution. However, even this work will be laid atop a clear evidentiary record and thus will not be able to misrepresent what the evidence reveals. With a reliable evidentiary record in place, the inevitable policy judgments will be more difficult to camouflage as technical algorithms or other nonjudgmental choices.

### Accessible and Transparent Decision Processes

Excellent regulators understand their audience is the public at large and endeavor to accurately and clearly communicate the underlying analyses to them. Rather than provide the bare minimum required by law, an excellent regulator is committed to transparency that advances the public interest. Accordingly, the excellent regulator will claim deliberative process protections sparingly rather than as a matter of course. The excellent regulator will also create strong presumptions against other exceptions to open access to information, such as permissive trade secret policies or reflexive national security privileges. And most important, the excellent regulator will proffer accessible explanations and records that the public can find and understand, rather than burying core assumptions in the technical minutiae.

Excellent regulators are also completely candid about their internal deliberations, even when they involve compromises. The excellent regulator will thus resist the temptation to misrepresent the role of backroom negotiations if the negotiations played a meaningful role in a decision. For example, if a president, minister, or other political actor changes the terms of a rule, the excellent regulator will ensure that the agency's decisionmaking is explained and linked to the record to ensure that the agency's own processes are not being manipulated or obfuscated.

### Adaptive Regulation

Excellent regulators constantly recalibrate their programs to ensure that the right processes, standards, and approaches are working. Foibles in requirements are corrected. Assumptions that turn out to be too generous—or conversely, assumptions that turn out to be too stringent—are updated. Regulatory excellence requires the agency to devise means for identifying important changes in public attitudes, technology, scientific techniques, and a whole range of other developments that must be confronted to ensure that their rulemakings advance the public good in the long term. Otherwise, assumptions and decisions can drift significantly from the public interest. Furthermore, because the goal is nimble reform, this recalibration process should be fluid, voluntary, transparent, and not laden with formal requirements.

While attentive regulators remain attuned to technological and policy shifts that may affect their regulatory programs, they also exercise their expert judgment in deciding when or whether such a shift warrants a change. In this way, the excellent regulator is able to distinguish fires from fire drills and avoids fostering a policymaking environment in which priorities are renegotiated on a daily basis.

### FORWARD MOVEMENT AND NOT GETTING STUCK IN THE MUD

The regulator's overarching task is to take care that the laws are implemented and enforced in a manner consistent with the broad directions laid down by the legislature, and to do so in ways that engage society in a larger conversation about the challenges ahead. To accomplish this, the regulator must move relatively swiftly. Mapping affected interests and summarizing the relevant evidence can be done simultaneously, and each can be equipped with "stopping rules" that focus and limit the searches. The engagement and education of affected parties must also be realistic, given time and resource constraints, and are likely to serve more as starting points for a larger political dialogue than as the means to reach definitive conclusions.

As regulators focus on summarizing the best available evidence and engaging all significant interests, some existing regulatory requirements may become superfluous or even counterproductive. Escalating paperwork and analysis hurdles are well positioned to ossify the productivity of excellent regulators, in some cases without producing countervailing gains.[30] These requirements may not need to be wholly eliminated in order to allow regulatory excellence to occur (exceptional people and teams can do exceptional things). But it is critically important to remember that one of the overarching qualities of the excellent regulator is to swim against the tide of these existing institutional requirements. Indeed, excellent regulators will identify the ways in which their efforts to follow the stars are sometimes impeded by well-meaning procedural requirements and, in so doing, will contribute to a larger conversation about how regulatory processes should be revised and reinvented. For example, analytic requirements that force a regulator to collect and include only peripherally related technical information bog down the decision process while adding little value. Indeed, by heaping additional information onto an already overloaded deliberative process, these superfluous analytics conflict with the important goal of ensuring rigorous engagement from all affected groups.[31]

An excellent regulator tasked with advancing the public interest in today's world must also be creative, determined, entrepreneurial, and able to seize any available and permissible opportunity to advance the public interest. Excellent regulators are not robots; they navigate various impediments in order to service the public along with accomplishing their legislative mission. This can mean advancing regulatory goals in unconventional ways or jumping frames and taking risks guided only by their desire to benefit the public interest. Some agencies, for example, may find they can set policies more swiftly and effectively through enforcement cases or recalls than rulemakings.[32] The U.S. Occupational Safety and Health Administration requests that parties reveal conflict of interest disclosures in their submissions, a novel approach that borrows from scientific journals.[33] The U.S. Office of Information and Regulatory Affairs developed a practice of prompting agencies to identify ways to advance the public interest within their mandates while minimizing the amount of time and money expended.[34] In a statutory mandate that required EPA to set elaborate health-based treatment standards for disposing of toxic substances on land, EPA recognized the failure of previous programs and adjusted its practices to use the much simpler technology-based standards instead.[35] Some agencies may realize that, as they consider promulgating rules on multiple issues, affected groups might be too divided to engage in all issues at once. As a result, a creative agency may promulgate a series of rules, knocking off a new issue every several years without attempting to resolve all controversial issues in a single rulemaking.

Excellent regulatory entrepreneurs also remain aware of the larger political, regulatory, and legal context within which they operate. For example, an excellent regulator seizes on opportunities to advance one of the many public-oriented projects when the political conditions are right. Rules that have been sitting in the pipeline can be pushed to the top of the agenda when they can be expected to prevent crises or disasters that have made headline news. Different presidential or legislative priorities may also cause some innovative ideas to be more promising than others. If a presidential candidate's electoral campaign is based on improving the integrity of agency science, for example, then innovations that advance public health programs could use that objective to prioritize some projects over others in the short run. Excellent regulators never give up on projects, but they do use their political savvy to gauge which issues are ripe and which issues will need more time in the pipeline.

Although excellent regulators work at the outer edge of what is possible, they also respect hard legal constraints and do not violate the letter of the law. Excellent regulators instead are careful to identify and respect the line between soft impediments that undermine public-benefiting regulation and hard legislative constraints. However, they continue to innovate and imagine possibilities up to that hard edge of statutory limitations. Indeed, they may, and perhaps should, call attention to legal limits or advocate for renewed thinking about the appropriate regulatory design when processes or laws undermine the public interest.

Finally, an innovative regulator appreciates that many of the best ideas will emerge from talented staff members who are familiar with the issues and not from the top-down edicts of senior management and politicians. Consequently, excellent regulatory leaders will work to inspire their staffs to be creative, energetic, and well informed. In order to foster this professional climate, the excellent regulatory official will provide rewards to those who solve challenges that advance the agency's mission of enhancing the public interest. Employees who do exceptional work—not simply in volume but in originality and outside-the-box thinking—should be singled out and compensated more richly. Those who simply work through their file folders and punch the clock without infusing creative ideas into the work should be thanked but redirected into less significant positions within the agency.

## IMPLICATIONS FOR PERFORMANCE MEASURES

In light of these aspirational goals, how can we determine whether an agency regulator is emerging as excellent or is falling short of expectations? The varying contexts, situations, and dynamics (not to mention budgets, political pressures, external conditions, interest groups, and legal constraints) make it not only difficult but treacherous to inject formal "measures" of excellence into regulatory processes. Moreover, innovation—one of the two most important features of agency policy—is likely to fly out the window as the agency becomes judged externally by measures that may impede creative problem solving, pragmatism, and original thinking on substantial public challenges.

Simplistic "output" measures designed to measure the quality and quantity of the regulator's work could also frustrate efforts to think outside the box. For example, a focus on lowering pollution levels may prevent the exploration of alternative industrial processes that abandon the use of certain chemicals entirely. Perhaps even more problematic, excellent regulators may not be able to control the output on which they are measured. Despite courageous and innovative policies, poor results may be achieved for any number of reasons that have nothing to do with the choices the regulator has made. Imperfect output measures thus run the risk of erroneously classifying excellent regulators as second-rate, a result that discourages and demoralizes excellence rather than rewarding it.

Specifying procedural benchmarks may nevertheless be helpful in identifying and rewarding excellent regulators: establishing a kind of "minimum bar" or checklist that any excellent regulator should have to meet in advancing the public welfare in rules and policies. For example, an excellent regulator must necessarily provide a rigorous and accessible statement of the evidence, ideally one that has been subjected to critical scrutiny by the public and experts. An excellent regulator must also identify all affected interests, including future interests, and ensure that their views are recorded in a rigorous, legally backed way. Finally, an excellent regulator must justify policy decisions against the evidentiary and deliberative record and explain how the choices embedded in those decisions are the best options for advancing the public interest. Table 3-2 offers a preliminary template for these and related process steps according to whether the regulator is bad, good, or excellent.

Beyond establishing process benchmarks, spotlighting the worst examples of regulatory practice can discourage repeat performances. Examples of subpar regulation could include:

- Documentation that key public beneficiaries of rules are not engaged or were not solicited to participate in decisions that affect their interests

- Agency rules that involve political decisions that were misleadingly presented as predominantly technical or scientific in nature

- Inaction in effectuating mandates in ways that are not explained solely by budget limitations or other unmovable constraints and that undermine the legislative goals of advancing the public interest

- Judicial decisions reversing and remanding agency rules because the rules not only violate the terms of the statute but undermine the interests of underrepresented groups

- False or fabricated reasoning on the part of the regulator

In addition to highlighting negative practices, a neutral, expert group of analysts could identify models of excellent regulation. Such positive case studies could highlight ways regulators have succeeded in remaining grounded, overcoming obstacles, and advancing the larger public interest. Regulators who address problems with creative approaches or resolutions, for example, might be selected out as particularly excellent.

**TABLE 3-2.** Regulatory Process Benchmarks

| | | Type of Regulator | |
|---|---|---|---|
| Stage in Decisionmaking | Bad | Good | Excellent |
| Public engagement/ deliberation | Passive | Outreach for obvious blind spots in participation | Educates and engages all major affected parties and includes a rigorous assessment of potential implications for future generations as well as underrepresented, significant groups |
| Technical analysis | Inseparable from and occurring with political deliberations | Kept distinct from political deliberations by instituting peer review on technical reports | Technical staff is firewalled with multiple rounds of public and peer review on their accessible reports |
| Bridging uncertainties | Adopts views of the dominant commenter | Gives ad hoc but transparent explanations | Creates default rules that create incentives for future information production |
| Methods for choosing policy outcomes | Analysis is largely divorced from the needs of significant affected groups | Analysis hinges on identifying the best option based on the major interests affected | Analysis follows the "good" path but also includes defaults that compensate for underrepresentation of significant groups |
| Reason-giving | Works backwards from ends to justify the means | Provides cogent reasons from the record | Provides publicly accessible explanations that are honest and candid and that also explain choices forgone with equally accessible explanations. Also identifies where external institutions and political pressures altered the outcome when appropriate |

## CONCLUSION

An unwavering commitment to the public good, a grounded and rigorous decision process, and an ability to make progress regardless of context and circumstances are the keys to regulatory excellence. And even though the concept of the public good will change with circumstances and regulators, basic process goals—such as engaging the most significant affected groups—are unequivocally at the core of the mission. Attaining excellence is difficult, but recognizing it shouldn't be.

### NOTES

1. For a list of such requirements in the United States, see Mark Seidenfeld, "A Table of Requirements for Federal Administrative Rulemaking," *Florida State University Law Review* 27 (2000): 533. Similar requirements have been recommended and implemented in many developed economies. See, for example, Organization of Economic Cooperation and Development, "Regulatory Reform in OECD Countries: Reports by Subject" (www.oecd.org/regreform/regulatoryreforminoecdcountriesreportsbysubject.htm).

2. See, for example, Ralph L. Keeney, *Value-Focused Thinking: A Path to Creative Decisionmaking* (Harvard University Press, 1992), pp. vii–ix, 29–30, 44–51.

3. Charles E. Lindblom, "The Science of 'Muddling Through,'" *Public Administrative Review* 19 (1959): 79; Keeney, *Value-Focused Thinking*.

4. Keeney, *Value-Focused Thinking*; see also Sidney A. Shapiro and Ronald F. Wright, "The Future of the Administrative Presidency: Turning Administrative Law Inside-Out," *University of Miami Law Review* 65 (2011): 577.

5. Theodore Roosevelt, "Speech at Groton School," May 24, 1904 (www.theodorerooseveltcenter.org/Research/Digital-Library/Record.aspx?libID=o285148).

6. Peter L. Strauss, "The Place of Agencies in Government: Separation of Powers and the Fourth Branch," *Columbia Law Review* 84 (1984): 578–80.

7. Colin Scott, "Accountability in the Regulatory State," *Journal of Law and Society* 27 (2000): 57.

8. Cynthia R. Farina and Mary J. Newhart, *Rulemaking 2.0: Understanding and Getting Better Public Participation* (Washington: IBM Center for the Business of Government, 2013), pp. 14–19, 21–37.

9. Amy Gutmann and Dennis Thompson, *Democracy and Disagreement* (Cambridge, Mass.: Belknap Press, 1996), pp. 12–16.

10. B. Dan Wood and Richard W. Waterman, *Bureaucratic Dynamics: The Role of Bureaucracy in a Democracy* (Boulder, Colo.: Westview Press, 1994), p. 145.

11. *Mississippi* v. *Environmental Protection Agency*, 744 F.3d 1334 (D.C. Cir. 2013); *American Trucking Associations* v. *Environmental Protection Agency*, 283 F.3d 355 (D.C. Cir. 2002).

12. Andrew J. DeBrin, *Essentials of Management,* 9th ed. (Independence, Ky.: Cengage Learning, 2011), pp. 1–35, 345–506.

13. James Madison, "The Federalist No. 10," in *The Federalist,* edited by Cass Sunstein (New York: Barnes and Noble Classics, 2006).

14. Kevin Stack, "The Paradox of Process in Rulemaking" (unpublished draft 2015); Wendy Wagner, "Participation in Administrative Process," in *Comparative Law and Regulation: Understanding the Global Regulatory Process*, edited by Francesca Bignami and David Zaring (Northampton, Mass.: Edward Elgar, 2016).

15. Administrative Procedure Act, § 706(2)(A).

16. James Q. Wilson, *The Politics of Regulation* (New York: Basic Books, 1980), p. 367; William T. Gormley Jr., "Regulatory Issue Networks in a Federal System," *Polity* 18 (1986): 607.

17. Jason Webb Yackee and Susan Webb Yackee, "A Bias towards Business? Assessing Interest Group Influence on the U.S. Bureaucracy," *Journal of Politics* 68 (2006): 128.

18. Wendy Wagner, Katherine Barnes, and Lisa Peters, "Rulemaking in the Shade: An Empirical Study of EPA's Air Toxic Emission Standards," *Administrative Law Review* 63 (2011): 128–29.

19. Ibid., p. 125.

20. See generally Wendy Wagner, "Administrative Law, Filter Failure, and Information Capture," *Duke Law Journal* 59 (2011): 1321.

21. Frank Ackerman and Lisa Heinzerling, *Priceless: On Knowing the Price of Everything and the Value of Nothing* (New York: New Press, 2005), p. 212.

22. See, for example, Keeney, *Value-Focused Thinking.*

23. Ackerman and Heinzerling, *Priceless*, pp. 218–27.

24. David M. Driesen, "Cost-Benefit Analysis and the Precautionary Principle: Can They Be Reconciled?," *Michigan State Law Review* 2013 (2013): 771.

25. See, for example, Lindblom, "The Science of 'Muddling Through.'"

26. Ian Ayres and Robert Gertner, "Filling Gaps in Incomplete Contracts: An Economic Theory of Default Rules," *Yale Law Journal* 99 (1989): 87, 91.

27. National Research Council of the National Academies, *Review of the Environmental Protection Agency's Draft Iris Assessment of Formaldehyde* (Washington: National Academies Press, 2011), p. 156.

28. Wendy Wagner, "Science in Regulation: A Study of Agency Decisionmaking Approaches," February 18, 2013 (www.acus.gov/report/professor-wendy-wagners-science-project-report).

29. Ibid., pp. 36, 39–40

30. See, for example, Curtis W. Copeland, "Length of Rule Reviews by the Office of Information and Regulatory Affairs," December 2, 2013 (www.acus.gov/sites/default/files/documents/Cope-land%20Report%20CIRCULATED%20to%20Committees%20on%2010-21-13.pdf); General Accounting Office, *Chemical Assessments: Low Productivity and New Interagency Review Process Limit the Usefulness and Credibility of EPA's Integrated Risk Information System* (Washington: Government Printing Office, March 2008).

31. See, for example, Cynthia R. Farina, Mary J. Newhart, and Cheryl Blake, "The Problem with Words: Plain Language and Public Participation in Rulemaking," *George Washington Law Review* 83 (2015): 1358, 1365.

32. Jerry L. Mashaw and David L. Harfst, *The Struggle for Auto Safety* (Harvard University Press, 1990).

33. Occupational Safety and Health Administration, Occupational Exposure to Respirable Crystalline Silica, Proposed Rule, 78 Fed. Reg. 56274, 56274 (2013).

34. John D. Graham and others, "Managing the Regulatory State: The Experience of the Bush Administration," *Fordham Urban Law Journal* 33 (2006): 974.

35. *Hazardous Waste Treatment Council* v. *EPA*, 886 F.2d 355 (D.C. Cir. 1989).

# 4

# Regulatory Excellence and Democratic Accountability

## KATHRYN HARRISON

**REGULATION IS A CHALLENGING** policy instrument from the perspective of democratic governance. It typically entails the imposition of costs or restrictions on some actors in order to protect the welfare of others. The exercise of the state's monopoly on coercion demands strong mechanisms for democratic accountability to ensure that the freedoms of those who are regulated are not limited without appropriate justification and due process. At the same time, obstacles to collective action present a very different democratic challenge.[1] Those who face compliance costs typically are smaller in number with more at stake than the beneficiaries of regulation. Regulated interests thus tend to be well organized to oppose strict standards and enforcement, while beneficiaries—whether consumers, workers, or breathers of the air—are often great in number with modest or uncertain individual stakes in the outcome. The challenge of collective action thus suggests a risk of unduly weak, rather than excessive, regulation.

In this chapter I consider the question of regulatory excellence through the lens of democratic accountability. In doing so, I do not intend to suggest that only process considerations are relevant to regulatory excellence, but rather that democratic legitimacy is an essential underpinning of any regulatory regime. Since my own research has focused on environmental regulation, and most recently energy and climate change, the chapter draws examples primarily from those fields, but the overarching principles I raise here would apply to any policy domain. Some of the examples describe instances of regulatory failure rather than excellence, as reflections on failure can often help to identify features of regulatory excellence that were lacking in those instances.

## WHAT COUNTS AS REGULATION?

The central question, "what makes an excellent regulator?," prompts two prior questions: what do we mean by regulation, and who is the regulator? Regulation involves a series of activities: the design of regulatory mandates and regulatory agencies via legislation, the adoption of rules using authority delegated by legislation, and the promotion of compliance with those rules. Studies of regulation typically focus on the second and third steps. However, this chapter occasionally revisits the first step, the design of regulatory institutions and mandates, since the original statute in which legislatures opt for the policy instrument of regulation can predispose the steps that follow to excellence or failure. After all, even the most capable and committed regulator will fail if her mandate is unattainable, her authority inadequate for the task at hand, or the process or institutions she inherits fundamentally flawed.

## WHO IS THE REGULATOR?

In envisioning "the regulator" one tends to think of stand-alone regulatory agencies, such as the Canadian National Energy Board, the U.S. Consumer Product Safety Commission, or the U.K. Civil Aviation Authority. However, regulation takes place in varied institutional settings, and the identity of regulators is accordingly more diverse.

The regulator is typically envisioned as a bureaucrat wielding the proverbial stick, or at least a clipboard and yardstick.[2] Yet if we consider regulation to comprise all three steps—design of legislative mandates, adoption of rules, and promotion of compliance—it is clear that there are different categories of regulators. Elected legislators write statutes that specify regulatory mandates, institutions, and processes. Those statutes delegate future decisions, to be enacted via regulations or permits, to executive actors, who may be elected (as in parliamentary systems) or appointed (as in the United States). Implementation is usually undertaken by public servants, but may even involve nongovernmental actors, such as professional bodies to whom public authority to regulate their profession is delegated. Any one of these actors—legislators, heads of regulatory authorities, or the staff who answer to them—can be considered regulators, and the criteria for excellence differ in recognition of the different roles each actor plays.

The legal or constitutional context has important implications for the identity of regulators and the mechanisms of accountability. In a parliamentary democracy, executive and legislative functions are fused. Ministers who wield regulatory authority are expected to hold seats in Parliament and are accountable, both individually and as a cabinet collectively, to the legislature. Indeed, ministerial responsibility to the elective House of Commons, rather than the crown, is *the* fundamental principle of parliamentary government. In contrast, in a presidential system with a separation of powers between the executive and legislature, as in the United States, executive actors typically are prohibited from holding seats in the legislature.

These structures have several implications. First, in a parliamentary system the director of the relevant regulatory body is usually an elected politician, not a bureaucrat. For instance, Canadian environmental statutes typically grant regulatory authority to either the minister of the environment or to the cabinet as a whole. In contrast, the director or administrator of a U.S. regulatory agency, such as the Environmental Protection Agency, is a bureaucratic official appointed by the president. While appointed bureaucrats presumably are, and should be, chosen primarily for their expertise, a politician will almost certainly be a layperson who has no specialized knowledge of the subject matter at hand yet a stronger claim to speak for the affected public. However, the flip side of democratic legitimacy is partisanship and political motives, which may render an elected regulator more inclined than a more independent bureaucrat to eschew publicly beneficial regulations that would incur the wrath of powerful or financially generous constituencies.

Second, mechanisms of democratic accountability differ. In both cases, accountability to voters is indirect. In a parliamentary system, ministers' immediate accountability is to the legislature, where they must answer publicly to hostile opposition parties. In acting on authority delegated by Parliament, individual ministerial responsibility is the fundamental mechanism of accountability. The minister answers first and foremost to the House of Commons. In a presidential system, regulators are directly accountable to the president. Although regulators often face criticism from the legislature, their authority and legitimacy derives from the elected president.

Third, the nature of regulatory statutes produced by parliamentary and presidential systems tends to differ. Faced with an independent executive, the U.S. Congress seeks to ensure fidelity to its intentions by tying the hands of those to whom it delegates regulatory authority via nondiscretionary statutory mandates.[3] It is common to find highly specific language with respect to regulatory triggers, factors to be considered in rulemaking, standards of decisionmaking, and deadlines, all backed by citizen suit provisions that invite judicial enforcement of any of those mandates. In contrast, the majority coalition that controls the legislature in a parliamentary system both drafts and implements legislation. They are, in effect, delegating regulatory authority to themselves (and future cabinets). As a result, regulatory statutes produced by Westminster parliamentary systems tend to *authorize* rather than *mandate* regulation by the executive via pithy statutes that grant broad discretion to the executive. While U.S. environmental statutes typically direct the EPA administrator via the word "shall," comparable Canadian legislation allows that the minister "may" undertake a variety of actions. With such discretionary authority there also is a weaker basis for legal challenges: the courts tend to be less active in the regulatory process in parliamentary systems, such as Canada's, than in the United States.[4]

Complicating matters further, regulatory agencies may be more or less independent of their political sovereigns in either system. Regulatory independence may be established by appointment of regulatory oversight boards with multiyear terms, narrow conditions for dismissal of directors, and statutory limits on political interference. There are two very different rationales for independence. The first is to take the politics out of rulemaking and enforcement by ensuring that decisions are made by experts, based only on their expertise. The second is predicated on awareness, if not explicit acknowledgment, that politics is unavoidable in regulation. In that case, well-intentioned (or fearful) legislators may choose to "pass the buck" for politically difficult decisions to arm's-length officials.[5] As discussed further in the following sections, the former rationale is compelling if regulatory decisions are in fact merely technical matters, guided by values set out in a statute by elected legislators. However, if that is not the case, there is a risk of depicting what are in fact value-based decisions as matters of facts alone, in so doing weakening mechanisms of democratic accountability.

### CLOSING THE SCRUTINY GAP

Regulation typically imposes costs on a discrete number of actors in order to deliver benefits for a much broader community.[6] Where regulatory decisions may have significant impacts on a subset of actors, a best-in-class regulator has a responsibility to consult those parties, to ensure that every decision is made with an understanding of the magnitude of potential impacts and of the means to mitigate costs. This typically applies to firms, sectors, or individuals that are the targets of regulation. In the Canadian context, there is also a constitutional duty to consult Aboriginal governments that have shared or unresolved claims to land or resources that may be affected by a project under review or an operating industry.

The diffuseness of benefits delivered by regulations that protect the environment or broad classes of consumers, investors, or workers presents a very different democratic challenge. As set out decades ago by Mancur Olson and applied in the regulatory context by James Q. Wilson, the logic of collective action should lead regulators to anticipate a scrutiny gap, in which those potentially regulated are more engaged and attentive than those who will benefit from regulation.[7] Consider the example of regulations to reduce industrial emissions of greenhouse gases, which would impose significant costs on a discrete number of polluters in order to achieve benefits for the public at large, and indeed for the entire planet, now and for decades to come. Those constrained by regulation typically are keenly aware of what is at stake for them and are motivated to defend their interests with regulators, whether on their own or via collective action with like facilities or industries. In contrast, the beneficiaries of globally diffused benefits tend to be ill-informed, inattentive, and unorganized.

This divergence in political engagement can yield an increasing gap between popular perception and reality as one proceeds through the regulatory process. The media, and thus the public, tend to be most attentive at the legislative stage. However, statutes that promise bold targets may win over voters with the promise of clean air, water, and food, while leaving critical decisions with respect to how, or even whether, to achieve those targets to a regulatory process that takes place after media scrutiny has subsided. This is particularly problematic when regulatory statutes are discretionary, as is common in parliamentary systems, since there is no guarantee that promised actions will ever materialize once public attention fades.[8] At the rulemaking stage, although media attention has often moved on, those who are adversely affected have even stronger financial incentives to learn about and speak on behalf of their interests in notice-and-comment or other stakeholder consultation processes. There is thus a risk that public support will be underestimated, and proposals relaxed or amended to offer significant concessions apparent only to regulated interests. If engagement of beneficiaries is an uphill battle at the legislative and rulemaking stages, the slope is even steeper as implementation of regulations moves from a single point of decision to the monitoring of compliance and enforcement actions against hundreds or thousands of facilities.

This dynamic underlies the phenomenon of regulatory "capture" documented by Marver Bernstein. In the absence of public scrutiny, regulatory authorities established to protect the public interest over time became sympathetic to the plight of regulated industries, to the point that regulations intended to protect the public became a means to protect existing firms from competition.[9] Of course, much has changed since Bernstein wrote in the mid-1950s. The 1960s and 1970s saw a veritable explosion of public interest groups that seek to represent the diffuse interests of the public in consumer and environmental protection. U.S. legislators themselves responded with nondiscretionary "action-forcing" statutes backed by citizen suits. There are stronger expectations for public reporting and greater media attention to new areas of social regulation. However, it remains the case that we live in an Olsonian world, where only a small fraction of those who nominally share the goals of environmental or other public interest groups join or donate to those organizations. Moreover, the specificity and citizen suit provisions of U.S. regulatory statutes typically are the exception to the rule globally. Regulatory capture may not be as easy in the past, but the structure of interests that allowed capture to occur is ever present.

An excellent regulator thus will endeavor to document and publicize the magnitude and distribution of costs and benefits of proposed actions. Efforts should be made to reach out to those who are diffusely affected, whether by costs or benefits, beyond mere publication in an official government register or gazette that only those with dedicated regulatory affairs staffs are in a position to monitor. This is particularly important for individuals in low-income communities, who often live in closest proximity to regulated facilities, but have more limited access to online sources and less free time to monitor them than individuals in wealthier communities. Polling, focus groups, and stakeholder consultations by invitation (possibly with financial assistance to facilitate participation) offer other vehicles for actively soliciting input from wheels that are less likely to squeak.

### HONESTY

It goes without saying that elected officials and public servants should not provide false information. It follows that it is also wrong to intentionally mislead, for instance by omitting relevant information or taking advantage of an audience's lack of expertise or inattention to details. In practice, however, and especially when the lead regulator is a politician, it is difficult to draw the line between where strategic "framing," the lingua franca of politics, leaves off and intentionally misleading voters begins. Those who present a selectively optimistic picture might argue that it is the job of opposition parties and critics in civil society to fill information gaps and offer alternative scenarios. Still, a regulator aiming for excellence, mindful that inattentive citizens will often misunderstand unfamiliar material, should not push those boundaries.

Unfortunately, there are many examples from Canadian environmental regulation that would seem to cross that line. For instance, the previous Canadian environment minister, Canada's lead environmental regulator, insisted repeatedly that the government was on track to meet its greenhouse gas emissions targets for 2020 based on its sector-specific regulatory strategy, even though her own department projected that only about half the reductions needed relative to a business-as-usual baseline would be achieved by 2020, and no additional federal regulatory proposals had been published that could even begin to close that gap by the deadline.[10] Canadian and U.S. governments at times have proposed what sound like ambitious greenhouse gas reduction goals that are, in fact, targets for reduction of emissions *intensity* relative to production, at a rate expected to yield continued emissions growth. For instance, Alberta's 2008 Climate Change Strategy promised to "reduce emissions by 50 Megatonnes by 2020" several times before clarifying only toward the end of a document that few voters would have read in its entirety that those reductions were relative to a business-as-usual projection, and that emissions in fact were expected to be higher, not lower, in 2020.[11] The statement by the then premier that "Alberta's greenhouse gas emissions will steadily decline" goes beyond mere framing, given that it was offered as a preface to a regulatory strategy that projected *increasing* emissions. As at the federal level, the Alberta environment minister's claim as late as 2015 that the province was on track to meet its 2020 emissions target challenged credulity, given reports by the province's own auditor general that the department had known since 2012 that it was not on track.[12]

### CLEAR RATIONALES: FACTS VS. VALUES

Regulatory standards rest on two types of questions. *Positive* questions concern the facts: what we know, and don't know, about the scope of the problem, what is causing it, what can be done about it, and at what cost. These questions are the province of experts, including scientists, doctors, engineers, and social scientists. In contrast, *normative* questions ask what ought to be done. What level of risk is acceptable? How great a cost or restriction on liberties is justified to address a given problem? Are proposed regulations fair? Scientists have no special claim to answering such questions. Their specialized training offers no particular insight into public values, nor is there a basis to assume that their values are representative of the public's. With respect to the second set of questions, in a democracy *politicians* are elected to represent voters' normative values.

There is no question that regulatory excellence demands reliance on the best available expertise and evidence. However, it would be a mistake to assume that regulatory decisions can be based on evidence or science alone. Rather, excellence in regulation requires thoughtful deliberation with respect to both facts and values and where to draw the sometimes blurred line between the two. At minimum, a best-in-class regulator will be explicit about both the factual and the value basis for regulatory decisions.

Failure to distinguish between facts and values can yield two distinct problems. The first is that value judgments will be made by subject-matter experts. This problem is greatest where experts themselves are unaware of or inattentive to where their expertise leaves off and their values begin. The line between the two is especially blurred in the realm of uncertainty, where experts may posit a range of plausible risks. In that context, the decision whether to adopt a risk-neutral, risk-tolerant, or risk-averse posture necessarily draws on values as well as facts.[13]

While the need to justify regulatory decisions in court has prompted attention to the fact-value distinction in the United States, in Canada it is still common to hear calls for regulatory decisions to be left to the experts alone. For instance, Canadian scientists and environmentalists lobbied for a scientific advisory body to be assigned exclusive authority over the listing of endangered species, even though the language of the proposed statute meant that the decision to list could have significant economic and distributive consequences. Although that effort was unsuccessful, in the case of Canadian National Energy Board (NEB) "expert panels" are granted broad authority to weigh both evidence and values in conducting environmental assessments of major oil and gas projects. The NEB typically defends its appointments based on the panelists' expertise, with little or no attention to their politics or values, even though a panel's recommendations would be expected to rely on both facts and values. One way to constrain experts' value judgments is for politicians to specify generic decision rules (for example, to ensure health protection with a "margin of safety" or to require adoption of "best technology economically achievable"). However, NEB expert panels set their own terms of reference, the implication being that the values of expert panelists weigh heavily not only in their assessment of the acceptability of the risks posed by a project, but also in the questions that get asked in the first place. The results can be problematic and inconsistent. For instance, a recent NEB review of Enbridge's proposal to build the "Northern Gateway" pipeline from the tar sands in Alberta to the Pacific coast in British Columbia took into account the economic benefits to Canada at the point of extraction but deemed the corresponding environmental costs of extraction to be beyond the scope of the review.

The second risk is that regulators will misrepresent their political or value judgments as science. Canadian regulators' project approvals and regulatory standards are often justified simply on the grounds that the projects or substances are "safe," in so doing concealing policymakers' judgments with respect to risk acceptability. The irony is that while it is entirely appropriate for elected representatives to make those judgments, there is nonetheless a temptation for policymakers to hide behind the credibility of science. That temptation may be particularly great where the underlying call is based on a political calculus, rather than an assessment of the fairness of the anticipated distribution of costs and benefits. This seems most problematic in a parliamentary system, where the head of a regulatory authority is often a politician, where statutes typically grant tremendous discretion to the executive, and where there are often stronger norms of confidentiality. Yet the need to justify regulatory decisions to critical judges can also prompt U.S. regulators to overstate the degree to which their decisions are driven purely by "the facts." Cary Coglianese and Gary Marchant, for example, conclude that in justifying its national ambient air-quality standards for ozone and particulate matter, the U.S. EPA "exaggerated the determinacy of science in an effort to mask contested policy choices and escape scrutiny."[14]

While regulatory independence is seen as a solution to the problem of political interference, independence can increase the risk of the first problem, namely, value-based or political decisions made by unaccountable experts. A solution sometimes employed is to rely on a governing board that combines expertise and representation of different interests. However, that strategy still leaves the question of which interests will be represented and by whom (discussed in the following section).

One clear implication, whether regulators are independent or not, is that they should provide a public rationale for their decisions, one that is sensitive to the distinction between questions of fact and value, as well as to the interactions between the two that occur in the realm of scientific uncertainty. Explicit consideration of distributional considerations is critical to provide confidence that fairness, rather than political influence, has carried the day. Where regulation will be carried out by relatively independent bureaucrats, it is critical for elected legislators to provide explicit guidance with respect to the values they intend to inform future rulemaking, and for decisionmakers to justify their decisions within those values.

## NEUTRALITY

An excellent regulator is unbiased, other than to ensure adherence to values specified by the statute. That can be a challenge, however, given the scrutiny gap noted above. Regulatory officials who disproportionately hear from regulated interests thus need to actively seek out other perspectives.

Legislators creating regulatory authorities must exercise care not to make matters worse by institutionalizing real or apparent conflicts of interest. First, it can be problematic for agencies to have conflicting mandates, particularly if one mandate is dominant. This was an underlying motive for transferring responsibility for pesticide regulation to the U.S. EPA in 1972 from the U.S. Department of Agriculture, as the latter organization's primary mandate, to promote agriculture and protect the interests of farmers, created at best a perceived and at worst a very real conflict of interest. Yet recent amendments to the Canadian Environmental Assessment Act reduced the role of agencies such as Health Canada and Environment Canada in favor of greater autonomy for line departments. Federal port authorities, such as the Port of Vancouver, are now exclusively responsible for conducting environmental assessments of a broad range projects within their purview. This is problematic given that the port itself claims that its core mandate is to promote trade. Moreover, the port is required to fully fund its own operations with revenues from port users and tenants, thus creating a financial disincentive to reject a project that would yield significant revenues for its own operations. The risk of conflicting mandates is also apparent in a recent decision to approve a coal port in British Columbia, not by the provincial Ministry of Environment, but by the Ministry of Mines, which did so by amending a decades-old permit for a *gravel* quarry.

Second, institutionalized bias may be created through appointment of directors that govern independent regulatory agencies. In the case of the Port of Vancouver, a majority of the board members are nominated by the industries that use the port. While this board composition is arguably well designed to avoid bias in the port's role of regulating access to the port by different users, it is woefully ill-suited to a mandate to regulate the environmental impacts of those same industries. In effect, the foxes have been charged with guarding the chicken coop.

Finally, even in an era where cooperation between government and business is celebrated, it is critical for regulators to distinguish between the roles of the state and the roles of regulated actors. When public comments are sought, it must be by the regulator, not by (or in addition to) the proponent or industry. Reflecting a long-standing model of cooperation, when a coal port was proposed in the Vancouver harbor, it was the private proponent, rather than the Port of Vancouver, that distributed information on corporate letterhead to neighbors and solicited public comments on the project. This sort of cooperation not only raises important questions about regulatory bias but also undermines the efficacy of consultations; one wonders how many households would even recognize that a leaflet from a private firm was intended to bring an issue of public policy to their attention.

Where regulatory goals are negotiated, there must be opportunities for diverse stakeholders to participate. When partnership agreements are struck by business and regulators, the terms of the agreement and compliance reports must be available to the public.

## COMMITMENT TO EVALUATION AND PUBLIC REPORTING

As already noted, the scrutiny gap tends to expand with each step in the regulatory process. Media attention at the legislative stage typically fades by the point of rulemaking, and it is a distant memory when the time comes to monitor compliance by hundreds or thousands of regulated entities (although there are of course exceptions for high-profile rules and instances of noncompliance). Implementation failures loom especially large in the context of permissive statutes, which authorize but do not require performance of regulatory actions. In that context, it is easy to promise bold action at the legislative stage yet fail to follow through at the more politically challenging implementation stage.

A best-in-class regulator will be committed to monitoring and reporting at each step of implementation. That suggests the need for two distinct, though related, forms of evaluation, both of which must be public: assessment of the efficacy of regulatory programs and reporting on compliance by private actors. Regulators' evaluation of their own performance is challenging, both analytically and politically. Politically, it is of course unappealing for any agency to publicly report on its own failures. For that reason, a commitment to periodic program evaluation and public compliance reporting ideally will be built into legislative mandates. Program evaluation also offers the advantage of reminding legislators of progress, or lack thereof, toward goals they set in years past. It can also be effective to rely on independent auditors. In Canada's parliamentary system, the office of the auditor general reports to Parliament, rather than to cabinet or individual ministers. That independence lends credibility to occasional regulatory program reviews, which often reveal failings that the executive branch has either not recognized or not publicized. The auditor general of Canada reported in 2012 and, disturbingly, again in 2014 that Environment Canada had failed to put in place mechanisms for tracking compliance and monitoring the impact of its regulations on greenhouse gas emissions. Similarly, in 2014, the Alberta auditor general "found no evidence that the [provincial environment] department regularly monitored performance between 2008 and 2012 against the 2008 [climate action] strategy targets" and that there was "no clear link between the implementation plan and monitoring and reporting."[15]

Analytically, if we are to understand what works and what doesn't, it is essential to control for other factors that might have affected outcomes, including technological progress and market forces. This challenge is particularly important in the case of voluntary or "beyond compliance" programs, which hold the appeal of promoting progress with a minimal commitment of agency resources. The challenge is that evaluation of such programs is fraught with problems of self-selection; those who "volunteer" to go beyond compliance may simply be those who are doing so for other reasons. Indeed, after controlling for selection, many voluntary programs that were once celebrated appear to have had minimal or no impact.[16] In the absence of those evaluations, regulators had drawn quite the opposite conclusion: that encouragement of voluntary action could offer a credible substitute for regulation. This illustrates the importance of a commitment not only to the evaluation of regulatory programs, but to making such evaluations public.

## TRANSPARENCY

Each of the foregoing dimensions—democratic accountability, honesty, clarity of rationale, neutrality, and performance evaluation—is enhanced by transparency. However, regulatory transparency presents special challenges in Westminster parliamentary systems. The traditional interpretation of individual ministerial responsibility is that the minister, and only the minister, must answer to the House for all actions by public servants that report to them. It follows that bureaucrats should be anonymous, accountable only through the minister they report to. Bureaucratic anonymity is further reinforced by the expectation of a permanent public service, in which even the most senior of officials retain their positions when there is a change of government. After all, it would be difficult for a government to trust officials who were clearly associated with regulations of which a new government disapproves. Finally, the doctrine of collective ministerial responsibility, such that members of a cabinet stand—or fall—as one, rests on a tradition of candid discussions reinforced by cabinet secrecy.

A growing struggle between transparency and secrecy is illustrated by the recent debate in Canada over cabinet "muzzling" of government scientists. Although government scientists routinely publish in peer-reviewed journals, the Conservative government that held a majority in Canada's parliament until 2015 required media interviews concerning scientists' research and even conference presentations to be approved in advance with responses vetted by the cabinet. An incredulous public asked why the government was trying to hide facts uncovered by science, not least when the research in question had already been published. Defenders of the government argued that government scientists often venture beyond the science to offer policy prescriptions, which is not the purview of experts, and also a violation of ministerial responsibility. Although this tradeoff is real, one would think that, short of vetting every public response by its own scientists, the government easily could have established guidelines reminding government scientists to stick to questions of fact, rather than policy, in media interviews.

Where regulators fail to document their success or failure voluntarily, it is critical that members of the public be able to obtain such records by other means, including freedom-of-information statutes. However, the exemption for "advice to cabinet," consistent with the norm of cabinet secrecy, again exemplifies the fundamental tension between traditional accountability to parliament and modern accountability to the public directly.

Jeffrey Roy notes that "the traditional doctrine of ministerial responsibility is simply no match for today's contemporary governance mosaic."[17] The ritual of a daily question period is inadequate for holding the executive to account for the complicated and diverse activities of a modern government, with the result that information essential to accountability simply does not emerge. Indeed, ministers themselves are hard-pressed to monitor the activities of their own departments, to say nothing of independent agencies that sit even less easily within the parliamentary tradition. At the same time, there has been a decline of public deference and an emergence of digital communications and social media that offer opportunities for direct citizen oversight of regulators to complement, rather than supplant, the work of Parliament. While there is no question that Parliament should continue to demand answers from ministers, given the inevitable limitations of that mechanism of accountability in a modern era of big government and complex policy decisions, it is time for regulators to throw open their doors to allow greater scrutiny of information by both legislators and citizens at large.

### PROCEDURAL FAIRNESS

In addition to fairness of outcomes, regulatory excellence demands a fair decisionmaking process, one in which a broad range of interests have an opportunity to share their perspectives and provide feedback on proposed standards and decisions. Ideally, consultations provide valuable information on both questions of fact (who is affected and how?) and questions of values (what is the range of public opinion?). Laypersons can contribute expert knowledge drawn from personal experience or oral history.

There is, however, a tradeoff between substantive and procedural goals, in particular between timeliness and cost-effectiveness and procedural inclusiveness. Where to draw the line is further complicated by competing interpretations. A campaign by a Canadian environmental group to "mob the mic" by signing up thousands of British Columbians to testify at NEB hearings concerning the Northern Gateway pipeline was depicted by some as healthy citizen engagement and by others as intentional obstruction of the regulatory process.[18]

Still, many recent regulatory processes fall well short of that gray area. In pursuit of "world-class regulation," Environment Canada itself has committed that "affected parties [will be] engaged throughout the [regulatory] process to give stakeholders a voice, enable market certainty, reinforce credibility, and engender public trust."[19] In stark contrast, the auditor general of Canada reports that detailed regulatory proposals have been shared with industry representatives only. The distinctive Canadian approach of inviting diverse stakeholders to "multistakeholder consultations" on regulatory proposals that prevailed for two decades appears to have been abandoned since 2006, while the terms of reference for National Energy Board pipeline reviews since the Northern Gateway controversy have excluded all but a narrow definition of "directly affected" citizens, including dozens of academic experts who unsuccessfully sought to testify concerning climate change.[20]

## CONCLUSION

Needless to say, it is difficult to establish quantitative measures for criteria such as honesty, transparency, and procedural fairness. In part, that is because there is a gray area between acceptable and unacceptable performance. Where is the line between strategic and misleading rhetoric? How inclusive is inclusive enough? How transparent is sufficiently open? In part, it is because it is difficult to measure performance on these criteria when only those making public statements know whether they are intentionally misleading their audience. However, the impossibility of devising quantitative measures does not mean that these criteria are less important. Indeed, they are the fundamental underpinnings of any regulatory regime.

Regulation is among the most politically challenging of policy instruments. Regulated entities actively resist strict mandates, while beneficiaries are often disengaged. In that context, it is easy to ignore discretionary mandates or decline to enforce unpopular standards. It is tempting to keep bad news private and to oversell program effectiveness. An excellent regulator is one who is aware of and resists those temptations. An excellent regulator goes looking for problems, and ways to solve them.

## NOTES

1. Mancur Olson, *The Logic of Collective Action: Public Goods and the Theory of Groups* (Harvard University Press, 1965).

2. Eugene Bardach and Robert A. Kagan, *Going by the Book: The Problem of Regulatory Unreasonableness* (Temple University Press, 1982).

3. Terry M. Moe and Michael Caldwell, "The Institutional Foundations of Democratic Government: A Comparison of Presidential and Parliamentary Systems," *Journal of Institutional and Theoretical Economics* 150, no. 1 (March 1994): 171–95.

4. Kathryn Harrison and George Hoberg, *Risk, Science, and Politics: Regulating Toxic Substances in Canada and the United States* (McGill–Queen's University Press, 1994).

5. R. Kent Weaver, "The Politics of Blame Avoidance," *Journal of Public Policy* 6, no. 1 (October–December 1986): 371–98; R. Kent Weaver, *Automatic Government: The Politics of Indexation* (Brookings Institution Press, 1988).

6. James Q. Wilson "The Politics of Regulation," in *The Politics of Regulation*, edited by James Q. Wilson (New York: Basic Books, 1980), pp. 357–94.

7. Olson, *The Logic of Collective Action*; Wilson, "The Politics of Regulation," pp. 357–94.

8. On the failure of Canadian governments to fulfill regulatory mandates, see Kathryn Harrison, *Passing the Buck: Federalism and Canadian Environmental Policy* (University of British Columbia Press, 1996).

9. Marver H. Bernstein, *Regulating Business by Independent Commission* (Princeton University Press, 1955).

10. See Shawn McCarthy, "Environment Minister Aglukkaq Vows to Fulfill 2020 Carbon Promise," *Globe and Mail*, November 18, 2013; Canada, Environment Canada, *Canada's Emissions Trends* (Ottawa: Minister of the Environment, October 2013); Office of the Auditor General of Canada, "Report of the Commissioner of the Environment and Sustainable Development," Fall 2014 (www.oag-bvg.gc.ca/internet/English/parl_cesd_201410_e_39845.html).

11. Alberta, "Alberta's 2008 Climate Change Strategy: Responsibility, Leadership, Action," January 2008 (http://environment.gov.ab.ca/info/library/7894.pdf).

12. Auditor General Alberta, "Report of the Auditor General of Alberta," July 2014 (www.oag.ab.ca/webfiles/reports/AGJuly2014Report.pdf). See also Matt McClure, "Alberta's Claims of Greenhouse Gas Success Don't Measure Up, Experts Say," *Calgary Herald*, March 22, 2015; James Wilt, "Alberta's New Head of Climate Change Plan, Diana McQueen, Blows Smoke while Province Fails to Act," March 30, 2015 (www.desmog.ca/2015/03/30/alberta-s-new-head-climate-change-plan-diana-mcqueen-blows-smoke-while-province-fails-act).

13. National Research Council, Committee on the Institutional Means for Assessment of Risks to Public Health, *Risk Assessment in the Federal Government: Managing the Process* (Washington: National Academies Press, 1983); Harrison and Hoberg, *Risk, Science, and Politics.*

14. Cary Coglianese and Gary E. Marchant, "Shifting Sands: The Limits of Science in Setting Risk Standards," *University of Pennsylvania Law Review* 152, no. 4 (April 2004): 1255, 1265.

15. Auditor General Alberta, "Report of the Auditor General of Alberta," July 2014.

16. Werner Antweiler and Kathryn Harrison, "Canada's Voluntary ARET Program: Limited Success despite Industry Cosponsorship," *Journal of Policy Analysis and Management* 26, no. 4 (2007): 755–74.

17. Jeffrey Roy, "Beyond Westminster Governance: Bringing Politics and Public Service into the Networked Era," *Canadian Public Administration* 51, no. 4 (December 2008): 541–68.

18. Canadian Press, "Northern Gateway Hearings Start in Kitimat on $5.5 Billion Oil Pipeline Proposal," *The Tyee*, January 8, 2012 (http://thetyee.ca/Blogs/TheHook /Environment/2012/01/08/Northern-Gateway-hearings-start/); Jenny Uechi, "British Columbians Urged to Pipe Up about Enbridge Northern Gateway Project," *Vancouver Observer*, September 20, 2011 (www.vancouverobserver.com/politics/news/2011 /09/20/british-columbians-urged-pipe-about-enbridge-northern-gateway-project).

19. Office of the Auditor General of Canada, "Report of the Commissioner of the Environment and Sustainable Development," Fall 2014 (www.oag-bvg.gc.ca/internet /English/parl_cesd_201410_e_39845.html).

20. Simon Donner, Kathryn Harrison, and George Hoberg, "Donner, Harrison, and Hoberg: Let's Talk about Climate Change," *National Post*, April 10, 2014.

# 5

# Beyond Process Excellence

## *Enhancing Societal Well-Being*

### JOHN D. GRAHAM AND PAUL R. NOE

**THERE IS MUCH CONFUSION** among academics, regulatory practitioners, and stakeholders over what it means for a regulator to be excellent. We suspect that there is even greater consternation over process—how regulations are made—than about the substantive outcomes. The confusion is so ingrained in both law and regulatory practice that regulatory programs frequently are not even designed to objectively determine, before or after enactment, whether a regulation enhances societal well-being.[1] We believe that the confusion is both a symptom and a cause of a large void in the architecture of administrative law: there is no general legal framework to require regulators to balance tradeoffs and design regulations that do more good than harm.

For more than twenty years, the Organization for Economic Cooperation and Development (OECD) has been promoting the use of regulatory impact analysis (RIA) and related analytic tools to increase the focus of regulators on societal well-being. Key OECD recommendations include a centralized regulatory oversight body in each country, a rigorous process of ex ante RIA, and some "look-back" process to modernize existing regulations. The response in Europe has been a "better regulation" movement that has made progress at the EU level and in some countries (for example, the United Kingdom and the Netherlands).[2] But the quality of RIA in Europe is highly uneven.[3] In the developing world, progress toward better regulation has been even slower, although the World Bank has played a constructive role with its annual *Doing*

*Business* report.[4] More recently, pro-environment interests have begun to see merit in promoting benefit-cost analysis in the developing world.[5]

Although executive directives have exhorted regulators to maximize societal well-being, political and institutional resistance is so strong that we believe it necessitates the enactment of judicially enforceable legislation requiring regulators to do more good than harm. In the United States, there is a long-standing presidential directive that agencies design regulations so their benefits justify the costs, but it does not trump presidential and interest-group politics.[6] Moreover, many regulators proceed from one regulation to the next without much focus on understanding the outcomes of their work; insofar as regulators are concerned about results, the yardstick tends to be whether they hear complaints from organized interest groups, judges, or elected officials. That is a pretty weak filter since, when citizens experience good or bad outcomes in daily life (such as a change in the price of gasoline or a new safety feature in their car), they rarely realize whether those outcomes relate to regulatory action or other factors.

Process considerations are by no means trivial or unimportant. They include adherence to the statutory language that authorizes agency action, as well as requirements around public and stakeholder participation and transparency about decisionmaking rationales. Process also encompasses political considerations such as whether the regulatory action is consistent with the priorities of the president or prime minister and, more crassly, whether the regulatory action advances the electoral interests of the political leadership or the (usually partisan) allies of the political leadership in the legislature.

As important as process considerations can be, the most important outcomes of regulation are the effects on citizens, businesses, and other organizations, and the social, economic, and natural environment. We presume the key outcomes are those that influence well-being, where well-being is understood to be determined by the overall welfare of citizens, as well as the distribution of that welfare. The quality of the natural environment, for example, is judged by the humans who experience it, recognizing that humans have a strong interest in the welfare of other species as well as the welfare of future generations. Likewise, the outcomes for citizens are of primary concern, but those citizens may have interests in the well-being of noncitizens in the nation-state or in other nations.

In drawing a sharp distinction between process and outcome, we do not intend to suggest that procedural requirements are unrelated to the quest for good outcomes.[7] When the U.S. Congress gave federal courts the power to overturn "arbitrary and capricious" regulatory actions, for example, it presumably did so, at least in part, with an eye toward protecting society from the perverse outcomes that could flow from "arbitrary and capricious" regulations.

A similar outcome-related justification could be made for other procedures that mandate public participation, transparency, and respect for legislative or administrative priorities.

In this chapter we argue that procedural criteria of regulatory excellence are relevant and important but should be understood as only the bare minimum: fidelity to process is the beginning rather than the end of the inquiry into regulatory excellence. The more important dimensions of excellence, which we acknowledge may be philosophically and scientifically more challenging, relate to the substance of the regulatory design and the ultimate impacts of a regulation on societal well-being. To be more responsive to well-being, regulatory procedural requirements should be supplemented with requirements that emphasize well-being. This issue is being raised in Europe as well as the United States.[8] One might argue, with some irony, that in this chapter we are advocating process reform to improve the substantive design of regulations and their outcomes for society. We would put it differently: we believe that administrative process needs to be supplemented with legally enforceable administrative substance requirements to ensure that regulations do more good than harm.

## SOCIETAL WELL-BEING AND CURRENT PROCEDURES: THE DISCONNECT

Although pursuing regulatory excellence based on societal well-being is not easy, procedural requirements alone are likely to have an imperfect relationship to well-being. A well-being approach to regulatory excellence is consequentialist because it presumes that the ultimate determination of regulatory excellence requires understanding how the regulator, through its rules, affects well-being. If one relies entirely on procedural notions of excellence, either one does not need to address consequences or one needs to have confidence that procedural requirements deliver excellent consequences. But a definition of regulatory excellence that restricts itself only to an open and participatory process provides no bulwark against the institutional and political forces that can all too frequently diminish, rather than enhance, societal well-being.

Since the current body of procedural requirements in many countries (including the United States) were adopted without explicitly considering the well-being approach to regulatory evaluation, it takes a large leap of faith—or an "invisible hand" in regulatory politics—to believe that current procedures maximize societal well-being. We believe, and show in this chapter with U.S. case studies, that regulatory politics can have the opposite effect. And if the United States is not sufficiently outcome oriented, the problem likely is more acute around the world, where RIA practices are less rooted in the political and legal culture.

A regulator's well-being inquiry has three major components: (1) the physical consequences of the regulation for citizens (often mediated through impacts on businesses, the environment, and so forth), (2) the valuation of those consequences (typically based on what citizens would prefer if they were well informed), and (3) a distributional check to ensure that, once aggregated, the distribution of societal well-being is acceptable (or, preferably, optimal).

Theorists argue that these steps can be embedded in a social-welfare function, where social welfare is determined by the well-being of each citizen and an aggregation system to account for distributional preferences (a special case is a function where the well-being of each citizen is weighted equally). Yet existing regulatory procedures in many countries are not well designed to implement the well-being criterion, and interest-group and electoral politics too often can undermine well-being.[9]

## High-Quality Scientific and Technical Information

To achieve excellence, regulators need access to the best available scientific and technical information, including objective and unbiased interpretation of that information. Unfortunately, regulatory procedures can fail to encourage, or even allow, regulators to gather the best available evidence and engage in the close coordination between scientists and regulators needed to achieve well-designed regulations. In a regulatory system where interest-group and electoral politics are dominant concerns, the quest for high-quality scientific and technical information can be diminished.

Although regulators possess substantial technical resources to assist in estimating the consequences of regulatory alternatives, the best available expertise is not necessarily located in the regulating agency. For example, when there was public concern about "sudden acceleration" in Toyota cars in the United States, the National Highway Traffic Safety Administration (NHTSA) of the Department of Transportation (DOT) realized that there were technical issues best addressed by another federal agency, the National Aeronautics and Space Administration. When the U.S. Environmental Protection Agency (EPA) regulates the energy industry, agency professionals sometimes seek (and at times resist) the technical contributions from analysts at the Department of Energy (DOE), because DOE has greater expertise on some questions. In the field of chemical risk assessment, DOE, the Department of Defense, and the Food and Drug Administration (FDA) have argued in various cases that EPA did not properly use the best available science, and in some cases the

National Research Council of the National Academy of Sciences has concurred with the criticism of EPA.[10]

When the U.S. Office of Management and Budget (OMB) reviews a proposed rule, it includes other relevant agencies, but current regulatory procedures do not always require or encourage the regulator with legislative authority to defer to, or even consult with, other regulators that have better access to relevant data and expertise. In the United States, the White House, practicing a unitary theory of the executive branch, typically discourages one agency from publicly criticizing the technical work of another agency. A promising approach would be for regulators to seek advice on, or peer review of, regulatory science by qualified experts organized by institutions that are separate from the regulatory body. Yet at present one cannot have great confidence that the first step in the well-being criterion—projecting the physical consequences of regulation—is handled with excellence since regulators are not expected to rely on the best experts inside and outside of government.

There are greater hurdles to regulators using scientific and technical information submitted by regulated entities, even when that information is the most relevant and authoritative. Regulatory procedures sometimes treat scientists and engineers in regulated entities as if they were more biased than experts in academia, think tanks, consulting firms, or the government. No compelling evidence supports such a general claim of bias, especially if regulators scrutinize the quality of information they obtain through different sources, such as the replicability of experiments and transparency of models.

Looking forward, regulatory excellence requires sound decisionmaking when scientific and technical information is uncertain—that is, when there is a cost (or risk) of waiting for better scientific information. The value-of-information (VOI) framework, a close cousin of benefit-cost analysis, is well suited to addressing this pervasive dilemma, but it is rarely used by regulatory agencies. The VOI stance provides a more promising framework for harmonizing U.S. and European regulations than does uneven application of a subjective precautionary principle.[11]

### Determining the Preferences of Informed Citizens

The valuation of the physical consequences of regulation is typically performed in monetary units, facilitating an apples-to-apples comparison of benefits and costs. Using methods such as revealed preference and stated preference, regulatory analysts strive to ensure that plausible monetary values are assigned to physical consequences.

The social sciences are making progress with these methods, but significant uncertainties remain, as indicated by the contemporary controversy over the "social cost of carbon" (that is, the estimated monetary damage to society of emitting a ton of carbon dioxide into the atmosphere). One of the key inputs to this calculation, the social discount rate for converting future consequences into present value, remains a source of contention among professional economists. There is some effort in the United States, led usually by OMB, to require best-available valuation methods and numerical values (see, for example, OMB Circular A-4, "Regulatory Analysis"), but such efforts are not routinely updated or followed. Regulatory agencies are not legally required to use OMB-recommended methods or to explain to courts why they deviated from OMB guidance.

Some Western-trained economists and libertarians confuse valuation efforts by assuming that consumer preferences observed in real-world markets are necessarily the preferences that should be honored by regulatory analysts implementing the well-being criterion. The assumption is fine in most cases, but there are exceptions when it is apparent (or likely) that the preferences revealed by consumers or workers are based on factual errors, poorly explained information, misperceptions, ill-considered emotions, or faulty reasoning processes. It is also reasonable to ask how regulators themselves can overcome such basic human frailties; the reason is presumably because the regulator has access to specialized knowledge and training (such as the findings of decision science and behavioral economics) and has practice in dealing with issues that consumers confront less frequently. Thus it is imperative that regulators pursue their craft in an objective and unbiased manner. A judicially enforceable requirement to do more good than harm would help maintain that focus.

### Aggregation and Distributional Concerns

The least-developed area in the well-being criterion is distributional weighting, and in the United States and elsewhere the design of the regulatory system is questionable on this point. Current procedural requirements often do require special consideration of specific interest groups, sectors, or subpopulations (for example, small businesses, children, aboriginal groups, state and local governments, farmers, and so forth), but such requirements seem to reflect interest-group politics more than a well-grounded philosophical stance on the fairness-based design of a social welfare function. Organized interest groups already are well represented through notice-and-comment procedures, public hearings, and face-to-face meetings with staff at regulatory agencies and oversight bodies like OMB, but the interests of the unorganized public (especially lower-income citizens, nonunion workers, ordinary taxpayers, and consumers) have remarkably little weight in current regulatory processes.

Fortunately, many current requirements for RIA or benefit-cost analysis provide some voice for the interests of the unorganized.

There are, however, serious limitations of the regulatory review process. In the United States, OMB review typically occurs late in the game, after the agency has determined the course of action it wants to take. (In fact, agencies too often treat benefit-cost analysis as a post hoc justification for regulatory proposals that were designed with other motivations.) OMB is given more power in some presidential administrations than in others. OMB also is short on staff and not backed up by any judicial review of agency compliance with the executive order on regulatory review or the Circular A-4 analytic guidelines. Perversely, presidential politics sometimes causes agencies and OMB to be deployed in a direction that could undermine societal well-being. And there is a large volume of "stealth regulation" that occurs without any OMB review or benefit-cost justification, and much of this activity is permissible under current procedural requirements.[12]

In fact, specialized U.S. procedures already have been established to facilitate "regulatory negotiation" whereby organized interest groups (for example, trade associations, labor unions, and environmental groups) can meet and draft a proposed regulation for consideration by the responsible agency. Once such interest groups agree on an approach, it is difficult for an analysis of societal well-being to have much impact. Thus there may be a disconnect between those who value regulatory negotiation and those who value societal well-being.

### Key Regulatory Design Issues

In many cases, the issue is not whether to regulate. Regulators rarely launch a regulatory initiative that has no merit because markets are working perfectly. And it is not common for regulators to fabricate economic and scientific information to justify a regulatory intervention where regulation is completely unnecessary.

The more prevalent questions concern the breadth and stringency of regulation, the proper choice of regulatory instrument, and the coordination of national regulation with related rules at the state, local, and international levels. It can be challenging to overcome political opposition and enact a stringent regulation even when called for by the well-being standard, but a benefit-cost ratio can make a difference.[13] Despite these key questions, many process requirements (such as consultation with stakeholders) relate only to the procedural steps of developing the regulation, not to the substantive issue of whether the regulation as designed increases societal welfare. Thus current and often-advocated procedures are insufficient for implementation of the well-being criterion and the meaningful attainment of regulatory excellence.

## REGULATORY CASE STUDIES: THE GOOD, THE BAD, AND THE UGLY

To illustrate the preceding conceptual themes, we present some brief regulatory case studies from the United States. Some of the cases highlight good practices for regulation that promotes societal well-being; others reveal shortcomings of process alone.

### *Trans-Fat Labeling for Foods*

A strong body of experimental and epidemiological evidence links the trans-fatty-acid content of food to a risk of coronary heart disease. In February 1994, the Center for Science in the Public Interest (CSPI), a nutrition and health advocacy organization, petitioned the FDA to include trans-fat on nutrition labels and set limits on the amounts of trans-fat in foods. Recognizing the growing body of evidence, the FDA finally proposed in November 1999 that the standard food label be modified to include information on trans-fat content.

The FDA's benefit-cost analysis showed that such a change would lead many companies to reduce the trans-fat content of their food products. The benefits from reduced heart attacks (about $2.9 billion per year) would more than pay for the extra labeling and food-processing costs (up to $275 million per year, then declining after the third year of compliance).

During the transition from the Clinton to the G. W. Bush administration, the FDA's momentum behind the trans-fat rule petered out. The well-organized baker and processing associations had filled the rulemaking record with numerous critical comments. The Bush administration was slow to appoint an FDA commissioner. Only one consumer group, CSPI, was working the issue aggressively, but it had limited influence in conservative administrations.

Despite the lack of support, based on the strength of the FDA's benefit-cost analysis, OMB decided to publicly prompt the FDA to finish the trans-fat rulemaking.[14] When the FDA did so in 2003, the rule helped stimulate a much broader movement in the United States and abroad to reduce the trans-fat content of foods offered everywhere from grocery stores to fast-food restaurants. Simply disclosing information helped transform the grocery store aisle into a platform for companies to compete on the healthy attributes of their food products.

The FDA's trans-fat labeling rule illustrates how faithfulness to the criterion of societal well-being can lead to favorable regulatory outcomes. Those outcomes might not have occurred—or at best would have occurred years later—under the model of interest-group pluralism that underpins much of the current procedural design of the regulatory system. One might argue there was a lack of leadership at the FDA, but there is no question that a favorable RIA helped to break the impasse.

### Reducing Interstate Transport of Air Pollutants

During the George W. Bush administration, the U.S. EPA issued the Clean Air Interstate Rule (CAIR), which required coal-fired power plants to reduce by 60–70 percent the emission of sulfur dioxide and nitrogen dioxide, pollutants that can be transported long distances and form smog and soot. (A similar regulatory program was enacted in Europe, called Clean Air Strategy Europe, with an RIA reaching similar conclusions.) Although CAIR was expensive (about $1.9 to $3.1 billion per year), EPA estimated that the benefits— primarily avoidance of premature deaths from fine particle exposure—were thirty times greater than the costs. Using more conservative (yet plausible) assumptions about benefits, OMB estimated that the benefit-cost ratio would be 1 to 3. OMB and EPA together argued unsuccessfully in the Bush White House, on benefit-cost grounds, that the sulfur cap should reduce sulfur by 90 percent rather than 70 percent.

The federal courts ultimately slowed implementation of the CAIR rule for legalistic reasons that are inconsistent with the societal well-being criterion. EPA under the Obama administration reissued the rule with somewhat greater coverage and stringency but also ran into judicial obstacles. Absent a statutory well-being requirement, litigation of rules often veers off in directions of questionable public value.

CAIR also illustrates how regional politics can contribute to regulatory outcomes inconsistent with faithful implementation of a societal well-being standard. If benefit-cost analysis supported a 90 percent sulfur reduction, why wouldn't the Bush EPA enact it? The answer to this question may be informed by an appreciation of how regional politics in "battleground states" influences presidential politics.

George W. Bush was elected president in November 2000 by the narrowest electoral college margin in modern political history. While the national press made much of Bush's victory in Florida (because of the controversy over "hanging chads" on paper ballots and the five-to-four Supreme Court decision against a Florida recount), Bush's 52–46 percent victory in West Virginia (with its five electoral college votes) was equally crucial to his election. In fact, Bush's defeat of Vice President Al Gore in West Virginia was the first win by a Republican presidential candidate in that state since 1928.[15]

The economy of West Virginia is heavily dependent on coal, which is used primarily to generate electricity. Throughout the 2000 campaign, Bush pledged his support of "clean coal" as an energy source and successfully painted Gore as an enemy of coal. During Bush's first term, there was a strong reluctance in the White House to issue burdensome regulations that might cause electric utilities to shift from coal to natural gas.

There certainly were principled policy concerns about overregulating energy (for example, fuel diversity, the reliability and affordability of gas when prices were high before the fracking revolution, and the need for affordable gas in manufacturing). It did not help EPA's cause that its benefit-cost estimate was viewed skeptically in the White House. Although the rule had a plausible case using more realistic estimates, there was room for varying interpretations, which illustrates the importance of agencies using objective and unbiased analysis in determining societal well-being.

However, it was apparent that Bush would fight hard to keep West Virginia when he sought reelection in 2004. One way that Bush succeeded was by moderating regulatory burdens on coal. Without a legal mandate to maximize societal well-being, electoral politics can trump such an outcome.

### The California Zero-Emission Vehicle (ZEV) Mandate

When Barack Obama campaigned for the White House in 2008, one of the base constituencies he courted was the network of West Coast advocates seeking to commercialize the electric vehicle (EV). The network includes organized pro-car environmentalists and their donors, California-based venture capitalists with interests in battery and electric drive-train technology, companies that produce the chargers and recharging stations (also based in California), investors in Tesla (the darling of EV companies), and Silicon Valley entrepreneurs who see EVs as a symbol of technological progress. To appeal to EV enthusiasts, Obama pledged to put one million plug-in vehicles on the road by 2015 and to force automakers to achieve an average of fifty miles per gallon (MPG) or more in new vehicles by 2025.[16]

When Obama took office in January 2009, he promptly delivered on his pledges. Obama's first budget supported the generous EV tax credits that Congress initiated in 2008. Depending on the vehicle's design, an EV purchaser was made eligible for tax credits of up to $7,500 for the purchase of a vehicle and up to $2,000 for the cost of purchasing and installing a home charger. On the supply side of the market, DOE, under the 2009 Recovery Act, allocated $2.1 billion in subsidies for battery manufacturing projects, vehicle component production, construction of production facilities, and community-based EV demonstration projects. Billions more in federal loan guarantees for EVs were granted to companies such as Ford, Nissan, and several suppliers.[17]

On the regulatory front, EPA and DOT undertook a joint rulemaking to increase the average fuel efficiency of passenger vehicles from 35.5 miles per gallon in 2016 to 54.5 miles per gallon by 2025. The EPA-DOT rulemaking was supported by an elaborate benefit-cost analysis. Tucked in the rulemaking were two little-noticed provisions for EVs that were not subjected to any benefit-cost analysis.

First, DOT/EPA encouraged vehicle manufacturers to comply with the tighter MPG requirements by installing EVs, rather than more cost-effective technologies such as the conventional hybrid engine (as commercialized by Toyota in the Prius) or the clean diesel engine (as championed by German vehicle manufacturers).[18] To tilt the compliance incentive toward EVs, DOT/EPA allowed vehicle manufacturers to count EVs as two vehicles instead of one in their MPG compliance calculations for the early years of the 2017–2025 program. Moreover, in the carbon-control aspect of the DOT/EPA rule, EVs are not penalized for any of the carbon dioxide emissions they induce at power plants by consuming electricity. EVs effectively are treated as ZEVs.

Second, and more important, in 2009 DOT/EPA granted a waiver to California (and to nine states aligned with California) under the Clean Air Act to proceed with an ambitious California ZEV program.[19] Normally only the federal government regulates motor vehicle emissions, but the Clean Air Act gives California the option to seek a waiver from EPA to be allowed to set its own, more stringent vehicle emission standards. After EPA granted California its waiver in 2009, the California Air Resources Board (CARB) issued a state requirement that vehicle manufacturers selling into California must offer for sale an increasing number of ZEVs starting in 2018, reaching by 2025 a required minimum of 15 percent of new vehicle sales that can meet the zero-emission standard. Under the state regulation, California-based Tesla, as a "low-volume" manufacturer, was exempted from ZEV burdens but was permitted to sell credits for its ZEVs to other manufacturers, thereby boosting its troubled balance sheet.

CARB did publish a rudimentary benefit-cost analysis of its ZEV mandate. It concluded that it would take roughly the ten-year life of a vehicle for the energy savings of a ZEV to pay for a ZEV's initial $10,000 cost premium.[20] A variety of the technical assumptions used in CARB's analysis likely would not have passed muster under OMB's guidelines for regulatory analysis, Circular A-4. More important, CARB's analysis focused only on the well-being of California; the analysis was not done from a national perspective.

EPA's waiver decision allowing CARB to adopt the ZEV mandate should have been subjected to a national benefit-cost analysis, with OMB review. Under the Clean Air Act, other states are permitted to sign on to the California ZEV program if they wish. About ten (including New York, Massachusetts, Oregon, and Washington) have done so. Thus, the California ZEV mandate now covers more than one quarter of all new vehicle sales in the United

States. EPA's ZEV waiver for California was a multibillion-dollar decision with national economic ramifications.

Moreover, car dealers find it very challenging to sell ZEVs, despite all of the subsidies and incentives; California, for example, gives ZEVs access to high-occupancy vehicle (HOV) lanes. A ZEV not only is more expensive than a conventional hybrid or diesel-powered car, but also has limited range (less than 100 miles for most pure EVs) and takes four hours to charge (assuming the user has an upgraded level-2 home charger).[21] Accordingly, manufacturers likely will have to cut prices on ZEVs to comply with the California mandate and compensate for the losses by raising prices on non-ZEV vehicles.[22] The resulting welfare losses will not be confined to California and the other ZEV states. Those losses will be felt partly by consumers and stockholders in all states and partly in the form of reduced compensation and layoffs of workers where plants are located (for example, Mexico, Japan, Germany, Missouri, Ontario, Michigan, Alabama, Tennessee, Kentucky, and Indiana).[23] Few employment losses will occur in ZEV states because those states have no vehicle assembly plants and few supplier plants.[24]

Finally, the ZEV program may not produce any significant environmental benefits because the market interactions between the ZEV mandate and the 54.5 MPG federal mandate were not analyzed carefully. If a manufacturer is compelled to sell an additional ZEV into the California market, it can count that ZEV twice(!) in its MPG compliance calculation at the federal level. That means the manufacturer may sell an additional gas-guzzler and still comply with the 54.5 MPG mandate. Adding the ZEV mandate to a federal program that encourages ZEVs could, under plausible assumptions, cause more carbon pollution than the federal program by itself (with or without the two-for-one sweetener).[25]

The sobering story of the California ZEV program illustrates the need for a legally enforceable mandate for regulators to do more good than harm. The quality of the benefit-cost decision must be scrutinized carefully, such as through robust judicial review, since regulators and their reviewers will be constrained from checking a poorly analyzed campaign pledge of a president or prime minister. A national benefit-cost requirement backed by judicial review would check the executive's misuse of regulatory power for base-pleasing purposes and promote meaningful regulatory excellence.

## IMPLICATIONS AND PRESCRIPTIONS

The focuses of administrative procedures (for example, faithfulness to statute, transparency as to the rationale for decisions, and opportunity for public and stakeholder participation) are not objectionable if understood as minimum standards for excellence that must be coupled with a substantive focus on well-being. An exclusive focus on administrative procedure, though, gives enormous weight to organized interest groups and politicians' policy preferences, neither of which is always a good proxy for societal well-being.

The first distortion, familiar to scholars of regulation, is the influence of interest-group politics (often in the form of "rent seeking"). History suggests that the legislature will be particularly vulnerable to the wishes of well-organized special interests that draw support from several regions of the country. Elected executive officials are certainly not immune from interest-group capture either, as illustrated by the ZEV mandate.

The second distortion follows from this last point. Although it is often viewed as legitimate ("democratic") for regulatory policy to reflect the priorities and electoral interests of elected politicians, especially national leaders, their views may have little to do with overall societal well-being. In the United States, the president's policy preferences are increasingly treated as legitimate because he is the only elected official who represents the entire nation, in contrast to individual senators and representatives who focus on the interests of their states or districts. The issues are different in a parliamentary system, where the executives are drawn from the Parliament, but still national ministers are sometimes granted greater deference because they are seen to represent the entire nation.

Unfortunately, there are ominous trends that may motivate chief executives to give relatively less attention to societal well-being than they might have in the past. At least in the United States, the contemporary bout of partisan polarization may lead chief executives to act contrary to societal well-being. Under polarization, chief executives are perceived as leaders of their political party as much as leaders of the country as a whole.[26] (In this respect, the United States is beginning to resemble a two-party parliamentary system.) That induces a particular presidential focus on the policy preferences of party activists, partisan-oriented media professionals, and party-oriented donors, as they are the most politically active and they offer cues to the ordinary partisan voter who does not pay as much attention to politics. As a result, chief executives work at least as hard at "base politics" (pleasing and turning out the faithful) as they do at appealing to the median voter (the true independent or moderate). Once elected, chief executives may seek policies that reward their base even if the policies are questionable from the perspective of societal well-being, as illustrated by Obama's commitment to a ZEV mandate.

If a chief executive from one party makes regulatory policy for societal well-being that happens to please interest groups aligned with the opposing party, there may be little political benefit. Bush's decision on labeling foods for trans-fat content raises this issue, and there are certainly pro-business regulatory decisions by Obama that were not effusively praised by the business community. The inability of chief executives to count on any public praise for decisions unless they are base-pleasing measures is a strong disincentive to focus on societal well-being.

A third distortion occurs because of the tremendous significance of electoral politics. The distorting effects of electoral politics on regulatory policy are particularly acute in the United States, as illustrated by Bush's defeat of Al Gore in West Virginia and relatively restrained regulation of coal in the Bush administration. In parliamentary systems, similar distortions arise from the ways votes are counted and coalition governments are formed.

A fourth distortion arises in many democracies because of the much too frequently noncompetitive nature of general elections. In the United States, the president is elected not by the national popular vote but by electoral college votes in a dwindling number of "battleground states": for example, Colorado (9), Florida (29), Iowa (6), New Hampshire (4), Nevada (6), North Carolina (15), Ohio (18), Virginia (13). As a gross rule of thumb, both parties have a good shot at about 190 electoral college votes with any decent presidential candidate. Most of the contested campaign occurs in ten or fewer swing states with about 100 electoral college votes. The victors are encouraged, owing to a reelection mindset that seems to pervade among both elected leaders and their advisers, to spend their terms in office focusing on policies that might give them an edge in subsequent elections in those battleground states. This distracts from a focus on societal well-being, which is the proper definition of regulatory excellence.

We close with two proposals consistent with OECD recommendations and recent developments in the European Union to give greater voice to societal well-being in legislative and executive deliberations. First, to promote greater substantive regulatory excellence, legislatures should recognize the essential role that they play in regulatory policy and take the modest step of imposing RIA requirements for new legislation. The establishment of dedicated offices within legislative bodies to implement those RIA requirements not only would provide benefit-cost information to legislators on regulatory legislation, but also could help in overseeing the work of regulatory agencies and providing analytic comments on rulemakings, particularly those that seem to have a weak benefit-cost rationale. Second, legislatures or other oversight institutions should supplement current rulemaking procedures with administrative *substance* requirements focused on societal well-being. Ideally, legislatures should make it crystal clear to reviewing courts that regulations will not pass muster unless they do more good than harm.[27]

NOTES

*Acknowledgments:* With respect to co-author Paul Noe, the views expressed in this chapter are his own and do not represent the views of AF&PA or its member companies.

1. Organization for Economic Cooperation and Development, *Report on Regulatory Reform* (Paris: OECD, 1997).

2. Jonathan B. Wiener, "Better Regulation in Europe," *Current Legal Problems* 59 (2006): 447–518.

3. Claudio M. Radaelli and Fabrizio De Francesco, *Regulatory Quality in Europe: Concepts, Measures, and Policy Processes* (Manchester University Press, 2007).

4. World Bank Group, *Doing Business*, Annual publication (Washington: World Bank).

5. Michael A. Livermore and Richard L. Revesz, *The Globalization of Cost-Benefit Analysis in Environmental Policy* (Oxford University Press, 2013).

6. President Reagan issued Executive Order (EO) 12291 in 1981 requiring benefit-cost analysis for major rules, followed by Clinton EO 12866 (1993) and Obama EO 13563 (2011).

7. On how administrative procedures can lead to good outcomes, see Steven P. Croley, *Regulation and the Public Interests: The Possibility of Good Regulatory Government* (Princeton University Press, 2008).

8. Alberto Alemanno, "A Meeting of the Minds on Impact Assessment: When Ex Ante Evaluation Meets Ex Post Judicial Control," *European Public Law* 17, no. 3 (2011): 485–505; Alberto Alemanno, "The Better Regulation Initiative at the Judicial Gate: A Trojan Horse within the Commission's Walls or the Way Forward?," *European Law Journal* 15, no. 3 (2009): 382–401.

9. For a classic statement of how interest-group politics and rent seeking detract from the benefit-cost state, see C. Boyden Gray, "Obstacles to Regulatory Reform," *University of Chicago Legal Forum* (1997): 1–11.

10. Cheryl Hogue, "EPA's Efforts Endorsed," *Chemical and Engineering News* 92, no. 20 (2014): 26–27.

11. On how Europe and the United States differ on science-based regulation, see Jonathan B. Wiener and others, eds., *The Reality of Precaution: Comparing Risk Regulation in the United States and Europe* (Washington: Resources for the Future Press, 2011).

12. John D. Graham and Cory R. Liu, "Regulatory and Quasi-Regulatory Activity without OMB and Cost-Benefit Review," *Harvard Journal of Law and Public Policy* 37, no. 2 (Spring 2014): 425–45; Paul R. Noe and John D. Graham, "Due Process and Management for Guidance Documents: Good Governance Long Overdue," *Yale Journal on Regulation* 25 (Winter 2008): 103, 104 and n7, 109 and nn28–30.

13. Richard L. Revesz and Michael A. Livermore, *Retaking Rationality: How Cost-Benefit Analysis Can Better Protect the Environment and Our Health* (Oxford University Press, 2008).

14. Judith Weinraub, "The Hidden Fat; Some Scientists Have Known about the Dangers of Trans Fats for More Than Two Decades. What Took the Government So Long?," *Washington Post*, September 10, 2003.

15. Michael Barone and Richard E. Cohen, *The Almanac of American Politics 2004* (Washington: National Journal Group, 2003), p. 1709.

16. Margaret Kriz, "Is Obama's Goal of Putting One Million Plug-in Hybrids on the Road by 2015 Achievable?," *National Journal*, May 2, 2009.

17. John D. Graham and others, "No Time for Pessimism about Electric Cars," *Issues in Science and Technology* 31, no. 1 (Fall 2014): 33–40.

18. On the superiority of conventional hybrids, see Jeremy J. Michalek and others, "Valuation of Plug-in Vehicle Life-Cycle Air Emissions and Oil-Displacement Benefits," *Proceedings of the National Academy of Sciences* 108, no. 40 (October 4, 2011): 16554–58; Shisheng Huang and others, "The Effects of Electricity Pricing on PHEV Competitiveness," *Energy Policy* 39 (2011): 1552–61.

19. U.S. Environmental Protection Agency, California State Motor Vehicle Pollution Control Standards; Notice of Decision Granting a Waiver of Clean Air Act Preemption of California's 2009 and Subsequent Model Year Greenhouse Gas Emission Standards for New Motor Vehicles, *Federal Register* 74 (July 8, 2009): 32,744.

20. California Air Resources Board/California Environmental Protection Agency, Staff Report: Initial Statement of Reasons: Advanced Clean Cars: 2012 Proposed Amendments to the California Zero Emission Program Vehicle Regulations, ES-2, December 7, 2011 (www.arb.ca.gov/regact/2012/zev2012/zevisor.pdf).

21. Sanya Carley and others, "Intent to Purchase a Plug-in Electric Vehicle: A Survey of Early Impressions in Large U.S. Cities," *Transportation Research Part D: Transport and Environment* 18 (2013): 39–45.

22. A price war in the EV industry has already begun. Jeff Bennett, "Volt Falls to Electric-Car Price War," *Wall Street Journal*, August 6, 2013.

23. Graham and Liu, "Regulatory and Quasi-Regulatory Activity," pp. 431–39.

24. See "Ten Busiest North American Assembly Plants," *Automotive News*, January 12, 2012.

25. Lawrence H. Goulder and others, "Unintended Consequences from Nested State and Federal Regulations: The Case of the Pavley Greenhouse-Gas-Per-Mile Limits," Working Paper 15337 (Cambridge, Mass.: National Bureau of Economic Research, 2009).

26. Alan I. Abramowitz, *The Disappearing Center* (Yale University Press, 2010).

27. See Caroline Cecot and W. Kip Viscusi, "Judicial Review of Agency Benefit-Cost Analysis," *George Mason Law Review* 22 (2015): 575–617, which finds that U.S. courts reviewing benefit-cost analyses for some regulatory decisions are doing so competently.

# 6

# Regulatory Equilibrium

## TED GAYER

**A NINETEENTH-CENTURY RABBI OFFERED** the following advice: In one pocket you should keep a slip of paper that says, "I am but dust and ashes," and in the other pocket a slip that says, "The world was created for me." The secret of living well, advised this rabbi, comes from knowing when to reach into which pocket.

In seeking an equilibrium between timidity and pride—an equilibrium that another religious scholar describes as humility[1]—I see in the rabbi's advice a useful analog to secular life, and even to the secular role of a regulator. The regulator should be humble about what regulatory actions can achieve, but not nihilistic to the point of neglecting to regulate when there is sufficient evidence. The regulator should appreciate its ability to effect great change, but should also recognize that its role is not to regulate all, or even most, problems, even if the law allows it to do so. My recommendations below lean more toward the need for humility, discretion, and regulatory restraint, since I think the nature of, and selection into, the role of a regulator leads to the tendency to see a societal problem and immediately conceive a regulatory response. This tendency presents a greater risk of unnecessary and harmful regulatory action than of regulatory inaction where it is advisable.

I will focus on one particular balancing goal of an excellent regulator, the need to be guided by scientific evidence, while also recognizing the limits of science in the making of sound regulations. Scientific evidence can provide powerful reasons for forceful regulations ("the world was created for me"), but science can only answer so much and must therefore be employed critically and selectively ("I am but dust and ashes"). The science I refer to includes biological studies (such as epidemiological studies of the health effects from pollution), economics studies (such as the valuation of the health benefits of reducing pollution), and psychological studies (such as the examination of cognitive biases that can lead people to make decisions that harm themselves).

## REGULATION AND THE EVALUATION OF EVIDENCE

The need for regulations to be guided by science should be self-evident, as knowing what and how much to regulate, and how people and the economy will respond to regulations, all require sound evidence. The limits of science might be less appreciated, and they take many forms. First, many regulatory decisions involve questions of values and ethics, which are not within the scope of scientific inquiry.[2] To take just one example, the question of what discount rate to use for valuing the effects of climate change, which will be borne heavily hundreds of years from now, involves ethical considerations of intergenerational equity. A critical question for the regulator, and one that empirical scientific studies cannot much help answer, is how best to incorporate the preferences of future citizens into regulatory decisions made today.

Also, some important questions needed for regulatory decisionmaking might not be amenable to credible empirical examination. For example, the usefulness of any environmental regulation rests squarely on the reliability of the estimates of the benefits and costs of reducing the targeted pollution. The biggest challenge arises in estimating the benefits of an environmental regulation—for example, the effect that a given reduction in a specific pollutant has on the health of affected individuals—because this requires an understanding of the causal relationship between that pollutant and an array of health outcomes.

The ideal, yet impossible, way to estimate a causal relationship would be to observe the same people in two different states of the world: one in which they are exposed to the pollutant and one in which they are not. (Even better from the standpoint of identifying causal relationships would be to study the same people under conditions in which they could be exposed to many different levels of the pollutant.) By comparing the same people in different states of the world, it is guaranteed that all factors other than the pollutant will be held constant, and the different outcomes will therefore reflect the causal impact of the pollutant. The impossibility of observing the same people in different states of the world is known as the fundamental problem of causal inference.

Given this problem, the most credible way to estimate the causal impacts of a pollutant or a regulation is by using a randomized control trial (RCT).[3]

An RCT randomly assigns subjects to a treatment group and a control group. In the pollution example, subjects would be randomly assigned either to one group that is exposed to the pollutant (the treatment group) or to another group not exposed to the pollutant (the control group). (Again, even better would be to have multiple treatment groups, each with different pollution exposures.) Because of the random assignment, with enough observations the treatment and control groups should be statistically identical in all dimensions except pollution exposure. Therefore, any differences in outcomes can credibly be ascribed to exposure to the pollutant. In medicine, for instance, we establish a credible causal relationship between a treatment and a health outcome using an RCT. By randomly dividing people into two groups and comparing the health outcomes after one group has received the treatment, we can be relatively confident that any differences in health in the two groups are caused by the treatment.

While RCTs offer the best means of credibly estimating a causal relationship, they are not foolproof. As Jim Manzi points out in his book, *Uncontrolled*, the applicability of the scientific method (even of controlled experiments) is often limited when we are studying social phenomena.[4] The researcher may confront what Manzi calls high "causal density," which means there are many causal chains and feedback loops at work in social processes, making it difficult to make reliable inferences from a single study, even a single RCT. Manzi argues for using multiple, replicated experiments for social phenomena.

Another possible problem with RCTs exists if the researcher conducting the evaluation does not specify the outcome of interest before the experiment, since it is then possible that the regulator will only witness the subset of outcomes that responded to the treatment. For example, in 2000, the National Heart, Lung, and Blood Institute (NHLBI) in the United States started requiring any studies that it funded to list all primary outcomes of interest before the evaluation was to take place. A recent study examined fifty-five clinical studies between 1970 and 2012 funded by the NHLBI and found that 57 percent of those published before 2000 showed a significant benefit in the primary outcome, but only 8 percent of the ones published after 2000 showed a significant benefit in the primary outcome.[5]

But a bigger impediment to RCTs, especially when examining environmental effects, is that they are seldom possible for ethical or practical reasons. The ethical objections apply to such things as randomized studies of the effects of pollution on health, although perhaps less so where the effect of the treatment is unknown. There are also many practical constraints to RCTs, including legal considerations that can prevent selectively applying regulations in the name of experimentation. The law frequently prohibits applying regulations on a small scale before applying them to the full population or applying regulations differently across regions.

The result is that many regulations have nothing close to the evidence underlying them that even a well-designed RCT might provide. They are also only analyzed before they are implemented and are never subsequently assessed by regulators after they are implemented to see whether they are effective. The Obama administration, in its Executive Order 13563, has attempted to address this issue by requiring agencies to conduct retrospective reviews of regulations.[6] Other observers of regulatory policy, more skeptical of the inclination or ability of the agencies to impartially examine their own existing regulations, have suggested that legislators adopt a more forceful legislative approach that sets a sunset window on regulations. No matter the likelihood of any widespread adoption of a sunset approach, an excellent regulator should embrace and attempt, whenever possible, to move toward the goal, as Michael Greenstone suggests, of "a culture of persistent regulatory experimentation and evaluation."[7]

Given the challenges of conducting retrospective RCTs of regulations, most analyses of regulations tend to compare health outcomes of those exposed to the higher level of pollution with health outcomes of those exposed to the lower level of pollution. This approach faces the problem that there may be other important differences between the two groups of people. For example, pollution levels in central cities, where the local population tends to have lower incomes, tend to be higher than in outlying suburbs, where residents are wealthier. Thus a comparison of high-pollution groups with low-pollution groups, in this example, would compare the health outcomes of low-income people with those of high-income people—groups well known to have very different health outcomes. So it would be misleading to attribute the differences in health to the different pollution levels. Analysts can attempt to control for the differences in characteristics, but there is substantial evidence that attempting to control for confounding factors while using cross-sectional data is unlikely to provide reliable estimates.[8]

The implication is not that the regulator should abandon all hope of understanding the problem at hand and assume that no regulation is the right response to pollution. Rather, the challenges of empirical estimation highlight the need for some humility and for careful choices about and scrutiny of the research designs used to estimate a causal link between treatment and outcome. RCTs still offer the best approach, whenever possible, especially where the number of observations is high, but even better would be multiple experiments with a variety of initial conditions. Even absent RCTs, there are alternative approaches such as "quasi-experiments," where the researchers rely on circumstances outside their control to mimic random assignment to the treatment and control groups.[9] More generally, the degree of credibility of an empirical study will vary based on the exogeneity of the treatment being examined; the researcher should examine carefully how well the empirical strategy employed isolates the treatment effect.

The regulatory impact analyses (RIAs) conducted by regulators should include basic information needed to assess the quality of the empirical studies used in the benefit-cost analyses contained in the RIA report.[10] Such basic information could include an overview of the research design employed (for example, RCT, quasi-experiment, panel data, repeat cross-sectional data, time-series data, cross-sectional data, theory, anecdote). It could also note whether the empirical studies report the averages of available variables for the treatment and control groups, and whether the available variables have statistically significant differences between treatment and control groups. For example, any RIA claiming health benefits of regulating emissions should include a comparison of the statistical distributions of the treatment and control groups for each health study used, noting how many characteristics were available to compare and the proportion of them that were statistically balanced between the treatment and control groups. If the observable characteristics of the treatment group are statistically similar to the observable characteristics of the control group, then we can have greater confidence that those characteristics that cannot be observed are also similar across the two groups, implying that any difference in outcomes is due to the treatment, not to confounding factors.

Unfortunately, many published studies lack a transparent presentation of the research design and of diagnostic tests that can help assess the reliability of the results. This lack of information makes the credibility of the findings more dubious, and they should be treated accordingly in regulatory analyses. A step in the right direction would be for regulators to require that any raw data, cleaned-up data, and statistical programs used in an analysis be made available and replicable in order for the results to be relied on in a regulatory impact analysis. Indeed, in the United States, the Office of Management and Budget (OMB) or the regulatory agencies themselves can easily make this information available online, affording anyone the ability to assess the empirical estimation and to replicate the findings. This movement toward greater transparency is already occurring in the academic literature, as exemplified by the *American Economic Review*'s data availability policy that requires data for studies published in the journal to be "clearly and precisely documented" and "readily available to any researcher for purposes of replication."[11]

The idea of using a checklist to track the characteristics of empirical analysis, and then providing greater data transparency to allow replication, should help regulators pay closer attention to the quality of the empirical studies underlying the benefit-cost analyses they use to justify regulations. But I confess to skepticism that even the best regulators will fully adopt such an approach. Regulators are people, not angels, so even the best of them are subject to biases, and limited information can lead them to incorrectly evaluate evidence. This problem is especially acute in the United States, where regulatory agencies are charged with conducting the benefit-cost analyses for the regulations they are considering. We all suffer from confirmation bias, so one would expect that those most deeply involved in the implementation of a regulation are likely to focus on evidence of the benefits of their preferred regulatory approach more than on the evidence of the costs of this approach, irrespective of the quality of the research designs. All organizations resist evaluation, and government organizations—which are not subject to market discipline to test their effectiveness—are in particular need of outside evaluation. In the United States, the role of the Office of Information and Regulatory Affairs (OIRA) within OMB is in part to serve as a check on regulatory agencies' benefit-cost analyses, and indeed my idea of a "quality checklist" is meant to beef up this role. But OIRA also has limited resources and is not itself an independent third party, since it is, like the regulatory agencies, part of the executive branch.

The desire for third-party validation of regulatory analyses has led to proposals in the United States to add the benefit-cost standard to the Administrative Procedure Act's criteria for judicial review. In effect, the benefit-cost standard, which has applied to major rules by executive order since 1981, would be made a statutory standard subject to judicial review. Chris DeMuth describes many benefits of this approach, primarily as a way of addressing what he sees as an unhealthy expansion of regulatory discretion and power due to Congress's delegation of responsibilities to the executive branch.[12] The appeal of this approach is that it would provide greater third-party assessment of benefit-cost analyses (in this case by the judiciary), which would increase the premium on credible and convincing empirical evidence on the benefits and costs of regulations in order to better justify either regulatory action or inaction. No matter the prospects of legislative changes to the Administrative Procedure Act, there are some signs that the judiciary is paying more attention to the benefit-cost analyses used to justify regulations, such as the recent Supreme Court ruling against regulation by the Environmental Protection Agency (EPA) of mercury and other hazardous air pollutants, in which the court found that the EPA unreasonably failed to "consider cost when making its decision."[13]

It is possible to improve the transparency of the regulatory review process irrespective of any changing role of the judiciary in reviewing benefit-cost analyses. One of the goals of Executive Order 12866, which required U.S. regulatory agencies to assess the benefits and costs of regulatory options, was to make the regulatory review process more "open to the public."[14] For economically significant rules, agencies are required to develop regulatory impact analyses "to provide to the public and to OMB a careful and transparent analysis" that includes "an assessment and (to the extent feasible) a quantification and monetization of benefits and costs anticipated to result from the proposed action and from alternative regulatory actions."[15]

Unfortunately, over time the regulatory review process has come to serve more as a public relations tool, in which it is used for supporting decisions that have already been made, rather than a tool for informing and contributing to the decisionmaking process. OIRA's ability to counter this is limited, since it frequently receives RIAs for proposed or final rules from the agencies with little time to require substantial changes, owing to delays by the agencies coupled with deadlines imposed by statutes or court orders. Indeed, in some cases, agencies submit draft RIAs for OIRA's review after submitting their draft rule language. This has led to proposals to institute a formal early review process that would allow at least six months of review in advance of proposed and final regulations.[16] Given the limited resources available to OIRA to conduct a more thorough and informative early review process, the early review process could only apply to a subset of regulations, such as those expected to have annual benefits or costs in excess of $1 billion.[17]

## REGULATING BEHAVIORAL FAILURES

As has long been advocated by economists, and institutionalized in U.S. government guidelines such as the Office of Management and Budget's Circular A-4, regulations should be motivated by the need to address a significant market failure (for example, externalities, market power, or inadequate or asymmetric information). Economists have long argued that regulators should rely, whenever possible, on market-based principles in designing regulations to address these market failures. For example, in the case of a pollution externality, a tax on production equal to the marginal external costs could lead producers to internalize the third-party costs stemming from production, which would result in an efficient outcome.

The modern regulator, however, must consider the emergence of the behavioral economics literature, which has focused on identifying cognitive limitations and psychological biases that lead people to make choices that cause self-harm, thus suggesting another type of market failure that justifies government intervention. These behavioral failures involve departures from the individual rationality assumptions incorporated in economists' models of consumer choice.[18]

Much of the evidence of behavioral failures is derived from laboratory experiments, stated preference studies, hypothetical classroom exercises, or narrowly defined decision contexts, so as with the empirical studies discussed above, there is a strong need for regulators to evaluate the quality and the applicability of any behavioral study before using it as a justification to regulate. Kip Viscusi and I have referred to the practice of applying results from a behavioral study in one context to a broader application of policy as "behavioral transfer" to recognize its similarity to the long-acknowledged challenge of "benefits transfer," in which the benefit estimation in one subpopulation is applied to another subpopulation being evaluated for a regulation.[19] We conclude that a higher level of scrutiny is required for behavioral transfers than for traditional benefits transfers, and that the results of behavioral studies are more relevant for indicating the presence of a potential behavioral failure than for credibly estimating the empirical magnitude of any failure.

While the behavioral economics literature does provide evidence that would point to another role for regulation, a prudent regulator should possess the self-awareness to recognize the two main reasons why regulatory responses motivated by behavioral economics findings might be suboptimal.[20] The first is that, as a behavioral agent herself, the regulator is not immune from the psychological biases that affect ordinary people. The second is that a substantial public choice literature suggests that a regulator is subject to political incentives that could lead to suboptimal policies, and even at times to the misuse of behavioral economics studies to enhance regulatory control or favor the influence of special interests rather than to promote social welfare.[21]

There are many public choice reasons why private decisions, even those subject to behavioral failures, might lead to better outcomes if left unregulated. The most obvious argument is that behavioral evidence of irrational and self-harming behavior in market transactions would suggest that bad decision-making also presents itself in political decisions, such as in voting practices. To the extent that policies are decided by the median voter, and the voting of the median voter is subject to behavioral failure, then this would suggest a tendency for policy to be suboptimal. Public choice theory also suggests that private decisionmakers have stronger incentives to acquire information—expending both time and money—to overcome behavioral biases, since the personal costs to the person who makes a bad decision are arguably higher than the personal costs to the regulator of a rule that leads to a bad outcome.

Again, humility, not dismissiveness, is in order for a regulator faced with evidence of behavioral failures. One way to approach the challenge is to consider Daniel Kahneman's description of two modes of thinking: System 1 thinking "operates automatically and quickly, with little or no effort, and no sense of voluntary control," while System 2 thinking "allocates attention to the effortful mental activities that demand it, including complex computations."[22] The biases that lead to suboptimal private actions typically stem from the "freewheeling impulses" of System 1 thinking. The impulse to regulate when there is evidence of a behavioral failure is motivated by the belief that government experts are, by nature, training, and employment, better disposed toward System 2 thinking and can therefore design policies that overcome the problems caused by System 1 thinking. The countervailing risk is that regulators' behavioral failures (such as those stemming from narrow expertise or overconfidence caused by the illusion of explanatory depth), as well as public choice pressures, could lead to suboptimal regulatory responses. The challenge then is to assess whether private decisionmakers acting in the marketplace are more or less prone to harmful biases than are the regulators. This approach parallels the traditional public finance calculus of weighing the inefficiencies caused by market failures against the inefficiencies caused by government failures in attempting to address market failures through regulations.[23]

Kip Viscusi and I have taken a "behavioral public choice" approach and identified many instances in which cognitive and psychological biases, combined with public choice pressures, lead to policies that institutionalize irrational behavior rather than overcome them.[24] For example, a well-documented bias is that people tend to overestimate low mortality risk and underestimate high mortality risk.[25] That is, threats to health—such as the risks of stroke, cancer, and heart disease—tend to be underestimated, while less consequential threats—such as the risks of botulism, lightning strikes, and natural disasters—tend to be overestimated. Experts in regulatory agencies could be better suited to making more accurate risk assessments if they had professional involvement in particular risks that the general public does not have. Government agencies have the expertise and staff to stay informed about the evolving scientific evidence related to risk, thus relying on Kahneman's System 2 thinking when evaluating these risks. Unfortunately, in the analysis Viscusi and I conducted, we found many regulatory policies (such as EPA's approach to remediating hazardous waste sites) in which the regulatory response demonstrated the same kind of biased risk perception that plagues individual risk judgments.

The point, again, is not that an excellent regulator should be dismissive of findings of behavioral failures. Doing so would mean forgoing regulatory opportunities to address real harms. Rather, the point is that there is a need for weighing the risk of leaving a behavioral failure unregulated against the risk of a policy response that institutionalizes the bias.

This cautionary approach would adopt the default position of respecting consumer sovereignty under the presumption that fully informed people are better able to make decisions that bear on their own well-being than are regulators. However, the insights of behavioral economics suggest that market failures indeed can arise when people make self-harming decisions, and Viscusi and I advocate estimating the benefits of correcting these actions relative to the outcome that would present if people were fully informed and fully rational actors. To take a simple example, regulators should prioritize remediating the high-risk hazardous waste site over the low-risk hazardous waste site, even if psychological factors lead residents to view the latter as riskier than the former. It is important that such an approach be grounded in systematic, well-documented, and context-specific findings of behavioral findings, and that the policy outcome to address self-harm be achieved through less intrusive and lower-cost regulations when possible.

A regulator should also attempt to guard against the temptation to misuse behavioral insights to achieve goals other than addressing self-harming behavior. For example, the behavioral literature on tax salience suggests that tricking people into thinking a tax does not exist could increase tax revenues by more than it harms the taxpayers who are making poor consumption choices based on lack of knowledge about the tax.[26] Although net benefits are increased, a policy of disguising taxes (or regulations) would be inconsistent with the approach of basing policies on fully informed, fully rational decisionmaking.[27] Regrettably, agencies sometimes disguise their lack of evidence by relying on weak claims of behavioral biases to justify a host of otherwise inefficient regulations.[28] The behavioral economics literature provides fascinating insights into systematic deviations from rational behavior, which can then be integrated into economics in a way that provides better predictions and ultimately better opportunities for improving social welfare. But the existence of these behavioral insights does not mean a regulator should be dismissive of the merits of individual choice when making policy prescriptions stemming from behavioral findings.

## CONCLUSION

The existence of an "excellent regulator" does not mean there will necessarily be excellence in regulation. Regulation does not, and should not, stem from individual decisionmakers or institutions, no matter what qualities they exhibit when exercising full discretion and using their authority to improve social welfare. As with the exercise of other governmental power, an excellent *overall* regulatory system should be subject to the full checks and balances of the larger governmental system within which it is situated, with the legislature maintaining ultimate authority for the regulatory powers it delegates to the regulator, and with courts helping to ensure that regulations are based on valid legal authority and do not violate protected legal rights. Such a regulatory system works well only insofar as it is robust to the existence of a decidedly nonexcellent regulator.

Despite my reservations about focusing too much on the characteristics of the regulator and paying too little attention to the full regulatory apparatus, I have attempted to recommend an approach that any regulator should take in evaluating the evidence brought to bear in the regulatory decisionmaking process. I have also recommended some key design elements in the regulatory process itself, such as the implementation of quality checklists and requirements for the disclosure of research methods. My recommendations would promote greater discernment in evaluating the quality of the scientific evidence used in the regulatory review process, and greater transparency and decentralized information sharing of the data and methods underlying this evidence. My approach also calls for a regulator to take seriously the insights of behavioral economics, insofar as these findings are systematic, well documented, and specific to the context under consideration for regulation, but also to be on guard against misusing behavioral findings as open-ended justifications for regulatory action.

The nineteenth-century rabbi's paper-in-each-pocket metaphor captures well what an excellent regulator must do. Keeping it always in mind should encourage regulators to find an equilibrium in which they are motivated to act on sound evidence, but still strive to mitigate the risk of confirmation bias and regulatory overreach.

### NOTES

1. In the words of Rabino Nilton Bonder, "Many people believe that humility is the opposite of pride, when, in fact, it is a point of equilibrium."

2. Cary Coglianese and Gary E. Marchant, "Shifting Sands: The Limits of Science in Setting Risk Standards," *University of Pennsylvania Law Review* 152 (2004): 1255.

3. Michael Abramowicz, Ian Ayres, and Yair Listokin, "Randomizing Law," *University of Pennsylvania Law Review* 159 (2011): 929.

4. Jim Manzi, *Uncontrolled: The Surprising Payoff of Trial-and-Error for Business, Politics, and Society* (New York: Basic Books, 2012).

5. Robert M. Kaplan and Veronica L. Irvin, "Likelihood of Null Effects of Large NHLBI Clinical Trials Has Increased over Time," *PLoS ONE* 10 (2015): e0132382.

6. Barack Obama, "Executive Order 13563: Improving Regulation and Regulatory Review," *Federal Register* 76 (January 18, 2011): 3821 (www.gpo.gov/fdsys/pkg /FR-2011-01-21/pdf/2011-1385.pdf).

7. Michael Greenstone, "Toward a Culture of Persistent Regulatory Experimentation and Evaluation," in *New Perspectives on Regulation*, edited by David Moss and John Cisternino (Cambridge, Mass.: Tobin Project, 2009), pp. 111–25.

8. See, for example, Kenneth Y. Chay and Michael Greenstone, "The Impact of Air Pollution on Infant Mortality: Evidence from Geographic Variation in Pollution Shocks Induced by a Recession," *Quarterly Journal of Economics* 118 (2003): 1121.

9. See, for example, Michael Greenstone and Ted Gayer, "Quasi-Experimental and Experimental Approaches to Environmental Economics," *Journal of Environmental Economics and Management* 57 (2009): 21, for a discussion and examples of the role of quasi-experiments in environmental economics.

10. Ted Gayer, "A Better Approach to Environmental Regulation: Getting the Costs and Benefits Right," Hamilton Project Discussion Paper 2011-06 (Brookings Institution, May 2011).

11. *American Economic Review*, "Data Availability Policy" (www.aeaweb.org/aer/data.php).

12. Christopher DeMuth, "Can the Administrative State Be Tamed?," *Journal of Legal Analysis* 8 (2016): 121.

13. *Michigan v. Environmental Protection Agency*, No. 14–46, slip op. (Supreme Court of the United States, June 29, 2015) (www.supremecourt.gov/opinions/14pdf/14-46_10n2.pdf).

14. William J. Clinton, "Executive Order 12866: Regulatory Planning and Review," *Federal Register* 58 (September 30, 1993): 51735 (www.archives.gov/federal-register/executive-orders/pdf/12866.pdf).

15. U.S. Office of Management and Budget, "Circular A-4: Regulatory Impact Analysis: A Primer," September 2003 (www.whitehouse.gov/sites/default/files/omb/inforeg/regpol/circular-a-4_regulatory-impact-analysis-a-primer.pdf).

16. Winston Harrington, Lisa Heinzerling, and Richard D. Morgenstern, "What We Learned," in *Reforming Regulatory Impact Analysis*, edited by W. Harrington, L. Heinzerling, and R. D. Morgenstern (Washington: Resources for the Future, 2009), pp. 215–38.

17. Arthur G. Fraas, "Comment Submitted to the Office of Management and Budget on the Executive Order on Federal Regulatory Review," March 16, 2009 (www.reginfo.gov/public/jsp/EO/fedRegReview/Arthur_Fraas_Comments.pdf).

18. William J. Congdon, Jeffrey R. Kling, and Sendhil Mullainathan, in *Policy and Choice: Public Finance through the Lens of Behavioral Economics* (Brookings Institution Press, 2011), offer a thorough summary and categorization of the deviations from standard economic assumptions found in the behavioral economics literature.

19. W. Kip Viscusi and Ted Gayer, "Rational Benefit Assessment for an Irrational World: Toward a Behavioral Transfer Test," *Journal of Benefit-Cost Analysis* 7 (2016): 69–91.

20. For other reasons against regulating based on behavioral failures, see, for example, Robert Sugden, "Why Incoherent Preferences Do Not Justify Paternalism," *Constitutional Political Economy* 19 (2008): 226; and Jayson L. Lusk, "Are You Smart

Enough to Know What to Eat? A Critique of Behavioural Economics as Justification for Regulation," *European Review of Agricultural Economics* 41 (2014): 355.

21. W. Kip Viscusi and Ted Gayer, "Behavioral Public Choice: The Behavioral Paradox of Government Policy," *Harvard Journal of Law and Public Policy* 38 (2015): 973.

22. Daniel Kahneman, *Thinking Fast and Slow* (New York: Farrar, Straus and Giroux, 2011).

23. Clifford Winston, *Government Failure versus Market Failure: Microeconomics Policy Research and Government Performance* (Washington: AEI-Brookings Joint Center for Regulatory Studies, 2006).

24. Viscusi and Gayer, "Behavioral Public Choice," p. 973.

25. Sarah Lichtenstein and others, "Judged Frequency of Lethal Events," *Journal of Experimental Psychology: Human Learning and Memory* 4 (1978): 551.

26. The model in Raj Chetty, Adam Looney, and Kory Kroft, "Salience and Taxation: Theory and Evidence," *American Economic Review* 99 (2009): 1145, demonstrates how net benefits can increase as a tax becomes less salient.

27. Amy Finkelstein, "E-ZTax: Tax Salience and Tax Rates," *Quarterly Journal of Economics* 124 (2009): 969, provides evidence that as tax salience goes down (in the case of a switch from a toll booth to an E-ZPass), tax rates go up.

28. Ted Gayer and W. Kip Viscusi, "Overriding Consumer Preferences with Energy Regulations," *Journal of Regulatory Economics* 43 (2013): 248.

# 7

# A Risk Regulation Perspective
# on Regulatory Excellence

### BRIDGET M. HUTTER

**REGULATION IS EXTRAORDINARILY DIFFICULT.** It is about balancing and achieving multiple objectives, as well as balancing the interests of multiple groups and stakeholders.[1] "Excellence" in regulation might be viewed differently depending on where you stand—for example, as a member of the public or as a business—and when and where you ask "What constitutes best regulatory practice?" This is because regulatory objectives and interests not only vary between groups, they also vary across time and across countries. Excellent regulators need to be able to handle this complex and shifting landscape, one that is often not of their own making.

I will consider these issues from the perspective of risk regulation, taking the view that a crucial feature of regulation is that it attempts to control and manage risk.[2] This perspective developed in the 1990s within a wider social science context, emerging as a distinctive interdisciplinary area bridging the studies of regulation and risk management across a number of social science disciplines.[3] The focus of this chapter is on the ways in which the definition and understanding of "risk regulation" are influenced by the broader contexts in which they are situated. It is not an approach that, for example, constructs mathematical risk models, but rather one that examines the social, economic, and political circumstances within which these risk models are constructed and surveys how they are used both within, and by, organizations. Such an approach partly reflects a more general trend in social science literature to view and make sense of the world through the lens of risk. It has also emerged along-side changes in regulatory practice.

This chapter considers different types of risk. In particular, it differenti-ates the risks that regulators oversee and manage—such as risks to health and safety, financial stability, the environment, aviation safety, and so on—from the risks that regulators themselves face, such as political risks. I argue that "excellent" regulators must address both the technical and the social aspects of the risk regulation task they are charged with undertaking.

## RISK REGULATION AND EXCELLENCE: ANTICIPATION

For many social scientists, risk regulation is a very modern phenomenon: a real expression of what some have termed the "risk society."[4] This is a society in which there is an orientation to the future and a belief that we can control and manage risks.[5] The social theorist Anthony Giddens argues, for example, that we live in a world where there is no longer a belief in fate but an "as-piration to control" future events, which leads to a growing preoccupation with the future.[6] From this perspective, regulation is one manifestation of a modern belief that risks can be anticipated and controlled. Moreover, risk has become a key organizing concept in such a society.[7] Excellent regulators, it follows, aspire to satisfy demands for the anticipation and control of risks. These are very great, and arguably unreasonable, expectations, which come to the fore when things go wrong and regulators are among those blamed for not foreseeing events.[8] There are many examples of this, ranging from the 2007–08 financial crisis to terrorist attacks. Witness the debate about whether the French police and intelligence services should have predicted the *Charlie Hebdo* murders,[9] or the 9/11 Commission's pronouncement that U.S. intelli-gence agencies and other governmental entities did not succeed in preventing the 9/11 attacks because of failures of "imagination."[10] Similar controversies surround the "failure" of regulators to predict the financial crisis. Indeed, most disasters that occur lead to a similar questioning of regulators, businesses, and others, which in turn creates an industry of "self-help" advice that spells out what was done wrong, what should have happened, and how things should be done better next time.[11]

Risk regulation can be a very normative and emotive topic, apparent in the political rhetoric, both pro- and antiregulation, that is employed. This rhe-toric is underpinned by different political philosophies about the relationship between the state and markets and is reflected in changing policies. Regula-tors are seldom free to make decisions about how best to manage risks free from political steering, and excellent regulators have to be adept at managing risks in association with these shifting agendas. A common political theme over recent decades has been the so-called better regulation agenda, with different regimes around the world exemplifying stronger or weaker variations of this. There have been repeated deregulatory initiatives since the 1980s, for example, with politicians using the changing language of "burden," "deregulation," "better regulation," and "regulatory impact."[12] The costs and benefits of regulation have been at the center of political debates in the form of normative claims about "burdens" and "red tape." In policy terms, such concerns are encoded in the tools regulators use, some of which have also become benchmarks against which they are judged. These include, for example, cost-benefit analyses, regulatory impact assessments, and risk-based regulation, all of which incorporate calculative and probabilistic thinking about regulation itself.

Such technocratic, apparently "rational," approaches aim to make regulation more efficient, objective, and fair for business. In so doing, they disguise some of the very real political and ethical decisionmaking that lies at the heart of regulation and that characterizes the regulatory process from its inception. For example, the definition of what is deemed to be "risky" can be controversial: it is frequently contested and negotiated. Identifying what constitutes a risk is not always straightforward because there may be conflicts in evidence, as well as competing interests. As Mary Douglas and Aaron Wildavsky once observed, there can be "substantial disagreement . . . over what is risky, how risky it is, and what to do about it."[13] Determining whether a risk requires regulation can be similarly controversial, as can determining, at the implementation stage, the correct regulatory approach to take.

Partly as a result of such controversy, many regulatory regimes have begun to explicitly design their operations using systematic risk assessment and prioritization.[14] The adoption of apparently rational, objective, and transparent ways of prioritizing work, and the deployment of limited regulatory resources, may be appealed to should a crisis require defensive measures to avoid blame and liability.[15] This practice has also arisen from other contemporary imperatives defining excellent regulation, some of which are discussed under the generic title of the "New Public Management," and which include the adoption of risk-based approaches by public sector departments. Excellent regulators thus become defined as excellent risk managers.[16]

## RISK REGULATION AND ORGANIZATIONAL RISK MANAGEMENT

There are a variety of ways in which regulatory and risk management templates have blurred. The most fundamental is through the use of risk assessment tools by regulators, especially those derived from natural science and economics. More recently, some jurisdictions have mandated a more general move to risk-based approaches as a way of organizing regulatory activities. In the United Kingdom, for example, the Hampton Report on "effective inspection and enforcement" led to risk-based regulation becoming the cornerstone of Treasury recommendations for regulation, enshrined and made mandatory by the Legislative and Regulatory Reform Act 2006.[17]

There is no firm definition of risk-based regulation, but the practice usually includes a commitment to a philosophy that takes the principles of risk management as a framework for governance, the organization of regulatory work, and an agency's resources. It involves the formalization of regulation through the employment of technical risk-based tools from economics (for example, cost-benefit approaches) and science (for example, risk assessment techniques).[18] As such, it usually involves cycles of risk identification, measurement, mitigation, control, and monitoring. Risks are identified and assessed, a ranking or score is assigned on the basis of this assessment, and inspection and enforcement are undertaken on the basis of these scores.[19] It is a systematic approach that takes a holistic view of regulation and risk management and conceptualizes risks as interrelated and as having potential consequences for broader social, economic, and political environments. It provides an overarching framework for governance, in contrast to systems in which risk management tools are used in an ad hoc, piecemeal way—for example, those that rely more on the expertise of individual regulatory officials or local offices and regimes.[20]

Achieving excellence in this context places numerous demands on regulators. Among them, regulators must have access to accurate information so that they have a clear idea of the risks they are regulating. This is not always straightforward, as—even in the simplest cases—the necessary data may not be available. Sally Lloyd-Bostock and I have discussed the difficulties encountered by the U.K.'s General Medical Council (GMC), the professional regulator for doctors in the U.K., in determining the risks they need to consider in a risk-based approach.[21] Their main data source has been recorded complaints, but while these can be a very rich source of risk-related information, they are not representative of all risks and may not, therefore, provide the most useful data for risk-based regulation purposes. For example, patients tend to report dissatisfaction in areas where they feel they are competent to judge, but research indicates that most risks to patients are not recognized by the patients themselves, let alone reported by them. The data that are recorded will be further filtered and constructed by methods and systems used for processing patient complaints, which will in turn reflect the perceptions and attitudes of members of the organization. It is highly questionable that such data can readily be used for risk-based regulation purposes. However, generating new sources of data can be very expensive.

At a technical level, there may be difficulties in how regulators rely on data. For instance, the past is not always a good predictor of the future. This is the case, for example, in environmental risks. Climate change may well be increasing the incidence and patterns of natural disasters, thus rendering their incidence and location less predictable. The 2007–08 financial crisis also reveals the ways in which social and political environments can distort our interpretation of data. The risk models used by the financial markets in the decades before the crisis were colored by a climate of optimism that encouraged mistaken assumptions about risk and the ability of markets to regulate themselves.[22]

At a political level, scientific data can be compromised by partisan interests. "Climategate" involved a politically motivated challenge to the status of scientific evidence and expert knowledge relating to climate change. The controversy began in November 2009, when a server was breached at the University of East Anglia's Climatic Research Unit (CRU), one of the research centers that compiled global temperature and precipitation analyses. Two weeks before the Copenhagen Summit on climate change, large amounts of data relating to the CRU's climate change research were posted on the Internet. Climate change skeptics alleged that the hacked emails showed evidence that climate scientists manipulated data and that the emails constituted evidence of a global warming conspiracy and the suppression of dissenting scientific papers. Despite the fact that successive inquiries refuted these claims, this was a damaging episode for scientists, especially given that international climate change talks were in progress at the time. This episode underlines the difficulties of securing a robust and agreed evidence base.

Excellent regulators are those who appreciate both the limitations of the data and the political context within which they operate. They need to be able to critically appraise the value and validity of available data sources and be able to manage and integrate these. Most particularly, excellent regulators recognize the need to employ staff with the technical skills to use risk-based tools and the ability to interpret and act in response to the data.[23] In short, excellent regulators require good data as well as analytical rigor and sound judgment to understand the restrictions of the approach and the levels of (un)certainty under which they operate. Achieving the ideals of risk-based regulation demands the resources to fund these levels of information collation, analysis, and interpretation. In recent years, as public sector budgets have been drastically reduced, this has become a difficult task.

Another crucial element of being an excellent regulator is appreciating the heuristic nature of the regulatory models the agency employs. In regulatory agencies, for example, risk-based regulation acts as a guide to decisionmaking about the prioritization of resources. But risk-based regulation has its faults too:

it simplifies complex data, and where there are insufficient data it relies on proxies. Cultural and other factors may also affect how risk-based tools are interpreted.[24] Indeed, the uncertainties and points of contestability around the more technical aspects of risk-based regulation can be exploited by interested parties. The very tools used by state regulators may be used to challenge their decisionmaking and authority. Regulatory models and tools may be forgotten over time, or it may be that they are well understood by those at the top of the organization but not understood by those operating the system at a lower level in the organization. More important in the context of this discussion, they may not be understood by those assessing the performance of regulators.

Regulation, however, is not just a matter of achieving technical excellence; far from it. As Mary Douglas explains in her seminal work on risk, while risk assessments may be presented as scientific and neutral, they are also inherently moral and political.[25] Regulation involves choices about the distribution of resources, such as the relative value given to individual or collective goods, and these choices may find themselves reflected in the technical tools of risk-based regulation. Similarly, determining acceptable costs in cost-benefit analyses has been a matter of dispute, with the argument being that indirect costs and benefits are rarely considered and that the interpretation of estimates depends on one's perspective.[26] Even if the causes and costs of risk are clear, acceptable levels of risk must still be defined, and that is essentially a political decision. Similarly, fundamental questions such as how much weight should be given to potential impact, how much to probability, and how much to public opinion are not simple technical decisions but are intrinsically political. Excellent regulators will be adept at managing this balancing act without compromising their regulatory mission. There are occasions, however, when doing so will prove very difficult. However robust the tools used in risk-based regulation may be, and however carefully they are used by regulators, much depends at the end of the day on the political will to act; and there are examples, such as the period before the financial crisis, of governments being reluctant to give regulation the support they need to fulfill their mission.[27] It is for this reason that we need to consider the political environment within which risk regulation takes place.

## RISK REGULATION AND POLITICS

Being an excellent regulator is in many senses aspirational, but it also requires pragmatism and realism. Risk regulation is a messy world. The regulator is seen by some as the "fall guy" in a system where governments distance themselves from difficult, sometimes irreconcilable problems, and so are at liberty to criticize the decisions made by regulators.[28] Regulators may be criticized for being too harsh when things are calm and being too lax when risks have been realized. Excellent regulators have to be aware of this. Governments and politicians are fickle: while they can speak an antiregulation rhetoric, they can be quick to regulate following a disaster. They can be keen to create complicated metaregulatory structures, including "better regulation" and "deregulation" organizations, the net effect of which leads to increased regulation.[29] Politicians and the citizenry exhibit a fundamental ambivalence around the topic of regulation.

Excellent regulators learn to deal with the ambivalence that is encoded in the word "regulation." Their role is about the management, as opposed to the elimination, of risk, about control and restriction, but also about adaptation and flexibility—reconciling risk with other factors. They must act in the interests of markets, organizations, stakeholders, and consumers, and also the national and global economy. Because such interest groups may not always share objectives, regulation can be a balancing act. The job of a regulator, therefore, involves negotiating and weighing both risks and partisan interests. Excellence in regulation demands impartiality in dealing with the series of difficult issues associated with managing this balancing act. However, this does not necessarily mean that all parties involved "win" and "lose" in equal measure: the interests of various groups and stakeholders are not equally weighted. Sometimes risk management tools can help give some broad indication of where the weight of evidence indicates the solution lies, and being open and transparent about this can be helpful. There are times when regulators have to consider taking a stand regarding the correct balance—even when there are strong political interests aligned against such a stand. These are occasions when strategic and negotiating skills can help, but there may be moments when regulators decide to take an ethical standpoint to protect weaker, less vocal groups. Ascertaining whether a regulator has struck the "right" balance is difficult, and there may be no easy solutions; in some cases, only time will tell. And it should be remembered that sometimes decisions are judged and proven erroneous many years after they were made. Witness, for example, the decision by U.K. regulators in the early 1990s to regard BSE (bovine spongiform encephalopathy, or "mad cow disease")—in the form of vCJD (variant Creutzfeld-Jakob disease)—as being nontransmissible to humans; this view was argued to be correct for nearly a decade before it was proven wrong. The evidence in that case was that scientific interpretations had been influenced by partisan interests and that this contributed to a defensive, rather than precautionary, stance by regulators.

The regulatory process holds many risks for regulators and the regulated alike.[30] There are the risks of failing to regulate serious problems on one hand,

and overregulating small risks on the other. Regulators need to judge when to intervene and when they should leave organizations to get on with managing risks on their own. This judgment involves appreciating the complexities of so-called stakeholder groups, which can be highly diverse in their constitution, abilities, and motivations. Businesses vary enormously in both their regulatory capacity and their views of regulation. Some businesses are very powerful players who are able to organize and put substantial sums of money into fighting regulation. Consider, for example, the debates over nutritional food labeling: some food businesses spent millions fighting a "traffic light" labeling scheme designed to give consumers readily identifiable information about the amount of fat, saturated fat, sugar, and salt in food products via easy to understand red, amber, and green traffic lights. The controversy over whether the labeling scheme should be implemented persisted for many years in the U.K. before eventually moving to Europe, where a proposal to adopt the system was rejected in June 2009 by the European Parliament, despite strong support from public health campaigners and some food chains. The debate is an example of an industry divided and underlines the need to appreciate the complexities of stakeholder groups. A similar debate over food labeling took place in Australia. At the other end of the spectrum are small and micro-businesses in which the risks associated with running a business are often ill-understood.[31] In these circumstances regulators may be the main source of information and education about risks. There are, of course, exceptions, such as small and micro-businesses with highly specialized workforces in technology sectors who function in an industry vulnerable to closure in the event of accidents.[32]

There are a variety of factors that explain variations in businesses' capacity to manage the risks they generate: motivation, organizational capacity, and changing circumstances, to name a few.[33] The optimal solution is to align, where possible, regulatory and organizational interests. In some sectors there may be a "natural" alignment of interests; for example, a major risk event could mean the destruction of a site and the possibility of going out of business. This does not necessarily mean that the business has the capability to manage regulation, but at least it has a strong motivation to do so. An alignment can also occur when organizations seek solutions to compliance problems that satisfy wider interests. A simple example: for many decades railways and regulators struggled to get workers to wear high-visibility vests when working on or near the tracks; the problem was solved by providing workers with comfortable protective clothing that was also highly visible. "Nudge" techniques, based on behavioral economics, offer a similar hope that individuals and organizations, when given the right nudge, will choose optimal solutions without the need to resort to costly regulatory processes.[34] But, notwithstanding the paucity of evidence demonstrating the success of these strategies, we do know that neither all risks nor all businesses are amenable to simple solutions. Excellent regulators help facilitate these solutions by leveraging a wide range of motivations to manage risks, such as those concerning reputational issues, education, and the threat of legal sanction.[35]

The "public" is not a homogeneous grouping either; it is even more disparate than a business. There are many publics with different risk concerns and varying risk appetites, and therefore publics can also exercise ambivalence about risk regulation.[36] They are selective and differential about the risks that concern them. Typically, their regulatory standards are higher in cases of involuntary risk than they are for voluntary risk-taking. Some risks do not generate concern (for example, mobile phones and nanotechnology), whereas other risks generate what some regard as disproportionate attention.[37] Publics may be loosely organized, as in the case of green markets, but this is atypical. More usually nongovernmental organizations are taken as representative of the public as a whole.[38] Yet despite their heterogeneity, publics are often portrayed as a uniform group by politicians and the media.

### RISKS TO REGULATORS

In past decades we have witnessed politicians discussing the "public" as a threat. With this in mind we turn to considering to what degree the public poses a risk to regulators. In the U.K. the public began to be regarded as a potential risk to regulators partly as a result of the BSE/vCJD incident, when public opinion was increasingly vociferous in contesting the official advice and the public were eventually proven correct in their concerns. This experience led to a massive loss of trust in regulators, experts, and government in the U.K. Since then, debates about the role of science and technological innovations have construed the public as a "new" risk and one which it is feared may be activated through exposure to various media outlets.[39] More recently, public perceptions of risk have become viewed as a potential source of risk to businesses, regulators, and governments, to the extent that the public are portrayed as increasingly risk averse and depicted as making spiraling demands for the public management of risks. Sally Lloyd-Bostock argues that political and media claims about this culture of risk averseness effectively blame "the public" for the potential consequences of a range of anticipated risks, such as excessive regulation.[40] There are groups that have an interest in promoting such myths: most prominently politicians, but also the press, who may regard public fears as a good media story. Certainly the term "public" can be hijacked by the media and conveniently presented as a homogeneous grouping.

In a similar way, the media can be used by particular interest groups to further their regulatory (or deregulatory) ambitions. An example of this is the manner in which a number of large airlines exploited the media during the April 2010 volcanic eruption in the Eyjafjallajökull area of Iceland. The resulting cloud of volcanic ash spread across Europe, and much of its airspace was closed to civil aviation for six days. The closure had far-reaching consequences, which included huge financial losses for airlines. The airlines successfully used the media to contest the regulatory decision to close airspace according to international protocols, their objective being to reopen the skies as soon as possible—a goal that was achieved by the renegotiation of regulatory limits.[41]

Regulators hold an important duty, sometimes explicit, sometimes implied, to protect the public. This presents another set of risks to regulatory agencies that excellent regulators need to be able to negotiate. For example, there are fine lines between enabling, directing, and restricting choice. Regulators need to be careful not to be seen to endorse particular products, but instead to provide impartial, evidence-based advice; they also need to be careful not to take responsibility for risks caused by others. If risks are not managed successfully, it is not always the "fault" of the regulator. Primary responsibility often lies with the generators of the risk, who may not have cooperated with regulatory demands or been capable of managing risks. Moreover, the social and political climate may have been such that it was difficult for regulators to do their job—for example, in situations where light-touch regulation was mandated. However, nuanced arguments around these issues in the event of an accident often fail to be heard. Excellent regulators therefore need to be adept not only at selecting policies and regulatory tools; they also need the skills to effectively communicate their decisions. They must know how to manage their audiences: diverse business organizations and diverse publics. They must also be able to communicate the intricacies of the legal and possibly financial constraints under which they operate, and very importantly, their political neutrality.

One means of aiding this communication, which has been increasingly advocated, is to be transparent about the reasoning used to make regulatory decisions.[42] Transparency is, in fact, one of the rationales for and attractions of risk-based regulation, but experience shows us that transparency does not necessarily protect regulators from criticism or blame should things go wrong.[43] One of the strongest proponents of a transparent risk-based regulatory system in the U.K. preceding the financial crisis was the Financial Services Authority. However, its approach was not accepted as a defense for its failure to predict the crisis in the financial markets. Partly for this reason, excellent regulators also need to think through their crisis management and contingency planning. Zero tolerance is not an option in a system of regulation which demands that regulators "regulate" rather than "eliminate" risk, where they are required to weigh costs and benefits and determine the tolerability of risk. Moreover, we cannot anticipate and manage everything all of the time: some things will be unknowns, some systems are too complex to completely manage, and—as we have seen—regulators do not always have the skills or information necessary to make their decisions.[44]

## CONCLUSION

Regulatory excellence is difficult to achieve in a national context, but in a transnational context the challenges are greatly exacerbated. Twenty-first-century regulators need to be able to operate on a world stage. They are increasingly asked to regulate risks that have no national boundaries, such as environmental, financial, and Internet risks. They are operating in arenas where there are powerful multinational companies with the capacity to shape regulation to their own advantage and who may threaten regulatory "shopping"—such as when some major financial institutions have threatened to relocate from cities like New York and London if more burdensome rules are imposed on their operations. These companies have the capacity to exploit global inequalities not just in regulatory regimes but also in cheap labor. Excellent regulators need to scale up all of their skills to grasp the complexities—technical, moral, and political—of operating on a global scale.

In this context, excellent regulators should be seen to set high standards of risk regulation, establish models that are recognized as exemplary and that other countries want to follow, and to engage in—and lead—transnational discussions. Excellent regulators will preferably be highly regarded in their own countries.

We live in a global landscape where risks, and the demands of regulatory excellence, are fast expanding. Embracing transnational cooperation and negotiation requires strong diplomatic skills. The world also demands an even greater appreciation of the social science aspects of risk regulation—namely an understanding that the ways in which problems are framed as "risks," and how decisions are made, are deeply embedded in social, economic, and political environments.

### NOTES

1. Best-in-Class Regulator Initiative, University of Pennsylvania Law School, June 2015 (www.law.upenn.edu/institutes/ppr/bestinclassregulator).

2. See Christopher Hood, Henry Rothstein, and Robert Baldwin, *The Government of Risk* (Oxford University Press, 2001); Bridget M. Hutter, *Regulation and Risk: Occupational Health and Safety on the Railways* (Oxford University Press, 2001).

3. For an account of the development of this perspective, see generally Bridget M. Hutter, "Risk, Regulation, and Management," in *Risk in Social Science*, edited by Peter Taylor-Gooby and Jens Zinn (Oxford University Press, 2006).

4. Ulrich Beck, *Risk Society: Towards a New Modernity* (London: SAGE Publications, 1992).

5. Peter L. Bernstein, *Against the Gods: The Remarkable Story of Risk* (New York: John Wiley, 1996).

6. Anthony Giddens, "Risk and Responsibility," *Modern Law Review* 62 (January 1999): 1–10.

7. Michael Power, *Organized Uncertainty: Designing a World of Risk Management* (Oxford University Press, 2007).

8. See, for example, Cary Coglianese, *Regulatory Breakdown: The Crisis of Confidence in U.S. Regulation* (University of Pennsylvania Press, 2012); Fiona Haines, *The Paradox of Regulation: What Regulation Can Achieve and What It Can Not* (Cheltenham, U.K.: Edward Elgar, 2011); Hutter, *Regulation and Risk.*

9. See John Mueller and Mark Stewart, "How French Intelligence Missed the 'Charlie Hebdo' Terrorists," *Time*, January 14, 2015 (http://time.com/3667663/charlie-hebdo-attack-terrorism-intelligence).

10. National Commission on Terrorist Attacks, *The 9/11 Commission Report: Final Report of the National Commission on Terrorist Attacks upon the United States* (New York: W. W. Norton, 2004).

11. Max H. Bazerman and Michael D. Watkins, *Predictable Surprises: The Disasters You Should Have Seen Coming, and How to Prevent Them* (Harvard Business Review Press, 2008).

12. Anneliese Dodds, "The Core Executive's Approach to Regulation: From 'Better Regulation' to 'Risk-Tolerant Deregulation,'" *Social Policy & Administration* 40 (October 2006): 526–42.

13. Mary Douglas and Aaron Wildavsky, *Risk and Culture: An Essay on the Selection of Technological and Environmental Dangers* (University of California Press, 1983), p. 64.

14. See Julia Black, "The Emergence of Risk-Based Regulation and the New Public Management in the United Kingdom," *Public Law* (Autumn 2005): 512–49; Bridget M. Hutter, "Risk Management and Governance," in *Designing Government: From Instruments to Governance*, edited by Pearl Eliadis, Margaret Hill, and Michael Howlett (McGill–Queen's University Press, 2005), pp. 303–21; see also Bridget M. Hutter, "The Attractions of Risk-Based Regulation: Accounting for the Emergence of Risk Ideas in Regulation," CARR Discussion Paper 33 (London: Centre for Analysis of Risk and Regulation, London School of Economics and Political Science, 2005).

15. Black, "The Emergence of Risk-Based Regulation."

16. Christopher Hood and Ruth Dixon, *A Government That Worked Better and Cost Less? Evaluating Three Decades of Reform and Change in U.K. Central Government* (Oxford University Press, 2015).

17. Philip Hampton, "Reducing Administrative Burdens: Effective Inspection and Enforcement," The Hampton Review, Final Report (London: Her Majesty's Stationery Office, 2005) (http://webarchive.nationalarchives.gov.uk/20090609003228 /http://www.berr.gov.uk/files/file22988.pdf).

18. Hutter, "Risk Management and Governance," pp. 303–21.

19. Julia Black, "Risk-Based Regulation: Choices, Practices and Lessons Learnt," in *Risk and Regulatory Policy: Improving the Governance of Risk* (Paris: OECD, 2010), pp. 185–224.

20. Hutter, "Risk Management and Governance," pp. 303–21.

21. Bridget M. Hutter and Sally Lloyd-Bostock, "Risk, Interest Groups and the Definition of Crisis: The Case of Volcanic Ash," *British Journal of Sociology* 64 (September 2013): 383–404.

22. See Clive Briault, "Risk Society and Financial Risk," in *Anticipating Risks and Organising Risk Regulation*, edited by Bridget M. Hutter (Cambridge University Press, 2010), pp. 25–45; Nassim Nicholas Taleb, *The Black Swan: The Impact of the Highly Improbable* (New York: Random House, 2007).

23. Hutter and Lloyd-Bostock, "Risk, Interest Groups and the Definition of Crisis," pp. 383–404.

24. See generally Black, "Risk-Based Regulation," pp. 185–224; Hutter, "Risk Management and Governance," pp. 303–21.

25. Mary Douglas, *Risk and Blame: Essays in Cultural Theory* (London: Routledge, 1992).

26. Frank Ackerman and Lisa Heinzerling, *Priceless: On Knowing the Price of Everything and the Value of Nothing* (New York: The New Press, 2004).

27. Bridget M. Hutter and Sally Lloyd-Bostock, *Regulatory Crisis: Negotiating the Consequences of Risk, Disasters and Crises* (Cambridge University Press, forthcoming).

28. Douglas, *Risk and Blame*.

29. See John Braithwaite, *Regulatory Capitalism: How It Works, Ideas for Making It Work Better* (Cheltenham, U.K.: Edward Elgar, 2008); Jacint Jordana, David Levi-Faur, and Xavier Fernández-i-Marín, "The Global Diffusion of Regulatory Agencies: Channels of Transfer and Stages of Diffusion," *Comparative Political Studies* 44 (October 2011): 1343–69.

30. Bridget M. Hutter, ed., *Anticipating Risks and Organizing Risk Regulation* (Cambridge University Press, 2010).

31. Bridget M. Hutter, *Managing Food Safety and Hygiene: Governance and Regulation as Risk Management* (Cheltenham, U.K.: Edward Elgar, 2011).

32. Filippa Corneliussen, "The Impact of Regulations on Firms: A Case Study of the Biotech Industry," *Law and Policy* 27 (July 2005): 429–49.

33. Christine Parker and Vibeke Lehmann Nielsen, eds., *Explaining Compliance: Business Responses to Regulation* (Cheltenham, U.K.: Edward Elgar, 2011).

34. Martin Lodge and Kai Wegrich, "Rational Tools of Government in a World of Bounded Rationality," CARR Discussion Paper 75 (London: Centre for Analysis

of Risk and Regulation, London School of Economics and Political Science, 2014).

35. This is at the heart of "smart regulation" and also responsive regulation. See Neil Gunningham and Peter Grabosky, *Smart Regulation: Designing Environmental Policy* (Oxford University Press, 1998); Ian Ayres and John Braithwaite, *Responsive Regulation: Transcending the Deregulation Debate* (Oxford University Press, 1992).

36. Roger E. Kasperson and others, "The Social Amplification of Risk: A Conceptual Framework," *Risk Analysis* 8 (June 1988): 177–87.

37. Matthew Eisler, "Perspective: Where Nano Came from," in *Nanotechnology and the Public: Risk Perception and Risk Communication,* edited by Susanna Hornig Priest (Boca Raton, Fla.: CRC Press, 2011), pp. 9–19.

38. Alan Irwin and Kevin Jones, "Creating Space for Engagement? Lay Membership in Contemporary Risk Governance," in Hutter, *Anticipating Risks,* pp. 185–207.

39. Ibid.

40. Sally Lloyd-Bostock, "Public Perceptions of Risk and 'Compensation Culture' in the U.K.," in Hutter, *Anticipating Risks,* pp. 90–113.

41. Hutter and Lloyd-Bostock, "Risk, Interest Groups and the Definition of Crisis," pp. 383–404.

42. Martin Lodge, "Accountability and Transparency in Regulation: Critiques, Doctrines and Instruments" in *The Politics of Regulation: Institutions and Regulatory Reforms for the Age of Governance*, edited by Jacint Jordana and David Levi-Faur (Cheltenham, U.K.: Edward Elgar, 2004), pp. 124–44.

43. Hutter, "Risk Management and Governance," pp. 303–21.

44. Charles Perrow, *Normal Accidents: Living with High-Risk Technologies* (New York: Basic Books, 1984).

# 8

# Regulatory Excellence and Lucidity

## ROBERT BALDWIN

**EXCELLENT REGULATORS PERFORM IN** a manner that raises them above the merely satisfactory or competent agencies. The hallmark of such excellence, I argue here, is lucidity—a clarity of approach in delivering on the essential tasks of regulation. The notion of regulatory lucidity is set out in detail in this chapter, and an explanation is given of both the challenges encountered in pursuing lucidity and some of the strategies that regulators can adopt in order to rise to those challenges. The idea of lucidity provides a framework for thinking about regulatory excellence and, at the same time, a practical approach to the delivery of such excellence. It can particularly help regulators faced with the challenges of performing excellently when applying a "risk-based" approach to regulation, as is increasingly the case around the world in a variety of regulatory realms. Regulatory excellence poses special challenges and calls for particular responses in risk-based regimes.

### REGULATORY EXCELLENCE AS LUCIDITY

There is a difference of kind between the satisfactory and the excellent regulator, and this distinction turns on the lucidity with which the excellent regulator discharges the array of tasks that it is charged to perform. The excellent regulator is marked by a level of conscious clarity that is systemic and sustained.

This lucidity, or conscious clarity, has three key qualities. In delivering the appropriate regulatory outcomes effectively and at the lowest cost, excellent regulators will be *attuned* to their settings insofar as they are heedful of such matters as differences in ideas and approaches, the constraints imposed by cultural and institutional settings, and the potential of different regulatory options. They will, overall, be highly conscious of the challenges they face.

They will be *intelligent* in that they know precisely what they are setting out to achieve; the systems they use will allow them to process information expertly so as to assess their own performance and to explain their actions to stakeholders and others to whom they are accountable. Such intelligence is thus inward- and outward-looking insofar as it serves as a basis both for ensuring that the regulator's own tactics are appropriate and for explaining and justifying regulatory actions to those inside and outside the agency.

Lucid regulators will also be *dynamic* and display both a sensitivity to changes in their regulatory environments and an ability to adapt their regime to such changes.[1] The excellent regulator, moreover, will not only perform well currently but will also offer assurance to regulatory stakeholders that such a level of performance is likely to continue into the future. It will do so by being able to show that it has developed high levels of institutional competence across all aspects of its work activities. This contrasts with the position in which the regulator relies on a charismatic leader rather than the deployment of a highly skilled team. (An organization whose performance depends on an individual, who may depart from the agency, cannot offer such institutional assurance.)

Regulatory excellence, accordingly, involves excellence in both performance and institutional qualities or characteristics. For reasons of space, however, the discussion below is confined to the issue of excellence in performance.

The excellent regulator will perform extremely well across the whole array of activities that it carries out. Lucidity, accordingly, will be demonstrated by the excellent regulator in discharging all of the essential regulatory tasks in an effective way: setting *objectives*; producing appropriate *substantive outcomes*; and serving *representative values* through processes that further such matters as accountability, procedural fairness, and justification.

Why is excellence to be judged in relation to these three tasks? First, the setting of *objectives* underpins and gives focus to all of a regulator's activities, and it provides a basis for stakeholders to plan their affairs. For this reason, setting objectives can be seen as a fundamental deliverable of regulation rather than a mere means to an end. It is an activity, moreover, that the excellent regulator will perform in a manner that is seen as legitimate by those affected by its regulation.

As for appropriate *substantive outcomes,* delivery of these might be considered at first glance to be the core measure of regulatory performance. If a regulator produces the mandated outcomes (at nonexcessive cost), why be concerned about anything else? We might be happy with this situation if the nature of such results were uncontentious and the regulatory mandate for these results were clear and beyond dispute. The reality, however, is that regulators' mandates tend to be imprecise and malleable, dynamic and contentious. These features mean that parties who are affected by regulation will demand the serving of *representative values* so that they can participate fairly and adequately in the construction, development, and implementation of mandates. They will, accordingly, want regulatory processes to be fair and open, transparent, and accountable.[2]

Regulators will face a series of challenges in setting objectives, delivering appropriate substantive values, and serving representative outcomes. The key to excellence lies in meeting those challenges lucidly through approaches that are attuned to regulatory settings, intelligent, and dynamic.

## LUCIDITY IN SETTING OBJECTIVES AND DELIVERING SUBSTANTIVE OUTCOMES

Excellent regulators will establish their objectives with lucidity but in doing so they will confront a number of hurdles. A lucid regulator's first need is to stay attuned to the challenges that it faces.

### *Challenges*

It is normal for regulators to be charged to further outcomes that are imprecisely defined. There are a number of familiar reasons why this is so. Legislatures and governments may know that there is a problem that needs to be controlled through regulation, but they will have limited expertise in analyzing that problem; they will normally not have information about how the problem will develop; and they will recognize the need to give the regulator a degree of discretion that will allow it to deal with issues as they arise.

On many issues, there will be multiple views on the nature of the problem to be addressed and the objectives that the regulator should be pursuing. Different groupings of regulated concerns will disagree about the legitimate objectives of the regulator and what constitutes "satisfactory," "good," or "excellent" regulation. Producers and consumers, as well as large and small concerns, for instance, will often diverge markedly in their views on objectives and mandates, and the regulatory mandate will not have been defined in legislation in a manner that resolves such differences. As a result, debates over the regulator's objectives may involve considerable contention, and what the mandate calls for may be uncertain.

Regulatory excellence demands that such uncertainties be resolved in a clear, effective, and acceptable manner. That this may be no easy task is demonstrated by considering an example. Many regulators around the world are charged to further sustainable outcomes, or to encourage sustainable development, or to recognize the value of sustainability.[3] Sustainability, however, is a principle understood in so many ways, and covers so many disciplines,[4] values, and time-periods,[5] that setting objectives with clarity is difficult. These challenges are compounded by conflicting priorities as well as evidential uncertainties on central issues.[6] They are perhaps at the severe end of the scale of regulatory difficulty, but similar hurdles are encountered by the many regulators who are called on to pursue such broadly stated ends as "the public interest" or "the satisfaction of reasonable consumer demands."

With many broadly stated objectives, a first issue is *content*: what is the meaning of the notion of such concepts as "sustainability" and "the public interest"? As noted, different regulated concerns and interests are likely to have their own readings of the mandates that are set out in legislative form, and a first difficulty for any regulator is to produce a vision of the mandate that is acceptable across the array of affected parties and external observers. A further challenge arises when different disciplines or conceptual frameworks offer varying approaches to achieving objectives. In the case of sustainability, for instance, economic, environmental, and social perspectives offer their own separate approaches to the formulation of sustainability objectives, and the relative priorities of economic, environmental, and social considerations is often unclear. Multiple objectives and values may be implicated, with trade-offs between present and future gains and losses. There is no readily available, uncontentious way to deal with such matters as the balance between the needs of today's less affluent consumers and the environmental interests of future generations.[7]

Where several regulators are involved in an area, it may be extremely difficult to ensure that all of them subscribe to a common conception of the values or the objectives in question.[8] When, moreover, there are such contests, powerful regulated concerns will have opportunities to seize the initiative in defining a regime's objectives.[9] In "metaregulatory" regimes that delegate frontline risk management functions to corporate operators, there is a special danger that those operators will seek to further conceptions of regulatory objectives that are self-serving.[10]

A further regulatory challenge can arise when the very idea that objectives can be established with precision is contested. Thus Bob Gibson and his colleagues argue that the principle of sustainability offers no clear prioritizing or resolution of conflicts between criteria to be taken into account in decisions but a set of, sometimes imprecisely defined, desiderata that are to be addressed in ways that will not necessarily prevail over other values and objectives.[11]

Regulatory excellence demands not merely that the content of objectives be captured clearly, it calls for clear thinking on the *status and force*, and *role*, of mandated objectives. Thus regulators need to avoid confusion over whether the objectives being set are legally binding, whether they are intended to have a degree of precision that underpins implementation, or whether they merely set out values to be accorded respect in decisions and policies. Further issues include whether the objectives serve to found enforceable rights or merely set aspirations down on paper.[12] The excellent regulator must also be certain whether a relevant aim is a principal or a secondary objective. The role of the objectives must be clearly envisaged insofar as the regulator knows whether they apply generally or only to specific projects, institutions, and policy areas.

All of these difficulties are compounded by data challenges and evidential uncertainties. Regulators have to collect and analyze data in order to set and pursue their objectives, but doing so may not be easy in some sectors or in relation to some risks. In the case of sustainability, for instance, valuations of future social and environmental effects—such as intragenerational equity and conservation of biodiversity—are especially difficult to quantify, and even current data levels often stand in the way of setting sustainability objectives.[13]

These kinds of difficulties are compounded when multiple governmental departments and agencies are involved in a regulated activity and they collect data by different methods and according to different framing values and assumptions. When, moreover, regulators have to justify their actions to other institutions, the ways in which they engage in dialogue with different bodies will affect how they construct arguments and use information.[14] For many regulators, the sheer number of institutions (governmental and nongovernmental, public and private) that have interests in the issues they address is likely to produce pressure to conceive of objectives in a plethora of ways. This point, it should be noted, applies not merely to relationships that are based on formal accountability arrangements; it has force whenever regulators engage in collaborative relationships with other institutions, engage in routine conversations with them, or seek legitimation from them. In addition, domestic and supranational courts are likely to have an impact on this front and may offer their own binding vision of objectives. All such pressures stand in the way of clear and consistent understandings of aims.[15]

A further set of challenges arises when regulatory objectives are set within political and governmental priorities, or business conditions, that are volatile. In such scenarios, even the most highly legitimate of regulatory objectives have to be adjusted in order to maintain credibility or to adapt to market changes. A challenge here is to balance two conflicting appetites of regulatory stakeholders:

for changes that will meet new expectations or economic circumstances and for the stability that allows businesses and others to plan their investments and affairs.[16]

Even where government contexts are not volatile, regulators may have to deal with the efforts of governments to take over the task of bringing objectives into focus. One governmental strategy that is designed to foster precision in regulatory missions is the promulgation of binding governmental guidance for regulators. The idea here is that central government office holders can flesh out legislative objectives in an authoritative and democratic manner so that regulators can work toward aims that have some certainty.

This system has been deployed in a host of areas, including the U.K. environment sector, but experience reveals that statutory guidance is not a device that guarantees regulators an easy route to lucidity. In the environmental domain, a system of statutory guidance was deployed in an effort to give content to statutory obligations on sustainability. The secretary of state for environment, food, and rural affairs was required under section 4 of the Environment Act 1995 to issue legally binding guidance to the U.K. Environment Agency on what the secretary of state saw as an appropriate contribution to sustainable development. The agency was bound to follow this guidance in pursuing agency objectives.

The 2002 statutory guidance, however, made manifest the difficulties involved in giving content to a broad notion such as that of furthering sustainable development. The agency's objectives did not, in themselves, flesh out any comprehensive concept of sustainable development. Some objectives referred to sustainability, some referred to the need to conserve certain resources, and many objectives were stated without reference to sustainability.

In this instance, questions of *status and force,* as well as *role,* compounded the difficulties of establishing the *content* of objectives. At some points, the agency's obligation to further sustainability called on the agency to produce certain outcomes; at other points it seemed to demand the serving of certain values or the government's policy objectives. The government's guidance, indeed, did not so much instruct the agency to follow a particular approach to sustainable development as suggest that the secretary of state's position on the appropriate agency contribution to sustainable development was revealed in a White Paper.[17] The difficulty was that the objectives referred to did not offer a great deal of help on *content, status and force,* or *role.* They played political policy as well as legal roles; and instead of offering an approach to understanding the legal requirements of sustainable development, they provided a cryptic list of ten policies to be considered in making policy. The secretary of state's guidelines thus did little to assist the agency in giving clear content to the objective of furthering sustainable development.[18]

The preceding account is thus an example of a failure to facilitate regulatory lucidity through the production of governmental guidelines on regulatory objectives. In the case recounted, the guidelines did not so much help the regulator to render objectives more clear as offer a cascade of subprinciples and subobjectives that purportedly derive from the highest level of principle and whose status and force as well as role were uncertain. For the excellent regulator, the challenge is to produce clarity of vision in the face of such governmental inputs.

With respect to the delivery of appropriate substantive outcomes, the excellent regulator will build on clearly identified and legitimated objectives before gathering information about problems, issues, and challenges that need to be overcome to further those objectives.[19] Regulatory excellence then demands devising positive strategies for dealing with identified problems and applying these strategies on the ground so as to modify behavior when necessary to produce the desired outcomes at the lowest feasible cost.

When gathering information on issues and problems, regulators often confront institutional structures and constraints that hinder detection and information collection, and that add to the difficulties of collecting data, especially in relation to issues that are intrinsically complex and contestable (such as matters of equity between generations or classes of consumer). Poor institutional coordination impedes information gathering,[20] as do differences of view on objectives that stem from differences between cultures and disciplines.[21]

With respect to the development of strategies, special challenges arise when there are varying conceptions regarding the *content, status and force,* and *role* of the values and objectives to be furthered. In relation to the example of sustainability, for instance, such variations will impact strategic choices: parties who see sustainability in political terms, for instance, will not see enforcement choices in the same way as those who see the principle as legally binding. Where numbers of agencies and departments are involved in an area, individual institutions may be wedded to particular intervention strategies and, again, this may stand in the way of coherent and coordinated approaches to strategic design.

Many of the challenges that regulators encounter in developing strategies will also be faced when interventions are made in order to modify behavior. Thus, the methods used to apply any given intervention tool may be subject to contestation. In any regulatory intervention regime it is difficult to ensure that common conceptions of risks, problems, and approaches can be fostered on different organizational levels (or horizontally across departments).[22] When regulatory concepts and objectives are contested, the challenges just noted will be all the more severe, as will producing reliable performance indicators. A similar point can be made regarding regulatory efforts to respond to changes in a timely fashion: where objectives are contested, regulators often have to negotiate settlements between many parties, and such complex renegotiations are an impediment to dynamism.

### Responding to Challenges

The excellent regulator will be aware of the challenges and will adopt lucid—attuned, intelligent, and dynamic—approaches. Lucidity demands an awareness that a variety of conceptions of objectives must be accommodated. How can regulators develop and sustain legitimate conceptions of objectives for all concerned? Commentators have suggested that the way forward lies in developing procedures for consultation and policy development that foster agreement even in the face of differences of discourse and interests.[23]

An early pioneer of this approach in the U.K. utility sector was Don Cruickshank who, as director-general of Oftel, the telecommunications regulator, instituted a practice in the 1990s of publishing the draft Annual Management Plan of Oftel and soliciting stakeholder comments on it. The aim of this strategy was to enhance transparency and foster legitimation of the regulator's vision of its annual objectives. The agency reported:

> There has been public debate on the work programme contents prior to publication. All interested parties were invited to comment on the shape, content and focus of this year's Management Plan. This process culminated in a well-attended public meeting. The public discussion by a regulator of its intended work plan is unique but we have found it to be an extremely valuable process and one I would recommend to others. This draft has benefited significantly from the constructive input of both consumers and companies and thus will ensure that Oftel makes the best use of limited resources.[24]

There is considerable potential in such approaches, but it is one thing for a regulator to develop and legitimize a statement of high-level regulatory objectives; it is another to ensure that such conceptions of aims are promulgated consistently through the regulatory organization, among the co-regulators (public and private), and at all governmental levels (corporation, state, local, and supranational) involved in controlling an activity or industry. The excellent regulator will be attuned to this issue and will develop and implement strategies for ensuring cross-organizational consistency of aims.

The basis for lucidity in the regulator's vision of objectives is not just staying attuned to differences of viewpoint; it lies in intelligence and dynamism. The excellent regulator will build on a strong, evidence-based analysis of issues, and there will be a dynamic aspect to the setting of objectives insofar as the excellent regulator will operate systems that are sensitive to *changes* in expectations, preferences, political constraints, and other aspects of the regulatory environment. Objectives will be adjusted when necessary to cope with these mutations.

Overall, a key mark of the excellent regulator is the ability to produce a statement of objectives that is clear not merely about the content of those objectives (what they demand) but also about their force and status as well as their role and scope. The excellent regulator, moreover, will be sensitive to the need to adjust objectives where necessary.

On the matter of producing substantive outcomes, lucidity calls, again, for an awareness of the challenges noted above, and for approaches that are attuned to the regulatory setting, intelligent, and dynamic. Successful information-gathering activities have to acknowledge that different organizations and interests will use different methods and assumptions in gathering and supplying information. The excellent regulator will develop appropriate strategies to address such challenges. It might, for example, take steps to bring greater consistency to information collection and expert analysis to the data. In the sustainability field, for instance, feedback systems have been said to be an especially effective way for the attuned, intelligent, and dynamic regulator to address the indeterminacies of sustainability-related policies.[25]

In developing strategies and applying these on the ground so as to produce the desired results at the lowest cost, lucidity means that the regulator will deploy intervention strategies that take account of the sensitivities of different regulated concerns and the need to customize intervention approaches so as to maximize their effectiveness and positive impact. The excellent regulator will display intelligence and dynamism by identifying regulatory strategies, priorities, and intervention methods that are supported by high-quality analysis of relevant evidence, that are sensitive to changes in markets, preferences, and so on, and that command support across the agency and within the body of regulated concerns as far as this is feasible. Such strategies and identified priorities will also provide the lucid regulator with a basis for both performance evaluation and the adoption of any required regulatory changes.

## SERVING REPRESENTATIVE VALUES

The greater the indeterminacies in the content, status and force, or role of regulators' mandated objectives, the greater the challenges they confront when they seek to both serve representative values appropriately and demonstrate that they have done so.

## *Challenges*

It is especially difficult for a regulator who faces high levels of indeterminacy in objectives to convince parties of its fairness. Complexities in, and contests over, unresolved mandates provide myriad opportunities for powerful parties to influence regulatory approaches and actions in a self-serving manner. Accusations of substantive bias are liable, accordingly, to be difficult to defend against.

As for procedural fairness, a special difficulty that many regulators face is that they operate within decentered, fragmented regulatory regimes in which interests and claims are made by a wide range of methods.[26] This makes it very difficult to create assurances of procedural fairness because comparisons cannot readily be made on a single plane; there is, simply, little obvious procedural equivalence. Similar issues arise in relation to fairness of access and participation. A message that is open and transparent to one kind of stakeholder may be opaque to another type. Again, the need to explain and justify regulatory actions involves mirroring challenges, since accountability is often rendered through a host of different types of conversations or claims.

## *Responding to Challenges*

The lucid regulator will respond to the above challenges in a manner that is attuned to the stakeholders, intelligent, and dynamic. Such a regulator will, accordingly, seek to demonstrate *substantive* fairness by showing that decisions and policies properly take into account and respect the interests of affected parties. It will have the evidence in hand to demonstrate the paying of such respect, and it will ensure that its ability to justify its actions will hold even in the event that the regulatory environment changes.

The lucid regulator will respond to the need to show *procedural* fairness by attuning itself to the procedural standpoints and expectations of its various stakeholders. It will take all feasible steps to demonstrate that, by employing a variety of procedures, it offers all stakeholders equivalent levels of fairness, representation, and opportunities to affect outcomes. The lucid regulator will also take steps to ensure informational fairness and will be prepared to act in a facilitative role, assisting and enabling participation where this is necessary for the required equivalence (where necessary by packaging information in the form most digestible for the party at issue). It may involve using best offices to organize negotiations and settlements between parties so that disagreements are minimized. Such efforts, moreover, will seek to straddle institutional divisions so that access to one decision or policymaker is not devalued by perceived exclusion from the processes of other agencies that are involved in the regulatory issue.

The lucid regulator will, moreover, recognize the need for dynamism and will be quick to act on changes that affect the fairness of participation. Thus, when a newly complex issue enters the agenda, an excellent regulator will take rapid steps to ensure that this new complexity does not exclude any parties from the relevant processes.

The lucid regulator will likewise respond to issues of access and participation in an attuned and intelligent way and will be prepared to ensure not only that all interested parties are identified but also that it develops and applies processes and information systems that facilitate understanding by the full range of stakeholders. This inclusiveness may require a good deal of individual and tailored interaction, and the resource implications of this will need to be kept in mind. Also considered, and addressed, will be the dangers that transparency in some aspects of a decision or policy may be undermined by activities controlled by another regulatory body. The dynamism of the lucid regulator will demand that fresh routes to transparency be developed as new kinds of issues come on to agendas.

In justifying its actions, regulatory lucidity will demand, in the first place, that the regulator remain attuned to the institutional context so that the different stakeholders are responded to with the appropriately tailored message. Securing strong justification is, however, a challenge for any regulator who faces indeterminacies, regime complexities, evidential uncertainties, vulnerabilities to change, and high levels of contestability. The intelligent regulator will focus on collecting information that will maximize the potential to make convincing justificatory claims and establishing the dynamic agency that will see the process of justification as an ongoing project.

## RISK-BASED REGULATION AND EXCELLENCE

As noted at the start, very many regulators operate "risk-based" regimes in which analyses of risks guide the regulators' interventions. This prompts the question whether regulatory lucidity poses special challenges when a regulator operates a risk-based regime. It may do so in a number of contexts and respects, and regulatory excellence calls for attention to those special challenges.

In setting operational objectives and making risk-based assessments, regulators have to work from their overall objectives down to key risk objectives. If the regulator in question is charged to deal with risks that involve high levels of indeterminacy (such as "risks to sustainability"), the identification of key risks is likely to be subject to supranormal levels of contention. In such instances, the selection of a particular basket of risks exposes the regulator to more acute political pressures than would otherwise be the case—an argument made in some jurisdictions in relation to the prefinancial crisis financial regulator.[27]

Problems may also be encountered in adjusting risk priorities. One danger in all risk-based systems is "model myopia," the tendency to overcommit to the existing model of risks so that updating does not take place.[28] In circumstances where the regulators need to engage in extensive deliberative procedures so as to create broad buy-in to a particular set of risk identifications, the hard-earned settlements and agreements that underpin regulation will have to be unpacked. Regulatory resistance to such unpacking may thus combine with model myopia to render their regimes doubly unresponsive to change.

Difficulties can arise when a risk-based regulator seeks to attune its interventions to cultural variations and to tailor intervention methods to different operators' understandings of regulatory objectives. Risk-based regulation focuses on identifying the operators that require priority attention (the high risks); it says little about the modes of intervention required, and a focus on targeting may draw the eye away from choices of intervention style—which may be highly contentious.

Numerous risks are systemic in nature; they often arise because of cumulative pressure from pervasive or multiple sources. As was seen in the financial crisis of 2007 onwards, however, the logic of risk-based regulation may naturally focus attention on individual "silos of risk" so that systemic or cumulative risks are neglected. In some regulatory fields, moreover, what constitutes a systemic risk is also contestable (by operators and regulators alike), compounding an already considerable difficulty. The more that the regulatory regime is a multiagency affair, the more serious this problem is likely to be.

Risk-based regulators face special difficulties, furthermore, in measuring their own performance in delivering outcomes. Many control tasks are delegated to operating firms when risk-based regulators monitor operators' risk management systems rather than take direct steps to control risks. In such "metaregulatory" systems, when actors use different models or "codes" to evaluate risks, risk evaluations become complex and opaque. Cultural differences among the regulated parties exacerbate this problem.

Risk-based regulators may also find that ensuring that their staff act (and are seen to act) in a fair and consistent fashion comes at a significant price. Assessments of the risks presented by different operators involve the exercise of considerable discretion. The more scope there is for judgment, the more difficult it will be to ensure a consistent approach. The processes for overseeing staff discretion may, accordingly, be costly, and centralized controls over these matters can make the regulator slow to respond to changes in the regulatory challenges it faces.[29]

As for the risk-based regulator's ability to justify its actions and secure support, there may be further worries. The priorities that risk-based regulation demands may render the regulator especially vulnerable to political attack, especially when opinions differ on the content, status and force, and role of objectives. When some risks are not given priority, the regulator may be liable to censure from groups or interests who see those risks as central to their conception of appropriate regulatory objectives.

Clashes of regulatory logic may also impede the use of deliberative procedures to generate consent and support.[30] The logic of risk-based regulation is that risk analyses dictate priorities for intervention and the urgency of intervention methods. In many regulated areas, however, careful negotiation of approaches and solutions is required to cope with the challenges discussed here (indeterminacies in content, status and force, and role of mandate, as well as evidential uncertainties and regime complexities). Careful deliberation and effective facilitation are required if regulators are to retain the stakeholder support they need in order to secure desired outcomes.[31] There is tension between the mechanical approach of risk-based regulation and the deliberative model necessary to deliver the goods in many areas of regulation.

Public expectations may also introduce a difficulty for risk-based regulators who face indeterminacies of mission. Risk-based regulation is often perceived as promising a technical, rational, systematic solution to control issues; however, where positions on objectives and risk priorities involve qualitative judgments, evidential uncertainties and indeterminacies, and a multiplicity of divergent opinions, all of these factors contribute to dramatic departures from this promise. Justifications are, moreover, not always strengthened by disclosures about risk priorities; these can have the effect of merely exposing the agency to further attacks for failures to attend to unprioritized risks. Commitment to a risk model may render the regulator unresponsive to stakeholders by blinding the regulator to changes in stakeholders' perceptions of priorities.

How, then, can excellence be achieved by the risk-based regulator? The answer is that the approach adopted should be the same as that of any regulator; namely, challenges should be addressed in an attuned, intelligent, and dynamic fashion in pursuit of lucidity. Risk regulators, like any other regulator, must stay attuned to the hurdles that have to be overcome, whatever the source. In the case of risk-based regulation, the excellent regulator will seek especially to select key risks, adjust the package of key risks, deal with systemic risks, gather the information necessary for intelligent assessments of performance, and adapt to change in a dynamic fashion. Finally, the lucid risk-based regulator will have a clear strategy for explaining and justifying its risk priorities and actions—a strategy that meets the pressures that flow from often unrealistic expectations that risk-based systems offer clear-cut answers to regulatory questions.

## CONCLUSION

The factor that marks regulatory excellence is lucidity, as manifested in a clear-sighted and highly conscious approach to the regulator's tasks and challenges. The lucid regulator will be attuned, intelligent, and dynamic across the full range of its activities. It will be aware of challenges, contexts, possibilities, and alternatives, and it will address debates over the proper regulatory objectives. It will build on the solid collection and analysis of evidence, and it will both deliver effectively on the substantive and procedural fronts and be able to evaluate its own performance and explain its actions. It will, moreover, be consciously dynamic, operating systems that allow it to recognize the need for change and to implement the necessary adjustments to its approach. In these ways, the concept of lucidity offers regulators an organized and practical approach to the delivery of excellence.

### NOTES

1. See Robert Baldwin and Julia Black, "Really Responsive Regulation," *Modern Law Review* 71 (January 2008): 59–94.

2. See generally Robert Baldwin, Martin Cave, and Martin Lodge, *Understanding Regulation,* 2nd ed. (Oxford University Press, 2012), pp. 25–39.

3. In the United Kingdom, Ofwat, for instance, has a duty under the Water Industry Act 1991 (as amended) to "exercise and perform . . . powers and duties . . . in the manner . . . best calculated to contribute to the achievement of sustainable development." The word "sustainability" is not invariably employed. See, for example, the duty of the Alberta Energy Regulator under the Responsible Energy Development Act 2012. Section 2(1) states: "The mandate of the Regulator is (a) to provide for the efficient, safe, orderly and environmentally responsible development of energy resources in Alberta." The Environmental Protection and Enhancement Act (Alberta) recognizes the principle of sustainable development at section 2(c).

4. See, for example, Bob Giddings, Bill Hopwood, and Geoff O'Brien, "Environment, Economy and Society: Fitting Them Together into Sustainable Development," *Sustainable Development* 10 (November 2002): 187–96.

5. Virginie Barral, "Sustainable Development in International Law: Nature and Operation of an Evolutive Legal Norm," *European Journal of International Law* 23 (July 2012): 377–400.

6. See evidence of the Country Land and Business Association to the House of Commons Environmental Audit Committee, *The Sustainable Development Strategy: Illusion or Reality?* Thirteenth Report of Session 2003–04, vol. 2 (London: House of Commons), Appendix 7, para. 5. In evidence reproduced in the same report, English

Nature argues that: "We do not get the sense overall that Government policy making recognizes, or knows how to resolve, potentially conflicting objectives" (Appendix 9, para. 4.3). See also Productivity Commission of Australia, *Implementation of Ecologically Sustainable Development by Commonwealth Departments and Agencies*, Inquiry Report 5 (Canberra, May 5, 1999), pp. 7–9 (www.pc.gov.au/inquiries/completed/ecologically -sustainable-development/report/esd.pdf), noting the difficulty of measuring costs and benefits far off in the future.

7. David Pearce, Anil Markandya, and Edward Barbier, *Blueprint for a Green Economy* (London: Earthscan, 1989).

8. See Adrian Cashman, "Water Regulation and Sustainability 1997–2001" *Geoforum* 37 (July 2006): 488–504. The Environmental Audit Committee in its Seventh Report censured Ofwat for demonizing environmental and quality investment by emphasizing its upward effects on prices.

9. Cashman, "Water Regulation and Sustainability," pp. 488–504. See also Gavin Bridge and Phil McManus, "Sticks and Stones: Environmental Narratives and Discursive Regulation in the Forestry and Mining Sectors" *Antipode* 32 (January 2000): 10–47.

10. On metaregulation generally, see Cary Coglianese and Jennifer Nash, *Regulating from the Inside* (Washington: Resources for the Future Press, 2001); Cary Coglianese and Jennifer Nash, eds., *Leveraging the Private Sector: Management-Based Strategies for Improving Environmental Performance* (Washington: Resources for the Future Press, 2006); Cary Coglianese and Evan Mendelson, "Meta-Regulation and Self-Regulation," in *The Oxford Handbook on Regulation*, edited by Robert Baldwin, Martin Cave, and Martin Lodge (Oxford University Press, 2010), pp. 146–68.

11. Robert B. Gibson and others, *Sustainability Assessment: Criteria and Processes* (London: Earthscan, 2005), pp. 88–121.

12. Sustainability, for example, is treated within many discourses as a principle of legal relevance, but it can be treated as a policy objective only, or as a political or philosophical, rather than a legal, principle. Ibid.

13. Ecologically Sustainable Development Working Group, *Final Report Fisheries* (Canberra: AGPS, 1991). See also Ronnie Harding, ed., *Environmental Decision-Making: The Roles of Scientists, Engineers and the Public* (Sydney: Federation Press, 1998).

14. Julia Black, "Constructing and Contesting Legitimacy and Accountability in Polycentric Regulatory Regimes," *Regulation & Governance* 2 (June 2008): 137–64.

15. The courts have yet to develop a strong role on sustainability issues; see Katia Opalka and Joanna Myszka, "Sustainability and the Courts: A Snapshot of Canada in 2009," *Sustainable Development Law and Policy* 10 (Fall 2009): 58–65; John Martin Gillroy, "Adjudication Norms, Dispute Settlement Regimes and International Tribunals: The Status of 'Environmental Sustainability' in International Jurisprudence," *Stanford Journal of International Law* 42 (Winter 2006): 1–52.

16. See generally Robert Baldwin, "Regulatory Stability and the Challenges of Re-regulation," *Public Law* (April 2014): 208–28.

17. *A Better Quality of Life: A Strategy for Sustainable Development in the U.K.,* White Paper (London: TSO, CM 4345, 1999).

18. House of Commons Environmental Audit Committee, *The Sustainable Development Strategy* (2010).

19. On the importance of an adequate informational base, see Productivity Commission of Australia, *Implementation of Ecologically Sustainable Development,* pp. 15–16.

20. See ibid., pp. 14–15, 97.

21. Ibid., p. 14.

22. See Robert Baldwin and Julia Black, "Driving Priorities in Risk-Based Regulation: What's the Problem?" *Journal of Law and Society* 43 (2016): 565–95.

23. See, for example, Derek Bell and Tim Gray, "The Ambiguous Role of the Environment Agency in England and Wales," *Environmental Politics* 11, no. 3 (Fall 2002): 76–98; Gibson and others, *Sustainability Assessment,* pp. 107–11.

24. Oftel, *Draft Work Programme for 1998/9 and Beyond* (London: Oftel, 1998).

25. Productivity Commission of Australia, *Implementation of Ecologically Sustainable Development by Commonwealth Departments and Agencies,* "Recommendation 7.2."

26. Black, "Constructing and Contesting Legitimacy," pp. 137–64.

27. See Julia Black, "Paradoxes and Failures: 'New Governance' Techniques and the Financial Crisis," *Modern Law Review* 75 (November 2012): 1037–63.

28. See Julia Black and Robert Baldwin, "Really Responsive Risk-Based Regulation," *Law & Policy* 32 (April 2010): 181–213, 189.

29. Ibid., p. 206.

30. Ibid., p. 199.

31. See Productivity Commission of Australia, *Implementation of Ecologically Sustainable Development,* pp. 97–122.

**PART II**

# Seeking Regulatory Excellence

# 9

# Regulatory Excellence

*Lessons from Theory and Practice*

DANIEL C. ESTY

**REGULATORY EXCELLENCE HAS MANY** facets. But what constitutes "best practice" in the governmental domain has been underpinned by too little theory and not much analysis of practice. In this chapter I try to fill in both gaps. I introduce a framework about what should matter in pursuing good governance in the regulatory arena drawn from the scholarly literature, most notably from the fields of public administration and management with an overlay from the realm of administrative law. I amplify this taxonomy of regulatory best practices with observations from my work in the business world (where there has been much more systematic focus on organizational excellence) and my recent government service as commissioner of Connecticut's Department of Energy and Environmental Protection (DEEP).

## MANAGEMENT EXCELLENCE: VISION AND EXECUTION

While regulatory excellence has been understudied, there has been considerable work done in the private sector on the elements of management excellence.[1] Although business school scholars and management gurus all have their own lists of what is critical, almost all agree that the fundamental requirements are *vision* and *execution*. I believe that the same core principles apply in the regulatory realm.

133

### Vision

Business leaders spend a great deal of time defining their organization's direction and "vision," often working with their management teams to spell this out in a mission statement.[2] Public policymakers should do the same. Too often, the direction of government agencies is defined by inertia. Without strong leadership that sharply focuses the work of a regulatory body, civil servants will do tomorrow what they did yesterday. So clarity of vision about the agency's mission, core values, future direction, priorities and goals, and strategy emerges as the starting point for regulatory excellence.

I think that there is also a consensus that a "customer focus"—indeed, some would say *compulsive* attention to customer satisfaction and a commitment to listening to feedback—must be at the heart of any successful organization's vision and culture.[3] Such a customer orientation—with a relentless focus on the needs of the public and the concerns of the regulated community—has not been at the heart of government practice, but should be.[4]

Most everyone in business recognizes the value of innovation and the need to constantly update and refine their strategies and tactics—and therefore their products, services, and business models. Government entities have been much less focused on this transformation imperative. This too is a mistake. Regulatory excellence requires a deep commitment to continuous improvement and occasional fundamental restructuring. At Connecticut's DEEP, I made transformation of the state's environmental regulatory model the central focus of my tenure as commissioner. As I discuss in detail below, we used a "lean" process (borrowed from manufacturing)[5] to completely reengineer all twenty-six of DEEP's permitting programs and dozens of other agency activities.[6] This streamlining of operations allowed the agency to cope with significant human resource and budget reductions while delivering dramatic improvements in permitting speed, better targeting of limited regulatory resources to the biggest risks, elimination of a substantial backlog of pending permits, and greatly improved reviews from the regulated community.[7]

### Execution

Nearly every set of core principles of quality management puts a premium on execution: implementing the business strategy to deliver against clear targets such as sales growth or improved profitability. Government needs to put the same priority on implementation.[8] Success should not be judged by laws passed, regulations written, treaties negotiated, budget growth, staff hired, or any other "input" metric. Progress must be gauged by changed behavior within the regulatory community and on-the-ground performance outcomes. For an environmental agency, for instance, success should be measured by improvements in air and water quality, evidence of properly managed chemicals and waste, and lower levels of greenhouse gas emissions in the atmosphere. Efficacy and efficiency both need to be part of this calculus.

Execution in any organization requires a number of strategy elements, including strong leadership with a visible commitment to improved performance and clarity about the need to do things differently and better. Almost every business has a sharp focus on delivering greater efficiency. Lower costs translate immediately into bottom-line results. Because they operate without profit targets, governments have not prized efficiency as much, but they should. The public's support for regulatory efforts varies with the perceived cost of regulations. When the burden is low, public support is easier to maintain. When regulatory costs are seen to be high relative to the gains, political and public scrutiny increases. One key to regulatory excellence is thus to reduce the regulatory burden without lowering standards. In this regard, regulatory bodies should pursue efficiency as a priority. Some of the same tools that the private sector has deployed, such as redesigning operations for greater speed, efficiency, effectiveness, and transparency through lean analysis, should be more widely adopted in government.[9]

Communication is also critical to implementation and thus to regulatory excellence. Transformation is hard to deliver under any circumstances, especially in government, where there has been so little reward for doing new things. Clear marching orders from top management, particularly on the urgency of the transformation agenda, will be required. This reality is why so much emphasis in business is placed on creating a sense of a "burning platform," which implies that there is no choice but to jump to something new and make changed practices succeed. Government leaders need to drive innovation just as hard and establish the same sense of urgency about transformation. Likewise, there needs to be strong bottom-up information flow—both because successful change requires buy-in from the staff who will have to carry out reengineered regulatory programs and other processes, and because the health of any organization depends on feedback (particularly bad news) getting from the staff to top management quickly.

The management literature almost universally emphasizes *people* as a critical input to organizational success.[10] This emphasis holds equal sway in government. Recruiting top talent is essential. And training (and retraining) at all levels of the organization is fundamental to execution. Of course, even the best people will not be able to perform at a high level without adequate resources and technology support such as computers, video links, and access to online materials and databases. But governments often stint on these critical resources in the face of budgetary challenges. At the Connecticut DEEP, with the governor's strong support, we committed new resources (even at a time of budget cuts) to staff training and the upgrading of information technology (IT) and communications equipment in parallel with our "lean" transformation initiative. These commitments helped ensure the buy-in of the regulatory staff and contributed significantly to the positive results achieved.

Getting alignment and commitment to the transformation required for excellence across a regulatory staff can be much more challenging than it would be in the private sector, where foot-dragging can lead to dismissal. But every organization can establish appropriate goals, incentives, and rewards to drive execution. Quantitative metrics and benchmarking are useful in this regard, both to judge individual performance and to gauge whether programs are delivering on their promise. In business, leaders are trained to be data-driven and tough-minded about what is working and what is not. Every day, they evaluate initiatives and double down on those that are delivering the best results. But they also know that they must make choices, and where programs are not producing the anticipated outcomes, they shut them down and redeploy those resources toward more promising strategies and projects. Government officials need to get better at "declaring failure" and redeploying scarce resources. Too often in a regulatory agency the status quo holds sway long after it is clearly not working.

Designing metrics for a regulatory agency takes more work than might be needed in a private sector entity, but the management benefits are just as significant.[11] Good data can help to identify best practices (which can then be disseminated more widely), flag underperforming groups, individuals, and managers (allowing top management to prioritize them for transformation investments), and help develop materials that allow the agency to better "tell its story" to the public, legislators, and the media.[12]

## GOVERNMENTAL CONSTRAINTS

While management principles offer a valuable starting point for what will be needed for regulatory excellence, the regulatory realm operates under some additional constraints. When one wields the power of the state, efficiency cannot be the only priority. Thus regulatory agencies must carry out their work in ways that reflect respect for procedural fairness, distributional equity, political accountability, and checks and balances on the exercise of power.[13] Likewise, government must operate with special attention to discipline on corruption and self-dealing as well as lobbying and special interest manipulation of outcomes, all of which have been catalogued elsewhere and therefore will not be reviewed in depth here.[14] Suffice it to say that the elements of administrative law that produce good governance—notice and comment processes, open hearing and public participation mechanisms, obligations to publish draft decisions and explain policy choices, and structures for appeal or the cross-checking of outcomes—are in some tension with efficiency goals and other aspects of the framework of regulatory excellence outlined in this chapter. But they are essential to governmental legitimacy and must be upheld as prerequisites for regulatory excellence.[15]

### STRATEGIES FOR DELIVERING REGULATORY EXCELLENCE

Going beyond the private sector management literature and building on my own government experience, I identify in the following text five additional components of regulatory excellence beyond vision and execution.

### *Integration*

Regulators are often called on to fix market failures and to "internalize externalities" so that our economy functions efficiently and nonmonetary priorities (such as safety or environmental protection concerns) do not get overlooked. They make decisions that define the terms of competition in the marketplace and impose significant costs (sometimes amounting to billions of dollars) on those they regulate. Getting the framework of decisionmaking right therefore matters a great deal. Fundamentally, this means having a systematic and carefully constructed process for summing the costs and benefits of regulatory interventions. This formula is simple to describe but hard to implement. There are many ways that the requisite calculus can get skewed.

Regulators need, in particular, to avoid "siloed" thinking. They must consider all of the relevant costs and benefits as well as the countervailing risks and impacts.[16] Those charged with reducing air emissions, for instance, must be sure that they do not make water pollution worse. But sadly, this seemingly obvious rule is often ignored. Indeed, to reduce vehicle emissions in the 1990s, the U.S. Environmental Protection Agency (EPA) required MTBE to be added to gasoline to improve octane and produce cleaner combustion, only later to discover that the additive caused severe water pollution.[17]

Regulators need to pay special attention to costs and benefits that are hard to capture because they are spread over time or space, or are otherwise uncertain.[18] Some of the worst environmental regulatory failures of the twentieth century arose from the difficulty of capturing and managing slow-to-emerge or disaggregated harms, such as fishing practices that depleted fish stocks across the world or the buildup of greenhouse gas emissions from millions of sources that now threaten to cause climate change.[19]

Regulators must be further trained to recognize tradeoffs and to take seriously opportunity costs. Simply put, money spent on toxic waste cleanup is not available for investment in sewage treatment systems. More fundamentally, a dollar spent on regulatory compliance cannot be spent for business expansion, so public officials must be attentive to the efficiency of their rules and the economic burden (and competitiveness impacts) of the requirements they impose.

When Governor Dannel Malloy offered me the position of commissioner of Connecticut's Department of Environmental Protection (soon to be reconfigured as the Department of Energy and Environmental Protection), he told me that I would be taking on the most reviled agency in the state government. The heart of the problem centered on the delay in getting permits issued and the sense on the part of the regulated community that the department did not take seriously benefit-cost tradeoffs and the regulatory burden imposed on business. The mistrust these problems engendered colored everything Connecticut's DEEP did. In response, I told everyone at the agency that we needed to think of ourselves as "DEEEP"—with the three "e's" indicating we were committed to progress on *e*nergy, *e*nvironment, and the *e*conomy simultaneously. This integrated agenda helped reframe how the staff understood their job, making it clear that regulatory progress depended on the agency being seen as attentive to regulatory costs and the state's economic growth imperative.

While the concept of "regulatory budgets," which limit the total regulatory compliance costs that a government can impose, has not taken off (and might not be a good idea), the willingness to pay for regulatory programs is not endless in the business world or in the political domain.[20] As noted earlier, a smart regulator will not push the limits of the public's tolerance, and will ensure that efficiency is a watchword with regard to both the cost of administration (the government's regulatory expenditures and staffing, which translate into a tax burden) and the regulated community's compliance costs.

Signals from public officials about their seriousness of purpose in reducing the regulatory burden and cutting red tape are critical to a regulatory agency's credibility. The across-the-board "lean" review of DEEP regulations that I led translated into faster processing times, less paperwork, and lower compliance costs, all of which produced significant goodwill in the Connecticut business community and dramatically reduced criticism of the remaining regulatory requirements.

I also worked with the DEEP management team to identify outdated, outmoded, duplicative, and otherwise unneeded regulations and statutes, which we then convinced the Connecticut General Assembly to repeal.[21] These "streamlining initiatives" paid further dividends. Business leaders were shocked. They claimed never to have seen a regulator repeal requirements wholesale. The value of convincing the business community that DEEP cared about the regulatory burden it was imposing and was seeking to minimize it meant that when the agency did impose a burden, it got the benefit of the doubt that the costs were justified.[22]

### Innovation

Inertia is a powerful force in every organization, but especially in government where there is often little incentive to innovate. But regulatory excellence requires that systems be regularly reviewed and updated, and sometimes completely overhauled. When new policymaking tools emerge, the regulatory process needs to be reengineered to take advantage of the advances that have been made. Innovations that are quickly implemented in the business world often move slowly into the governmental realm. For instance, the information technology revolution that has transformed many aspects of society—how baseball teams pick their players,[23] how businesses advertise and market their products, and so forth—has been slow to take root in the policy domain.[24]

In this spirit, I put innovation and changed modes of operation at the heart of my vision for DEEP. I understood that transformation was essential not only in light of perceived limits to the agency's past performance but also as an inescapable reality given the governor's commitment to shrink the size of state government, which meant that I had to plan for staff attrition over three years of about 10 percent and an overall budget shrinkage of 15 percent. But thoughtful budget cutting turns out to be another critical element of regulatory excellence—and a crisis that can be converted into an opportunity. Specifically, budget cuts offer a way into the difficult conversation about priorities and which programs have outlived their usefulness, as well as the need to transform regulatory practices. Could Connecticut afford to spend thirty person-hours on each underground oil tank inspection? Not under the budget realities laid out by Governor Malloy. But it would have been hard to get the DEEP oil tank inspection team to shift to new ways of doing business (getting field inspectors to use tablet computers and transfer their reports electronically to all those in headquarters who needed to review them for simultaneous action) without the "burning platform" of budget cuts and shrinking personnel counts. Today, those same inspections each take about four person-hours to complete.[25]

The Connecticut DEEP's lean initiative required the staff who managed each process to lead the redesign charge, which some found burdensome but ultimately resulted in significant buy-in from those who were being asked to remake their own work lives. The results were dramatic. Permitting time dropped by an average of about 75 percent. The backlog of permits was reduced by 97 percent. And the Connecticut Business and Industry Association's annual survey of agency performance revealed a strong uptick in the business community's assessment of the agency's performance. Of particular note, these efficiency gains were achieved while maintaining environmental standards.[26]

Regulatory excellence in the twenty-first century requires a real commitment to using IT tools and to delivering on the promise of "e-government."[27] Where regulatory decisions once required a paper file to be reviewed by five different people within an agency, today an electronic file can be parallel-processed by all five, cutting the time required for review by up to 80 percent.

Likewise, using the Turbo Tax model, government agencies can create "smart forms" that help those applying for permits get their applications filled out right the first time. The opportunity to bring best practices from the business world and from emerging academic theory (notably behavioral economics ideas such as "choice architecture" and default rules) has just begun to be tapped.[28] But the only way that these breakthroughs will penetrate is if agencies promote a culture of innovation.

Similarly, access to public information can be completely restructured in the digital age. Rather than keeping paper files and responding to Freedom of Information Act (FOIA) requests, it makes more sense to put all of the material that is in the public realm online so that people can find the files they want at any time without coming to the agency offices or getting help from agency staff. This sort of innovation offers the promise of lower document costs, less space allocated to files, and reduced staff time. Indeed, my effort to make DEEP "paperless" was met with great enthusiasm—particularly my further proposal that the basement file space would be converted to a coffee bar.

More generally, public participation processes should be reconfigured for the twenty-first century. Where sixty or ninety days of review might have been needed in the past for interested parties to file comments by mail, today's instant communication options mean that thirty days of time should be the norm for notice-and-comment procedures, with extended time granted only for particularly complicated issues. Some consumer groups and environmental organizations may claim that compressed review timeframes limit regulatory oversight. But their objections cannot be squared with the fact that "time is money" and the reality that many past processes moved far too slowly, adding cost and regulatory burdens that cannot be justified, especially as companies face growing global competition from enterprises operating abroad under much lighter regulatory requirements.

To put a finer point on this competitiveness concern, the regulatory burden on business has been of little interest to many nongovernmental organizations (NGOs) who fashion themselves as watchdogs for the public interest. This insensitivity to regulatory efficiency and costs has translated into competitive disadvantage for the United States in many markets and helped to fuel the present political backlash against regulations broadly. The environmental community must commit to an agenda of helping to reform and "lighten" the regulatory burden without lowering standards as a way to ensure ongoing public and political support for environmental protection and other regulatory goals. Simply put, it is much easier to sustain a commitment to robust regulation under conditions of economic vitality and job growth than in circumstances of recession and employment insecurity.

Some innovation efforts must be led from the top. But many innovation opportunities will be missed if there is not a parallel commitment to bottom-up efforts to find breakthroughs. Regulatory excellence thus requires that a regulator's leadership team encourage fresh thinking and risk taking at all levels so as to ensure that new approaches will be put forward, experimentation undertaken, and better ways of doing business identified. Given the prevailing "CYA" attitude of most government workers (who have decades of *not* being rewarded for creativity), innovation will not come easily.[29] It must be reinforced constantly by ensuring that breakthroughs are publicly celebrated.[30]

At the Connecticut DEEP, I pushed the management team to challenge the prevailing wisdom every day—and to take risks. I urged the middle managers in particular to offer up their ideas on how things might be done differently and promised to run interference for them with their bosses or the EPA supervisors outside the agency. From this commitment to honor innovation came dozens of new initiatives, including, for example, a restructured approach to removing asbestos from schools—*without* a threat of penalties for Clean Air Act violations and *with* a funding mechanism to support energy efficiency improvements for the schools. This emphasis on compliance rather than "gotcha" enforcement, along with cost savings for schools through lower energy bills, made principals and superintendents (and thus local officials as well as state representatives and state senators) big fans of the transformed approach to asbestos abatement.

### Incentives

At the heart of regulatory excellence lies a need for careful attention to incentives,[31] the signals that change behavior in the regulated community as well as the structure of rewards and penalties for those in government.[32] The evidence is mounting that when a business sees its profit logic and the government's regulatory agenda in alignment, much more gets done than when these interests are pulling in opposite directions.[33] In the environmental arena, for example, the "command and control" approach to regulation is giving way to market-based regulatory strategies. But the change is happening more slowly than it should. Government leaders need to make incentive analysis a top priority so that their staffs understand how the regulatory framework shapes behavior in the marketplace—with a special focus on unintended consequences.[34] Harnessing economic incentives and competitiveness pressures offers the prospect for improved regulation in many circumstances.

Failure to think about the real-world impacts of regulatory requirements has caused enormous problems. For example, the federal Superfund program in the United States, launched in 1980 with a hope that it would induce greater care in the disposal of hazardous waste, has trapped thousands of properties in regulatory limbo and made redevelopment of "brownfields" very difficult.[35]

President Obama's Executive Order 13563 directs federal agencies to review their existing rules and regulations to determine if they "should be modified, streamlined, expanded, or repealed" so as to make the regulatory framework more effective and less burdensome. This valuable effort to institutionalize a commitment to understanding the real-world impacts of past regulatory efforts and to ensure systematic attention to reform should be applied broadly. Every regulatory body should commit to the same sort of systematic review of the efficiency and effectiveness of its existing framework of rules and requirements.

### Investment

Where the money will come from to fulfill public policy goals now requires much greater focus than it did when governments at all levels had bigger budgets. Increasingly, to get brownfields cleaned up, clean energy projects built, or any number of other public investments undertaken, the regulatory structure must be carefully crafted so that limited government resources and incentives can be used to leverage private sector capital.

Much of the regulatory framework of the twentieth century ignored the question of where money for investments would come from. In the environmental arena, for example, the regulatory system has long centered on "red lights"—rules that spelled out what polluters were told to *stop* doing. Today, it is clear that we need an equally well developed structure of "green lights" that give a *go* signal to the business world and engage the entrepreneurial spirit of the private sector in solving problems—whether developing renewable energy technologies or making investments in new infrastructure such as water systems.[36]

In the spirit of enticing private capital into needed clean energy projects, the Connecticut DEEP shifted from the prevailing twentieth-century "subsidy" model for promoting renewable power and energy efficiency to a new approach centered on clean energy "finance." Rather than trying to pick winners and fund their projects, Connecticut launched a "green bank" with the express mission of using limited public funds to leverage private investment in clean energy projects, with a new focus on "cheaper, cleaner, and more reliable" energy. By "de-risking" clean energy investment in Connecticut, encouraging entrepreneurial activity, and harnessing the discipline of private capital and market forces, DEEP was able to deliver a tenfold increase in renewable power projects in the state and vastly greater support for energy efficiency while lowering project costs.[37]

The new approach demonstrates several additional elements of regulatory excellence. First, rather than seeking new money, existing funds were redeployed. Second, market forces were harnessed to produce better results. The keys to the expanded renewable energy portfolio (covering solar, wind, and fuel cells) were reverse auctions and marketplace competition across technologies, as well as specific projects to drive down costs.[38] Third, the state recognized that creating more certainty in the marketplace was a critical government role as clarity and predictability helps to reassure private investors and reduce their perception of the risk of putting up capital. DEEP launched a number of efforts in this regard, notably providing the winners of the reverse auctions with ten- and fifteen-year power purchase agreements that they could literally "take to the bank" and get low-cost financing as well as other efforts. In addition, the green bank helped to standardize clean energy contracts; launched the Property-Assessed Clean Energy (PACE) program, which provided for repayment of commercial energy loans on local property taxes; led an initiative with cities and towns to lower the "soft costs" of oversight and regulation; and took a tranche of default risk from the private banks putting up funds, which reduced their perceived risk and led to a lower cost of capital and a dramatic increase in the flow of private finance for clean energy projects.[39]

### Implementation

As noted earlier, regulatory excellence must be judged not by good intentions or money spent but rather by on-the-ground results achieved. Efficacy matters. And so does efficiency. It turns out to be important to remind all those working on regulatory matters that getting good outcomes (which protect the public) should be a priority, but so should speed.[40] And clarity about what should be done is also important. In fact, getting an answer of "no" from a regulatory agency quickly is often better than a drawn-out review because it allows a filing to be redone in a manner that will work.

In delivering regulatory programs, moreover, the public must believe that the standards imposed make sense and that enforcement of the rules is done in a predictable, efficient, and neutral manner. All of this requires a focus on transparency and metrics that clearly explicate the requirements, standards, and expectations.

We now live in a world that is data-driven and fact-based. Directionally correct environmental regulation is not good enough. Regulatory mandates must be narrowly tailored to statutory goals and implemented in a cost-effective manner. Demonstrating these elements of regulatory excellence requires carefully designed metrics.[41] In the past, too many performance measurement systems tracked activity or inputs rather than results. The EPA, when I was there in the 1990s, tracked "enforcement" progress by counting the number of cases brought—which led to a spike at the end of each quarter in asbestos violation notices going out, representing the easiest sort of case to bring but not necessarily the most high-risk behavior to redirect.[42]

Good metrics must be aligned with the regulatory agency's vision and goals and designed to focus attention on the most critical priorities.[43] As noted earlier, care must be taken in the performance measurement design; otherwise incentives will be created to "teach to the test," which directs effort away from strategic goals that require sustained effort toward those with short-term payoffs. In addition to proper framing, any system of performance measurement must be undergirded by statistical best practices. For example, metrics need to be normalized to ensure that unlike circumstances are not being compared. And sensitivity analysis should be deployed to highlight the assumptions and factors that determine outcomes.

Good implementation requires more than robust metrics. Regulators must be committed to a program of continuous improvement in their work. It is critical that everyone in the regulatory body be focused on productivity gains. Performance needs to be benchmarked both internally and externally, and lagging performers need to be coached on how to improve. Best practices need to be systematically identified both within the regulatory agency and by others doing similar work in other regulatory organizations.

## CONCLUSION

Bringing a degree of analytic rigor to the quest for regulatory excellence offers the promise of much better results in a variety of settings. A body of theory about what is required for improved regulatory performance has begun to emerge. Now the practice needs to follow with a further commitment to tracking progress and creating an empirical foundation for additional refinements to the theory.

As this chapter suggests, a number of regulatory best practices can now be identified, starting with clarity about the organization's mission and a businesslike commitment to execution. In many regulatory bodies, the vision and direction will need to center on transformation and innovation in the regulatory process and the critical job of making the organization both more effective and more efficient. In terms of execution, appreciation for the inevitable tradeoffs that regulation entails, and more broadly, attention to "customer" expectations, need to be top priorities. In addition, best-in-class regulatory bodies focus on the incentives their rules create, recognize the importance of transparency and predictability in their actions (which build trust with stakeholders), emphasize data and metrics to track performance, and commit to benchmarking and continuous improvement.

### NOTES

1. There has been, of course, some important scholarly work on regulatory reform from James Q. Wilson, Stephen Breyer, Jerry Mashaw, Peter Schuck, and Cary Coglianese, among others.

2. John P. Kotter, "Leading Change: Why Transformation Efforts Fail," *Harvard Business Review* (January 2007): 4–5.

3. Leonard L. Berry and A. Parasuraman, "Listening to the Customer: The Concept of a Service-Quality Information System," *MIT Sloan Management Review* 38 (Spring 1997): 73.

4. Aamer Baig, Andre Dua, and Vivian Riefberg, "How U.S. State Governments Can Improve Customer Service," McKinsey & Company, December 2014, pp. 2–4.

5. Pascal Dennis, *The Remedy: Bringing Lean Thinking Out of the Factory to Transform the Entire Organization* (Hoboken, N.J.: John Wiley, 2010).

6. Eric A. Scorsone, "New Development: What Are the Challenges in Transferring Lean Thinking to Government?," *Public Money and Management* 28 (March 2010): 61–64.

7. Connecticut's Environmental Quality Scorecard (CT DEEP, 2014); resignation letter of Commissioner Daniel C. Esty to Governor Dannel P. Malloy (January 15, 2014) (both available from the CT DEEP Public Affairs Office).

8. Cary Coglianese and Jennifer Nash, eds., *Leveraging the Private Sector: Management-Based Strategies for Improving Environmental Performance* (Washington: Resources for the Future Press, 2006).

9. See OECD Best Practice Principles for Regulatory Policy, "Regulatory Enforcement and Inspections" (2014) (www.oecd.org/gov/regulatory-policy/enforcement -inspections.htm).

10. Elizabeth G. Chambers and others, "The War for Talent," *McKinsey Quarterly*, (2007): 2.

11. Particular care must be taken to ensure that the incentives created do not lead to unintended consequences.

12. Daniel C. Esty, "Why Measurement Matters," in *Environmental Performance Measurement: The Global Report 2001–2002* (Oxford University Press, 2001).

13. Peter H. Schuck, *Why Government Fails So Often: And How It Can Do Better* (Princeton University Press, 2014), p. 92.

14. Stephen G. Breyer, *Administrative Law and Regulatory Policy: Problems, Text, and Cases* (New York: Wolters Kluwer Law and Business, 2011); Jerry L. Mashaw, *Greed, Chaos, and Governance: Using Public Choice to Improve Public Law* (Yale University Press, 1997); Eric Posner and Cass Sunstein, "Institutional Flip-Flops," Working Paper 501 (University of Chicago, 2015).

15. Daniel C. Esty, "Good Governance at the Supranational Scale: Globalizing Administrative Law," *Yale Law Journal* 115 (2006): 1490–1562.

16. John D. Graham and Jonathan B. Wiener, *Risk vs. Risk: Tradeoffs in Protecting Health and the Environment* (Harvard University Press, 1997); Stephen G. Breyer, *Breaking the Vicious Circle: Toward Effective Risk Regulation* (Harvard University Press, 1993).

17. John D. Graham, *Bush on the Home Front: Domestic Policy Triumphs and Setbacks* (University of Indiana Press, 2010), pp. 149–50.

18. Christopher Carrigan and Cary Coglianese, "Oversight in Hindsight," in *Regulatory Breakdown: The Crisis of Confidence in U.S. Regulation*, edited by Cary Coglianese (University of Pennsylvania Press, 2012), pp. 12–17; Daniel Farber, "Uncertainty," *Georgetown Law Journal* 99 (2011): 901–60.

19. Howard Kunreuther and others, "Fast and Slow Thinking in the Face of Catastrophic Risk," Working Paper 2014-6 (Philadelphia: Risk Management and Decision Processes Center, Wharton School, August 2014); Daniel Kahneman, *Thinking, Fast and Slow* (New York: Farrar, Straus and Giroux, 2011).

20. Nick Malyshev, "A Primer on Regulatory Budgets," *OECD Journal on Budgeting* 2010/3 (2010): 1–10; Philip Wallach, "An Opportune Moment for Regulatory Reform," Strengthening American Democracy Series (Brookings Center for Effective Public Management, April 2014).

21. Connecticut Department of Energy and Environmental Protection Regulatory Report (Hartford, 2014).

22. Mariana Mazzucato, *The Entrepreneurial State: Debunking Public vs. Private Sector Myths* (New York: Anthem Press, 2013).

23. Michael Lewis, *Moneyball: The Art of Winning an Unfair Game* (New York: W. W. Norton, 2003).

24. Daniel Esty, "Environmental Protection in the Information Age," *New York University Law Review* 79 (April 2004): 115–211. See also Daniel Esty and Reece Rushing, "Governing by the Numbers: The Promise of Data-Driven Policymaking in the Information Age" (Center for American Progress, 2007) (https://cdn.americanprogress.org/wp-content/uploads/issues/2007/04/pdf/data_driven_policy_report.pdf).

25. Streamlining the UST Inspection Process through Technology and the Lean Process, New England Annual Meeting for Enforcement, Compliance and Assistance, Lori Saliby, Supervising Environmental Analyst, June 4, 2014.

26. DEEP Deputy Commissioner Macky McCleary, "Outcomes from Permitting Process Meetings," February 15, 2012.

27. See White House, "Office of E-Government and Information Technology" (www.whitehouse.gov/omb/e-gov/).

28. Richard Thaler and others, "Choice Architecture," in *The Behavioral Foundations of Public Policy*, edited by Eldar Shafir (Princeton University Press, 2010).

29. Michael Gibbs, "Four Ways Companies Can Encourage Innovation," *Chicago Booth Review* (June 2015): 1.

30. Brad Power, "How Toyota Pulls Improvements from the Front Line," *Harvard Business Review* (June 2011): 2.

31. Madhu Khanna and William Anton, "Corporate Environmental Management: Regulatory and Market-Based Incentives," *Land Economics* 78 (November 2002): 539–58.

32. Ian Ayres and Amy Kapcyznski, "A New Meaning of the Light Bulb," *Forbes*, January 21, 2015.

33. Daniel C. Esty and Andrew S. Winston, *Green to Gold: How Smart Companies Use Environmental Strategy to Innovate, Create Value, and Build Competitive Advantage* (Yale University Press, 2006).

34. Schuck, *Why Government Fails So Often,* p. 127.

35. Steven Ferrey, "Allocation and Uncertainty in the Age of Superfund: A Critique of the Redistribution of CERCLA Liability," *New York University Environmental Law Journal* 3 (1994): 36–98.

36. See Clifford Winston, "Government Failure vs. Market Failure: Microeconomics Policy Research and Government Performance" (Washington: AEI-Brookings Joint Center for Regulatory Studies, 2006) (www.brookings.edu/~/media/research/files/papers/2006/9/monetarypolicy-winston/20061003.pdf).

37. See Connecticut Department of Energy and Environmental Protection, "Restructuring Connecticut's Renewable Portfolio Standard," April 26, 2013 (www.ct.gov/deep/lib/deep/energy/rps/rps_final.pdf). See also Clean Energy Finance and Investment Authority, "Connecticut's Green Bank: Energizing Clean Energy Finance," 2013 (www.ctcleanenergy.com/annualreport/CEFIA_AR_2013-Final.pdf).

38. Schuck, *Why Government Fails So Often*, p. 240.

39. See Clean Energy Finance and Investment Authority, "Connecticut's Green Bank," p. 6.

40. Schuck, *Why Government Fails So Often,* p. 404.

41. Cass R. Sunstein, *Simpler: The Future of Government* (New York: Simon and Schuster, 2013).

42. Shelley H. Metzenbaum, "Performance Management: The Real Research Challenge," *Public Administration Review* 73 (November 2013): 857–58.

43. Robert Rodgers and John Hunter, "A Foundation of Good Management Practice in Government," *Public Administration Review* 52 (January 1992): 27–39.

# 10

# What Makes a Regulator Excellent?

*Mission, Funding, Information, and Judgment*

SHELLEY H. METZENBAUM AND GAURAV VASISHT

THE QUESTION "WHAT MAKES a regulator excellent?" is not easy to answer. Is "excellent" synonymous with "effective"? How does a regulator's judgment factor into the equation, given that one person's "tough, but fair" regulator may be perceived by another to be "politically motivated," or another person's "careful and deliberate" regulator may be perceived in some circles as "captured" by industry?

Mindful of these important questions raised by the concept of "regulatory excellence," and at the risk of attempting to answer questions that perhaps can never be definitively answered in the abstract, we offer this: An excellent regulator is one that is adequately funded, that wisely manages its resources, and that effectively navigates its external relationships so as to act even under difficult circumstances for the purpose of furthering its mission.

Notably, our measure of excellence would judge regulators on the decisions they make based on information available to them, or on factors that were reasonably foreseeable to them, at the time of their decisions. However, a regulator's zealous pursuit of information to sharpen its analysis and foresight, and its efforts to work proactively to get ahead of issues to tackle them effectively, are themselves important characteristics of regulatory excellence. In addition, we do not measure excellence on the basis of regulatory philosophies, which may reasonably differ even among excellent regulatory agencies. This is not to say, however, that a regulator that is equipped with relevant information but fails to act on it because of a rigid belief in some regulatory "philosophy" gets a free pass; clearly, such a regulator would not be one that has achieved excellence.

In this chapter we unpack our definition of an excellent regulator while remaining mindful of crucial practical considerations, such as the role of agency leadership, historic culture, and political context, all of which are influenced by many other factors and contribute to an agency's overall effectiveness. Specifically, we focus on issues that affect a regulator's pursuit of its mission—a focus that brings to the fore such topics as the articulation, interpretation, and scope of core missions; funding adequacy; priority setting; the ability to influence regulatory outcomes, including by leveraging a regulator's horizontal (industrywide) perspective across regulated parties; and the capacity and skills to communicate issues, options, and choices.

## A REGULATOR'S PURSUIT OF ITS MISSION

It is axiomatic that an excellent regulator acts to further its mission, often articulated in the form of an overarching statement that has taken shape over time. Also axiomatic is that the absence of a clearly stated and understood mission statement makes it difficult to achieve regulatory excellence because it renders an organization directionless. The excellent regulator is guided by its organizational mission and taps the power of goals to advance that mission, but also respects and anticipates the limits of missions and goals.

### The Core Mission

Legislators often specify in law the core mission of a regulatory organization. The U.S. Congress, for example, defined the mission of the Federal Reserve System as "provid[ing] the nation with a safer, more flexible, and more stable monetary and financial system."[1]

Other times, legislators leave it to the executive or ministerial part of government to define mission statements, expecting it to make coherent the patchwork of purposes laid out in the laws the organization has been mandated to implement. In the United States, when Congress has not done so, every U.S. federal government entity must articulate a mission statement in its strategic plan.[2] The U.S. Environmental Protection Agency (EPA), for example, created by executive order, describes its mission as "protecting human health and the environment."[3]

A mission statement, on its own, cannot guarantee regulatory excellence. Such a statement is just words. Organizational excellence necessitates making sure different parts of an organization understand how they contribute to the core mission.[4] Toward that end, excellent organizations translate their mission into specific goals, objectives, strategies, and suites of indicators, which they use to gauge progress on achieving their missions and to know when mid-course corrections are needed. EPA, for example, identifies five strategic goals supporting its core mission: (1) addressing climate change and improving air quality; (2) protecting America's waters; (3) cleaning up communities and advancing sustainable development; (4) ensuring the safety of chemicals and preventing pollution; (5) and protecting human health and the environment by enforcing laws and ensuring compliance.

Excellent organizations translate general goals into specific targets that lay out how much they hope to accomplish of what by when; they then share that information with people in the organization, delivery partners, and other interested external parties. In addition, they assign responsibility for managing progress on each goal to specific individuals or organizational units.

Goals—especially when specific, ambitious, and not too numerous—offer many benefits. They focus, energize, encourage persistence, and stimulate discovery through four mechanisms: a directive function; an energizing function; persistence; and indirectly by leading to the discovery or use of task-relevant knowledge and strategies.[5] They do this not only for individuals but also for organizations.[6]

Efforts to clean up the Charles River in Massachusetts illustrate the innovation-driving, persisting power of a well-framed goal, especially when the goal is described in a way that excites a community. In 1995, the New England regional administrator of EPA set a specific goal: the Charles River would be swimmable in ten years. He announced it on the eve of the annual Head of the Charles Regatta, which brings hundreds of thousands of people to the river's edge. Beyond that, he assigned one person (part-time) to manage progress on the goal, who assembled a team (initially, two other part-time employees) to achieve the goal.

The regional administrator did not hesitate to set this place-specific goal. It clearly contributed to EPA's national organizational mission (protecting human health and the environment) as well as to one of its national strategic goals (protecting America's waters.) He also appreciated that setting an outcome-focused goal would energize people more than would a goal to issue a specific number of permits, write a new rule, take a specific number of enforcement actions, or achieve a higher compliance rate. Beyond that, it would not limit EPA to the tools it traditionally used, but rather would invite discovery and innovation.

Six months later, on Earth Day and with great fanfare surrounded by community leaders, the regional administrator gave the river a "D" grade. At the same time, he described EPA's planned next steps and explained why those steps were being taken. These actions established the expectation that EPA would issue a similar Charles River report card every year and not wait until the end of the ten-year period to report on progress.[7]

Driven by the goal and a desire to show progress every year, the EPA's "goal leader" and his team sought timely data to understand more precisely possible causes of water quality problems. They turned to data posted online by a local watershed association whose trained volunteers had recently started collecting samples every month at thirty-seven points along the eighty-mile stretch of the river. These data revealed downstream water quality readings that were worse than upstream ones that could not be explained by the pollution contributed by permitted dischargers in between. Finding these anomalies triggered follow-up inquiries to understand why they were happening. Early on, one such anomaly led EPA to a wastewater source illegally hooked up to the storm sewer that was sending untreated waste directly into the river instead of into the wastewater sewer system for treatment.

Using volunteer-collected data departed from past practice. EPA and state regulators traditionally favored data collected by government and government-approved parties, but the temporally frequent and geographically dispersed data collected by volunteers helped EPA discover previously unknown problems. Before looking at these data, EPA and local activists had assumed that most of the river's pollution problems came from "nonpoint sources" such as runoff from roads and fertilizer from fields. The data revealed that "point sources," including regulated parties holding wastewater discharge permits, continued to be a problem. It also helped EPA discover other point sources that were operating illegally and needed controls.

The Charles River goal and annual report card not only led to the discovery of previously unknown problems, but also encouraged innovative approaches to address them. EPA wanted to find more systematic ways to look for and eliminate illicit connections and brainstormed how best to do that. One person suggested lifting manhole covers on storm sewer systems when it was not raining to look for running water. This idea led EPA to adopt a wholly new way of working with local governments to encourage them to look for, and then fix, illicit hookups. The result was an unprecedented improvement in water quality over five years: from being swimmable 19 percent of the time in 1995 to 59 percent of the time in 2000.[8]

Twenty years, multiple regional administrators, and two presidents later, EPA continues to issue an annual Charles River report card. It continues to search for the most significant problems and innovate to improve the water quality.[9]

In certain situations, of course, goals can introduce systematic harms such as neglect of areas not specifically identified in the goals, a rise in unethical behavior, distorted risk preferences, corrosion of organizational culture, and reduced intrinsic motivation.[10] Some crime-reduction efforts in the United States, for example, likely suffered because of insufficient attention to police abuse data and community concerns. Teachers in many communities have been charged, at best, with teaching to the test and, at worst, with cheating to help students get better test scores. Linking incentives to goal attainment often tempts measurement manipulation, as has been the charge against some teachers, and can lead to the adoption of timid targets.[11]

In some circumstances, the mission itself may not be broad enough to keep up with innovation in the world it regulates. Following the financial crisis of 2008, for example, it has become clearer that there are significant risks in the capital markets outside the reach of the Federal Reserve—but within the jurisdiction of the Securities and Exchange Commission (SEC)—that could spill over into the broader financial system. Given the lessons of the crisis, should the SEC look to expand its mission of investor protection, maintaining fair, orderly, and efficient markets, and capital formation to include financial stability? The SEC may find some limited support for such an interpretation in existing law, or it might lobby Congress to give the agency that mandate more clearly. Alternatively, should the Federal Reserve, the ostensible systemic risk regulator, which some have argued has been given the mandate to maintain stability without the necessary jurisdiction or tools, seek to expand its focus into the capital markets, where it traditionally has not paid significant attention? A broadened focus in this regard might arguably be necessary if the Federal Reserve is to fulfill its financial stability mandate.

Another challenge arises when innovations in the regulated sector spurred by technological advances or other factors require new applications of regulatory tools. In the world of high-frequency trading, virtual currency, cybersecurity threats, complex derivatives products, data privacy concerns, and other emerging matters, it might be necessary to broaden an agency's traditional focus into unfamiliar areas or use authorities in new ways. Regulatory excellence requires a regulator that is capable of adapting to changes in the institutions and industries it oversees.

We do not take a position on the judgments an agency may make in tackling the specific scenarios raised here. Indeed, whether it is prudent for the SEC or the Federal Reserve to expand their focus, or necessary for regulators to adapt to specific industry innovations, is debatable from different perspectives. We provide these examples to suggest that an excellent regulator at times might need to diverge from pursuit of its core mission and adapt to fill a void in regulation, address lessons learned from past failures, or respond to innovation. A rigid approach to achieving the mission or goals, or to using the available tools, could overly constrain regulators as the world around them changes and risks accumulate.

Moreover, we believe that an excellent regulator is acutely aware of its powers and jurisdictions (beyond their traditional use) and is willing to exercise those powers in new ways, albeit in limited circumstances and only where appropriate and necessary, to achieve the desired regulatory outcomes. Importantly, where a regulator does apply its powers in novel ways, it should prioritize communication with regulated industries to restore the element of predictability and expectation, which may otherwise be lost in the process.

### *Funding Adequacy*

Regulatory excellence is difficult to achieve when an agency lacks the resources necessary to accomplish its basic work. Even the best-intentioned regulators, when faced with budgetary challenges, will not be able to accomplish their core missions. The challenge of doing more with less is not easily overcome—corners need to be cut, resources likely become overwhelmed, expertise is not gained (or might be lost), and morale suffers. Over time, agency culture can deteriorate while risks continue to build in the regulated sector.

Regulatory agency funding is a complex issue, however. Most government agencies are funded through legislative appropriations, although a fortunate few are funded by fees not subject to subsequent vote by elected officials.

Funding adequacy has a direct and profound impact on whether a regulator can be effective. Speaking about the inadequacy of funding at the SEC and the Commodity Futures Trading Commission (CFTC)—two agencies in the financial regulatory sphere that are funded through congressional appropriation—U.S. Treasury Secretary Jack Lew has said:

> Even with the best rules, illegal behavior or excessive risk taking will go unchecked unless regulators have the resources to conduct regular examinations, monitor suspect behavior, and go after those who break the law. The point is, this is not an either/or proposition. The best rules will fall short without effective supervision and enforcement. And effective supervision and enforcement are only possible with sufficient resources.[12]

With such profound consequences one might wonder why some regulators—typically those funded through legislative appropriations—are in many cases so woefully underfunded. There are many answers: in some cases, legislators wish to control what they perceive as excessive spending on misjudged priorities, while in other cases spending might be restricted as a punitive measure for agencies that failed in the run-up to a regulatory failure. But some have argued that funding challenges have sometimes arisen as part of the messy budget process by industry lobbyists who wish to impair the work of an agency in a specific area. As a former chair of the Federal Deposit Insurance Corporation, Sheila Bair, has written:

> Regrettably, industry lobbyists have found that the best way to harass the SEC and CFTC and block efforts at financial reform is through convincing appropriations committees to restrict how these agencies can use their money. For instance, in the House, there have been attempts to prohibit the CFTC from using its funds to implement rules forcing more derivatives onto public trading facilities, and other measures.[13]

In short, the politics of appropriations can make managing the necessary resources exceedingly difficult.

On the other end of the spectrum are agencies that are independently funded through fees and assessments on regulated parties, such as the Office of the Comptroller of the Currency (OCC), the former Office of Thrift Supervision (OTS), and the Board of Governors of the Federal Reserve System. These agencies have a different set of challenges, including establishing strong safeguards to prevent the waste of resources. In addition, regulatory capture has proven to be a challenge for such agencies, particularly where regulated institutions fund the agencies but retain the choice of their regulator. This construct creates a conflict of interest that, in the past at least, has resulted in perverse incentives for regulators to apply a lax form of regulation on regulated institutions.[14]

Indeed, under this construct some regulators may market themselves to institutions and compete with each other to enhance their jurisdictional reach and power. These regulators may also fear at times that tough regulation could result in financial institutions changing regulators, which would have an immediate impact on the agency's finances, reduce the agency's power and jurisdiction, and perhaps even call into question the very need for the agency, particularly if it has a shrinking jurisdictional footprint. In the realm of financial regulation, the OTS and the OCC are examples of agencies that succumbed to these challenges in the period leading to the financial crisis, according to some observers.[15]

Given the importance of resources to regulatory agencies, and the sometimes whimsical nature of congressional appropriations, an excellent regulator must be adequately funded, most likely without being subject to appropriation, and be effectively managed so that its resources are not expended on priorities beyond its mission. The regulator must also be confident enough in the exercise of its jurisdictional power that it does not fear that regulated parties will shop for "friendlier" regulators or otherwise fall prey to inappropriate incentives. Effective legislative oversight (outside the appropriations process) can also ensure that resources are adequately targeted and deployed and that the agency is not engaged in any waste or abuse of its resources.

All this is not to say that a regulator subject to the appropriations process cannot be excellent; it certainly can be. But given the poor track record for funding many agencies that do not have independent funding sources, it will be much more difficult for these agencies to achieve the level of excellence that could more reasonably be expected of their independently funded counterparts.

### *Priority Setting*

Still, no agency has infinite resources. Given this state of affairs, priority setting takes on a critical role. Four core categories of information should influence an agency's ability to set appropriate priorities for itself. A regulator must understand:

- the characteristics of risks and conditions affecting an agency's mission;

- the industries and institutions it regulates, including their risk profiles, business models, and activities;

- its own risk profile, taking into account its needs for staffing, expertise, and technological capabilities, mindful of such things as upcoming retirements, attrition, and other medium- to long-term considerations; and

- how to deploy its resources in high-needs areas in a manner that will have the greatest impact.

#### UNDERSTANDING RISKS AND CONDITIONS THAT AFFECT MISSION ACCOMPLISHMENT

Excellent regulators assemble and study information about the risks they seek to prevent and the conditions they hope to improve to inform a risk-based setting of priorities. This information can also help them decide how best to design actions and treatments that will have the greatest impact using the available resources.

Most regulatory agencies work to advance two missions: improving (or pre-venting the deterioration of) conditions that would threaten the health of complex systems (for example, the ecosystem, financial markets); and reduc-ing the frequency and consequence of harmful incidents (for example, bank failures, oil spills, permit violations, traffic and workplace accidents).

The large number of regulatory organizations that seek to prevent bad things from happening while keeping their costs as low as possible seem to do especially well when they: consistently collect and code information about harmful incidents and their characteristics; analyze those data to look for patterns, anomalies, and relationships; and disseminate the analysis broadly so others can use it to set priorities for their own preventive or corrective ac-tions. One strong framework for organizing harmful incident information is the Haddon matrix used by the National Highway Traffic Safety Adminis-tration (NHTSA). NHTSA codes information gathered by the states about characteristics of the equipment, operators, the physical environment, and the social environment for every traffic fatality before, during, and after the event. This allows identification of the highest-risk cars, drivers, and road designs, nominating them for priority attention. The same information can also help local public works departments set priorities for road redesign projects.

Inspection and examination findings can be similarly coded to detect com-mon types of noncompliance problems and the most noncompliant parties.[16] So, too, can near misses, which are especially important for low-frequency, high-consequence events.[17]

Savvy regulators have also seen great benefit when they more systemati-cally monitor changes in complex systems, such as water quality, human health, or financial system health, then share the data broadly along with planned strategies and the impact of past "treatment" or intervention efforts. This kind of information has informed priority setting at the local level in Massachusetts and the state of Washington, but has also worked well at the national level, as demonstrated by the Healthy People initiative started by the U.S. Department of Health and Human Services in 1979.[18]

There is broad recognition that financial regulators do not fully understand the risks in the financial system. To help them better understand those risks, the Treasury Department's Office of Financial Research in conjunction with the Federal Reserve and other agencies is compiling data about various financial activities, products, and entities and then standardizing that infor-mation across agencies. In the long run, this effort will help regulators ana-lyze the risks in the financial sector and help policymakers and regulators identify and address threats to financial stability.

## UNDERSTANDING REGULATED INDUSTRIES AND INSTITUTIONS

It is not enough to look at harmful incidents, near misses, and the conditions of complex systems. A regulator's ability to understand the business models and institutional risk profiles and vulnerabilities of those it regulates is fundamental to priority setting. A knowledgeable regulator uses this information to deploy its resources where they are likely to be needed most and in a manner that will have the greatest impact. It also seeks to anticipate where problems may percolate in the future and tries to get ahead of them.

Without a clear understanding of the regulated sector and the factors that influence its decisions and actions, a regulator might wind up misallocating resources and rely too heavily on checklist methodologies instead of focusing on the regulated parties and products that pose the greatest risks. Inadequate understanding of the characteristics of the regulated community can result in significant gaps in supervision and regulation that lull regulators into complacency.

Consider, for example, the OTS's supervision of American International Group (AIG). In that case, the OTS focused myopically on the thrift side of AIG's business and failed to understand the risks that AIG's derivatives business posed to the entire organization, let alone the financial system at large. Virtually every postmortem of the financial crisis cites OTS's failure to understand AIG's business as a critical component of AIG's near demise and its subsequent bailout. It is clear that a regulator that is so much in the dark about the institutions it supervises cannot possibly allocate its resources effectively to do its job well.

Another example is the SEC's oversight of the stand-alone investment banks Lehman Brothers and Bear Stearns under a voluntary program called the Consolidated Supervised Entities (CSE) program. Through the CSE program, the SEC gained oversight of the investment banks, but deployed minimal resources to examine and supervise them. Had it understood the risks that the investment banks posed, it would have either not launched the CSE program or allocated more resources to the program to ensure proper supervision of the firms.

An excellent regulator understands the complexities of the firms and industries it regulates, including size and location but also ownership structure, suppliers, subsidiaries, and employee characteristics. In addition, it seeks to understand factors that influence key decisionmakers, such as the information channels they use and the regulated parties who most influence their peers.[19] The excellent regulator then uses that knowledge to allocate resources in a more targeted, risk-focused manner.

## A REGULATOR'S UNDERSTANDING OF ITS OWN RISK PROFILE

Another critical component of priority setting is to understand where the holes are within the regulatory organization itself. Some have basic challenges, such as an aging workforce eligible to retire in the near future and many entry-level recruits, but few mid-level or high-level supervisors to mentor and supervise those recruits. Other regulatory agencies may lack expertise in specific areas, such as emerging technologies and products. Many others have weak information systems and analytic capacity that make it hard to gather, study, and share relevant information about the characteristics of risks, regulated parties, and the results of inspections.

There can be many reasons for an agency's workforce challenges. For example, mid-level supervisors may have been poached by industry for high-paying jobs. At the state level, mid-level examiners can be fertile ground for federal agency recruitment. Long-standing hiring freezes due to budget challenges can also cause or exacerbate these challenges even further. Civil service laws and collective bargaining agreements can perpetuate the problem by preventing the transfer of resources from one area to another, limiting promotion opportunities, and creating obstacles to the hiring of mid-level industry professionals in anything but junior-level positions.

Navigating these conditions is critically important for regulatory agencies to be effective. Failure to obtain and deploy resources effectively can lead to a significant buildup of risk and problems with agency morale, with some in the workforce feeling overworked and overwhelmed while others treat the lack of resources as an excuse. Over time, if these conditions persist, agencies might lose their culture as vigorous pursuers of regulatory aims and become beholden to the industries they regulate. Worse yet, they may not be taken seriously by their regulatory counterparts or by the industries and institutions they regulate.

Fundamental to all of this is the ability of regulatory agencies to hire and retain talented people. In general terms, this means compensating agency staff satisfactorily and creating a satisfying work environment and career path for them. Also fundamental is the need to train agency personnel to understand the innovations taking place in the industries they regulate so they can negotiate the complex tradeoffs required of regulators. Less experienced regulatory staff need multiple opportunities to practice, with expert feedback, the exercise of discretion and the selection of regulatory tools and targets.[20]

A well-paid, well-trained workforce that is satisfied with the work it performs and is driven, among other things, by career growth can be energized and fulfill its regulatory obligations more fully than one that is poorly trained or that believes that rewards for performance are unfairly distributed.

Special attention must be given to agency culture, which takes many years to cement and can be very difficult to change. Culture is a function of all of the factors mentioned above, but perhaps is influenced the most by agency leadership. The tone at the top matters, and communicating effectively through the ranks of an agency is the only way to effect deep change. Moreover, an agency's leadership must empower the workforce to challenge situations in the field, ask questions, and recommend solutions; the regulatory staff must feel they have a seat at the table and the ability to influence the outcome of important decisions.

Finally, a core part of priority setting involves establishing mechanisms to monitor agency and industry performance not only to detect the most prevalent and emerging problems but also to learn about promising developments and to guide the search for ways to reduce risks and improve conditions. Robust information systems that make it easy to collect, study, and share information about regulated parties, including self-reported data, information about incidents, and the results of inspections and examinations are invaluable. Also important are people who regularly analyze the data and share these analyses with others. Especially important is not falling into the trap of treating the number of examinations conducted or number of enforcement actions taken as performance indicators rather than as merely information documenting regulatory activity.[21] Key performance indicators must instead focus on risks, especially within the regulated industry but also within the regulatory agency, appropriately calibrated to reflect the realities on the ground.

### *Ability to Influence Outcomes*

An effective regulator finds ways to influence change in the regulated sphere, using both proven means and creative new approaches. Although there are many ways of influencing a change in industry, in this section we highlight three of them. The first leverages the regulator's ability to assume a horizontal perspective by looking across regulated parties to detect common patterns, detect noteworthy variations across regulated parties, make constructive comparisons in order to find better or lagging performers, and then encourage adoption of what works and adjustment of what does not. The second idea, closely related, involves the disciplined collection and use of data, measured trials, and other evidence to assess the impact of prior actions and test new actions to find increasingly effective and cost-effective ways to reduce risks and improve conditions. The third involves discretion in selecting tools to prevent and remediate problems at individual institutions and perhaps even across the regulated industry.

*The Horizontal Perspective.* Regulators benefit when they assume a "horizontal perspective," looking across those they regulate to identify the better performers, both on an absolute scale and in terms of the improvement rate. Industry often describes this as "benchmarking," and it is a common practice for cost cutting and process improvement that can readily be applied to regulatory objectives. NHTSA, for example, looks across the data it collects to see when changes in law in one jurisdiction correlate with reductions in the frequency and cost of traffic fatalities, spotlighting practices worth trying to replicate. When such practices can be replicated with similar favorable results, NHTSA then uses grants, campaign materials, and information to encourage uptake.[22] Policymakers at all levels of government use the information NHTSA collects to decide whether to adopt new rules or campaigns to reduce risks (such as educational campaigns about seat belt usage or the dangers of cell phone use). A horizontal perspective can also reveal outliers, those with the worst practices that need assistance or enforcement, depending on the circumstances. Excellent regulators build information systems with incident, condition, and compliance data that support this sort of analysis.

*Collection of Data.* On occasion, excellent regulators complement the information they routinely collect with discrete surveys. Environmental agencies, for example, have tried measuring intermediate outcome indicators, such as awareness, attitudes, and understanding. Oregon randomly sampled regulated parties to measure their awareness of regulatory obligations.[23] The United Kingdom's environmental agency conducted surveys of small and medium-sized enterprises and learned that three-quarters were not well-versed in environmental legislation.[24]

Mandatory online surveys of similarly situated financial institutions could be used to give real-time, confidential feedback to financial institutions about their cybersecurity practices; the shared results could implicitly encourage improvements by those who perform relatively poorly. Since regulators would also have access to these results, examiners might follow up to determine whether the institutions had taken steps to improve. The regulator could also aggregate the data to look for shared problematic practices that could be addressed with a broader brush.

*Effective Use of Tools.* A fundamental question is whether an excellent regulator is bound by the traditional use of its authority to pursue its core mission or whether it can exercise discretion in the application of its tools and authorities. Put simply, it is not bound. Instead, its leaders should stay relentlessly focused on the organization's mission and flexibly select the tools likely to work best in each situation.

### Communication for Impact and Accountability

Excellent regulators need to master the science and art of communication. Too often, communication is treated as the purview of a press office. Communication, in fact, should be treated as a critical regulatory skill needing as much capacity among regulators as marketing, sales, and internal communications functions do in private firms.

When regulators do their job well—especially when they successfully prevent harmful incidents, associated risks, and deteriorating conditions—few pay attention. A plane landing safely is not newsworthy. The harsh reality, though, is that the absence of attention to accomplishments brought about by regulatory organizations allows the public to forget too easily why a regulator exists. Even worse, because regulators attract public attention when problems arise and often get blamed for falling down on the job, public views about regulators are often biased toward the negative.[25] This not only affects key political support for funding adequacy, but it also hurts the prospects for making necessary changes to a regulator's legislated authority.

Excellent regulators realize the need to communicate successfully to the public why they exist, what they do, and why it is important. This is what EPA did with its Charles River initiative. It is noteworthy that despite failing to meet the agency's ambitious goal to make the river swimmable by 2005, EPA not only escaped criticism, but the goal has garnered over two decades of attention and action from regional administrators of different political parties.

Regulators have many opportunities to communicate effectively about their organizational mission: when they announce goals and report progress on them, when new incidents arise or a new regulatory action is taken, and even on key anniversary dates associated with the organizational mission. Beyond communicating to inform, excellent regulators communicate to enlist and engage the public—especially regulated parties, their employees, and those affected by those parties—in understanding and reducing the risks the regulated entity seeks to address.

Regulators have increasingly come to appreciate the value of communication to ensure awareness of regulatory requirements and understanding of why they are needed.[26] Awareness, understanding, and acceptance of the need for a regulation, though, does not always lead to needed behavior changes. Other factors related to persuasion, such as an interest in following others who have changed their practices, are often more influential.[27]

Communication can be a powerful deterrence tool, too. Industry participants may be reluctant to change their practices if they believe their competitors are engaged in the same behavior. At the same time, awareness that a violator got caught raises the sense of fairness among those in compliance and fear among those who are not.[28]

In a few areas of regulation, regulatory decisions, and even a regulator's words, can move markets. When that happens, strong communication skills are critical. Former U.S. Treasury secretary Timothy Geithner, for example, was acutely aware that the way he and his colleagues talked, or failed to talk, about regulatory actions directly affected investor confidence and, ultimately, the stability of the financial system.[29] Similarly, officials at the U.S. Food and Drug Administration know that their actions and words can make or break a product being reviewed, so they must choose their timing and language carefully, balancing the need for transparency and fairness.

It is tempting to ignore regulators' need to master communication skills, but it is costly to overlook it. This is an area that has received woefully little attention. Regulatory excellence necessitates not only an understanding of the science of communication but also, given the complexity of the situations in which most regulators work, better awareness of opportunities and the evidence about how to do it well.[30]

### CONCLUSION

Although there are many key elements of regulatory excellence, several appear to be the most significant—mission, funding, information, and judgment. Mission, and the associated goals and strategies, define the direction for regulatory action. Funding provides a regulator with the ability to act in pursuit of its mission. The regulator can then use its resources to hire a talented workforce, retain that talent by paying people decently, and create a motivating career path in the government and an environment within which to adapt to technological innovation. Information is key to setting priorities and influencing outcomes, as is judgment. Excellent regulatory judgment calls for choosing the right regulatory and supervisory tools to solve problems, informed by relevant information. The mix of mission, information, resources, and judgment lead to actions taken by an excellent regulator to drive positive change.

Moreover, excellent regulatory leaders must not fear taking on these challenges nor hesitate to let others receive some of the credit for their good work. This need is particularly acute for regulatory leaders who follow in the footsteps of others who pursued lax regulation strategies but were the beneficiaries of good economic times and, fairly or not, received plaudits for supporting a good economy and job creation.

NOTES

1. Board of Governors of the Federal Reserve System, *Strategic Framework 2012–15* (2013) (www.federalreserve.gov/publications/gpra/files/2012–2015-strategic -framework.pdf).

2. Government Performance and Results Act of 1993 (GPRA), Pub. L. No. 103–62, 107 Stat. 285 (codified as amended in scattered sections of 5 U.S.C., 31 U.S.C., and 39 U.S.C.).

3. U.S. Environmental Protection Agency, FY 2014–2018 EPA Strategic Plan (2014) (www2.epa.gov/sites/production/files/2014-09/documents/epa_strategic_plan _fy14-18.pdf).

4. Robert S. Kaplan and David P. Norton, *The Strategy-Focused Organization* (Harvard Business School Press, 2001).

5. Edwin A. Locke and Gary P. Latham, "Building a Practically Useful Theory of Goal Setting and Task Motivation: A 35-Year Odyssey," *American Psychologist* 57, no. 9 (2002): 705–17; Gary P. Latham, "Motivate Employee Performance through Goal-Setting," in *The Blackwell Handbook of Principles of Organizational Behavior*, edited by Edwin A. Locke (Malden, Mass.: Blackwell, 2004), p. 108.

6. Alvin Zander, *Motives and Goals in Groups* (New Brunswick, N.J.: Transaction, 1996), p. xvi.

7. U.S. Environmental Protection Agency, Charles River Initiative (www2 .epa.gov/charlesriver/charles-river-initiative#ReportCard).

8. Shelley H. Metzenbaum, "Measurement That Matters: Cleaning Up the Charles River," in *Environmental Governance: A Report on the Next Generation of Environmental Policy*, edited by Donald F. Kettl (Brookings Institution Press, 2002).

9. U.S. Environmental Protection Agency, History of Human Impacts on Charles River (www2.epa.gov/charlesriver/history-human-impacts-charles-river).

10. Lisa D. Ordóñez and others, "Goals Gone Wild: The Systematic Side Effects of Over-Prescribing Goal Setting," Working Paper 09-083 (Harvard Business School, 2009).

11. For a summary of the literature and a discussion of how to use goals and minimize problems associated with their use, see Shelley H. Metzenbaum, *Performance Accountability: The Five Building Blocks and Six Essential Practices* (Washington: IBM Center for the Business of Government, 2006).

12. Jacob L. Lew, Remarks of Secretary Lew at Pew Charitable Trusts, December 5, 2013 (www.treasury.gov/press-center/press-releases/Pages/jl2232.aspx).

13. Sheila Bair, *Bull by the Horns: Fighting to Save Main Street from Wall Street and Wall Street from Itself* (New York: Free Press, 2012), p. 342.

14. See generally Daniel Carpenter and David A. Moss, *Preventing Regulatory Capture: Special Interest Influence and How to Limit It* (Cambridge University Press, 2013).

15. See, for example, National Commission on the Causes of the Financial and Economic Crisis in the United States, *Financial Crisis Inquiry Report*, January

2011(http://fcic-static.law.stanford.edu/cdn_media/fcic-reports/fcic_final_report
_full.pdf).

16. National Center for Environmental Innovation, U.S. Environmental Protection Agency, "ERP States Produce Results: 2007 Report States' Experience Implementing the Environmental Results Program" (December 2007) (www.epa.gov/erp
/files/2007reportfull.pdf).

17. James Phimister and others, "Near-Miss Incident Management Systems in the Chemical Process Industry," *Risk Analysis* 23, no. 3 (2003): 445–59.

18. In the state of Washington, the Puget Sound Partnership has created "vital signs" and a "report card" to track progress in improving various environmental conditions. See, for example, Puget Sound Partnership, "Puget Sound Action Agenda Report Card" (http://gismanager.rco.wa.gov/ntaportal). The Clean Charles Initiative in Massachusetts also used a water quality report card. See, for example, Shelley H. Metzenbaum, "Measurement That Matters: Cleaning Up the Charles River," in *Environmental Governance: A Report on the Next Generation of Environmental Policy*, edited by Donald F. Kettl (Brookings Institution Press, 2002). The U.S. government's Healthy People initiative now tracks twenty-six leading health indicators. See Office of Disease Prevention and Health Promotion, "Healthy People 2020" (www.healthy people.gov). On the use of information more generally in priority setting, see Shelley H. Metzenbaum, "From Oversight to Insight: Federal Agencies as Learning Leaders in the Information Age," in *Intergovernmental Management for the 21st Century*, edited by Timothy J. Conlan and Paul Posner (Brookings Institution Press, 2008).

19. Michael Wogalter and others, "Research-Based Guidelines for Warning Design and Evaluation," *Applied Ergonomics* 33 (2002): 219–30; Robert Cialdini, *Influence: The Psychology of Persuasion* (New York: HarperCollins, 2009).

20. Louis Deslauriers, Ellen Schelew, and Carl Wieman, "Improved Learning in a Large-Enrollment Physics Class," *Science* 332 (May 2011): 862–64.

21. Shelley H. Metzenbaum, "More Nutritious Beans," *Environmental Forum* 20 (2003): 19–41.

22. Shelley H. Metzenbaum, "Strategies for Using State Information: Measuring and Improving Program Performance," IBM Center for the Business of Government, Managing for Performance and Results Series (December 2003) (www.businessofgovern ment.org/sites/default/files/MeasuringandImprovingPerformance.pdf).

23. Les Carlough, "General Deterrence of Environmental Violation: A Peek into the Mind of the Regulated Public" (Oregon Department of Environmental Quality, 2010) (www.deq.state.or.us/programs/enforcement/DeterrenceReport.pdf).

24. NetRegs, U.K. Environment Agency, "SME-nvironment 2003" (www.netregs .org.uk/pdf/sme_2003_uk_1409449.pdf).

25. Cary Coglianese, ed., *Regulatory Breakdown: The Crisis of Confidence in U.S. Regulation* (University of Pennsylvania Press, 2012); Cary Coglianese and Margaret Howard, "Getting the Message Out: Regulatory Policy and the Press," *Harvard Journal of Press/Politics* 3 (1998): 39–55.

26. See also Shelley H. Metzenbaum, "Compliance and Deterrence Research Project: Measuring Compliance Assistance Outcomes," State of Science and Practice White Paper (EPA, 2007).

27. Robert B. Cialdini, *Influence: The Psychology of Persuasion* (New York: William Morrow, 2006).

28. Dorothy Thornton, Neil A. Gunningham, and Robert A. Kagan, "General Deterrence and Corporate Environmental Behavior," *Law and Policy* 27 (2005): 262.

29. Timothy Geithner, *Stress Test: Reflections on Financial Crises* (New York: Crown, 2014.)

30. For the complex challenges of physics and other science and engineering tasks, Carl Wieman recommends 10,000 hours of complex decisionmaking practice to get to a world-class level of expertise. See Bob Roehr, "Nobel Laureate Carl Wieman: Effective Teaching Should Create Students Who Think Like Scientists," American Association for the Advancement of Science, June 8, 2012 (www.aaas.org/news /nobel-laureate-carl-wieman-effective-teaching-should-create-students-who-think -scientists).

# 11

# Beyond Best-in-Class

## *Three Secrets to Regulatory Excellence*

ADAM M. FINKEL

**HOW COULD A SOCIETY** build the best regulatory organization the world has yet to see? One possible blueprint for such an endeavor would be to identify the best component parts from regulators around the world and put together an institution using the "best of the best." Basketball aficionados sometimes engage in this kind of daydreaming, imagining the result if one could create a player with, say, Michael Jordan's athleticism, Larry Bird's eyes, Julius Erving's hands, Allen Iverson's reflexes, and Wilt Chamberlain's strength.[1] Perhaps a regulatory organization starting from scratch, or able to rebuild itself with no constraints, would try to emulate the best risk-informed (or solution-informed)[2] priority-setting system it could find in any other regulatory organization around the world and in any policy domain, and then also look for and emulate the best set of processes for encouraging broad and deep public comment, the best method for targeting scarce enforcement resources, the best internal whistleblower protection system, and so forth.

The idea is of course unrealistic, because no regulator, given its finite resources, can ever be outstanding in every conceivable way simultaneously; in practice, the regulator would likely overspend on the attributes it assembled first, having nothing left over for other important pieces of the puzzle. But I see three reasons why setting out to improve a regulator by assembling the "best of the best" component parts might not even be *desirable*:

166

1. It fundamentally assumes that each component should be *only as good* as today's best examples. Raising the level of any regulatory authority's operations to "best-in-class" status is laudable, but it is cold comfort if the best is not particularly effective.[3] Even when there are widely recognized icons to emulate, settling for their standards will preclude a step change to a higher and hitherto unrealized level of performance. The best-in-class typewriter is still inferior to even an average personal computer in speed and lacks the capacity to remember documents for subsequent editing. In the same way, the list of "best of" basketball attributes that I presented above, drawn from players who all retired years ago, does not anticipate the transformative attributes of a player like Stephen Curry, who is changing the game because he must be guarded at spots on the floor that few had ever thought of as reasonable places to shoot from.[4]

2. Each component part emulated by a new or rebuilt regulatory agency would likely be construed in only one of the three forms of what Cary Coglianese has called the "TAO" of regulatory excellence—as a *trait*, an *action* (or a set of actions), or an *outcome*.[5] These three aspects, which are akin to different parts of grammatical speech, are different ways to describe the same concept, in terms of what an agency values, what it does, or what it achieves.[6] For example, the attribute of honesty can be construed as a trait, in adjectival form: "we are (or 'we pledge to be') trustworthy." It can be construed as an action, in verb form: "we keep our promises" (or "we have kept this particular promise thus"). Or it can emulate an outcome, in participial form: "we are trusted" (for example, surveys of stakeholders reveal this). It is hard to see all three facets at once, and tempting to think that any one invocation of a virtue covers all three, as if they are redundancies. But more important, there are six *connections* among the three facets—each one relates mutually to the other two—and in this chapter I argue that true regulatory excellence is more about the *introspective and careful alignment* of each form than it is about what they are per se. Returning to the basketball analogy, a regulator should be wary of assembling a showy collection of stars who are not interested in working together as a team, a task that requires aligning their philosophies and calibrating their actions to learn from untoward outcomes.

3. The sports analogy, ported over to constructing a public organization, is not wholly apt because it views each desired attribute as existing on a one-dimensional ordinal scale. In sports, a speedy player is unambiguously better than a plodding one, and a player who can leap over a boulder is clearly better than one who cannot jump over a brick. In contrast, for nearly all of the important attributes of a public regulatory agency, *we*

*should not seek superlative versions of average traits, actions, or outcomes, because the very virtues one might simple-mindedly seek to maximize have opposite poles that are **also** virtues.* Consider the simple attribute "speedy" as it might apply to a regulatory agency. Is being "deliberate," which is the polar opposite of speedy, a vice? Clearly not—speed is desirable but to the same extent so is thoroughness, and this is quite different from a "good, better, best" scale where nothing is lost by moving toward the superlative. Maximizing virtues that regulatory agencies correctly see as attractive is perilous, because it means minimizing or repudiating as many competing virtues.

For these reasons, a regulator might set its goal as going "beyond best-in-class" to true excellence, and might better achieve it by focusing on two visions of continuous improvement: (1) aligning its TAO to achieve coherence and synergy; and (2) finding the elusive equilibrium, for each of a long list of attributes, between two *competing virtues,* which can also be thought of as "reconcilable demands." But true regulatory excellence cannot be attained without a third and final leap, the third "secret" offered in this chapter. An excellent regulator must not merely be "mission-driven," but "mission-ruthless," rejecting to the fullest extent possible any behavior that elevates any other goal above that of maximizing public value according to its mission. Building a regulatory organization that does these three things well is the key to comparative and absolute success. In this chapter, I discuss each of these three themes, while offering some practical advice for how the leaders of regulatory agencies and their staffs can gauge whether they are doing the aligning, the equilibrating, and the focusing in ways that sustain and improve their organizations.

### ALIGNING THE REGULATORY TAO

The leaders of a regulatory organization should imagine themselves standing at each of the three vertices of a triangle (see figure 11-1), looking "both left and right," and asking themselves: "Have we aligned this set of attributes to each of the other two?" To answer this question, the leaders could rely on appraisals from the organization's staff, its overseers, its various publics, or neutral experts convened for the purpose. The key is for the regulator to appraise whether the traits it espouses are leading to purposive actions consistent with attributes of excellence, whether those actions are begetting outcomes in causal, direct, and efficient ways, and whether those outcomes represent changes in the world (or the maintenance of desirable states of nature) that it should be proud of, given its stated traits.

**FIGURE 11-1.** Aligning the "TAO" of Regulatory Excellence

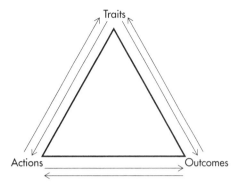

These questions of appraisal may be more easily posed if the regulator appreciates the signs and symptoms of misalignment. To spur reflection, I offer in table 11-1 six cautionary statements about what can happen, for each of the six connections, when the connection is misaligned (as in a railroad train fast approaching a poor link between two sections of track) or absent (as in the train approaching a river where the bridge has washed away). In order to suggest the kinds of lapses these misalignments can lead to, I offer an example for each from the point of view of a hypothetical agency that professes to embody a "risk-based" orientation.[7]

A world-class regulator asks the "Who are we?," the "What should we do?," and the "What should we achieve?" questions in concert. It "inspects" the connections (as a pipeline owner would inspect its network) between each kind of attribute for gaps and misalignments.[8] It seeks "not just the confidence and drive to act, [but] having engraved inner criteria to guide action."[9] Aligning the three attributes thus responds to the hopes of many stakeholders that regulatory agencies will not merely push raw information for the sake of transparency, but let the public in on their rationales in the name of "apparency."[10] Being forthcoming about a decisionmaking rationale, especially when the agency explains a particular decision as grounded in a *prearticulated* statement of philosophy and predilection, can transform stakeholder disappointment into something affected parties regard as "disadvantageous to me personally, but acceptable broadly." An "engraved inner criterion" need not be a straitjacket, because the goal is not to describe *how* tradeoffs will be balanced, just that the agency will do so with certain values in mind.[11]

Aligning the regulatory attributes can also change the entire context of how constituents view agency success and failure. Consider, for example, a regulator that explicitly professes a philosophy (a trait) of being willing to take institutional risks that have small (or even slightly negative) *expected* net benefit

#### TABLE 11-1. Regulatory Misalignments

1. Traits without aligned actions are *hypocrisies* (the agency is not what it says it is). For example, the agency claims to have an efficient "worst risks first" priority-setting system, but consistently and without rationale eliminates small risks at great expense while ignoring inexpensive ways to reduce large risks.

2. Traits without aligned outcomes are *platitudes* (the agency is what it says it is, but that does not do society any good). For example, the agency's rhetoric emphasizes the most efficient opportunities for maximal risk reduction, but evidence shows that the risks it says it targets are in fact rising rather than falling.

3. Actions without aligned traits are signs of *capture* (the agency "goes along to get along"), which casts a shadow on the actions themselves; they are likely to change with the tide. For example, the agency abandons otherwise worthwhile rulemaking or enforcement projects when affected stakeholders complain.

4. Actions without aligned outcomes are *drudgery* (the agency is very busy, but probably just moving sand from one proverbial pile to another). For example, the agency is blind to the risk-increasing side effects of its interventions and ends up foisting risks off onto other subpopulations.

5. Outcomes without aligned traits are *capricious*, easily undone or reversed (the agency is effecting change for change's sake). For example, the agency could be approving a string of risky products and having to preside over recalls when some of them are found to cause harm far in excess of the benefits they confer.

6. Outcomes without aligned actions are *signs of inertia* and easily become raw material for a self-satisfied agency. For example, each of the first twenty-three times that the Space Shuttle flew without incident (at least according to the subsequent evaluation by the Rogers Commission), NASA arguably had convinced itself that the inherent risks were acceptable and perhaps even becoming smaller; yet in fact the risk per launch remained quite high, so the program was coasting along on the (temporarily) good outcomes preceding the nearly inevitable failure of the *Challenger* mission.

*Note:* For each of the six possible pairings of attributes in figure 11-1, this table characterizes the failure to align as a particular kind of regulatory pathology.

but that have a very large upside best-case scenario. For such a regulator, a "failure" (an outcome that goes awry) may well be seen as "a bold gamble that did not pay off this time," whereas the exact same course of events presided over by a regulatory agency with a reputation for passivity may be seen as "what happens when you let that agency out of your sight."

### FINDING THE "SWEET SPOT" WHEN VIRTUES COMPETE

In addition to alignment, regulatory excellence requires the organization's leaders and staff recognize that most of the qualities they seek to instill in their organization will coexist with competing virtues of the opposite sign. The excellent regulator arrays these reconcilable demands into pairs so that it can periodically calibrate its behavior, communications, and planning in order to navigate wisely between them, and to make conscious choices that optimize, rather than one-dimensionally maximize. These choices arise in all facets of a regulator's operations, but I have organized them into three groupings in table 11-2: those that arise in planning and problem solving; those that affect internal management decisions; and those that must be confronted in conducting analysis and responding to evidence.

In table 11-2, each row is divided into five columns. Columns 2 and 4 represent competing virtues; columns 1 and 5 represent the negative manifestations of each virtue, where actions have "crossed the line" into excess. The middle column describes some form of equilibrium embodying some of each desirable quality. Consider, for example, the first row in the table. Regulators should engage with stakeholders from a position of open-mindedness and humility, being willing to modify or abandon a policy or science-policy position in the face of convincing, compelling, or poignant argument. However, agencies should also lead, opining with confidence based on their expertise and their unique responsibility to amass evidence and manage competing claims when rights clash (for example, freedom to pursue profit versus freedom from involuntary risks without commensurate benefits). The leftmost and rightmost entries in this row describe how each competing regulatory virtue can spiral into a vice if taken to excess: here, a confident agency can become so enamored with its own voice (becoming arrogant or haughty) that it fails to listen at all.[12] At the other extreme, a regulatory agency can be so humble and so careful not to offend that it becomes an empty vessel, bowing to the first or the loudest argument it hears.[13] For example, I recently criticized the U.S. Occupational Safety and Health Administration (OSHA) for issuing back-to-back Requests for Information on chemical exposure limits as the sole output of five years' work on that issue. The agency said it was "having a dialogue,"

**TABLE 11-2.** Some of the Competing Virtues That Regulators Must Navigate

| Virtue taken to excess | Virtue | Sweet spot | Virtue | Virtue taken to excess |
|---|---|---|---|---|
| **A. Regulatory Process, Planning, and Engagement** | | | | |
| Groveling; self-loathing | Open-mindedness; humility | Empathic leadership | Confidence | Arrogance/Haughtiness |
| Resorts to hysterics (no reasoning) | Reasons intuitively | Conducts humane analysis | Reasons quantitatively | Coldly automatic |
| Hides from the media | Is cautious with the media | "Pushes" information judiciously | Cozy with the media | Relentlessly self-promoting |
| Is obsessive-compulsive | Works meticulously | Solves small problems easily, or not at all | Sees big picture | Is blasé |
| Sloughs responsibility | Does only what it must | Grows slowly | Fills voids | Grabs turf, with or without tools to succeed there |
| Takes punitive actions | Forces strict compliance | Prods the best to do a little better; prods the worst to do a *lot* better | Is flexible | Is captured |
| Micro-manages with specification standards | Considers best available technology | Allows regulated to meet *either* a specification or a performance standard | Considers exposure and risk | Rigidly enforces performance standards |
| Works too quickly, heedlessly | Works quickly | Finishes 80% of the agenda items in 20% of the time, and considers stopping | Is thorough and meticulous | Glacial; catatonic |
| Cares only about eliminating regulations and reducing burdens | Seeks to relieve unnecessary or outdated burdens | Sets agenda containing a mix of forward-looking and backward-looking priorities based on incremental net social benefit | Seeks to add new regulations based on "unfinished business" | Cares only about adding to the rulebook |

| Virtue taken to excess | Virtue | Sweet spot | Virtue | Virtue taken to excess |
|---|---|---|---|---|
| Hounds industry leaders to make trivial improvements | Leaves industry leaders alone | Engages industry leaders so as to leverage better behavior among their customers, suppliers, etc. | Promotes industry leaders to show good examples to others | Uses industry leaders to aggrandize the agency |
| | Is determined to promulgate uniform ("one size fits all") regulatory requirements | Develops rules with a small number of different "tiers" that accommodate large differences in circumstances among the regulated | Disburses so many exceptions and variances that "one size fits one" | |
| | Is reluctant to change features of a proposed rule (narrow definition of "logical outgrowth") | Engraves a process for what constitutes compelling evidence to change a major feature of a proposal | Proposes regulations that contain open-ended "details to be added later" so as to maximize public input | |
| **B. Internal Management** | | | | |
| Promotes a free-for-all of internal chaos and sabotage | Encourages dissent | Engraves a process for whistleblower protection | Is regimented | Is para-militaristic (crushes dissent with prejudice) |
| Blatantly favors long-time staff with little turnover | Values institutional memory | Plans and adapts to balance new skills and old knowledge | Values "new blood" | Fosters churn for its own sake, especially to encourage veterans to quit |

(continued)

**TABLE 11-2.** (continued)

| Virtue taken to excess | Virtue | Sweet spot | Virtue | Virtue taken to excess |
|---|---|---|---|---|
| **C. Science and Risk Management** | | | | |
| Protects the most vulnerable sub-interest, regardless of cost | Keeps an eye on equity | Develops analytic process to give additional weight to tails of distribution ("equity improves efficiency") | Keeps an eye on maximizing total net benefit | Declares victory whenever benefits exceed costs by a little or a lot, regardless of equity |
| | Emphasizes modeling/inference rather than measurement | Promotes Bayesian learning that integrates (with uncertainty) the findings of models and measurements | Emphasizes monitoring as the gold standard | |
| Is unwilling to risk any regulatory cost or job loss ("inverse precautionary principle") | Is averse to low-probability, high-consequence (LPHC) economic costs | Explicitly weighs the spectrum of possible values of net benefit, considering the probability of each | Is averse to LPHC health and environmental harms | Unwilling to risk any harm (traditional precautionary principle) |
| | Sets environmental/health/safety (EHS) goals and seeks to achieve them at minimum cost | Considers a range of options of varying degrees of cost and benefit | Sets cost constraint and seeks to maximize the amount of EHS benefit achievable under that constraint | |

but my reaction was that "it is time for the agency to stop asking for input and reveal something about its preferred path forward—if you want to have a dialogue, the way to start it is to speak."[14]

Somewhere in between the mirror-image qualities of humility and confidence lies the trait (and the accompanying actions) of "empathic leadership,"[15] which might be represented as a regulatory agency with officials who can sincerely say to the interested public: "We have listened to your point of view, and to yours over there as well, but we were not established as a tabula rasa—we have views of our own; and in light of those prior views and how they have been informed by your views, we come out here on this decision, for these reasons."

Table 11-2 contains roughly twenty additional spectrums representing competing virtues that may be taken to excess, or where an agency may simply focus on one to the exclusion of the other; in either case, the regulator will end up far from the "sweet spot" that balances the demands thoughtfully.

But how can the regulator find such a balance in each of these many cases? No general answer could apply to all regulatory organizations across the world's varied political systems, regulating a vast array of economic, environmental, or other externalities. However, I offer three principles that may aid the process of moving away from one virtue partially (but no further) toward its opposite number.

1. Simple, first-order strategies are more likely to fail. "Balance," unfortunately, often connotes splitting the difference, or employing other tactics to "even out" the extremes. The exact midpoint of a spectrum is just a special case of an equilibrium point where the endpoints happen to be of equal size or intensity, or where the costs of error do not depend on the sign of the deviation.[16] There is no reason to assume these special conditions hold for the kind of navigation that regulators must undertake between virtues and among disparate publics.[17] Similarly, a strategy of trying to smooth out controversy on average, by following one decision made near one tail of the spectrum of virtues with another one at the opposite end, will succeed only by luck, not by design. Excellent regulators are very wary of the bromide that says "If you've made everyone unhappy you must be doing something right." This may hold true on occasion, but certainly it is equally valid (though less prominently uttered) to conclude that "If you've made everyone unhappy, you might be doing everything wrong."

Regulators are often led to strategies of compromise or overcorrection for sound reasons, by explicit requests from competing stakeholder groups, or even by strategic requests from the same group over time, so it is easy to sympathize with regulatory agencies that pursue these paths. For example, David Kessler's strategy in the mid-1990s of asserting that the Food and Drug

Administration (FDA) had jurisdiction over tobacco, but only regulating with respect to sales and marketing to youth,[18] arguably was grounded on sound reasons. But it may have also failed initially because it introduced a legal inconsistency. In the Supreme Court decision rejecting the FDA's authority to regulate tobacco, the majority noted that, had the FDA's statute given the agency authority to regulate tobacco, the decision to treat cigarettes as a drug delivery device with risks but no benefits would have compelled the FDA to ban them outright.[19] Here the "foot in the door" strategy may have caused the door to slam on the agency's foot.

A few years later, OSHA made a strategic mistake (or perhaps it fell for a trap) when it promulgated an ergonomics rule that was in almost every respect the mirror opposite of a draft rule, put forward by the agency years before, that the regulated industries had roundly denounced. The first proposal was specification-based in the extreme, causing a flood of complaints about how it did not let firms innovate and solve problems on their own. By contrast, the ultimate ergonomics rule was designed entirely around management-based innovation, and the complainants then reversed themselves and denounced the rule for lacking specificity.[20] These critics ultimately succeeded in convincing Congress to invalidate OSHA's final rule. Clearly, regulators that fail to articulate and follow an "engraved inner criterion" for navigating these channels are supremely vulnerable to the "no good deed goes unpunished" reaction to their attempts at compromise or at win-some-lose-some balance.

2. There are several different kinds of equilibria, and physical analogies may provide some guidance for choosing among them. There are actually several "sweet spots" on the face of a tennis racket, none of which is located exactly at the center of the face, and each of which has different physical properties.[21] One point, located near the center, allows the player to hit the ball with the minimum of vibration transmitted back to her arm, while a ball hit at a different point (the "center of percussion") nearer to the bottom of the face transmits the least "shock."[22] A third point, closer still to the throat of the racket, offers the maximum return velocity for a given incoming velocity. An excellent regulator will have some insight into whether it most wants to avoid "vibration" (which could be analogized to low-level but chronic criticism), avoid "shock" (a dramatic short-term setback), or assert more influence ("velocity") over the debate—and may well choose an *asymmetric* balance between one virtue and another based on its own experience, and that of sister agencies it converses with, in order to find the particular "sweet spot" needed in each case.

Another example of an asymmetric equilibrium comes from astrophysics: when one astronomical body orbits another, there are several locations in between the two where a spacecraft can take advantage of certain special properties.[23] The first such "Lagrange point" between the earth and the sun allows a craft to make stable observations without overtaking or slowing down relative to a fixed point on earth. This point is located much closer to the earth than to the sun (about 1 percent of the distance between them). This is not quite the same as the point where the gravitational forces exerted by the two bodies are equal, but the analogy may be useful; the craft must "keep its distance" from the stronger pull of the sun, in the same way that any regulator *might deliberately choose a behavior that moves only a small distance toward the more powerful attractor of the two competing virtues.* Perhaps in the clash between speed and thoroughness, for example, it can be tempting to rush and take credit for some regulatory achievement; the thoughtful regulator will recognize this and choose to move somewhat more deliberately than it otherwise might prefer to.

3. In some cases, the ideal may involve offering both faces to the world, rather than an intermediate position between them. The leap from best-in-class to truly excellent may depend on the regulator creatively seeking game-changing responses to various demands so as to recast them as win-win opportunities. For example, the tension between design standards (opposed by those who decry "micro-managing" by bureaucrats) and performance standards (opposed by stakeholders who call for guidance and decry the "arrogance" of issuing vague requirements) can sometimes be sidestepped by issuing regulations that combine the two regimes. Specification standards could be combined with a "safe harbor" design that allows anyone to innovate as long as equivalent or better performance emerges. Similarly, the tension in benefit-cost decision-making between efficiency and equity is usually portrayed as zero-sum; but by deriving utility functions that recognize the disproportionate harm of subjecting individuals to concentrated risks or to inordinate costs, a regulatory agency can seek solutions that maximize an enriched conception of net benefit that maximizes welfare rather than expected monetized value.[24]

## FINDING "COMFORT IN THE CAUSE"

To this point, I have argued that an excellent regulator needs to articulate not only a mission statement but also an "alignment statement" and a "values statement."[25] The synergy among these aspects of policy and practice could permeate every major objective of the agency: for example, the U.S. Environmental Protection Agency (EPA) could foreshadow the next five years of one of its major Clean Water Act programs by stating something like: "We will increase the mileage of U.S. rivers that are fishable and swimmable by [X] percent per year during 2015–2020; we will do so with a portfolio of the following [Y] actions; and we will prioritize, plan, fine-tune, implement, and evaluate these actions within a public process dedicated to [Z] values." In order to make statements such as these meaningful and worthy, the regulator needs above all to understand its mission and seek to advance it single-mindedly—to "will one thing."[26]

Mindful of the litany of examples of "regulatory breakdown,"[27] I remain concerned that regulatory agencies too often expend their limited financial, human, and political resources in service of masters other than their core missions. Incisive self-evaluation may reveal that what appears to be, or is rationalized to be, action in service of the mission turns out instead to be in service of the leadership of the agency, the executive overseeing the government, one favored constituency alone, the personal ambition of a decision-maker or adviser, or the preservation of the institution—rather than the principles the regulatory organization was established to serve.

As one of many possible examples, early in my time as OSHA's director of health rulemaking, the Department of Labor's chief OSHA lawyer entered the morning executive meeting with news of an exciting "win" for the agency: an appellate court had upheld OSHA's right not to make progress on a proposed rule reducing levels of hexavalent chromium (Cr-VI) in U.S. workplaces, despite the plaintiffs' demonstration that three years had elapsed without any tangible reason for OSHA's failing to meet a self-generated deadline for proposing the rule.[28] According to OSHA's own risk estimates, more than 68,000 U.S. workers were exposed to concentrations of Cr-VI sufficient to increase their lifetime excess risk of lung cancer by more than one chance per 100 (in contrast to the level of 1 chance per million that EPA usually considers de minimis). I recall asking, I now see naively, whether we might accommodate two things: our desire to assert our newly upheld right to exercise considerable discretion and the poignancy of this particular issue on any reasonable risk-based priority list. We could wait a decorous interval and then announce that, despite the court decision, we would exercise our discretion by *restarting* this moribund rulemaking—not because we were petitioned to do so, but because we had studied the issue further and concluded that promulgating a reasonable standard was in the national interest. This flabbergasted my colleagues, who did not accept the premise that we would ever react to a grant of authority *not* to do something by turning around and doing it anyway, even at a more leisurely pace.[29] Defending the primacy of the regulatory agency (and perhaps promoting the narrow interests of a reduced workload) had clashed with defending the mission of the agency. And here the mission lost.

What are the forces that push or tempt regulators to forget or cloud their missions? The scholarly literature has tended to focus on two bugbears that can warp the regulator from without:

- excess dependence on (perhaps, but not necessarily, culminating in "capture by") interest groups that are no longer (or never were!) central to the mission;[30] and

- "goal ambiguity," wherein the simultaneous duty to police a regulated industry and promote it economically, or to deter harmful conduct while assisting firms already in compliance to further improve their performance, causes agencies to become "jacks of all trades but masters of none."[31]

As important as these sorts of forces are, I think the more powerful one is *chauvinism*—the insular banding together of agency personnel to defend the institution and only incidentally the mission. Chauvinism, or its more toxic cousin, tribalism, is the suspension of higher functions that can make a sports fan root for a player with an unsavory personal life, until the day that player wears another uniform and the fan suddenly realizes how blind he has been to his own cherished beliefs.[32] This pathology in the regulatory world can exist within a vicious circle: it sometimes only develops when the organization is truly under siege from self-interested external groups, but the "bunker mentality" reflex tends to frustrate and goad on the critics, resulting in yet more perceived need to defend the organization as the de facto mission of the staff and management.

The first step to breaking out of this vicious circle is for the leaders of regulatory organizations to admit (to themselves and to their publics) that they have made a mistake. As the U.S. secretary of transportation said in 2015 in response to the recall of millions of cars with defective air bags: "Defective agencies, like defective people, need the capacity for self-reflection and to make room for self-improvement. . . . And that is what NHTSA is doing today."[33] I have no special insight into how more regulatory officials can awaken to the need for such reflection, although I am not sanguine about prospects for this in regulatory organizations that discourage constructive criticism from staff and that view dissent as a form of treason.[34] In line with Cary Coglianese's comment that a regulator is in some respects like a parent,[35] I think that one of the hardest but most necessary questions parents must ask themselves periodically is whether what they are recommending or insisting their child do is motivated truly by what is best for the child, or what allows the parents to experience vicarious success or enjoyment.[36] Of course it is possible that those interests coincide, and that in the regulatory realm what is good for the organization is also what is best for the nation, but a regulator (like a parent) that occasionally imagines itself forced to justify its behavior to skeptical evaluation will be less likely to confuse the two.[37]

This advice begs the question of how a regulator can distinguish with confidence among competing conceptions of its mission. Clearly a primary source of a regulator's mission can be found in the text of its authorizing legislation, including any legislative history, other ancillary accounts, and judicial interpretations. For this reason, altering these fundamental statements may smack of tampering; witness the swift and broad denunciation of Wisconsin governor Scott Walker's attempt in 2015 to delete the clause in the state university system's statutory mission referring to the goal of "extend[ing] knowledge and its application beyond the boundaries of its campuses and to serve and stimulate society" at the same time that he attempted to add the words "to meet the state's workforce needs."[38] And sometimes, an important clue to a regulatory organization's mission can be found in an obvious place. In response to an assertion that EPA's risk assessment techniques should be calibrated so as to yield "best estimates" that strive to accurately *predict* the magnitude of health and environmental harms,[39] I observed that the acronym "EPA" does not stand for the "Environmental Prediction Agency." I believe EPA's mission, as contrasted, say, with that of the National Institute for Environmental Health Sciences, embodies a concern not only for accuracy, but also for the value of guarding preferentially against errors that underestimate risk and thereby lead to insufficient public protections.

Beyond this, although no set of observations could possibly apply as given to the entire panoply of regulatory agency types and circumstances, it is possible to offer some elaborations on regulatory agency missions that may be useful broadly. Most regulatory officials could use the following questions as starting points for self-reflection about their fidelity to their mission, with any negative answers needing either correction or special justification:

- *Does your organization avoid maximizing value along only one dimension?* (When regulatory agencies protect the environment without regard to cost, or promote industry without regard to externalities, they construe the agency mission to exclude concern over tradeoffs but still leave society with tradeoffs that are managed in ad hoc, opaque, or capricious ways.)

- *If your organization is required to ignore something important in its decision-making (regulatory costs, distribution, feasibility, or the like), does it nevertheless inform society about what it must omit from the decision calculus?*[40]

- *Does your organization regard "small" net changes in the economy as objects for special scrutiny to promote justice instead of just as a "rounding error"?* (For example, is a finding that "few net jobs are created or lost," but many citizens may still be forced to change jobs, the beginning of further analysis rather than the end of the story?)[41]

- *Does your organization live up to the principles it holds up for the rest of society?* (For example, does an environmental agency reduce its own water use or carbon footprint? Does a worker-safety agency maintain a low internal injury and illness rate?)[42]

- *Does your organization respond to new and asymmetric burdens not by fulfilling them half-heartedly, but by volunteering to* add *processes that equalize the playing field?* (For example, while Congress has required EPA, OSHA, and the Consumer Financial Protection Bureau to create panels composed of small business representatives to "preview" proposed regulations, there is no reason these agencies could not voluntarily create parallel panels of, respectively, community members *affected* by environmental impacts of small businesses, employees of small companies, or customers of small lenders.)[43]

- *Does your organization regard the "porting" of problems so they fall outside of the agency's narrow jurisdiction as an unacceptable shortcut instead of as a victory?*[44]

- *Is your organization willing to devolve authority to another agency that can do the job better, and to sunset programs that have succeeded and do not need to be continued?*

- *Does your organization resist exhortations to ignore "paper violations" of its regulations?* (Without a reliable system for reporting conditions within regulated entities, evidence-based problem solving is stymied.)

- *Does your organization seek to facilitate broad discussions whose goal is "coming to mature public judgment," as opposed to airing "raw mass opinion"?*[45] (A regulatory agency that engages stakeholders in discussions that highlight rather than bury information about uncertainties, limited resources, opportunity costs, and alternative solutions will foster light rather than heat, and can encourage disappointed stakeholders toward reluctant acceptance rather than frustrated acquiescence.)

## CONCLUSION

The heading for the previous section of this chapter, "Finding Comfort in the Cause," comes from a William Wordsworth poem called "The Character of the Happy Warrior," in which the poet describes someone

> *Who, with a toward or untoward lot,*
> *Prosperous or adverse, to his wish or not—*

*Plays, in the many games of life, that one*
*Where what he most doth value must be won . . .*
*Finds comfort in himself and in his cause;*
*And, while the mortal mist is gathering, draws*
*His breath in confidence of Heaven's applause:*
*This is the happy Warrior; this is he*
*That every man in arms should wish to be.*

A regulatory organization that aligns its traits, actions, and outcomes, that navigates thoughtfully between competing virtues, and that keeps its core mission in its sights (and in its rearview mirror as it evaluates) can and should be an edifice full of personnel who will find comfort in their tasks and be confident that they will *merit* applause even if they do not hear it often.[46] How different this vision of institutional comfort is from the mood that too often characterizes regulators in an era of increasing expectations and diminishing resources! The folly of the spiral of downheartedness—"we have too few tools to get the job done, and no one appreciates what we do"—is that it begets resentment on the part of the public, which in turn reinforces beleaguered feelings within the regulatory agency.

No one wants a bureaucracy stuffed with self-satisfied workers pursuing happiness as an end in itself. But there is much to be said for a system that can attract, nurture, and validate workers who view public service as a source of pride, motivation, and comfort. In the special arena of regulatory public service, no one is (or at least no one should be) "born to regulate,"[47] but a "beyond-best-in-class" regulatory organization should attract people who are "trained to protect," or "sworn to optimize," or "born to shed light on, and diminish, tragic choices."[48] These workers, and the publics they serve, deserve regulatory organizations that equip them to pursue this high calling.

## NOTES

1. John Denton, "Creating the Perfect NBA Player," *Florida Today*, February 8, 2003 (http://enquirer.com/editions/2003/02/08/spt_wwwspthoopsnbaperf8.html).

2. Adam M. Finkel, "'Solution-Focused Risk Assessment': A Proposal for the Fusion of Environmental Analysis and Action," *Human and Ecological Risk Assessment* 17, no. 4 (August 2001): 754–87.

3. For example, the U.S. Government Accountability Office (GAO) has released more than three hundred reports over the past several decades criticizing the whistleblower protection policies and practices of dozens of federal agencies. Although GAO reports tend to offer constructive criticism rather than unalloyed praise, looking at

the titles of these reports suggests that no major regulatory agency has a whistle-blower program worthy of emulation.

4. Nate Scott, "You Know Those 35-Footers Stephen Curry Was Practicing? He's Sinking Them in Games Now," *USA Today,* November 12, 2015 (http://ftw.usatoday .com/2015/11/you-know-those-35-footers-stephen-curry-was-practicing-hes-sinking -them-in-games-now).

5. Cary Coglianese, *Listening, Learning, and Leading: A Framework for Regulatory Excellence* (University of Pennsylvania, Penn Program on Regulation, 2015) (www .law.upenn.edu/live/files/4946-pprfinalconvenersreportpdf).

6. Adam M. Finkel, Daniel Walters, and Angus Corbett, *Planning for Excellence: Insights from an International Review of Regulators' Strategic Plans* (University of Pennsylvania, Penn Program on Regulation, 2015), pp. 7–9 (www.law.upenn.edu /live/files/4460-finkel-walters-corbett-strategic-plan-analysis-ppr).

7. "A key determination for the modern regulatory agency is to define what the ill-defined notion *risk-based* will actually mean to the agency, the regulated industry, and stakeholders." Greg Paoli and Anne Wiles, *Key Analytical Capabilities of a Best-in-Class Regulator* (University of Pennsylvania, Penn Program on Regulation, June 2015), p. iii (www.law.upenn.edu/live/files/4710-paoliwiles-ppr-researchpaper 062015pdf).

8. It is also possible that an agency will exhibit a quality that is out of step with *both* of the other vertices rather than just one. For the sake of completeness, I offer these adjectives to describe the three possible cases: (1) outcomes without either actions or traits are *random* (and certainly imply that no credit for outcomes is warranted); (2) actions without either traits or outcomes are *purposeless*; and (3) traits without either actions or outcomes are *vapid*.

9. David Brooks, "The Agency Moment," *New York Times,* November 14, 2014.

10. A recurring observation from stakeholders in Alberta who participated in the Penn Program on Regulation's Best-in-Class Regulator Initiative was that they did not care nearly as much about "data" and other factual information proffered by the agency as they cared about being privy to the underlying rationale for key agency decisions. Coglianese, *Listening, Learning, and Leading*, p. 84. In clinical psychology, "congruent communication involves more than transparency [but rather] apparency, . . . 'which has a more active, relational, transitive quality.'" Paul Wilkins, "Congruence and Countertransference: Similarities and Differences," *Counseling* (February 1997): 40.

11. For example, an agency might issue an update to its current five-year strategic plan in light of an unexpected economic recession, stating that, for the time being, it would be more risk-averse with respect to rulemaking and enforcement actions that could tend to cause significant net job losses (and more likely to favor actions that would tend to create significant net new jobs).

12. Of the many possible examples of agency actions that were criticized for perfunctory and insincere engagement with interested stakeholders, one might consider

the account in Lisa Heinzerling, "The FDA's Plan B Fiasco: Lessons for Administrative Law," *Georgetown Law Journal* 102 (2014): 927–89.

13. The competing virtues of humility and confidence are somewhat unusual, in that stakeholders may *perceive* one extreme as actually being an incarnation of the other. An agency that sincerely wants the public to shape its policies can end up being perceived as passive-aggressive, especially by the regulated community, as if the regulator is hiding its true conclusions and requirements rather than waiting for the public to help define them. When OSHA promulgated an ergonomics rule in 2000 that was unusually flexible and open-ended, conservative members of Congress denounced the agency for having a "secret plan" its inspectors would use to flesh out what was never made explicit in the rule itself, and this perception contributed significantly to the unprecedented congressional veto of the rule. What was probably intended to be a true concession ended up looking like a Trojan horse. Adam M. Finkel and Jason W. Sullivan, "A Cost-Benefit Interpretation of the 'Substantially Similar' Hurdle in the Congressional Review Act: Can OSHA Ever Utter the E-Word (Ergonomics) Again?," *Administrative Law Review* 64, no. 4 (Fall 2011): 707–84.

14. Robert Iafolla, "OMB Releases PEL Information Request to Begin Update of Chemical Exposure Limits," *BNA Occupational Safety and Health Reporter* 44 (October 2, 2014): 917.

15. Coglianese, *Listening, Learning, and Leading*, p. 24.

16. Adam M. Finkel, "The Cost of Nothing Trumps the Value of Everything: The Failure of Regulatory Economics to Keep Pace with Improvements in Quantitative Risk Analysis," *Michigan Journal of Environmental and Administrative Law* 4, no. 1 (Winter 2014): 108–09.

17. For an excellent discussion of the pitfalls of gravitating toward the "happy medium," see Peter Vanden Bosch, "The Goldilocks Fallacy," *PHALANX: The Magazine of National Security Analysis*, March 2014, pp. 28–32. Bosch also cautions against the related tendency for analysts to propose three decision options to managers and steer them toward the middle one by accentuating undesirable features of the other two. He explains in a related presentation (www.iup.edu/WorkArea /DownloadAsset.aspx?id=182319) that the maximum value of the function defined as the sum of the desirable characteristics of two competing virtues may lie near the 50/50 balance, but in other cases that point may in fact be the worst stopping place, depending on the shape of the two individual functions.

18. David Kessler, *A Question of Intent: A Great American Battle with a Deadly Industry* (New York: Public Affairs, 2001).

19. *FDA* v. *Brown and Williamson Tobacco Corp.*, 529 U.S. 120 (2000).

20. Finkel and Sullivan, "A Cost-Benefit Interpretation," pp. 767–70.

21. I thank Eric Rich, a student of mine at Penn Law, for calling this to my attention.

22. Richard M. Berger, "Tennis for Seniors" (2015) (http://tennis.bergerweb.net/ SeniorsBook/racquetscience.shtml); Nicholas James Savage, "Vibration Absorption in the Tennis Grip and the Effects on Racquet Dynamics" (PhD diss., RMIT Uni-

versity, 2006) (www.sensorprod.com/news/white-papers/2006-08_vat/wp_vat-2009
-08.pdf).

23. See European Space Agency, "What Are Lagrange Points?" (www.esa.int/Our
_Activities/Operations/What_are_Lagrange_points).

24. Carl F. Cranor and Adam M. Finkel, "Toward the Usable Recognition of Individual Benefits and Costs in Regulatory Analysis and Governance," *Regulation &
Governance* (2016) (http://dx.doi.org/10.1111/rego.12128).

25. In our exploration of features of regulatory agency strategic plans around the
world (Finkel, Walters, and Corbett, *Planning for Excellence*), we found one agency—
the U.S. Environmental Protection Agency—whose plan specifically highlighted "core
values" separate from discussions of mission, goals, and objectives. EPA articulated the
three values of "science, transparency, and the rule of law," although its eighty-page
document mentions these words in only a couple of places in the narrative and offers
no elaboration on why they were chosen or how the agency will embody them.

26. Søren Kierkegaard, *Purity of Heart Is to Will One Thing* (1846; New York:
Harper TorchBooks, 1964).

27. Cary Coglianese, ed., *Regulatory Breakdown: The Crisis of Confidence in U.S.
Regulation* (University of Pennsylvania Press, 2012).

28. *Oil, Chemical, and Atomic Workers Union and Public Citizen's Health Research Group* v. *OSHA*, Third Circuit, No. 97-3532, decided March 13, 1998.

29. OSHA made zero progress on this rulemaking during the subsequent four
years, until the U.S. Court of Appeals for the Third Circuit (314 F. 3d 143, decided
December 24, 2002) ordered the agency to issue a proposed rule forthwith: *"At some
point, we must lean forward from the bench to let an agency know, in no uncertain
terms, that enough is enough . . . .* We conclude that now is such a time. While competing policy priorities might explain slow progress, they cannot justify indefinite
delay and recalcitrance in the face of an admittedly grave risk to public health" (emphasis added).

30. For an evergreen example, see Samuel P. Huntington, "The Marasmus of the
ICC [Interstate Commerce Commission]: The Commission, the Railroads, and the
Public Interest," *Yale Law Journal* 61, no. 4 (April 1952): 467–509.

31. Young Han Chun and Hal G. Rainey, "Goal Ambiguity in U.S. Federal Agencies," *Journal of Public Administration Research and Theory* 15, no. 1 (2005): 1–30.

32. See, for example, Robert N. Kharasch, *The Institutional Imperative: How to
Understand the United States Government and Other Bulky Objects* (New York:
Charterhouse Books, 1973). According to the author, "The man at the top of the institution has the nondelegable duty to be moral. This duty is shirked when the most
important control, the man at the top, is absorbed into the institution itself" (p. 227).

33. Anthony Foxx, quoted in Ashley Halsey III, "Federal Regulators Admit They
Bungled Investigation of Deadly Auto Ignition," *Chicago Tribune*, June 5, 2015.

34. Even agencies that tolerate dissent could go further and actively encourage
risk taking. For a discussion of how the U.S. Department of State has encouraged

use of an anonymous (or attributed) "Dissent Channel" for more than forty years, with salutary results, see Neil K. Katyal, "Internal Separation of Powers: Checking Today's Most Dangerous Branch from Within," *Yale Law Journal* 115 (2006): 2314–49. See also Mary Rowe, Linda Wilcox, and Howard Gadlin, "Dealing with—or Reporting—'Unacceptable' Behavior," *Journal of the International Ombudsman Association* 2 (2009): 2–24.

35. Cary Coglianese, "Rating Governmental Excellence," p. 5 (www.law.upenn .edu/live/files/4380-coglianesediscussion-draft2march-2015pdfpdf).

36. Alice Miller, *The Drama of the Gifted Child: The Search for the True Self* (New York: HarperCollins, 1980).

37. Perhaps an excellent agency could not only promote the kind of "learning forums" Donald P. Moynihan describes in chapter 17 in this volume, but also use them explicitly to ask, "Are we doing this in service of something other than the mission?"

38. Karen Herzog, "Walker Proposes Changing Wisconsin Idea—Then Backs Away," *Milwaukee Journal-Sentinel*, February 4, 2015.

39. George Gray, "Characterizing Uncertainty for Better Decisions," presentation to the EPA IRIS Workshop on the NRC Recommendations, October 16, 2014 (www.epa.gov/sites/production/files/2015-01/documents/session3b_02_gray.pdf).

40. Cass R. Sunstein, *Risk and Reason: Safety, Law, and the Environment* (Cambridge University Press, 2002), pp. 191–228.

41. Cary Coglianese, Adam M. Finkel, and Christopher Carrigan, eds., *Does Regulation Kill Jobs?* (University of Pennsylvania Press, 2014).

42. See the discussion of "walking the walk" in Finkel, Walters, and Corbett, *Planning for Excellence*, pp. 13–14. An agency that requires of itself what it seeks to require from the regulated community, of course, will likely avoid charges of hypocrisy and find its enforcement tasks easier to carry out.

43. Adam M. Finkel, Testimony before the House Committee on Small Business (Regulatory Flexibility Act Improvements Hearing), June 15, 2011, p. 7 (http:// smallbusiness.house.gov/uploadedfiles/finkel_testimony.pdf).

44. John D. Graham and Jonathan B. Wiener, eds., *Risk versus Risk: Tradeoffs in Protecting Health and the Environment* (Harvard University Press, 1995).

45. Daniel Yankelovich, *Coming to Public Judgment: Making Democracy Work in a Changing World* (Syracuse University Press, 1991).

46. Here I refer to positive feedback (overt or more tacit) from both external constituencies and from the staff's own political leadership. High-level managers need to discourage reckless innovation, but could often do much more to encourage calculated risk taking. Agency staff (in my experience, particularly lawyers representing their agencies in enforcement cases or in defense of litigated regulations) should not see finishing their careers with "three victories and no losses" as preferable to finishing (say) with a record of thirty and three.

47. During the congressional veto of the OSHA ergonomics rule, several members of Congress remarked disapprovingly on a magazine interview with OSHA's

then director of safety standards (Marthe Kent), who told the interviewer, "I was born to regulate . . . . So long as I'm regulating, I'm happy. . . . I think that's really where the thrill comes from."

48. Guido Calabresi and Philip Bobbitt, *Tragic Choices* (New York: W. W. Norton, 1978).

# 12

# Compliance, Enforcement, and Regulatory Excellence

## NEIL GUNNINGHAM

EXACTLY *HOW* SHOULD AN excellent regulator intervene in the affairs of regulated organizations to ensure compliance (and arguably overcompliance) and facilitate enforcement? That question motivates this chapter, which is about the "intervention strategies" used for compliance and enforcement rather than about "resource allocation." In the absence of any consensus as to what criteria an excellent intervention strategy should satisfy, I accept the convention that the principal criteria for choosing an intervention strategy should be effectiveness and efficiency. In the majority of cases, the effectiveness of any intervention in reaching a social or economic target (that is, reducing social or economic harm) and its efficiency (doing so at least cost) will be the primary concern of policymakers. Legitimacy or political acceptability, including positive public perceptions of the regulator, is also important.[1] As will become apparent, though, regulators inevitably must make tradeoffs between all of these criteria.

There are, of course, many other aspects of regulatory excellence beyond compliance and enforcement. But compliance and enforcement are core concerns for any regulator, because laws that are not effectively implemented will rarely achieve their social and economic goals. This chapter proceeds by summarizing seven different intervention strategies before identifying the strengths and weaknesses of each. It then goes on to argue that different strategies are suited to different contexts, that account must be taken of the differing characteristics and motivations of various types of regulations and regulators, and that combinations of strategies often provide better outcomes than single strategies. Attention then turns to the role of "beyond compliance" mechanisms, to the potential to harness third parties as regulatory surrogates, and to the need for adaptation and resilience. Although no single template exists for achieving regulatory excellence in all regulatory fields, various signposts can be identified that point regulators toward that goal.

## CHOOSING INTERVENTION STRATEGIES

Regulators from the United States, the United Kingdom, Australia, and other countries have adopted a variety of distinctive intervention strategies—or ideal types—that have been discussed widely in the literature:[2]

- Advice and persuasion
- Deterrence
- Responsive regulation
- Risk-based regulation
- Smart regulation
- Metaregulation
- Criteria strategies

Each of these strategies, elaborated in table 12-1, will be readily recognized by students of regulation. Most of them apply exclusively or primarily to implementation, but metaregulation and smart regulation are constructs that apply equally to regulatory design. In addition, there is always the possibility of using a hybrid approach that combines elements of more than one strategy.

Which approach or approaches to intervention would an "excellent" regulator adopt? The relative strengths and weaknesses of various implementation strategies shown in table 12-1 vary substantially with the context. The sheer variety of regulatory programs, rules, market structures, political environments, and social contexts precludes definitive generalizations about when and to what extent any individual strategy is likely to "succeed" or "fail" in shaping the behavior of regulated entities.

Nevertheless there is much that is known, both about the strengths and limits of individual intervention strategies and about the likely responses of regulatees. Drawing on this knowledge will enable excellent regulators to avoid

From a review of the regulatory literature, seven distinct (but often mutually compatible) regulatory enforcement and compliance strategies can be identified.

Advice and persuasion. Negotiation, information provision, and education characterize this strategy. The threat of enforcement remains, so far as possible, in the background, only to be invoked in extreme cases where the regulated entity remains uncooperative and intransigent.

Deterrence. This strategy is accusatory and adversarial. Energy is devoted to detecting violations, establishing guilt, and penalizing violators for past wrongdoing. It assumes that profit-seeking firms take costly measures to comply with public policy goals only when they are specifically required to do so by law and when they believe that legal noncompliance is likely to be detected and harshly penalized.

Responsive regulation. This strategy is premised on the view that the best outcomes will be achieved if inspectors adapt to (or are responsive to) the actions of regulatees. Regulators should explore a range of approaches to encourage capacity building but must be prepared to escalate up a pyramid of sanctions when earlier steps are unsuccessful. Escalation occurs only when dialogue fails, and regulators de-escalate when met with a positive response. Indeed, it is preferable to escalate up a pyramid of supports, praising and rewarding good behavior and resorting to the pyramid of sanctions only when such behavior is not forthcoming. Implicit in responsive regulation is a dynamic model in which the strengths of different forms of regulation compensate for each other's weaknesses.

Risk-based regulation. This strategy involves the targeting of regulatory resources based on the degree of risk that duty holders' activities pose to the regulator's objectives, and it calls for applying principles of identifying, assessing, and controlling risks in determining how inspectors should intervene in the affairs of regulated enterprises.

Smart regulation. This strategy is a form of regulatory pluralism that embraces flexible, imaginative, and innovative forms of social control, harnessing businesses and third parties acting as surrogate regulators in addition to direct government intervention. The underlying rationale is that, in the majority of circumstances, the use of multiple rather than single policy instruments, and a broader range of regulatory actors, will produce better regulation. As such, it argues that the implementation of complementary combinations of instruments and participants tailored to meet the imperatives of particular issues, can accomplish public policy goals more effectively, with greater social acceptance, and at less cost to the state.

**Metaregulation.** This strategy involves government "regulating at a distance" by risk managing the risk management of individual enterprises. The regulator requires or encourages enterprises to put in place their own systems of internal control and management (via systems, plans, and risk management more generally). These are then scrutinized by regulators who take the necessary action to ensure that the mechanisms are working effectively. The goal is to induce companies to acquire the specialized skills and knowledge to self-regulate, subject to external scrutiny. Accordingly, the regulator's main intervention role is to oversee and audit the plans put in place by the regulated organization.

**Criteria strategies.** These strategies provide inspectors and other decision-makers with a list of criteria they should consider in arriving at a decision in any given case. There is no prescribed formula, and the mechanisms used in any particular case will depend on the circumstances.

common pitfalls and maximize the chances of success, as measured by the criteria identified earlier.

For example, the evidence suggests that *advice and persuasion*, while valuable in encouraging and facilitating those willing to comply with the law to do so, may prove disastrous against those who are not disposed to voluntary compliance. More broadly, advice and persuasion may actually *discourage* better regulatory performance among actors if agencies permit lawbreakers to go unpunished. Conversely, while a *deterrence strategy* can play an important positive role, especially in reminding firms to review their compliance efforts and in reassuring them that, if they comply, others will not be allowed to "get away with" noncompliance, as its impact is very uneven. Deterrence is, for example, more effective against small organizations than large ones, and better at influencing rational actors than the incompetent. Unless it is carefully targeted, it can actually be counterproductive, particularly when it prompts firms and individuals to develop a "culture of regulatory resistance."[3] Moreover, "the psychological research evidence showing that rewards and punishments routinely accomplish short-term compliance by undermining long-term commitment is now overwhelming."[4]

Could the problems of these strategies be overcome by building on their strengths while compensating for their weaknesses? This is one of the multiple aspirations of *responsive regulation,* which means that because regulated enterprises have a variety of motivations and capabilities, regulators should invoke compliance and enforcement strategies that successfully deter egregious offenders, while simultaneously encouraging virtuous employers to comply voluntarily and rewarding those who are going "beyond compliance." This is to be achieved by a variety of mechanisms, including the pyramids of sanctions and supports referred to in table 12-1.

However, in practice, a responsive approach, and the application of a "pyramid of sanctions" involving escalating intervention against regulatees who do not cooperate, is best suited to the regulation of organizations with which the regulator has frequent interactions. Only in such situations can a strategy of "tit for tat" play out,[5] or (as in later iterations) can regulation be rendered "more relational where it counts."[6] While this problem can sometimes be mitigated,[7] the less intense and the less frequent the level of inspection, and the less knowledge the regulator is able to glean about the circumstances and motivations of regulated organizations, the less practicable it becomes to apply responsive regulation.[8] Others have raised a number of other problems, not least the question of "whether responsive regulation can be scaled up to more diffuse, multiparty, logistically complex contexts, such as financial regulation."[9] Where responsiveness *is* applied, in practice there is qualified evidence of its virtues,[10] although in its "tit-for-tat" form it has more effect on behavior than on attitudes.[11]

Like responsive regulation, *risk-based regulation* provides a strategy for regulators to determine their response to particular regulated entities, but it does so on the basis of risk to the regulator's objectives rather than on the basis of the regulatee's degree of cooperation or responsiveness to the regulator. Typically risks are identified and assessed, a ranking or score is assigned on the basis of this assessment, and inspection and enforcement are undertaken on the basis of these scores. Risk-based regulation has the attraction of enabling regulators to prioritize their regulatory efforts and to maximize cost-effectiveness. However, while "risk scoring may provide a very ready basis for detecting high-risk actors . . . it may offer far less assistance in identifying the modes of intervention that are best attuned to securing compliance."[12] This is clearly a serious shortcoming of intervention strategy. There is also a paucity of empirical evidence demonstrating the positive impact of this approach,[13] leading to the conclusion that a risk-based intervention strategy scores much higher on legitimacy (providing a seemingly rational, cost-effective justification for regulatory responses) than it does on demonstrated effectiveness.

*Smart regulation* seeks to overcome the challenges for intervention strategy where interactions between regulators and regulatees are infrequent or otherwise problematic, by harnessing third parties as surrogate regulators.[14] Those who might fulfill this role include local communities and nongovernmental organizations (NGOs) by bringing complaints or shaming recalcitrant businesses into compliance, or even business associations by policing their members. To date the empirical research on smart regulation is supportive but not conclusive.[15] Perhaps the greatest challenge for this approach is coordinating government and third-party pressure, since this approach contemplates escalation of pressure by government, business, and third parties acting in tandem. While the research proposes ways that such coordination might be achieved, the proponents of smart regulation concede that coordination will not always be possible.[16] The role of third parties in effective intervention strategy is revisited later in this chapter.

*Metaregulation* also seeks to extend the reach of the regulator and, like risk regulation, is both a resource allocation strategy and an intervention strategy. In intervening, the role of the regulator is to oversee the effective development, implementation, and monitoring of risk or other corporate management plans by the regulated organization itself. Metaregulation has tended to be used explicitly,[17] in limited areas to which its application is particularly suited, such as major hazard facilities.[18] The highly targeted use of metaregulation is in part a consequence of the limited circumstances in which it is likely to be effective. It requires specialist, high-quality regulators to oversee the risk management strategies of the regulated organization, and sophisticated and motivated regulated organizations to develop and implement such strategies successfully and to regulate themselves effectively. At the very least, a receptive corporate culture is a necessary, though not sufficient, condition for its success.[19] Overall there is evidence that metaregulation has a positive impact on corporate behavior in targeted organizations, although relatively little is known about how this comes about.[20]

Finally, although a *criteria strategy* (or something closely approximating it) was identified as a policy option in some of the early writings on regulation,[21] it has not subsequently found any identifiable academic advocates. This is likely because it is primarily a list of different criteria that a field officer can take into account in decisionmaking. As such, it is not a coherent intervention strategy in its own right, neither capable of being developed theoretically nor (given the vast discretion it provides to field officers) tested empirically.[22]

## SIGNPOSTS FOR REGULATORY EXCELLENCE

Taken overall, an examination of the various intervention strategies suggests that some have considerably more merit than others, while the impact of a third group remains unproven. There are, at the very least, a number of help-ful signposts provided by the theoretical and empirical literature that will assist the regulator striving for excellence, though there exists no single mechanism and no simple formula that will permit such a regulator to dem-onstrate that it has indeed achieved regulatory excellence. These signposts are mapped out in the following sections, which also identify the importance of contextual factors in determining which strategy or strategies to use in par-ticular circumstances.

### *Invoke Different Strategies to Engage Effectively in Different Circumstances*

One striking feature of the intervention strategies described here is that they assume that a single strategy is appropriate to all. Certainly some strategies are flexible enough to take account of different motivations. For example, a criteria strategy usually includes culpability as one criterion but provides no coherent means for choosing between different criteria. In a far more coherent way, responsive regulation also takes account of different motivations as part of the "tit-for-tat" interaction, and risk-based regulation regards motivation as one important risk factor. Even so, each strategy prescribes a single approach—whether it be the application of criteria, escalating up an enforcement pyramid or a pyramid of virtue, or taking action on the basis of risk—for all regulatees in all circumstances. In short, none of the strategies described fully recognizes that different intervention strategies might be appropriate in different circum-stances (although responsive and smart regulation come closest to doing so).

This is unfortunate because there is unlikely to be a single identifiable best-practice approach that should be applied to all duty holders across the board. Because different duty holders confront different external pressures, and have different skills, capabilities, and motivations, what constitutes a best-practice intervention strategy will vary with the context. Risk-based regulation, for example, is of little use when the regulator knows so little about the target population that it cannot make any reasonable assessment of the risks caused by different types of enterprises within it (as may be the case with small enter-prises). Similarly, its use is problematic where only the risks of "routine" com-pliance failures can be measured, but not low-frequency, high-consequence events, as with the global financial crisis of 2008–09. In addition, risk-based regulation may be far better at dealing with some risks (such as occupational injuries) than with others (such as diseases that are hard to identify and have long latency periods).

Responsive regulation, too, is likely to work better when the regulator has the opportunity to make repeat visits than when a single engagement is all that is practicable. For example, large enterprises are readily identifiable, and their size and impact often justify repeat visits from regulators, the building of trust, and an iterative strategy such as responsive regulation. In contrast, small and medium-sized enterprises (SMEs) are often hard to identify, let alone difficult to visit given the high ratio of such enterprises to the number of regulators. *An excellent regulator, therefore, has regard to the strengths and weaknesses of different intervention strategies and to the "fit" between a particular strategy and the characteristics of the regulatory challenge.*

### Take Account of the Drivers of Regulated Enterprises

By implication, an excellent regulator needs to understand why regulated enterprises behave the way they do. What makes regulatees cooperate with regulators? What makes them resist?

Robert Kagan, Dorothy Thornton, and I identified two sets of variables as critical, based on three empirical research projects over a nine-year period and consistent with other emerging strands of other research.[23] First, consistent with sociological explanations of law-abidingness in individuals, we found that regulatees are motivated by: (1) fear of detection and punishment by government enforcement agents; (2) fear of humiliation or disgrace in the eyes of family members or social peers (social license); and (3) an internalized sense of duty—that is, the desire to conform to internalized norms and beliefs about the right thing to do.

The second set of variables is what we termed a multisided "license to operate" involving an often-demanding "social license" along with economic pressures and the demands of government regulators. In combination, the social, economic, and regulatory licenses were found to be critical factors in shaping the behavior of regulatees. For example, social license pressures can affect regulatory performance by pushing managers to comply with their regulatory obligations and tightening the regulatory license by bringing political pressure to bear on lawmakers. This social license, moreover, is monitored by a variety of stakeholders. Environmental groups, for example, not only enforce the terms of the social license directly (for example, through shaming and adverse publicity) but also seek to influence the economic license (for example, by generating consumer boycotts) and the regulatory license (for example, through citizen suits).

These findings have important policy implications. They suggest that business firms' social licenses provide a particularly powerful point of leverage, a point explored in discussing "beyond compliance" initiatives below. They also conclude that some significant level of legal enforcement is essential to generate and ensure compliance: first, by communicating regulatory norms and threatening credible levels of monitoring and legal sanctions for noncompliance; second, for its reminder effect ("check your speedometer!"); and third, for its reassurance effect ("you're not a fool to comply; we are really looking for, and finding, the bad apples").

Overall, the good news is that "regulation-induced fear of legal punishment, social license pressures, and the normative commitments of a great many regulated enterprise managers, acting together, are sufficiently powerful to induce relatively high levels of regulatory compliance in a great many regulatory programs and contexts."[24] Leveraging the license terms, and harnessing fear and duty, provides regulators with many opportunities to pursue excellence, examples of which are provided in the sections that follow.

### Apply Combinations of Compliance and Enforcement Strategies

Because all strategies have both strengths and weaknesses, there may be value in using combinations of complementary strategies to compensate for the weaknesses of one strategy with the strengths of another.

For example, Julia Black has shown how one agency deliberately created a more effective interventionist approach to regulation by requiring different inspectoral stances for organizations with different risk profiles.[25] This effort suggests that a metaregulatory intervention strategy (relying on risk profiles) can be effectively connected to a strategy of responsive regulation by applying a pyramid of enforcement mechanisms based on the degree of cooperation of the regulated organization; cooperation results in a de-escalation of enforcement and resistance leads to the converse response.[26]

However, some combinations can be problematic. For example, to what extent can a criteria and a risk-based strategy be successfully integrated? The answer is: it depends. If risk trumps other criteria in the event of any inconsistency between them, then those criteria are rendered meaningless by the introduction of risk. This outcome seems unlikely to have been the intent of policymakers. If, on the other hand, risk is simply one more factor to be taken into account (with no indication as to how conflict between different factors will be resolved), then the indeterminacy of the criteria approach is not addressed and the role of risk may be modest, perhaps at most tipping the balance in cases where other factors are equally weighted.

Another option is to combine risk-based regulation with responsive regulation. However, they are not necessarily comfortable bedfellows. A risk-based strategy implies that the higher the risk to the social and economic objectives of regulation, the tougher the enforcement action that should be taken, with past experience of the individual operator being taken into account as one indicator of future risk. In contrast, under responsive regulation the regulator should approach the regulated entity assuming virtue and certainly without an evaluation of risk shaping its decision about the appropriate form of intervention. Its normative basis is also quite different from that of risk-based regulation. Not least, responsive regulation appeals to the better nature of the regulatee and appears (and is) just, in a way that risk-based regulation, based as it is on utilitarian assumptions, is not. However, if these two strategies are used sequentially (resource allocation being determined on the basis of risk, responsive regulation as an intervention strategy), any such inconsistency is avoided.

Finally, it should be noted that the complementarity of the policy mix may vary over time, even in dealing with the same enterprise, because a firm's own motivation, corporate culture, or social, economic, or regulatory license may itself change. The result may be that intervention mixes that were appropriate at one time need to be adjusted at another to take account of changed circumstances.

### *Encourage Regulatees to Go beyond Compliance*

Strategies to encourage, facilitate, and reward beyond-compliance behavior may resonate with only a relatively small number of large, reputation-sensitive corporations, and in particular circumstances where they can identify "win-win" opportunities. Nevertheless, should an excellent regulator aspire to nudge good companies (further) beyond compliance? Or is it a misuse of scarce regulatory resources to focus on making the top 5–10 percent even better rather than concentrating on the most serious problems or on underperformers?

Much will depend on the regulator's overall intervention strategy. A risk-based regulator, for example, would seek to identify and target the largest risks, and such risks are unlikely to involve refinements in the practices of already high-performing regulatees. In contrast, a metaregulator might identify companies that go beyond compliance as particularly suited to "regulating at a distance." However, two other approaches are much more likely to deliver effectiveness and efficiency.[27]

Responsive regulation, in its later iterations, would see the preceding approaches as failing to realize opportunities to raise the performance of *all* regulatees, from leaders to laggards. John Braithwaite has argued that regulators should first look at the strengths of societal actors and then seek to expand them. In his view:

> Most environmental, healthcare or safety problems, for example, get solved by expanding the managerial capacities of regulated actors to solve them for themselves. . . . The idea of pyramids of supports is not just getting the performance of the most innovative actors through new

ceilings, it is also about these players finding better ways of solving problems that make it easier to increase demands upon laggards.[28]

Another potentially fruitful way for regulators to see the role of beyond-compliance strategies might be through the lens of the license-to-operate framework described earlier.[29] What a company decides to do in going beyond compliance can be explained largely by how it interprets and responds to the various license terms. Importantly, those terms are interconnected. For example, corporations fear that not meeting the requirements of the "social license" will result in increased regulation or greater economic costs to the company. Conversely, if regulators can provide not only economic rewards for going beyond compliance but also reputational benefits that strengthen the social license, then the combined effects will often exceed the impact of focusing on the regulatory license in isolation. As will be apparent, such an approach is consistent with responsive regulation's supports-based pyramid, which would equally applaud the provision of reputational rewards for "good apples" who have gone beyond compliance. A mechanism such as the U.S. Toxic Release Inventory, which mandates the estimation and reporting of major toxic releases, can of course reward the best performers while at the same time threatening the reputation of laggards.[30]

However, the preceding analysis should not be taken to suggest that existing beyond-compliance initiatives have necessarily achieved all that they promise. On the contrary, many of the programs introduced by the Clinton administration in the United States, which placed particular emphasis on this approach, appear to have either made only marginal differences to regulatory outcomes or failed to demonstrate any material difference and are unable to justify the resources devoted to them.[31] Equally, some have failed to distinguish between those businesses that are committed to going beyond compliance and those that simply seek the reputational benefits of participation in such initiatives without commitment to delivering beyond-compliance outcomes. So, too, there may be substantive and procedural rule-of-law issues if firms can be granted beyond-compliance privileges in the absence of clear and transparent criteria for inclusion in the program.[32] However, these problems are more a reflection of particular design flaws than of any inherent inefficiency or ineffectiveness of beyond-compliance initiatives.

On this point, the findings of John Mikler's study of vehicle fuel efficiency standards in Europe, the United States, and Japan are salient.[33] Although the United States performs poorly in this regard and Europe somewhat better, the clear leader is Japan, which "presents a dramatic case of easily exceeding standards . . . [where] the industry appears to continuously improve the fuel efficiency of its cars even in the absence of increasingly strict government regulation." Mikler's explanation suggests that "the state set[s] the strategic direction, to which industry responds as a challenge."[34] As one company or another develops a technological innovation that increases fuel efficiency, this best-practice standard becomes the minimum requirement for all companies, thereby "raising all boats." This approach—namely, moving up a pyramid of supports guided by responsive regulation,[35] but underpinned by a strengths-based pyramid—provides better outcomes than traditional direct regulatory approaches, at least in the Japanese context.

*Excellent regulators, therefore, should seek out opportunities to encourage enterprises to go beyond compliance, where these hold out the prospect of lifting the performance of all regulatees, or at the very least, of improving the performance of those who go beyond compliance in a cost-effective manner.* Given the insights of past research, measurement and monitoring to demonstrate both costs and outcomes, coupled with external audit and review, will be crucial.[36]

### Harness Third Parties

Excellent regulators recognize that they must use their scarce resources wisely and well and that this involves, among other things, what smart regulation would refer to as harnessing the capacities of third parties to act as surrogate regulators and engaging in what responsive regulation would call networked escalation.[37]

A substantial body of empirical research reveals that numerous actors influence the behavior of regulated groups in complex and subtle ways, and that mechanisms of informal social control often prove more important than formal ones. For example, in the case of the environment, there is a case for focusing attention on the influence of: international standards organizations; trading partners and the supply chain; commercial institutions and financial markets; peer pressure and self-regulation through industry associations; internal environmental management systems; and civil society in a myriad of different forms. In practical terms, this last category usually means NGOs and local community groups.[38]

Much will still depend on the context, of course. In the case of pesticide use by vegetable growers, supply chain and community pressure can play important roles; in the case of motor vehicle crash repairs, the insurance industry's role could be pivotal; and in the case of ozone protection, industry self-management may be the critical instrument.[39] Arguably the most powerful forms of "civil regulation" are those in which environmental NGOs or communities have the capacity to threaten the social license and reputation capital of large corporations.

However, the participation of third parties, particularly commercial third parties, in the regulatory process is unlikely to arise spontaneously, except in a very limited range of circumstances where public and private interests substantially coincide. What is needed is strategic government intervention to create incentives for third parties to operate as surrogate regulators.

To illustrate, for many years, the regulatory regime for the prevention of intentional oil spills (pursuant to an international treaty) was almost wholly ineffective, due in no small part to the difficulties of monitoring and, in some cases, to a lack of either enforcement resources or political will on the part of member countries. Furthermore, in the absence of government intervention and the imposition of penalties, third parties had no incentives to contribute significantly to the reduction of oil spills. All this changed when a new regime required tankers to be equipped with segregated ballast tanks (SBTs), thereby facilitating initial surveys and inspections by nongovernmental classification societies and making it hard for nonconforming tankers to receive the classification and insurance papers needed to trade internationally. The new regime facilitated coerced compliance by three powerful third parties— nonstate classification parties, ship insurers, and shipbuilders—and it achieved almost 100 percent compliance.[40]

The broader point is that, by expanding intervention strategies to harness third parties, some of the most serious shortcomings of traditional approaches to compliance can be and are being overcome. Third parties are sometimes more potent than government regulators. For example, the threat of a bank to foreclose a loan to a firm with low levels of liquidity is likely to have a far greater impact than any existing government instrument. Third parties are also often perceived as more legitimate. Farmers, for example, are far more accepting of commercial imperatives to reduce chemical use than they are of any government-imposed requirements. In any event, government resources are necessarily limited, particularly in an era of fiscal constraint. Accordingly, it makes sense for government to reserve its resources for situations where there is no viable alternative but direct regulation. *An excellent regulator, therefore, facilitates, catalyzes, and commandeers the participation of second and third parties to the cause of improving regulatory outcomes.*

### Develop Adaptive Learning and Resilience

As indicated earlier, much of our knowledge about compliance and enforcement strategies, and in particular about what works and when, remains tentative or incomplete. This suggests that excellent regulators need to engage in adaptive learning and treat policies as experiments from which they can learn and which in turn can help shape future strategy.

From this perspective, it is important to ask, as Dan Fiorino has: "How may mechanisms that promote policy learning . . . be strengthened? To what extent do policy-making institutions provide mechanisms for learning from experience and altering behavior based on that experience?" This might imply, for example, monitoring, ex post evaluation, and revision mechanisms. In Fiorino's terms, it means "building reliable feedback mechanisms into policy-making, strengthening learning networks, creating conditions that would lead to more trust and more productive dialogue and enough flexibility into the policy system so that it is possible to respond to lessons drawn from one's own experience or that of others."[41]

In particular, adaptive learning is heavily dependent on the depth and accuracy of an agency's statistical database and other information sources. Only with adequate data collection and interpretation can a regulator know how effective a particular regulatory strategy has been. Moreover, in the absence of credible self-evaluation, regulators will be unable to demonstrate to themselves, to regulatees, or to external audiences whether or to what extent they are achieving their objectives or whether the resources at their disposal are being well spent. Such a failure accordingly will also threaten their legitimacy.

Given the pervasiveness and inevitability of changing circumstances, part of the challenge might be to build resilience into an implementation strategy. Resilience thinking and resilience management have been influential in areas such as natural resource management, and there is now an extensive literature addressing how social and ecological resilience might be achieved.[42] However, there has been little written about how regulation and governance could gain from the insights of the wider resilience literature,[43] and even less about how it might be applied to implementation strategy. Having said this, it is worth noting that the strategy of using combinations of instruments advocated earlier is essentially a resilience strategy: compensating for the weaknesses of individual strategies by integrating them with others that have complementary strengths.

Measured in terms of adaptability and resilience, different intervention strategies would score very differently. Responsive regulation in particular "assumes the strategies advanced in its name will fail very often. It is designed to learn from these failures by repairing pyramids through adding layers that cover the weaknesses of failed strategies with varieties of new or reformed strategies."[44] Smart regulation, too, with its reliance on harnessing multiple parties and a comparable escalation strategy, in conjunction with industry sequencing, triggers, and buffer zones, is better capable of adapting to changing circumstances than, for example, risk-based regulation. The latter is often focused on established risk and may miss emerging problems. It also faces the inherent danger of "model myopia": the possibility "that regulatory officials become committed to a historically captured set of risk indicators and assessment criteria" that inhibit the regulator from taking account of data not captured by that model.[45] *Accordingly an excellent regulator needs to be constantly self-evaluating, learning, and adapting its approach, identifying emerging problems and acting promptly when it does so.*

## Maintain Legitimacy

Maintaining legitimacy is of particular importance for regulatory agencies, even where this conflicts with what might otherwise be judged to be the most appropriate strategy. Simply put, proposals that cannot gain political acceptance are unlikely to be adopted, no matter how effective they may be.[46] The point for present purposes is that legitimacy usually trumps effectiveness, and any intervention strategy must take account of this reality.

For example, consider responsive regulation, under which the regulator is expected to intervene initially at the bottom of an enforcement pyramid (assuming virtue on the part of the regulatee) and only escalate to enforcement action if the assumption proves incorrect. There may well be circumstances where the regulator cannot credibly maintain this strategy in the face of threats to its legitimacy, such as when there is political risk in doing so or when it is under community pressure. For example, suppose there has been a major incident or "near miss" involving an industrial facility situated close to a residential area. Here there will be considerable pressure to take decisive and immediate action, and to do so in ways that are visible to external audiences—the most obvious being the initiation of a prosecution—with the consequence that the matter will be publicly adjudicated. Even if there is evidence that the regulatee had very limited culpability (their past record being exemplary, the causes of the incident not being reasonably anticipated), the need to preserve legitimacy will be paramount.

For the regulator who wishes to maintain the trust of a regulatee who is a "good apple," the situation is a challenging one. Its difficulties may be lessened if the relevant compliance and enforcement policy *requires* advice, persuasion, or enforcement action in specified circumstances, in which case the regulator can legitimately plead that the decision is out of its hands. The regulator may also seek to preserve its relationship with the regulatee by exercising discretion as to what enforcement action it takes, such as by prosecuting for a less serious offense or agreeing on a "reasonable" penalty. By whatever means a regulator tries to maintain its relationship with the regulatee, the need to maintain legitimacy in the eyes of the broader community and to minimize political risk will almost certainly prove more compelling. So too with beyond-compliance initiatives that do not demonstrably treat like firms alike; they risk a legitimacy deficit that may ultimately be their undoing.[47]

### CONCLUSION

In this chapter I have sought to advance the debate over *how* to intervene by arguing, contrary to conventional wisdom, that rather than seeking to identify a single intervention strategy, an excellent regulator needs to apply different intervention strategies according to their suitability to particular regulatory contexts. Different types of regulatees confront different external pressures and have different skills, capabilities, and motivations. The economic and social risks posed by different operations are also intrinsically different. Accordingly, there is no single formula for achieving regulatory excellence.

Although excellent regulators will apply different intervention strategies in different circumstances, there are nevertheless numerous signposts that can steer all regulators toward the goal of regulatory excellence. These signposts include: invoking different strategies to engage effectively with different circumstances; facilitating, catalyzing, and commandeering the participation of second and third parties as surrogate regulators; and constantly self-evaluating, learning, and adapting their approach.

### NOTES

1. Procedural legitimacy is not considered in this chapter.

2. Neil Gunningham, "Enforcing Environmental Regulation," *Journal of Environmental Law* 23, no. 2 (2011): 169–201.

3. Eugene Bardach and Robert A Kagan, *Going by the Book: The Problem of Regulatory Unreasonableness* (Temple University Press, 1982).

4. John Braithwaite and Peter Drahos, *Global Business Regulation* (Cambridge University Press, 2000), p. 558.

5. Ian Ayres and John Braithwaite, *Responsive Regulation: Transcending the Deregulation Debate* (Oxford University Press, 1992), pp. 62–63.

6. John Braithwaite, "Relational Republican Regulation," *Regulation & Governance* 7 (2013): 124.

7. Ibid.

8. Neil Gunningham and Richard Johnstone, *Regulating Workplace Safety: System and Sanctions* (Oxford University Press, 1999), pp. 123–29.

9. Cristie Ford, "Prospects for Scalability: Relationships and Uncertainty in Responsive Regulation," *Regulation & Governance* 7 (2013): 14. See also Braithwaite, "Relational Republican Regulation."

10. For reviews, see Robert Baldwin and Julia Black, "Really Responsive Regulation," *Modern Law Review* 71 (2008): 59–94.

11. Vibeke Lehmann Nielsen and Christine Parker, "Testing Responsive Regulation in Regulatory Enforcement," *Regulation & Governance* 3 (2009): 376–99; see also Peter Mascini and Eelco Van Wijk, "Responsive Regulation at the Dutch Food and Consumer Product Safety Authority: An Empirical Assessment of Assumptions Underlying the Theory," *Regulation & Governance* 3 (2009): 27–47.

12. Julia Black and Robert Baldwin, "Really Responsive Risk-Based Regulation," *Law & Policy* 32, no. 2 (2010): 189–90.

13. Julia Black, "The Development of Risk-Based Regulation in Financial Services: Just 'Modelling Through'?," in *Regulatory Innovation: A Comparative Analysis*, edited by Julia Black, Martin Lodge, and Mark Thatcher (Cheltenham, U.K.: Edward Elgar, 2005), p. 156; Black and Baldwin, "Really Responsive Risk-Based Regulation," pp. 181–213.

14. See generally Neil Gunningham, Peter Grabosky, and Darren Sinclair, *Smart Regulation: Designing Environmental Policy* (Oxford University Press, 1998), chap. 6.

15. See, for example, Judith van Erp and Wim Huisman, "Smart Regulation and Enforcement of Illegal Disposal of Electronic Waste," *Criminology & Public Policy* 9, no. 3 (2010): 579–90.

16. Gunningham, Grabosky, and Sinclair, *Smart Regulation*, chap. 6.

17. Implicitly, as Julia Black has argued, metaregulation may be inevitable because of the massive disparity between regulatory resources and the number, size, and complexity of regulated enterprises. See Julia Black, "Paradoxes and Failures: 'New Governance' Techniques and the Financial Crisis," *Modern Law Review* 75, no. 6 (2012): 1037–63.

18. On metaregulation generally, see especially Christine Parker, *The Open Corporation: Effective Self-Regulation and Democracy* (Cambridge University Press, 2002). For a review of the "safety case" literature, see Neil Gunningham, "Designing OHS Standards: Process, Safety Case and Best Practice," *Policy and Practice in Health and Safety* 5, no. 2 (2007): 3–24.

19. Neil Gunningham and Darren Sinclair, "Organizational Trust and the Limits of Management-Based Regulation," *Law & Society Review* 43 (2009): 865–900.

20. For a review, see Neil Gunningham, *Mine Safety: Law, Regulation, Policy* (Sydney: Federation Press, 2007), chap. 3.

21. See in particular two early and classic studies: Keith Hawkins, *Environment and Enforcement* (Oxford University Press, 1984); Bridget M. Hutter, *Compliance: Regulation and Environment* (Oxford University Press, 1997).

22. A criteria strategy does bear a superficial resemblance to "principles-based" regulation, on which see Julia Black, "The Rise, Fall and Fate of Principles-Based Regulation," in *Law Reform and Financial Markets*, edited by Kern Alexander and Niamh Moloney (Cheltenham, U.K.: Edward Elgar, 2011).

23. Robert A. Kagan, Neil Gunningham, and Dorothy Thornton, "Fear, Duty and Regulatory Compliance: Lessons from Three Research Projects," in *Explaining Compliance: Business Responses to Regulation*, edited by Christine Parker and Vibeke Lehmann Nielsen (Cheltenham, U.K.: Edward Elgar, 2011), pp. 37–58.

24. Ibid., p. 54.

25. Julia Black, "Managing Regulatory Risks and Defining the Parameters of Blame: A Focus on the Australian Prudential Regulation Authority," *Law & Policy* 28, no. 1 (2006): 1–30; Black, "The Development of Risk-Based Regulation in Financial Services," p. 156.

26. See also John Braithwaite, "Meta Risk Management and Responsive Regulation for Tax System Integrity," *Law and Policy* 25, no. 1 (2003): 1–16.

27. The large majority of beyond-compliance initiatives tend to score well on legitimacy because they are voluntary and encourage dialogue with local communities concerning beyond-compliance goals and the means of achieving them.

28. John Braithwaite, "The Essence of Responsive Regulation," *University of British Columbia Law Review* 44, no. 3 (2011): 480–81.

29. Neil Gunningham, Robert A. Kagan, and Dorothy Thornton, "Social License and Environmental Protection: Why Businesses Go beyond Compliance," *Law & Social Inquiry* 29, no. 2 (2004): 307–41.

30. For a related discussion of how information can motivate environmental progress, see Shelley H. Metzenbaum and Gaurav Vasisht, "What Makes a Regulator Excellent? Mission, Funding, Information, and Judgment," chap. 10, this volume.

31. See, for example, Neil Gunningham and Darren Sinclair, *Leaders and Laggards: Next Generation Environmental Regulation* (Sheffield, U.K.: Greenleaf, 2002); Cary Coglianese and Jennifer Nash, "Performance Track's Postmortem: Lessons from the Rise and Fall of EPA's 'Flagship' Voluntary Program," *Harvard Environmental Law Review* 38 (2014): 1–86.

32. Coglianese and Nash, "Performance Track's Postmortem," p. 80.

33. John Mikler, *Greening the Car Industry: Varieties of Capitalism and Climate Change* (Cheltenham, U.K.: Edward Elgar, 2009).

34. Ibid., pp. 101, 106.

35. Braithwaite, "The Essence of Responsive Regulation," pp. 480–90.

36. Coglianese and Nash, "Performance Track's Postmortem."

37. On surrogate regulators, see Gunningham, Grabosky, and Sinclair, *Smart Regulation*, pp. 408, 413. On networked escalation, see Braithwaite, "The Essence of Responsive Regulation," pp. 507, 512.

38. See generally Gunningham, Grabosky, and Sinclair, *Smart Regulation*, chap. 6.

39. See Gunningham and Sinclair, *Leaders and Laggards*.

40. Ronald B. Mitchell, *Intentional Oil Pollution at Sea: Environmental Policy and Treaty Compliance* (MIT Press, 1994).

41. Dan Fiorino, "Rethinking Environmental Regulation: Perspectives on Law and Governance," *Harvard Environmental Law Review* 23, no. 2 (1999): 468.

42. See, for example, Lance H. Gunderson, Craig R. Allen, and C. S. Holling, eds., *Foundations of Ecological Resilience* (Washington: Island Press, 2009); Brian Walker and David Salt, *Resilience Thinking: Sustaining Ecosystems and People in a Changing World* (Washington: Island Press, 2006).

43. Perhaps the closest in this regard is Ahjond S. Garmestani and Craig R. Allen, eds., *Social-Ecological Resilience and the Law* (Columbia University Press, 2014).

44. Braithwaite, "Relational Republican Regulation," p. 135.

45. Black and Baldwin, "Really Responsive Risk-Based Regulation," p. 23.

46. Fiona Haines, "Regulatory Failures and Regulatory Solutions: A Characteristic Analysis of the Aftermath of a Disaster," *Law & Social Inquiry* 34, no. 1 (2009): 34.

47. Dennis D. Hirsch, "Bill and Al's XL-ENT Adventure: An Analysis of the EPA's Legal Authority to Implement the Clinton Administration's Project XL," *University of Illinois Law Review* 1 (1998): 129–72.

# 13

# The Role of Policy Learning and Reputation in Regulatory Excellence

## DAVID VOGEL

**A CRITICAL CHARACTERISTIC OF** an excellent regulator is the ability to engage in policy learning. Policy learning has two key dimensions. First, policy learning requires that a regulator recognize the accomplishments and shortcomings of both the decisions made by other regulators and its own decisions. Second, policy learning requires that the regulator demonstrate responsiveness to new information as it emerges. Engaging in policy learning is especially important for a regulator responsible for addressing health, safety, and environmental risks because risk management decisions are often based on provisional or contested scientific data. Such regulations may require making predictions or assumptions about the seriousness of the harms or dangers policymakers are seeking to ameliorate or prevent, which may or may not prove to be accurate.

The ability of a regulator to engage in policy learning may be influenced by two factors: the demands the public places on the regulator, and the agency's reputation. Reviewing the decisions of other agencies that were not subject to the same public pressures may give a regulator the opportunity to critically reassess and revisit its own decisions. Equally important, an agency's reputation can affect the willingness of officials from other agencies to learn from it. But the factors that shape an agency's reputation are complex. Not all regulatory policy failures undermine an agency's reputation, nor do all policy accomplishments necessarily enhance it. Much depends on how the public responds to or perceives the policy outcomes of an agency's decisions.

This chapter explores three case studies of policy learning and reputation. Two case studies involve transatlantic regulatory policy learning, or the lack thereof—namely, comparisons of the regulation of ozone-depleting chemicals and pharmaceutical products in the United States and Europe. The third case study examines the dynamics of regulatory reputation and learning within a single jurisdiction, focusing on the performance and impact of the agency responsible for regulating air pollution in California.

## REGULATING OZONE-DEPLETING CHEMICALS IN THE UNITED STATES AND EUROPE

In 1974, two American scientists, Sherwood Rowland and Mario Molina, published a study suggesting that the release of chlorofluorocarbons (CFCs), widely used chemical compounds in both consumer products and industrial processes, might be depleting the ozone layer. This in turn would allow more ultraviolet light to penetrate the earth's atmosphere, thus increasing the risk of skin cancer. Scientists on both sides of the Atlantic met Rowland and Molina's analysis with skepticism. At the time, there was no evidence that the ozone layer was actually thinning or, even if it was, that human activity was causing it. However, because the study was released at a time when public concerns about the environmental causes of cancer were politically salient, the U.S. Congress held several hearings to explore the policy implications of Rowland and Molina's research.

These hearings attracted considerable media attention. The American public quickly became persuaded that the use of CFCs in personal-hygiene products such as aerosol hair sprays and deodorants posed credible and unacceptable environmental and health dangers.

As Peter Morrisette noted, "The fear of skin cancer from the depletion of stratospheric ozone due to the use of CFCs as aerosol propellants in spray cans personalized the risk for many people."[1] Sales of aerosol products fell sharply. In 1975, a federal task force supported the CFC ozone-depletion theory and its links to skin cancer. It went on to make the precautionary recommendation that ozone-depleting emissions should be regulated unless new scientific evidence emerged to clearly refute the finding of the Rowland and Molina study. The following year the National Academy of Sciences confirmed the risk assessment of the task force, but also indicated that was unable to specify the urgency of the health and safety risks posed by CFCs.

In 1977, federal legislation granted the Environmental Protection Agency (EPA) the authority to regulate "any substance . . . which . . . may reasonably be anticipated to affect the stratosphere, especially ozone."[2] In March 1978, three U.S. regulatory agencies, namely EPA, the Food and Drug Administration (FDA), and the Consumer Product Safety Commission (CPSC), issued regulations banning all nonessential uses of CFC. These regulations affected nearly $3 billion worth of consumer products and ended half of all CFC domestic production in the United States.

European policymakers were of course aware of both the scientific findings and the public and policy responses to them in the United States. But they chose *not* to learn from them. Denmark was the only European Union (EU) member state to adopt a ban similar to that of the United States. For its part, the European Council, after two years of delay, approved a compromise resolution that imposed restrictions on CFC production that were largely symbolic. In May 1983, after a further review of scientific evidence, the EU concluded that no additional regulation was necessary.

Why were European policymakers unwilling to learn from the United States? Part of the explanation was the lack of comparable public pressure. While sales of aerosol personal-hygiene products had experienced a major drop in the United States, they remained stable in Europe. Indeed, American firms that had stopped using CFC propellants in consumer products they marketed in Europe saw their sales decline. But equally important, European officials did not trust American regulators, as the latter had developed a reputation in Europe for issuing "overhasty regulations" based on "scientifically disputed" evidence.[3]

This mistrust of American risk regulation was reflected, for example, in the comments of a British journalist who wrote in 1972: "We saw the Americans thrashing around from one pollution scare to the next. . . . One moment it was cyclamates, mercury, the ozone, lead, cadmium—there they seem set on working their way in a random manner through the whole periodic table."[4] A British social scientist observed in 1979, "Americans seem to have taken an excessively strict interpretation of risk, reducing 'reasonable risk,' to practically 'zero risk.'"[5] In part, this was true. The 1958 Delaney Clause in the Federal Food Drug and Cosmetic Act had established a policy of zero tolerance for any residue of carcinogenic pesticides or additives in processed food found to cause cancer, and it also established an extremely low threshold for designating a substance as a carcinogen. Neither standard had been adopted by any European country. European officials had chosen to interpret the results of animal testing much more flexibly, and as a result many substances that were banned in the United States remain permitted in Europe. When the CFC controversy emerged, it seemed to European policymakers that the American (excessively) low threshold standard was now being applied to risk regulations beyond food additives, including chemicals.

European officials believed that their insistence on a higher level of scientific proof or certainty was more responsible since it reduced the likelihood that costly, unnecessary, or unnecessarily stringent regulations would be adopted. In short, what they learned from the U.S. approach to regulating health, safety, and environmental risks was what *not* to do. In this context, the Europeans clearly thought they were being excellent by not overreacting to what they considered to be a speculative risk assessment. It was only after the dramatic 1985 announcement that a British scientific team had found a large hole in the ozone layer over Antarctica that European officials judged their standard of scientific risk proof to have been successfully met. As one scientist observed, "Now we've got a hole in our atmosphere that you could see from Mars . . . it is harder to label [it] as just a computer hypothesis."[6] Accordingly, European officials were now willing to work with the United States to harmonize international risk regulations, which led to the signing of the Montreal Protocol in 1987 that imposed global restrictions on ozone-depleting chemicals.

In this case, the reputations and credibility of American regulatory agencies were enhanced: their risk management decisionmaking—in particular their decision to impose significant restrictions on the basis of a plausible but not yet scientifically established risk—was vindicated: the ozone layer was in fact thinning, CFC emissions were the cause, and the depletion of the ozone layer had increased the incidence of skin cancer. But the precautionary American approach to the risks of ozone depletion can be judged "excellent" only in retrospect. Had future scientific research disproved the ozone-depletion hypothesis, then the credibility and judgment of U.S. regulatory officials would have been undermined and the more cautious European approach would have proven to be more responsible. The important lesson this outcome suggests is that there are times when the excellence of a regulation, or the extent to which it has improved public welfare, might not be immediately apparent.

One reason the American officials were able to make what turned out to be the "right" decision was the public pressure they received: a highly risk-averse American public considered the risks of CFCs to be both credible and unacceptable. Had the American public not supported, or demanded, this particular risk regulation, American policymakers might have been less willing to act against the use of CFCs in consumer products.

Significantly, the United States did not restrict other industrial or "essential" uses of CFCs, such as for refrigeration and in air conditioners. The costs of doing so were considered excessive, in large measure because the United

States would have been acting alone. Since the Europeans had not imposed comparable regulations, a more sweeping ban would have placed American firms at a comparative disadvantage. It would have forced firms operating in the United States to change their production methods. From this perspective, Americans did "learn" from Europeans: U.S. regulations were less stringent than they would have been if European policymakers had initially taken the risks of ozone depletion more seriously.

While the risk assessments on which European regulatory officials initially relied proved to be mistaken, they did not suffer any loss of reputation for two reasons. First, their risk assessments were consistent with the preferences of the European public. Indeed their reputation might well have suffered had they decided to restrict the use of aerosol in personal-hygiene products, despite the insufficiency of the scientific evidence of a public health threat and in the face of strong public demand for these products. From this perspective, they could be seen as exhibiting an important dimension of regulatory excellence, namely protecting their legitimacy and reputation by making decisions that were responsive to or consistent with public preferences. Second, as soon as there was compelling evidence of the CFC ozone-depletion theory, they did review and revise their risk assessment and entered into negotiations with the United States, which led to a new international agreement that phased out most uses of CFCs. Thus European regulators were willing to "learn," but they required a higher scientific threshold of evidence before they were willing to act. Nonetheless, the fact that they were willing to revise their initial risk assessment when the scientific evidence became conclusive exhibited an important dimension of regulatory excellence, namely the ability to learn from new information.

What makes this case somewhat ironic is that subsequently the European Union and the United States "traded places." The United States moved away from a precautionary approach to assessing and managing risks, instead increasingly demanding a high level of scientific "proof" before issuing new risk regulations, as European officials had earlier required with respect to CFCs. By contrast, over time the EU increasingly embraced the precautionary principle, which permitted regulatory action when "potentially negative effects" had been identified but it was still "impossible to determine with sufficient certainty the risk in question."[7] Had the risks of ozone-depleting chemicals emerged on the policy agendas on both sides of the Atlantic a decade later, it is entirely possible that the policy responses of the European Union and the United States would have been reversed.

It is, almost by definition, impossible to know in advance that a precautionary approach is justified, since its appropriateness depends on the "certainty" of future scientific evidence. Initial risk regulations clearly can later prove either too stringent (false positives) or too lax (false negatives). Regardless of regulators' initial actions or inactions (decisions that are likely to be shaped by the public's risk perceptions), regulators should be both able and willing to adjust their actions as new scientific information emerges. Thus, had new scientific evidence emerged to discredit the Rowland and Molina study, it would have been incumbent on U.S. officials to revise and review the regulatory restrictions they had earlier imposed. In this case, it was the Europeans who were challenged to revise and review their earlier risk assessments, which they did.

## PHARMACEUTICAL DRUG REGULATION
## IN THE UNITED STATES AND EUROPE

The era of modern drug regulation can usefully be dated from the thalidomide disaster of the early 1960s. The approval and widespread use of this sedative by pregnant women in several European countries led to a dramatic increase in children born with birth defects, most notably in Germany where it was available without a prescription. Half of exposed children died by their first birthday. In the United States, Frances Kelsey, a physician and scientist working for the FDA, had concerns about the drug's safety and had not yet approved the drug when its risks became public. Then, however, a front-page story in the *Washington Post* highlighted the fact that it *might* have been approved; in other words, the article claimed that there had been a near policy failure. This revelation led to the widespread public concern that the U.S. standards were too lax, and there was substantial political pressure to strengthen federal drug approval requirements.[8] Congress responded by enacting the 1962 Kefauver-Harris amendments to the Federal Food Drug and Cosmetic Act, which made American standards for drug approval "the most stringent in the world."[9]

Although the regulatory responses to the thalidomide disaster in Europe were more modest, the episode did prompt several European countries to reexamine the quality and independence of their regulatory institutions, as well as their policies and standards for drug development, approval, and surveillance. While European countries had been as likely to reject as to emulate the American model of drug regulation before the thalidomide disaster, afterwards, "nation by nation, introspection was quickly accompanied by extended gaze at the United States and the FDA, for it was widely perceived that American regulators had gotten matters 'correct' in the thalidomide affairs. . . . [The FDA] became the 'gold standard' to which other nations referred in constructing new models and institutions."[10] Thus the FDA's handling of thalidomide clearly strengthened its global reputation and policy impact.

Nonetheless, the FDA's widely perceived near policy failure due to its previous drug approval standards had placed the public spotlight on the risks of approving unsafe drugs. Accordingly, agency officials now clearly understood that their approval of any drugs that turned out to have harmful side effects would result in substantial media, public, and congressional criticism. As legal scholar Frances Miller explains, "Precaution was the FDA's official watchdog in part because congressional oversight committees habitually announced hearings to rake the agency over the coals whenever the media accuses it of failing to protect the public from unsafe drugs and devices."[11] Consequently, both the costs of meeting the FDA's strengthened premarket testing requirements and the time required for a new drug to be approved increased substantially. During the 1960s, the development costs for a new chemical entity increased from $1.2 million to $11.5 million, while between the 1960s and 1980s average drug development time grew from 8.1 years to 14.2.[12]

By contrast, while regulatory institutions and some procedures were strengthened in Europe, the essential British and German approaches to drug approval did not fundamentally change. As a senior British regulatory official put it: "The role of regulators is in fact to achieve the release on to the market of those products which have had peer review which has chosen them to be satisfactory."[13] In 1986, the chairman of a British drug approval body described his work as "concerned strictly with scientific issues," pointedly adding that "drug regulatory authorities should be immune from political or public pressure."[14] The latter two comments suggested that what some European regulatory officials *had* learned from the United States was the importance of *not* allowing public pressures to influence—and thus distort—the regulatory process.

Rather than strengthening their premarket requirements, regulatory officials in Europe instead chose to enhance their ability to monitor the adverse health effects of previously approved drugs. In essence, while the United States sought to prevent harms to public health *before* they occurred by relying on experimental or scientific data, European officials placed greater emphasis on reducing harms to public health *after* they occurred by relying on actual evidence of harms to humans. Predictably, many more approved drugs were subsequently removed from the market in Britain than in the United States.[15]

However, the latter development did not undermine the reputation of European regulatory officials in their home countries, nor did it persuade them of the superiority of the FDA's regulatory approach. On the contrary, British officials remained highly critical of the costly and time-consuming U.S. standards for new drug approval. According to one official, it led to "inflexibility, rigidity, polarization and irrationality."[16]

As memories of the thalidomide crisis began to fade, the relative lack of availability of new drugs in the United States became increasingly salient. For critics of the FDA's "drug lag," a term first coined in 1972, it was now the Europeans whose more permissive drug approval standards appeared to be better at protecting public health. A report by the U.S. General Accounting Office tracked the introduction of fourteen significant new drugs. It found that thirteen were available for use in Europe before they were approved for use in the United States. A German study found that while the United States was, by a large margin, the leading producer of new drugs, it ranked ninth out of twelve countries in being the first to make new drugs available to its citizens.[17] In 1985, nearly half of U.S.-discovered new chemical entities had yet to be introduced in the U.S. market, and more were being marketed in Germany than in the United States.[18] That same year it took more than thirty months for marketing approval to be granted in the United States and only six months in both Britain and France.[19]

The FDA now found itself increasingly criticized for denying Americans access to drugs that were already available in Europe. In 1980, U.S. Representative James Schuerer, a Democrat, accused the FDA of "contributing to needless suffering and death for thousands of Americans because it is denying them the life-enhancing and lifesavings drugs available elsewhere."[20] Two pharmacologists specifically cited the case of the drug nitzarepam, which was used to treat severe insomnia. It had been approved for use in Britain five years earlier than in the United States. They contended that thousands of American lives might have been saved during those five years, concluding, "in view of the clear benefits demonstrable from some of the drugs introduced into Britain, it appears that the United States had lost more than it had gained from adopting a more conservative approach than did Britain in the post-thalidomide era."[21] Somewhat ironically, the agency's domestic critics now argued that the health and safety of Europeans had been enhanced precisely because European drug approval authorities had *not* emulated the FDA by tightening their drug approval requirements.

Yet these criticisms had little impact on the FDA's practices and priorities. Why was the agency unwilling to learn from the health impact of drug approval policies in Europe? Part of the reason was that the FDA had historically defined its strategy for fulfilling its core mission (protecting public health) as preventing the public from being harmed by consuming unsafe drugs, a policy approach that had been reinforced by the public furor over thalidomide and the resultant 1962 legislation. This focus made it difficult for the FDA to recognize that the public could also be harmed by drug approval standards and requirements that were *too* stringent. Put more formally, the FDA's priority had been to avoid the risks of false-negative policy errors; however, this made it insufficiently attentive to the risks of false positives—that is, of taking too long to approve drugs that turned out to be both safe and effective.

Two other factors were also at work. One was the agency's long-standing role as the global leader or international standard-bearer in drug regulation. Its reputation as the "gold standard" had made the FDA uninterested in following, and possibly learning from, policy developments in other political jurisdictions, particularly those whose experience and expertise it considered inferior to its own drug approval authority.

The second factor was political. As the *Wall Street Journal* insightfully editorialized: "It is now clear that the FDA bureaucrats will never take any risks they can avoid. They have nothing to gain from approving an effective drug and everything to lose from making a mistake."[22] This view was echoed by a former FDA commissioner, who recalled: "The message to the agency staff was very clear. Whenever a controversy over a drug is resolved by approval, the agency and the individual involved will likely be investigated. Whenever a drug is disapproved, no inquiry will be made."[23] This somewhat cynical assessment made sense. Those whose health and safety were harmed by approved drugs were easily identified; they and the public knew who they were. But those patients who suffered owing to the unavailability of beneficial drugs were much more difficult to identify or to mobilize politically, as they themselves often did not know who they were.

Not until the AIDS epidemic of the mid-1980s did the FDA become willing to review and revise standards for new drug approvals. AIDS was a fatal disease for which there were no approved drugs. Those who had contracted AIDS were unwilling to wait for new drugs to be thoroughly tested for safety and efficacy, since they might not be alive by the time the agency had completed its lengthy approval process. In 1987, the FDA approved a drug for the treatment of AIDS in only eighteen months. While this approval was faster than for any drug in the FDA's history, it still failed to placate the highly mobilized activists in the AIDS community and their supporters, who accused the agency of "prolonging the roll call of death."[24]

Subsequently, the agency approved new rules designed to significantly reduce the time necessary to approve drugs developed to treat life-threatening illnesses. While adopted in direct response to the AIDS crisis, these rules were also designed to speed up the commercial availability of drugs for other illnesses for which there was no effective treatment. Consequently, the median approval times for new drugs that fell within this classification declined from 26.7 months in 1993 to 19 months in 1994.[25]

Policy learning across the Atlantic—in this case from Europe to the United States—began to accelerate. In 1992, Congress approved legislation that required firms to submit a user fee to the FDA for each new drug application. These fees would then go into a fund used to expedite the drug approval process. As part of the agreement that produced this legislation, the FDA promised to measurably reduce drug approval times, which it did: median approval time for all drugs fell to a little over a year.[26] Paying fees for drug approvals had long been the practice in several European countries. Subsequently, the FDA also began to authorize the use of third-party assessment for drug safety, a policy approach that it had resisted for several years but that had also previously been adopted in Europe. With these and other policy changes, Europe and American drug approval standards have converged. The drug lag has essentially disappeared, and a new drug is now as likely to first be approved in the United States as in Europe.

This case underlines both the importance of policy learning and the complex factors that can facilitate or impede it. To achieve regulatory excellence, regulators must be willing to learn, by continually monitoring and reassessing both their own policy impact and that of other regulatory authorities who face similar challenges. Regulatory policies cannot remain static or be based on what the agency has or has not achieved in the past. Rather, they must continually be reviewed and reassessed. In this context, it is important for regulators to recognize that more stringent regulations may not necessarily be more effective. Many important regulatory decisions involve tradeoffs: reducing some risks may increase others. Thus what it takes to be an excellent regulator can change over time. Excellence may at times be associated with being extremely cautious, while at other times caution can be viewed as a mistake. An important dimension of regulatory excellence involves being responsive to changes in the public's policy preferences and risk assessments, as well as to policy outcomes.

While all regulators should aspire to maintain excellence by learning and adapting, earning a reputation for regulatory excellence can produce mixed policy results. Some regulatory officials in other agencies might be more likely to "learn" from the regulator with an excellent reputation; however, the agency with an excellent reputation might be less willing to learn from the experiences of other agencies and less likely to review and reconsider the policies and practices that led it to be known as excellent.

## THE CALIFORNIA AIR RESOURCES BOARD

In 2006, the state of California enacted the Global Warming Solution Act. Described as "the most ambitious climate legislation enacted anywhere in North America and among the most aggressive policies in the world," this statute required the state to reduce its emissions of greenhouse gases (GHG) back to 1990 levels by 2020.[27] What was particularly striking about this legislation is that it was only ten pages long. The task of formulating the detailed and complex rules that would be needed to implement this broad goal was delegated to a state regulatory agency, the California Air Resources Board (CARB). Why were the state's elected officials willing to vest so much authority in an administrative body established by the state legislature in 1967 to address the state's unusually poor air quality?

The most obvious explanation is CARB's track record of accomplishing its primary regulatory responsibility, namely to improve air quality by reducing automobile emissions. By 2003, the main components of smog had been reduced by 99.3 percent for hydrocarbons, 96.2 percent for carbon monoxide, and 88.2 percent for nitrogen oxides.[28] This in turn led to substantial reductions in air pollution, most notably in southern California, where the air quality had historically been the worst in the United States. In this region, between 1973 and 1980 there were 644 violations of the federal ozone standard, while between 2003 and 2011 the standard was violated only twice.[29] While the region's population has doubled in size since 1970, the amount of smog in southern California declined by 50 percent. This was, literally, a highly visible regulatory policy accomplishment. The legal scholar Ann Carlson wrote: "The sky is bluer and the air easier to breathe. The exhaust from tailpipe from new cars is invisible not black." These impressive accomplishments had made CARB into "one of the most sophisticated and well-regarded environmental agencies in the world," one whose influence has extended far beyond the state's borders.[30]

It was its formidable policy accomplishments that had enabled CARB to win the confidence of the public and elected policymakers, and to be trusted with so much regulatory authority over the state's ambitious climate change regulatory policy initiatives.[31] According to State Senator Fran Pavley, an influential environmental legislator, "It seems hard to imagine that the Legislature would have vested power in CARB to devise an economic-wide program that will regulate all aspects of the state's economy unless it had tremendous confidence in CARB's regulatory capacity."[32] Indeed it is quite likely that without the regulatory reputation CARB had developed during the previous four decades the legislature would have never approved the Global Warming Solution Act in the first place. For had the state's elected officials been unable to delegate such substantial regulatory authority to CARB, they would have been forced to engage themselves in the politically challenging, and likely impossible, task of formulating and agreeing on a detailed plan for reducing carbon emissions. Moreover, it was the state's demonstrated success in reducing air pollution that gave policymakers the confidence that it also had the capacity to address the risks of global climate change.

CARB was able to develop early expertise over automotive emissions in California because of the federal government's 1967 decision to permit

California, and only California, to develop its own regulatory standards beyond those set at the federal level. This enabled CARB to function as an American laboratory for innovation on emission control technology and regulation. Indeed, the federal government has subsequently adopted virtually all of the state's innovative and more stringent emission standards, typically with a lag of a few years. In 1977, the federal government recognized the importance of CARB's regulatory leadership by giving other states the option of adopting California's more stringent automotive emissions standards or the laxer ones issued by the federal government. Approximately one quarter of the states have chosen to do so, which has also led to improved air quality in much of the United States.[33]

CARB has clearly benefited from the automotive industries' and the United Automobile Workers' relative lack of political influence within the state, as both would have strongly opposed many of the agency's policy initiatives. Also, CARB has cultivated and benefited from a close relationship with independent manufacturers of pollution control equipment. Many important innovations in the regulation of motor vehicle emissions were first developed by firms in California, including the two-way catalytic converter and unleaded gasoline. Because of CARB's commitment to steadily strengthening emission standards, a cluster of firms located in the state specialize in the development of new emission control technologies. These firms in turn have been important business backers of CARB. Its close working relationship with the business community has enabled CARB to become a leader in identifying and implementing new approaches, technologies, and requirements for regulating air pollution from vehicles in the United States.

Two other factors have also played an important role in strengthening CARB's impact, reputation, and effectiveness. One has to do with its sources of funding. Importantly, CARB is not dependent on state appropriations for financial support. Rather, its funds come directly from the fees it imposes on the parties it regulates. This support structure has made it possible for the agency to steadily increase the size of its staff to cope with its growing set of regulatory responsibilities, and also to engage in long-term planning. It has enabled the agency to hire and retain a well-paid staff of technically trained engineers, sophisticated lawyers, and policy experts. A second factor is CARB's administrative structure. Its governing board, which is appointed by the governor with Senate approval, consists of technical, scientific, and policy experts, as well as representatives from the state's largest regional air pollution control districts. This combination of expertise and political accountability has allowed the agency to develop leadership that is "both expert and politically sensitive."[34]

In sum, CARB's unusually high reputation as a regulatory agency stems from a variety of factors, including a few that bear on thinking about regulatory excellence more generally. First, it is important that an agency have a clear policy objective and that its ability to achieve this objective is publicly recognized and politically supported. In short, it must "deliver" measurable and valued public benefits. Second, an excellent agency must have substantial policy expertise, which in turn requires adequate and secure funding. Third, it needs to be situated within a political system in a way that balances political or public accountability with regulatory autonomy and independence. Fourth, it needs to cultivate a good working relationship with firms in the private sector that are likely to be important sources of technological innovations.

Finally, an excellent regulator needs to be in a position to experiment with policy innovations and assess their effectiveness. In this context, the regulatory autonomy given by the federal government to the state of California, and thus to CARB, has been an important asset in the making of environmental policy in the United States. It has enabled the United States to have *two* important air pollution control regulatory agencies, namely EPA and CARB, with the former able to benefit and learn from the track record of the latter. This case study thus provides support for the diversity or decentralization of regulatory policymaking within a country and the critical opportunities this can provide for policy learning.

## REGULATORY EXCELLENCE AS REGULATORY LEARNING

The case of CARB also suggests that regulatory excellence may be a property not only of a single organization, but also of a system of regulating. In other words, what has helped make the American system of auto emissions regulation excellent is a structure that allows for experimentation and thus domestic policy learning. In this context, California may be in a position to offer lessons to other states and possibly the federal government with respect to innovative policy approaches to address the risks of climate change. Clearly California continues to function as a regulatory laboratory: the rest of the United States can be expected to closely follow California's accomplishments, and its shortcomings, in order to assess which of CARB's ambitious and wide-ranging efforts to reduce greenhouse gas emissions are worth emulating.

The future of climate change regulation in the United States will likely be significantly affected by CARB's track record. What lessons then, might CARB learn from the FDA if it is to maintain its reputation for excellence? One critical lesson would be to closely monitor the impact of its policy choices on both public opinion and the achievement of its policy goals. To maintain its reputation, the agency must avoid overconfidence. It must proceed carefully and recognize that not all its policy choices will be wise or prudent. There is still much to learn about how greenhouse gas emissions can be most effectively and efficiently reduced, and as new economic and scientific data emerge, CARB must be willing to adjust its regulatory strategies.

It also must recognize that public acceptance of its legitimacy and authority cannot be taken for granted. The FDA paid too little attention to critics who argued that its too-stringent drug approval standards were undermining its core mission of protecting the public's health. CARB must not make a similar mistake: it must learn to listen and respond to public criticisms of its performance and adjust its policy choices accordingly. For example, if particular regulations issued by CARB were seen as hurting California's economy, or unduly interfering with the lifestyles of its residents, then its reputation and its policy effectiveness would suffer. It must also be willing to learn from the other governments, both domestically and internationally, that have embarked on a wide range of climate change policies, some of which differ from California's. Unlike the FDA, CARB should not assume that its policies and programs represent the "gold standard" for efforts to address the risks of global climate change. An excellent agency recognizes that it does not have a monopoly on expertise, and that a reputation for excellence in the past, or the present, does not guarantee one in the future.

In contrast to ozone depletion there is a broad scientific consensus regarding the risks of climate change. Nonetheless, the ozone case study does emphasize the importance of treating all specific risk regulations as provisional: as new information about the sources and consequences of greenhouse gas emissions and the technologies for addressing them emerge, as they surely will, CARB will need to modify some of its regulations. An excellent regulatory agency can never be complacent: it must keep learning.

Excellent regulatory regimes engage in both exogenous and endogenous policy learning. In other words, such regimes learn from the experiences of others, as well as from their own trials and errors. This learning process demands that the regulator be responsive to new information as it emerges. For health, safety, and environmental risk regulators, the learning process is particularly important because such agencies often must make regulatory decisions based on equivocal or uncertain information. Thus regulatory excellence may be provisional: it may often be difficult to initially assess which decision is the right one. At times it might make sense for an agency to wait before taking action, and at other times the agency might decide to act on the basis of limited information. In either case, it must be ever willing to change its actions in light of new information. What makes an agency excellent is less the quality of its decisions than its willingness and ability to respond to new information—information that either confirms or challenges its initial policy choices.

The need for regulators to engage in continuous policy learning as new information becomes available has been noted by influential students of public policy and administration such as Charles Sabel, Jonathan Zeitlin, and Peter May.[35] In particular, Sabel and Zeitlin's influential concept of experimentalist governance emphasizes the critical role of policy feedback in enabling officials to assess, review, and revise their policy prescriptions, while May reminds policymakers that policy failures represent important learning opportunities too.

Moreover, the track records, decisions, and experiences of other agencies subject to different public pressures, functioning within different legal environments, or relying on different scientific advice, are important sources of policy learning and thus an important dimension of regulatory excellence. External sources can help an agency assess and evaluate its own processes and decisions. This does not mean that regulatory excellence can only be determined by reference to the decisions of other regulators. But since the challenges faced by any regulatory body are unlikely to be unique, monitoring the decisions made by regulatory officials in different political jurisdictions is critical: it can help regulators learn both what to do and what not to do.

## CONCLUSION

Three major lessons can be drawn from the case studies in this chapter, contributing to our understanding of the dimensions of regulatory excellence.

First, excellent regulatory officials must maintain public confidence in the mission, work, and decisions of their agencies. Regulatory officials are not (typically) elected. The very establishment of regulatory bureaucracies is intended to give officials a substantial degree of autonomy. They should not base every decision on public opinion polls or seek to avoid public controversy at all costs. But at the same time, they must recognize that they are embedded in democratic political systems and that therefore they need to be aware of and broadly responsive to public preferences, especially as these may shift. In the case of ozone-depleting chemicals, both U.S. and European authorities were able to retain their reputations precisely because each of their actions, even though they differed from one another, were broadly consistent with the risk perceptions of their respective publics. The same has been true of CARB. That agency has been successful in large measure because Californians have strongly supported its policy goal of improving air quality. By contrast, while the FDA's initial focus on avoiding false negatives was clearly consistent with public preferences, as the focus and direction of public pressures on the agency began to change, it was too slow to adjust. It did eventually do so, thus once again bringing policies into better alignment with those of the broader American public. Taken together, the case studies show that if public preferences differ, as was true in the cases of both ozone-depleting chemicals and transatlantic drug approval policies after 1962, different agencies (or the same agencies at different times) may reach very different decisions. But this does not necessarily diminish the value or excellence of the choices they made. If societies differ, then their regulators can and should act differently too, while still striving for excellence.

Second, excellent regulatory officials are never complacent: they must be continually open to and engaged in policy learning. Regulators are always presented with a wide range of policy options and often have to act in the face of scientific or technological uncertainty. Some enjoy better reputations than others. Nonetheless, there is no substitute for policy learning, both from one's own experiences and from that of other agencies. In a sense, all regulatory policies and decisions are experiments: they are always provisional and they can also be improved. Much of CARB's success can be attributed to its ability to engage in continuous policy learning about how mobile source pollutants can be more effectively and efficiently controlled. Likewise, the U.S. Environmental Protection Agency has been willing to learn from CARB. European pollution control authorities were willing to change their regulations for ozone-depleting chemicals as new scientific data emerged, and, over time, the FDA demonstrated its regulatory excellence by exhibiting a willingness to learn from its counterparts in Europe.

Finally, regulatory excellence requires maintaining an appropriate relationship between regulatory agency officials and the businesses affected by their decisions. Here a balance must be struck. On one hand, the agency must avoid becoming the captive of business interests. On the other hand, it must be cognizant of the economic impact of its regulatory policies and be willing to learn from the knowledge and expertise of the private sector. CARB has been so successful precisely because it has been able to strike such a balance: it has challenged the interests of the major automotive manufacturers and at the same time worked closely with them and with other business innovators in pollution control technologies. Many of the accomplishments of California's climate change initiatives to date are due to CARB's support of and its close working relationship with private sector firms with a financial stake in reducing greenhouse gas emissions, especially investors in clean technology. Too cozy a relationship with industry can undermine an agency's reputation and legitimacy, but so can a relationship that is too adversarial. An excellent regulatory agency must recognize that its effectiveness will be enhanced if it is able to develop business allies and can demonstrate that its policies create economic as well as social value.

NOTES

1. Peter M. Morrisette, "The Evolution of Policy Responses to Stratospheric Ozone Depletion," *Natural Resources Journal* 29 (1989): 803–04.

2. Quoted in Miranda A. Schreurs, *Environmental Politics in Japan, Germany, and the United States* (Cambridge University Press, 2003), p. 119.

3. Ibid., p. 124.

4. Quoted in Stanley Johnson, *The Politics of Environment: The British Experience* (London: Tom Stacey, 1973), pp. 170–71.

5. Timothy O'Riordan, "The Role of Environmental Quality Objectives in the Politics of Pollution Control," in *Progress in Resource Management and Environmental Planning*, edited by Timothy O'Riordan and Ralph C. D'Arge (Chichester, U.K.: Wiley, 1979), 1:236–37.

6. Quoted in Srini Sitaraman, "Evolution of the Ozone Regime: Local, National, and International Influences," in *The Environment, International Relations, and U.S. Foreign Policy*, edited by Paul G. Harris (Georgetown University Press, 2001), p. 123.

7. European Commission, "Communication from the Commission on the Precautionary Principle" (European Union, 2000), p. 14.

8. See Mark Nadel, *Politics of Consumer Protection* (Indianapolis: Bobbs-Merrill, 1971), p. 123.

9. Fredrik Andersson, "The Drug Lag Issue: The Debate Seen from an International Perspective," *International Journal of Health Services* 22, no. 1 (1992): 70.

10. Daniel Carpenter, *Reputation and Power* (Princeton University Press, 2010), pp. 693–94.

11. Frances H. Miller, "Medical Errors, New Drug Approval, and Patient Safety," in *The Reality of Precaution: Comparing Risk Regulation in the United States and Europe*, edited by James Hammit and others (Washington: Resources for the Future Press, 2013), p. 260.

12. Henry G. Grabowski, John M. Vernon, and Lacy Glenn Thomas, "Estimating the Effects of Regulation on Innovation: An International Comparative Analysis of the Pharmaceutical Industry," *Journal of Law and Economics* 21, no. 1 (1978): 136. See also American Enterprise Institute for Public Policy Research, *Proposals to Reform Drug Regulation Laws*, AEI Legislative Analysis 8 (Washington, 1979).

13. Quoted in John Abraham and Graham Lewis, "Citizenship, Medical Expertise and the Capitalist Regulatory State in Europe," *Sociology* 36, no. 1 (2002): 71.

14. Ibid., pp. 71–72.

15. Mary E. Wiktorowicz, "Emergent Patterns in the Regulation of Pharmaceuticals: Institutions and Interests in the United States, Canada, Britain, and France," *Journal of Health Politics, Policy and Law* 28, no. 4 (2003): 625.

16. Frances B. McCrea and Gerald E. Markle, "The Estrogen Replacement Controversy in the USA and U.K.: Different Answers to the Same Question?," *Social Studies of Science* 14, no. 1 (1984): 14.

17. American Enterprise Institute for Public Policy Research, *Proposals to Reform Drug Regulation Laws.*

18. Andersson, "The Drug Lag Issue," p. 57.

19. Wiktorowicz, "Emergent Patterns in the Regulation of Pharmaceuticals," p. 625.

20. John Kelly, "Bridging America's Drug Gap," *New York Times,* September 13, 1981.

21. William Wardell and Louis Lasagna, *Regulation and Drug Development* (Washington: American Enterprise Institute, 1975), p. 205.

22. Quoted in Carpenter, *Reputation and Power,* p. 368.

23. Kelly, "Bridging America's Drug Gap," p. 19.

24. Thomas Kiely, "Rushing Drugs to Market," *Technology Review* 90, no. 6 (August/September 1987): 12.

25. "FDA Reform and the European Medicines Evaluation Agency," *Harvard Law Review* 108, no. 8 (June 1995): 2015.

26. Ibid.

27. Barry G. Rabe, "A New Era in States' Climate Policies?," in *Changing Climate Politics: U.S. Policies and Civic Action,* edited by Yael Wolinsky-Nahmias (Washington: CQ Press, 2015), p. 55.

28. Mary D. Nichols, "California's Climate Change Program: Lessons for the Nation," *UCLA Journal of Environmental Law and Policy* 27, no. 2 (2009): 191.

29. Ann E. Carlson, "Regulatory Capacity and State Environmental Leadership: California's Climate Policy," *Fordham Environmental Law Review* 24 (2013): 83.

30. Ibid., p. 65.

31. Ibid.

32. Quoted in ibid., p. 79.

33. Nichols, "California's Climate Change Program," p. 185.

34. Carlson, "Regulatory Capacity and State Environmental Leadership," p. 81.

35. Charles F. Sabel and Jonathan Zeitlin, eds., *Experimentalist Governance in the European Union: Towards a New Architecture* (Oxford University Press, 2010); Peter May, "Policy Learning and Failure," *Journal of Public Policy* 12, no. 4 (1992): 331–54.

**14**

# Regulatory Excellence via Multiple
# Forms of Expertise

DAVID LEVI-FAUR

*All of them are right; what is wrong is only what
they deny, not what they affirm.*

—Abraham Kaplan, *The Conduct of Inquiry*

**THE SEARCH FOR EXCELLENCE** in administrative governance appears on the
policy agenda for many good reasons. Some of these good reasons are known
as government or regulatory governance failures. Still, the extent to which
these governance failures are avoidable or even a fair representation of regulatory reality, rather than a pure reputational shift or ideological debate, is unclear and contested. The same goes for the question of whether government
failures are more widespread, severe, or costly than market failures.[1] Still, whatever the relative merits (and costs) of different strategies of governance and
welfare maximization, one thing is clear: excellence in regulation responds well
both to "real" governance failures and to the perceptions that they are pervasive. In one way or another, excellence seems the right, perhaps the most important, response when trust in government is low and when the delegitimation
of regulation is strong.

Moreover, excellence of any kind—personal and organizational—has
become enshrined in liberal Western societies, so it is hardly surprising that
aspirations of excellence now appear widely on regulatory agencies' mission
statements. In a certain sense, excellence is not a leadership choice anymore.

It is not even an organizational choice. It is taken for granted. It has become a core value that shapes identity, mission, and strategy. Excellence is actively promoted and nurtured by global organizations that act sometimes as "model missionaries" and other times as "model mongers."[2] Excellence strategies are often promoted in the language and forms of the diffusion of "best practices" and nurtured via "twinning."[3] One should take it for granted that excellence will remain high on the agendas of, or at least in the public discourses of, regulators around the world.

Still, the search for regulatory excellence, while commendable on moral and institutional grounds, often leads to disappointment. Disappointment will emerge because there are many, often conflicting, dimensions of excellence, and because excellence comes with substantive material costs. These costs include the costs of expertise, in both human capital and research and coordination capacities. Furthermore, excellence requires some difficult internal decisions about a regulatory organization's priorities, even with respect to excellence itself. As noted, there are many dimensions of excellence. Excellence in risk analysis is not excellence in public participation; excellence in prevention of risks is not necessarily excellence in risk spreading and risk mitigation; and excellence in reducing red tape does not necessarily equate to excellence in developing political strategies. On top of all this comes an understanding of the problems associated with the production, organization, dissemination, and translation of knowledge that make expert-based decisionmaking in the field of regulation particularly risky.

Public policy processes in general, and regulatory processes in particular, are increasingly dominated by experts. Excellence does not come on its own. It assumes, even embeds, the idea of expertise and is tightly coupled with it. Not many, especially in academic circles, would dispute the suggestion that a necessary condition for a best-in-class regulator is "world-class knowledge" and access to "world-class experts." More than at any time in the past, we live in a "knowledge economy" and a "knowledge society," which favor "reason-based" political and organizational processes. Even if one does not personally accept these suggestions, I doubt many would dispute the argument that current social, economic, and political processes (not to mention scientific and technological processes) are taking government and governance in this direction. Expertise has become the sine qua non of excellence. This is all part of a growing dominance of knowledge- and expert-based legitimacy.[4]

To a large extent, this chapter aims at coupling, decoupling, and recoupling the two "e"s: "excellence" and "expertise." A growing tendency to favor both agency independence and so-called risk-based regulation reinforces the dominance of a certain type of expertise, often that held by economists with advanced technical capacities in econometrics and modeling. The chapter's main argument is that regulators instead would do well to design institutions that allow other professions to perform creative and useful roles in regulatory decisionmaking, implementation, and evaluation. Regulatory excellence comes from fostering the institutional capacities that bring diverse kinds of expertise into the decisionmaking process and in this way allow different and multiple rationalities to play out within the regulatory organization.

## AGENCY INDEPENDENCE AND THE SEARCH FOR EXCELLENCE

Since the 1990s, independence has become a worldwide "gold standard" for regulatory agencies, treated as a prerequisite for excellent performance and outcomes. Independence is expected to provide for pure professional decisionmaking at the level of rulemaking, monitoring, and rule enforcement. It is not a new idea. The origins of "agency independence," and the set of interests, institutions, and ideas that promote it, are as old as bureaucracy itself. Still, the idea has gained dominance in recent years and nowadays holds the status of "taken for granted" in the field of regulation. The movement for central bank independence, together with the expectation that central banks will adopt increasingly narrow mission goals, led the way in the 1980s and 1990s and fostered in other realms the creation of hundreds of so-called independent regulatory agencies.[5]

The model of agency independence originated primarily in the United States in the financial sector, with its central banks and institutions supervising stock markets. But it is now the dominant organizational form for agencies in numerous spheres and nations around the world. Independence, like "agencification" more generally, is supposed to shield expert decisionmaking from undue influence and prevent two important kinds of capture: capture by politicians, and capture by business and other narrow interests. Capture biases the regulatory decisionmaking process. Accountability, transparency, and regulatory competition are often proposed, and rightly so, as characteristics that reduce the vulnerability of agencies to capture.

In many respects, the diffusion of independence as best practice and the separation of regulatory functions from other functions of government are evident in the rise of a special type of regulatory experts: the "regulocrats." Like bureaucrats, the regulocrats build on the notion that their expertise is superior to that of nonspecialists. Still, unlike many of the postwar bureaucrats, the regulocrats of today manage to keep one leg in their professional group, be it engineering, planning, law, economics, public administration, management, sociology, or science. Not only do the regulocrats regulate rather than provide services and manage delivery, but they also have an affiliation with professional groups and peers outside the state. (There are, of course, differences across nations and sectors.) Regulocrats' mobilization, promotion, role perceptions, and career patterns are shaped with at least one eye always on the norms and ideas in their respective professions and academic disciplines.

The growing importance of professional groups, and more generally the growing influence of academic knowledge, on the preferences and worldviews of the regulocrats suggests, on the face of it, more rational decisionmaking. But this expectation for greater rationality finds its limits. One of these lies in the fragmented organization of knowledge production in academia and the professions. Academia and the professions are organized around sets of skills and jurisdictions, not around problems. Because problems usually, perhaps always, are not confined to the domain of one profession or knowledge domain, actors with a strong reliance on professional or academic expertise may find themselves unable to solve them. If capture by outsiders—politicians or narrow interests—suggests the need for greater agency independence, then the current state of the production and application of knowledge suggests that the heads of regulatory agencies also need to carefully assess the limits of integrating expert knowledge into decisions.

## DEPOLITICIZED AGENCIES? DEPOLITICIZED EXPERTS?

The separation between "politics" and "expertise" is not as clear as portrayed in an idealistic account of expert-based decisionmaking. Regulatory agencies are highly politicized, even if politics within these organizations seem different than in the electoral arena. Knowledge, rationality, and reason are always mediated (not to say mobilized or abused) by political processes within and outside organizations. It is common to contrast experts with politicians, and to bring forward the tensions inherent in democratic policymaking, where different types of legitimacy and authority are conflicting. These tensions are real and should be discussed in any analysis of regulatory policymaking. Still, our focus here is not on a dichotomy between the experts and the politicians. Professionals have political skills and use them frequently even if they do not "run" for office.[6] Experts are involved with political struggles within and outside their professions. These struggles represent legitimate and even useful competition between ideas as long as they do not result in "professional domination" and a culture of unreflective knowledge and monorationality.

Perhaps the best example of professional domination nowadays is the hegemony that economists enjoy in regulatory policy.[7] This hegemony is expressed in economists' proprivatization, promarket, and proliberalization recommendations in many policy spheres, including finance, where other points of view and rationalities are presented on only a limited basis. Still, the challenges of professional domination are not confined to the role of economists. They unfold in struggles between managers and physicians, physicians and nurses, psychiatrists and psychologists, psychiatrists and social workers, engineers and lawyers, lawyers and field workers, planners and engineers, and so forth.

The negative effects of professional domination increase with the role of knowledge in decisionmaking, on the one hand, and the combination of "agency independence" and jurisdictional monopolies or cartels, on the other hand. Perhaps we need to develop indexes, measures, and ranking techniques to measure and assess diversity and professional domination in organizations. Such measures would capture the ability of agencies to nurture diversity, to maintain open debate, and to develop strategies for nurturing both in-house diversity and the hiring and mobilization of external professional device. Such measures and studies require, of course, better knowledge of the scientific composition of agencies and the role that science-based knowledge plays in an agency's professional profile.

While we can expect variations across countries, agencies, and sectors, some forms of professional domination are prevalent. One of these can be examined and assessed against the growing tendency to adopt risk-based regulation as a strategy for excellence. From food safety to financial regulation to climate change, regulators are using the language of risk assessment, risk-based regulation, risk communication, and risk analysis.[8] Risk approaches are today more than ever before "promoted as a universal organizing concept for improving the quality, efficiency, and rationality of governance."[9] It is beyond the scope of this chapter to provide an in-depth analysis of risk regulation, but what makes risk regulation useful here is the role it holds for experts. Risk-based regulation reflects the growing dependence of agencies on academic knowledge.

Still, risk-based regulation unavoidably prioritizes some harms over others at the same time that it requires the calculation of probabilities and impacts of adverse outcomes. The criteria for regulatory action are typically not based on legal or moral rights, but on utilitarian principles. Like any other imperialist approaches for governance, risk-based regulation creates its own privileged actors, institutional arrangements, and requirements for decisionmaking and divisions. More important, it rests heavily on the requirement for expert-led decisionmaking. More dependence on academic knowledge may mean increasing the risk of jurisdictional cartelization or even monopoly. Hence, excellence creates its own risks. It is important to clarify that this is not a problem of risk-based regulation, only that risk-based regulation is more prone to this kind of failure than other strategies, such as the adoption of benefit-cost analysis.

Risk-based regulation creates privileged actors: experts with high capacities in econometrics and mathematical modeling. As risks are being calculated, frameworks for risk assessment are being introduced to organizations; risk experts' tools and assumptions, unknown to others, gain advantage. With it, new roles of risk officers are carved into the organizational structure, and new debates and challenges around terms such as "the precautionary principle" emerge. Risk-based regulation is a fascinating phenomenon, and so is the new and innovative understanding of the state's role as a "risk manager."[10] One important element in the debate around risk-based regulation that is rarely discussed, however, is that it increases the reliance on experts in the decision-making process and that its strong reliance on modeling and econometrics increases the dangers of professional dominance.

Professional hegemony or dominance is clearly a characteristic of the processes of professionalization and expert-led decisionmaking. As Abraham Kaplan observes in *The Conduct of Inquiry*:

> In addition to the social pressures from the scientific community there is also at work a very human trait of individual scientists. I call it the law of the instrument, and it may be formulated as follows: Give a small boy a hammer, and he will find that everything he encounters needs pounding. It comes as no particular surprise to discover that a scientist formulates problems in a way which requires for their solution just those techniques in which he himself is especially skilled. . . . The fragmentation of a science into "schools" is by no means unknown even in as rigorous a discipline as mathematics; what is striking in behavioral science is how unsympathetic and even how hostile to one another such schools often are. . . . For the experimentalist science progresses only in the laboratory; the theoretician views experiments rather as guides and tests for his models and theories; others see the most important task making counts and measures, or arriving at predictions, or formulating explanations; the field worker and clinician have still other viewpoints. All of them are right; what is wrong is only what they deny, not what they affirm.[11]

The ideas that experts have interests, compete for hegemony, and suffer from tunnel vision will not be strange to sociologists of the professions, such as Andrew Abbott, or to political economists who worked on the politics of knowledge and the relations between politics, think tanks, and the distributive allocation of positions and funding to certain professions and rationalities at the expense of others.[12] They are also confirmed by studies of "institutional logic" that compete for attention and prominence and are studied mainly by institutional sociologists.[13]

Nothing of this sort is usually taken into account in the institutional designs of agencies. But regulatory leaders and the designers of regulatory agencies should consider more seriously the tendency of professions to monopolize "jurisdictions" and thus to capture the agency. The probability of agency capture by one profession may rise with an increase in agency independence and with approaches like risk-based regulation that strengthen the role and functions of experts in policy processes.

## EXCELLENCE VIA MULTIPLE RATIONALITIES

What is the solution to the problems created by monolithic forms of expertise? It is expertise itself—but different kinds of expertise. Recognizing the problems associated with professional domination by fragmented, narrow, and specialized forms of academic knowledge, I propose that a managed competition of ideas will provide an ideal strategy for achieving regulatory excellence. The managed competition of ideas recognizes the need to balance dominant expertise and rationalities via leadership strategies that nurture open competition between different kinds of expertise. This should be done using a careful institutional design that protects less privileged forms of expertise within the layers of organizational space. I focus my attention on three professions that are less privileged within regulatory agencies: criminologist, historian, and political scientist. The selection of these three professions is not necessarily systematic, but is based instead on my understanding that they either are not commonly represented in regulatory agencies or are not privileged within the discursive domains of regulatory policy.

### *Can Criminologists Make a Difference?*

There are many reasons why the Securities and Exchange Commission (SEC) failed repeatedly to prevent and to act in a timely fashion against fraudulent behavior in high-profile cases such as those involving Enron, Bernie Madoff, and AIG. One plausible reason, according to criminologist William K. Black, is the scarcity of criminologists in the U.S. financial regulatory systems:

> No federal, state, or local government agency has a "chief criminologist" (or a junior criminologist) position—yet most of them do (or should) serve as "civil law enforcement" agencies. The federal government does

not even have a position entitled "criminologist." In our [that is, the criminologist's] absence, regulatory decisions are frequently made that unknowingly create intensely criminogenic environments that produce widespread fraud and other ills. . . . But a subtler public policy failure has occurred in part because criminologists are excluded from the policy debates on regulation.[14]

How could well-trained criminologists help the SEC or any other regulatory agency? Criminologists, more than any other profession, have expertise in criminal behavior, deviation, and compliance, an expertise that extends beyond traditional criminal domains. Where some professions examine regulation and compliance strategies via procedural justice, political feasibility, or cost-effectiveness, criminologists approach regulation by seeking to understand fraud: fraud prevention, detection, and mitigation. They also have a better idea of the characteristics and signals that are typical of criminogenic environments and how to design architectures that are less subject to noncompliance. These include rapid growth, rapid change, shifts in the organization of industries, and new technologies that destroy old institutions and existing clubs and other types of networks. If regulation is ultimately about enhancing compliance, and indeed it is, then criminologists have a lot to contribute.

The idea that criminology matters to regulation goes hand in hand with the transformation of criminology itself.[15] There were times when criminology was mainly about social deviance, "street-level" individual crimes, deterrence, prisons, and punishment. But not anymore. Even if the traditional subjects still define the field overall, the criminology agenda today includes compliance, the emergence of social norms, corporate crimes, white-collar crimes, a wide range of mechanisms for dispute settlement, and a wide range of enforcement strategies, such as naming and shaming. What criminologists bring to the regulatory process is an understanding of deviant behavior and compliance strategies in organizations. In this regard, they have perspectives, capacities, and types of knowledge that are highly relevant to regulatory agencies that prioritize compliance, whether with finance and antitrust rules or with food safety and other forms of risk regulation.

It seems only logical that every regulatory agency would benefit from having a compliance department and a "chief criminologist." Even if a chief criminologist would not have prevented the Enron, Madoff, and other financial scandals, the rationale for institutionalizing the functions of a chief criminologist is so compelling that one must wonder why criminologists do not occupy more prominent positions in regulatory agencies. The answers lie in the realm of professional power, the internal organization of academic knowledge, and institutional path dependence rather than in the realm of necessity, usefulness, and regulatory excellence.

### *Does an Excellent Regulator Need a Chief Historian?*

While many of us know the histories of our respective countries, only some of us know well the histories of our own organizations, and even fewer of us systematically and authoritatively use lessons from our organizations' histories in decisionmaking and argumentation. The same is true for most people who work in regulatory organizations, and yet their lack of a thorough understanding of their organizations' histories makes them susceptible to repeating significant mistakes of the past. Excellent regulators will incorporate historical knowledge into their practices, "thinking in time" to make more effective decisions.

Historians are the custodians of an organization's memory of events, decisions, procedures, and conflicts that define the inside and outside of the organization from the moment it is first conceived. An organization's history is probably best understood in comparison with other organizations' histories and with an eye toward political, economic, and social developments that shape the organization's legitimacy, capacities, and legal and political mandates. We need organizational history in order to avoid the mistakes of the past as well as to extend our views and understanding of the options for action and inaction at any given moment. We need to form strong "organizational memories" and use the processes that create and enhance organizational memory in a manner that will allow the regulators and regulatory agencies to connect their "memory" to current practices of "knowledge management" and decisionmaking.

Organizational history can also help form a strong organizational identity. By "strong," I do not mean a manipulated image and the abuse of disciplinary tools, but strong in the sense of possessing a reflexive understanding of the organization's history. Such an identity-building process should allow flexibility and adaptation in the organizational identity itself. The benefits of a strong organizational identity include the promotion of organizational ethos and commitment to the basic values and goals of the organization. Both organizational memory and organizational identity facilitate the role of regulatory organizations as learning organizations. They may also help the organization meet its basic intellectual and social legitimacy concerns. The intellectual awareness and capacities of a historian should enhance regulators' courage to speak truth to people in power.

We need "chief historians" in regulatory agencies because historical reasoning or thinking is useful in decisionmaking. True, historical knowledge may well be lacking in "the predictive precision that is usually claimed by quantitative or social science models," but "what it offers instead is a systematic way to understand the changing context of organizations, communities, and policies within which planners pursue their profession."[16]

Of course, there are no easy ways to make historical knowledge more prominent in the life of organizations. It is certain, though, that the job should not be automatically entrusted to the "chief archivist" of the organization. The "chief historian" job in organizations should be elevated from the basement to the higher floors of the organization, closer to where strategy is shaped and decisionmaking takes place.

### Might Regulators Need a Chief Political Scientist Too?

A "chief political scientist" can be useful to regulatory agencies in a variety of ways. I'll focus here on two. The first is to advise on agency strategy in three key political arenas—the regulatory, parliamentary, and judicial—and in decisions that affect the stakeholders who are integral to the agency's work. Regulatory excellence means not only success in getting support for the agency's goals but also success in nurturing the political environment of the agency. Regulators need to understand the political environment in which the social and business stakeholders are working and design proactive responses to the most pressing and important aspects of those environments. Excellent regulators understand the interests and constraints of their stakeholders, have a realistic understanding of political capacities, and work to enhance those capacities in the relevant arenas and with key stakeholders. The chief political scientist would help with all of these tasks. He or she would also help the agency to develop a clear political identity and to escape the myth that regulation must be depoliticized. Although political strategies can be designed by non–political scientists, the expertise and professionalism of a capable political scientist provides a basis for successful formulation and implementation of the agency's political strategies and for the legitimacy of the function itself within the organization.

The second way a chief political scientist could help is by advising on, and advocating for, public participation in the regulatory process. The increasing role of regulation in the policymaking process and the accompanying process of professionalization of policymaking requires regulators to think differently and creatively about the meaning of democracy in the regulatory state. The expectations for democratic control via transparency, mechanisms of accountability, and the direct and open participation of different stakeholders in all aspects of their agencies' work will require new institutional designs. The experts in these institutional designs are often political scientists, and perhaps also social psychologists. These social scientists can and should be able to integrate into regulatory processes democratic innovations such as deliberative polls, town meetings, e-democracy, and citizen juries. They also know how to systematically learn from regulatory experiments in democratic deliberation. In doing so, they would not only add democratic criteria to the assessment of the agency's performance but also turn attention from measures of output legitimacy to process and input legitimacy.

### CONCLUSION

We have no need today to justify the search for excellence. Aspirations of excellence might even be taken for granted in the work of government in general and regulatory agencies in particular. It makes perfect sense to strive for excellence as long as agencies and their leaders are professionals. We expect excellence to be one of the core principles that is embedded in the identity and mission of every respectable agency; excellence matters even more than other norms and ideals, such as transparency and accountability, which are themselves stepping stones toward excellence.

The key challenge of regulatory excellence centers on how to achieve it. Asking "how" implies that excellence must actively be sought and does not come for free. Achieving excellence most likely will require some tradeoffs with other good aims: tradeoffs between excellence on one dimension or another; excellence in the short term or the long-term; and excellence through debate and professional competition or through unity and professional consensus. In other words, the search for excellence is necessarily more open-ended and difficult than one might assume. To make this observation is not a call for institutional conservatism, stagnation, or incrementalism. It is not to proclaim cynicism or engage in "excellence denial." Instead, it is to recognize the importance of organizational strategies that emphasize excellence in regulators' *capacities*, alongside the day-to-day investment in short-term performance. Building the capacity to deploy different kinds of expertise will provide the best chance of achieving excellence in the long and medium terms.

What makes a regulator excellent? Excellent regulators invest in broadening the capacities of their organizations, recognizing that academic and professional knowledge is highly specialized. Any single expert possesses only a narrow knowledge about specific aspects of a regulatory problem. But regulatory problems are in fact multidimensional and can be framed and understood differently by experts from different professions. Even within a single profession, knowledge is transitory and dynamic. Different generations of experts bring with them new and different ideas and values. Most important, excellent regulators recognize that knowledge itself is political, at least in the sense that the production of academic knowledge depends on the funding priorities of powerful institutions and individuals. Given these realities, the excellent regulator learns to allow for different problem definitions and different solutions, and then to transform different points of view through open, and possibly adversarial, discussions that chart a path toward more legitimate and coherent agency strategies.

**NOTES**

1. Charles Wolf Jr., "Market and Non-Market Failures: Comparison and Assessment," *Journal of Public Policy* 7 (January 1987): 43–70.

2. See Albert Bandura, *Social Foundations of Thought and Action: A Social Cognitive Theory* (Englewood Cliffs, N.J.: Prentice Hall, 1985); David Levi-Faur, "The Global Diffusion of Regulatory Capitalism," *Annals of the American Academy of Political and Social Science* 598 (March 2005): 12–32; David Levi-Faur, "'Agents of Knowledge' and the Convergence on a 'New World Order': A Review Article," *Journal of European Public Policy* 12 (October 2005): 954–65.

3. See Claudio M. Radaelli, "The Diffusion of Regulatory Impact Analysis—Best Practice or Lesson-Drawing?," *European Journal of Political Research* 43 (August 2004): 723–47; Dimitris Papadimitriou and David Phinnemore, "Exporting Europeanization to the Wider Europe: The Twinning Exercise and Administrative Reform in the Candidate Countries and Beyond," *Southeast European and Black Sea Studies* 3 (May 2003): 1–22.

4. Gili S. Drori and others, *Science in the Modern World Polity: Institutionalization and Globalization* (Stanford University Press, 2002).

5. Levi-Faur, "The Global Diffusion of Regulatory Capitalism," pp. 12–32; Jacint Jordana, David Levi-Faur, and Xavier Fernandez i Marín, "The Global Diffusion of Regulatory Agencies: Channels of Transfer and Stages of Diffusion," *Comparative Political Studies* 44 (October 2011): 1343–69.

6. James Q. Wilson, ed., *The Politics of Regulation* (New York: Basic Books, 1980).

7. See Yves Dezalay and Bryant G. Garth, *The Internationalization of Palace Wars: Lawyers, Economists, and the Contest to Transform Latin American States* (University of Chicago Press, 2002); Marion Fourcade, *Economists and Societies: Discipline and Profession in the United States, Britain, and France, 1890s to 1990s* (Princeton University Press, 2009).

8. Bridget M. Hutter, *Regulation and Risk: Occupational Health and Safety on the Railways* (Oxford University Press, 2001).

9. Henry Rothstein, Olivier Borraz, and Michael Huber, "Risk and the Limits of Governance: Exploring Varied Patterns of Risk-Based Governance across Europe," *Regulation and Governance* 7 (June 2013): 215–35, 218.

10. David A. Moss, *When All Else Fails: Government as the Ultimate Risk Manager* (Harvard University Press, 2004).

11. Abraham Kaplan, *The Conduct of Inquiry: Methodology for Behavioral Science* (New Brunswick, N.J.: Transaction, 1973), pp. 28–30.

12. See Andrew Abbott, *The System of Professions: An Essay on the Division of Expert Labor* (University of Chicago Press, 1988); Levi-Faur, "The Global Diffusion of Regulatory Capitalism," pp. 12–32.

13. Chad Michael McPherson and Michael Sauder, "Logics in Action: Managing Institutional Complexity in a Drug Court," *Administrative Science Quarterly* 58 (April 2013): 165–96.

14. William K. Black, "Why Doesn't the SEC Have a 'Chief Criminologist'?," *The Criminologist* 29 (November/December 2004): 2.

15. See David H. Bayley and Clifford D. Shearing, "The Future of Policing," *Law and Society Review* 30 (November 1996): 585–606; John Braithwaite, "The New Regulatory State and the Transformation of Criminology," *British Journal of Criminology* 40 (March 2000): 222–38.

16. Carl Abbott and Sy Adler, "Historical Analysis as a Planning Tool," *Journal of the American Planning Association* 55 (Autumn 1989): 472.

# 15

# Insurance and the Excellent Regulator

## CARY COGLIANESE AND HOWARD KUNREUTHER

**REGULATION STANDS AS ONE** of society's primary tools for managing the risks that pervade modern life. But regulation is not the only tool; insurance is another important risk management tool. In addition to providing a source of compensation for losses after risks have materialized, insurance can serve a regulatory role, helping to prevent risks from arising in the first place. When insurance premiums are risk-based, they encourage policyholders to invest in cost-effective loss reduction measures—an appropriate benchmark for regulatory excellence. Using risk-based insurance as a model, regulators can aspire to develop and enforce rules in such a way that they provide regulated firms with similar incentives to reduce their risk, yielding cost-effective outcomes for society.

Regulators seeking excellence can learn much from insurance. As Bridget Hutter argues in chapter 7, "excellent regulators" today have come to be "defined as excellent risk managers." Insurance as a model for regulatory excellence follows quite naturally from scholars' and policy advisers' recommendation that regulation become more *risk-based*.[1] If regulation is to do so, then regulators should design their rules and target their enforcement resources in ways that better mimic a well-designed insurance market operating in conjunction with well-designed liability rules.

Insurance markets themselves, though, do not always satisfy the fundamental precept of premiums reflecting risk, something that is clearly the case when it comes to low-probability, high-consequence events—the very kind of events that regulation often must address. Furthermore, there is empirical evidence that many individuals faced with low-probability, high-consequence events do not purchase insurance, even when premiums are subsidized.[2] This implies that insurance markets for these events will not work unless regulations mandate the purchase of insurance with risk-based premiums. For this reason, governments at times impose requirements that individuals buy health insurance, businesses pay workers' compensation premiums, or property owners in areas subject to flooding purchase flood insurance.

And yet, compelling people to buy insurance where premiums reflect risk can impose very high costs on individuals with low incomes. For individuals with significant budgetary constraints, financial assistance for insurance premiums may need to be provided through general public funding, such as means-tested vouchers. The best public policy strategy in these cases will depend on the coordinated use of different tools: insurance, regulation, and redistributive subsidies.

Our main purpose in this chapter is to draw lessons from insurance for regulators seeking excellence. The most important of these lessons lies in the need to align public policy effectively with private markets. Both insurance and regulation can benefit each other when public and private strategies are deployed synergistically. The excellent regulator must ultimately understand that it is part of an entire system of both public and private actors and that its success depends on more than just its own policies and practices.

## RISK MANAGEMENT AND RISK-BASED REGULATION

Although the word "risk" is often associated with dangerous activities— whether daredevil acts or complex industrial operations with narrow margins of safety—nearly every human endeavor poses some risk of harm. As a result, no one can go through life avoiding risk altogether, nor can societies protect their members from all risk. But risk can and must be managed. Sometimes specific risks can be virtually eliminated through regulation, such as when products or work practices are banned. For example, the U.S. experience with mandating the phase-out of lead as a gasoline additive in the 1970s eliminated that particular exposure pathway and its associated public health risks. More often, though, regulation manages risks rather than eliminating them.

Risks can be managed in many different ways. Consider the risk of physical damage, injuries, and fatalities associated with automobile accidents.[3] Regulation aims to reduce this risk through actions that lower the chances of accidents occurring, such as through driver training, speed limits, and equipment standards. It also works to reduce the consequences of an accident through protective measures, such as having manufacturers install seat belts or air bags.

Harms can also be lessened by responsive actions taken in the wake of accidents, such as when emergency medical responders and hospital staffs treat accident victims. Across the gamut of activities that make up modern life—from the construction of buildings to the consumption of food and drugs, and from the lending practices of banks to the operation of industrial facilities—regulation works to manage the risks that arise in the private marketplace.[4]

Sometimes the need for regulation arises due to individuals' lack of knowledge of the risks associated with products and services, which justifies regulation to require sellers to disclose relevant information to buyers. Other times regulation addresses what are often inevitable spillovers of risks, where a third party not involved in a market transaction for a good or service must bear some of the harms associated with that transaction. Pollution is a classic example of such a spillover, and environmental regulations are the principal means by which society manages this risk.

But just because regulations are designed to manage risk, this does not mean that they easily achieve their desired objectives. Risks are challenging to regulate not only because markets fail in classic terms due to information asymmetries and negative externalities, but also because humans are not very good at processing information, something particularly prone to occur with respect to low-probability events.[5] Furthermore, a focus on short time horizons often leads people to avoid taking costly action today to mitigate risks that would not materialize for some time to come.[6]

When faced with these and other challenges, what are regulators to do? Many scholars and policy commentators advise that regulation become "risk-based," by which they generally mean that regulators should analyze risks more carefully when making decisions.[7] Indeed, regulators around the world are pursuing rigorous risk analysis before they create new regulations, and thinking about risk priorities when deciding how to allocate scarce enforcement resources. Examples of risk's ascendancy in regulatory circles range from elaborate governmental procedures requiring the use of regulatory impact assessments[8] to Malcolm Sparrow's beguilingly simple admonition that regulators should "pick important problems and fix them."[9]

Sometimes risk-based is taken to mean that regulators should address the worst risks first.[10] Although such a strategy has a powerful common-sense appeal, it leaves important questions unanswered. For example, even if a regulator targets the worst risks first, nothing in a worst-first principle tells the regulator what exactly to do about those targeted risks. Should the aim be to eliminate those risks completely? Or should the worst risks be reduced to the level of, say, the second-worst risks? How much should society spend to make reductions in the worst risks? If the worst risks are too costly to address in relation to their expected, discounted benefits—and the risks of asteroids hitting planet earth might be an example—they may not be worth devoting as much attention to as moderate risks, where the expected, discounted benefits from regulation are higher than the expected, discounted costs.[11] What regulators need is a framework for defining what is meant by excellent, risk-based regulation. The theory of insurance can help provide such a framework.

## INSURANCE AS A RISK MANAGEMENT TOOL

Insurance, operating against a backdrop of clear liability rules, constitutes a "regulatory" vehicle for managing risk by compensating harmed individuals and encouraging those who engage in risky behavior to invest in mitigation efforts.[12] Background liability rules impose a duty of care on risk producers, requiring that they pay damages to anyone they are found to have harmed. Insurance can cover those damages and in so doing achieve outcomes similar to an ideal regulatory system. By setting premiums that reflect risk, insurance encourages investments in cost-effective protective measures to reduce future losses from untoward events. Even a brief review of how optimal insurance markets operate can reveal important insights about how risk regulation should ideally function and can provide a basis for regulators seeking to use insurance as a regulatory tool.

Insurance premiums are considered to be risk-based when the price charged to cover an event that has a loss $L$ with a probability $p$ is set equal to the expected loss (that is, $pL$).[13] An insurer will also usually charge an additional cost to cover its own expenses and generate a profit. An insurer normally relies on risk pooling and the law of large numbers when providing coverage against a specific risk. If the risks are independent and there are a significant number of policyholders, then the variance in the expected loss is very small, so the insurer can estimate with some degree of accuracy how large its annual claims payments will be *on average*.

A benchmark model of insurance supply assumes that insurance companies are maximizing long-run expected profits for their owners in a competitive market. In this environment, there are many insurance firms, each of which is free to charge any premium for a specified amount of coverage. The assumption of competition implies that their premiums will be high enough to allow the insurers to cover their costs and make a reasonable profit.

For a risk to be insurable, the insurer must have the ability to identify and quantify, or estimate at least partially, the chances of the event occurring and the extent of losses likely to be incurred; it will specify a premium for which there is sufficient demand and incoming revenue to cover the development, marketing, operating, cost of holding capital and claims processing, and yield a net positive profit over a specified time horizon. In setting a premium, an insurer must consider problems associated with asymmetry of information (*adverse selection* and *moral hazard*) and with the degree of *correlation of the risk.*

If the insurer cannot differentiate the risks facing two groups of potential insurance buyers, and if all buyers know their own risk, then the insurer is likely to suffer unsustainable losses if it sets the same premium for both groups by using the entire population as a basis for its estimate. This situation, referred to as *adverse selection,* can be rectified by the insurer charging a high enough premium to cover the losses from the "bad" risks. In so doing, the "good" risks might purchase only partial protection, or no insurance at all, because they consider the price of coverage to be too expensive relative to their risk.[14]

*Moral hazard* refers to an increase in the expected loss (probability or amount of loss conditional on an event occurring) due to individuals and firms behaving more carelessly as a result of purchasing insurance. A firm with insurance protection may alter its behavior in ways that increase the expected loss relative to what it would have been without coverage. If the insurer cannot predict this behavior and relies on past loss data from uninsured firms to estimate the distribution of claim payments, the resulting premium is likely to be too low to cover expected losses. The introduction of deductibles, co-insurance, or upper limits on coverage can be useful tools in reducing moral hazard, encouraging insureds to engage in less risky behavior because they know they will incur part of the losses from an adverse event.

The potential for a *high correlation of the risk* of extreme events has an impact on the tail of the distribution and normally requires the insurer to hold additional capital in liquid form to protect itself against large losses. The prices charged for disaster insurance must be sufficiently high to cover not only the expected claims costs and other expenses but also the costs of allocating capital to underwrite this risk. Moreover, because large amounts of risk capital are needed to underwrite catastrophe risk, the resulting premium will be high relative to an insurer's loss expenses simply to earn a fair rate of return on equity and at the same time maintain the insurer's credit rating.

When adverse selection, moral hazard, and correlated risks can be adequately addressed, the setting of risk-based premiums should result in an optimal level of risk reduction by insured firms. If premiums reflect expected losses, and if businesses must purchase insurance because of either regulatory mandates or the threat of subsequent tort liability, then premiums will operate much like a Pareto tax—one set at an amount equal to the expected marginal social costs of the behavior being taxed—forcing firms to internalize the full costs of their business activity. Firms can then be expected to undertake risk prevention strategies whenever the expected costs of doing so will be lower than the decrease in their risk-based premiums.

## WHAT REGULATORS CAN LEARN FROM INSURANCE

The way insurance can perform a regulatory function provides a model for regulators when they approach their work. Regulators can draw at least five lessons from the theory of insurance markets.

First, insurance markets operate efficiently if premiums are risk-based, and regulation also works well when it is risk-based. Insurance, in other words, provides one useful model for operationalizing the widely touted but ambiguous term, "risk-based regulation."[15] Regulators will be more likely to achieve outcomes that are efficient when regulations and their enforcement mimic an optimal insurance market by inducing regulated firms to internalize the full expected losses from their activities.

Second, risk-based insurance encourages policyholders to take actions that reduce their losses because they reduce insurers' expected claims payments and insurers can lower the premiums they charge. In this way, insurance is performance-based, in that the incentives it provides to policyholders are tied to outcomes. Regulators would do well also to focus on outcomes. In appropriate cases, they should use performance standards or market instruments.[16] They also should rely more extensively on mechanisms that measure how well regulations are working.[17]

Third, insurance markets in theory achieve an *optimal* level of risk management in society, which is not always the same as *eliminating* risks. The excellent regulator has a similar objective: to manage a risk so that the expected costs of risk reduction do not exceed the expected benefits of reducing the risk, taking into account the impact this has on other risks.

Fourth, because even excellent regulation will not eliminate most risks, society will need effective ways of compensating those who are harmed. Insurance has a dual function in this regard: providing incentives for reducing risks and compensating individuals through claims payments should one suffer a loss. Although regulators may not have any direct authority or responsibility for providing compensation, a well-ordered society within which a regulator operates will need to have some means of promoting equity and compensation for those who are negatively affected by regulatory decisions. Background liability rules can provide a useful supplement to regulation.

Finally, in the same way that insurance companies must invest in research and actuarial analysis if they are to compute risk-based premiums, excellent regulators need to build strong in-house analytic capacity to understand their risk environments. Regulators need to make a commitment to delivering public value in ways that comport with sound, neutral, risk analysis; they will fail if they are driven by short-term or parochial interests rather than the well-being of the public.


## BEHAVIORAL CHARACTERISTICS OF INSURERS

Although the theory of insurance as a risk management tool provides useful lessons for regulators, insurance markets themselves do not always operate precisely as theory would predict. Insurance firms themselves can deviate from the ideal model due to behavioral factors.

In the case of terrorism, for example, notwithstanding the World Trade Center bombing of 1993, the Oklahoma City bombing of 1995, and other costly terrorist attacks outside of the United States, the likelihood of large claims payments from attacks in the United States was still deemed by insurers in the country to be quite small because, prior to September 11, 2001, the insurance industry in the United States had never suffered catastrophic terrorism losses. In fact, actuaries and underwriters did not price the risk associated with terrorism nor did they exclude this coverage from their standard commercial policies.[18]

Following the terrorist attacks of September 11th, most insurers discontinued offering terrorism coverage given the refusal of global reinsurers to provide them with protection against severe losses from another attack. The few companies that did provide insurance charged extremely high premiums to protect themselves against a serious loss.[19] Concern about high premiums and limited supply of coverage led Congress to pass the Terrorism Risk Insurance Act at the end of 2002 that provided a federal backstop up to $100 billion for private insurance claims related to terrorism.[20]

The ambiguities associated with the likelihood of an extreme event occurring and the resulting outcomes raise a number of challenges for insurers with respect to pricing their policies. Actuaries and underwriters use rules of thumb that reflect their concern about those risks where past data do not indicate with precision what the loss probability is. Consider estimating the premium for wind damage to homes in New Orleans from future hurricanes. Actuaries will first use their best estimates of the likelihood of hurricanes of different intensities to determine an expected annual loss to the property and contents of a particular residence. When recommending a premium that the underwriter should charge, they will increase this figure to reflect the amount of perceived ambiguity in the probability of the hurricanes or the uncertainty in the resulting losses.

A recent web-based experiment provided actuaries and underwriters in insurance companies with scenarios in which they were asked to seek advice and request probability forecasts from different groups of experts and then determine what price to charge for coverage for flood damage and wind damage from hurricanes. It found that the average premium insurers would charge was approximately 30 percent higher for coverage against flood or wind damage risks if the probability of damage was ambiguous rather than well specified and if the experts were conflicted over their estimates. The data reveal that insurers would likely charge more in the case of conflict ambiguity (that is, when experts disagree on point estimates) than with imprecision ambiguity (when experts agree on a range of probabilities, recognizing that they cannot estimate the probability of the event precisely).[21]

Regulatory officials can exhibit similar behavioral tendencies. They may avoid necessary action for fear of the consequences to their organization if they make a mistake or an unpopular decision. These tendencies will likely be exacerbated when there is ambiguity and uncertainty, precisely the conditions in which regulators must often operate. The best regulators, like the best insurers, will be aware of their behavioral tendencies and strive to counteract or overcome them.

## SYNERGIES BETWEEN INSURANCE AND REGULATION

Achieving the regulatory effect of risk-based premiums will often depend on background liability or a mandate to purchase insurance, highlighting the synergistic relationship between insurance and regulation. This relationship can manifest itself in two ways: well-enforced regulation can improve insurance markets, and insurance markets can reinforce regulation.

### How Well-Enforced Regulation Can Reduce Insured Losses

After Hurricane Andrew devastated parts of Florida in 1992, the state government started to reevaluate its building code standards and enforcement. In 1995, officials in the state's coastal areas stepped up their efforts to enforce existing high-wind design provisions in the code for new residential housing. In 2002, the state adopted a new building code that incorporated hurricane-resistant design features and required all licensed engineers, architects, and contractors to take training courses on these new standards.

When Hurricane Charley made landfall at Port Charlotte in the same state in 2004, the value of the more robust regulation of building construction became clear in the form of lower insurance claims. The Institute for Business and Home Safety reported data from an insurer with more than five thousand policies in effect at the time in heavily hit Charlotte County. According to an analysis of the approximately 2,100 hurricane-damage claims filed on these policies, homes built after 1995 had an average claim severity 60 percent *lower* than homes built in prior years.[22]

### How Insurance and Third-Party Inspectors Can Support Regulation[23]

One of regulatory agencies' biggest challenges lies in inspecting facilities, as typically a regulator does not have enough inspectors to audit all the firms under its purview. When a regulator inspects compliant, low-risk firms, it wastes scarce inspection resources, not to mention the time of firms' managers. But without a well-designed inspection process, how can the regulator know that any firm is low risk? At the same time, low-risk firms need a credible way to distinguish themselves from high-risk competitors. One way to do this would be for the regulator to delegate part of the inspection process to the private sector, through insurance companies and third-party auditors. If a firm chose not to avail itself of such an opportunity to be inspected by third parties, the regulator could reasonably infer that the firm is more likely to be high risk. In this way, insurance and third-party inspection not only could substantially reduce the number of firms the regulator has to audit, but the regulator could deploy its inspectors more efficiently. As more low-risk firms credibly reveal themselves to the regulator, the likelihood would increase that regulatory inspectors would be auditing more of the high-risk firms.

In practice, the use of third-party inspections and insurance has demonstrated beneficial effects. The Hartford Steam Boiler Inspection and Insurance Company (HSB) initiated private boiler inspections coupled with insurance as far back as the 1860s. HSB always viewed insurance as secondary to loss prevention, with a large part of insurance premiums used to cover engineering and inspection services. To reduce future risks, HSB conducted extensive research on boiler construction, which eventually led to much more safely designed boilers. In addition, one of the key factors contributing to the reduction in boiler accidents over time has been a regulatory requirement adopted in all states that boiler owners submit to an annual inspection by a licensed third-party inspector.[24]

Insurance has also played a positive role in the regulation of workplace accidents. The U.S. Occupational Safety and Health Administration (OSHA) has been regulating workplace safety directly since 1971. Although OSHA regulation promotes safety to some extent, research shows that market-based workers' compensation insurance has created significant incentives for firms to maintain safer workplaces.[25] Today, almost every wage and salary earner in the United States is covered by some kind of workers' compensation system that requires employers to buy insurance to compensate their workers who are injured on the job. Since premiums are usually linked to performance, firms have financial incentives to invest in reducing safety risks. It has been estimated that, if the incentives of workers' compensation were removed, there would be an increase of over 30 percent in work-related fatalities in the United States; this translates to an annual increase of 1,200 workers who would die from job-related accidents.[26]

### THE NEED FOR EFFECTIVE PUBLIC-PRIVATE PARTNERSHIPS

Given the synergistic relationship between insurance and regulation, government officials and insurers must forge effective public-private partnerships to achieve societal goals.[27] The United States' experience with its National Flood Insurance Program (NFIP) illustrates the vital need for effective coordination between the public and private sectors in addressing risk management problems.[28]

After the Great Mississippi Flood of 1927, there developed a widespread belief among private insurance companies that flood peril was uninsurable. It was thought that floods could not be insured by the private sector alone for several reasons: adverse selection; exceedingly high risk-based premiums (so high that no one would be willing to pay them); and catastrophic flood losses that would cause insurer insolvencies.[29]

In response to concerns that private flood insurance was not widely available, Congress created the NFIP in 1968 to make insurance available to homeowners and small businesses. Administered through the Federal Emergency Management Agency (FEMA), the NFIP offers flood insurance to residents and businesses in participating communities, written and serviced by qualified private insurers at rates set nationally by the NFIP. Homeowners in designated flood-prone areas who have a mortgage from a federally backed or federally regulated lender are required to purchase flood insurance for the duration of the loan; however, it appears that this requirement is not evenly and robustly enforced around the country. In addition, policyholders who own older buildings that do not meet local floodplain building standards pay premiums discounted roughly 40–45 percent from the actuarially fair or risk-based price, although their premiums are still higher than those paid by owners of compliant structures.[30] In the aftermath of major hurricanes that made landfall in 2004, 2005, 2008, and 2012, the NFIP has had to borrow a total of nearly $27 billion from the U.S. Treasury to meet its claims obligations. In addition, because premiums have not reflected risk, property owners have not faced adequate incentives to undertake cost-effective risk mitigation.

In July 2012, President Obama signed the Biggert-Waters Flood Insurance Reform Act to reform and improve the NFIP. This law, which passed with overwhelming bipartisan support, recognized that flood insurance premiums should reflect risk and took steps to put the NFIP on a more financially sound foundation. But as higher premiums began to be phased in for some properties, many legislators wavered in their commitment to risk-based pricing given concerns raised by many of their constituents that they would not be able to afford coverage or that they were being treated unfairly. In response, Congress passed and President Obama signed the Homeowner Flood Insurance Affordability Act in March 2014, which eliminated or delayed the implementation of many of the rate changes made in the Biggert-Waters Act, leaving the financial soundness of the NFIP still in jeopardy and reducing the incentives for property owners to take needed risk management measures.

The NFIP is an example of a public-private cooperation to achieve risk management objectives. The program still needs a better way of aligning public and private action to maintain financial stability, promote optimal mitigation, and ensure equity and affordability. Going forward, insurance premiums need to be risk-based to communicate accurately the degree of the flood hazard and to encourage investments in loss-reduction measures. To address affordability concerns of low- and middle-income homeowners, means-tested vouchers can be coupled with hazard mitigation requirements to be financed with low-interest loans. The requirement for hazard mitigation would reduce future disaster losses both for the NFIP and for low- and middle-income families. The voucher program would cover a portion of the higher insurance premium as well as the costs of the loan for mitigating damage to the residential property. Homeowners who invest in mitigation measures would be given a premium discount to reflect the reduction in expected losses from floods, whether or not they had an insurance voucher. Well-enforced cost-effective building codes and seals of approval would provide an additional rationale for undertaking these loss-reduction measures.[31]

The need for a coordinated, well-designed public-private partnership to manage flood risks provides a broader lesson about regulatory excellence. As discussed in chapter 1, success for regulators ultimately depends on more than just the actions that the regulator takes. Regulatory success depends to a large extent on the actions that regulated entities take, as a regulator's raison d'être is to shape those entities' behavior so as to improve societal outcomes.

In addition, regulators need a supportive and well-designed legislative mandate and infrastructure. If the optimal solution to a regulatory problem is for regulators to compel businesses to internalize high spillover costs—much like the NFIP needs to charge premiums that reflect risk—regulation can only be effective if the legislature remains committed to the underlying objectives. If legislators backslide in the face of political pressures, they can blunt the credibility of needed regulation. In the forty-year history of the implementation of the U.S. Clean Air Act, for example, Congress extended legislative deadlines for compliance with national ambient air-quality standards, presumably slowing the pace of air-quality improvements.[32] Today, some firms may be less likely to take seriously the need to invest in steps to lower greenhouse gas emissions if their managers anticipate legislative capitulation once significant compliance costs start to accrue.

The legislative backlash against the Biggert-Waters Act arose because the premium increases authorized by that law were not paired with other mechanisms to help low- and middle-income property owners. The NFIP saga not only reveals the need for ways to make risk-based insurance affordable through mechanisms such as means-tested vouchers and low-interest loans; it also offers another lesson for regulatory excellence. Even when regulations' benefits outweigh their costs, these impacts will not be evenly distributed throughout society. Some segments of society will end up bearing more of regulations' costs or suffering more of their other direct or indirect adverse effects.[33]

Sometimes distributional considerations can affect the design and implementation of a regulation, such as when the U.S. Environmental Protection Agency developed a new source performance standard for coal-powered utilities in the 1970s that required the installation of expensive scrubbers, rather than the use of lower-cost, low-sulfur coal, in part to protect coal operations in central and eastern parts of the United States, which produce high-sulfur coal.[34] The distribution of regulatory impacts cannot be ignored, but the better way to address them may be through separate, means-tested transfer programs or tax adjustments.[35]

## CONCLUSION

This foray into the world of insurance offers important lessons for the regulator seeking excellence. At one level, the theory of insurance provides a model set of aspirations for the regulator, namely to reduce risk to optimal levels and create incentives that will induce cost-effective change. Of course, insurance cannot be a substitute for all regulation. In reality, insurance markets often do not operate as they should in theory. Indeed, for that reason, insurance it-self often depends on effective regulation, including well-enforced mandates that risk producers or risk bearers buy insurance.

How the burdens of both insurance premiums and regulatory costs are distributed matters, particularly when the costs of insurance and regulation weigh disproportionately on individuals with already limited resources. Find-ing appropriate means of redressing inequities is essential for effective sys-tems of social insurance as well as regulation, but the best way to deal with these distributional considerations may be through independent governmental programs, such as means-tested vouchers or tax credits. Even though such re-source distribution programs are often administered by separate governmen-tal entities, this does not detract from their relevance to the regulator. It only reinforces the notion that an excellent regulator does not operate in isolation.

In the end, regulation and insurance aspire to much the same objective: optimal risk management, with due attention to equity concerns. It makes sense, then, to coordinate insurance with regulation when developing soci-ety's overall risk management portfolio. Regulators seeking excellence can take from insurance markets a model for how to operate, and they can also search for appropriate opportunities to use insurance and third-party inspections to supplement their own regulatory efforts. Excellent risk regulation cannot be undertaken in a vacuum; it needs to work in alignment with liability rules, insurance markets, and the rest of society.

### NOTES

*Acknowledgments:* The authors thank Carol Heller for her excellent editorial assistance with this chapter.

1. As early as 2005, Bridget Hutter noted "the popularity of risk-based regu-lation." Bridget M. Hutter, "The Attractions of Risk-Based Regulation: Account-ing for the Emergence of Risk Ideas in Regulation," CARR Discussion paper 33 (London: London School of Economics and Political Science, Centre for Analysis of Risk and Regulation, 2005) (http://www.lse.ac.uk/accounting/CARR/pdf/DPs /Disspaper33.pdf). That popularity has not abated. In 2012, the regulatory body within the Organization for Economic Cooperation and Development (OECD) adopted a set of internationally affirmed principles of regulatory reform that ex-pressly urged countries to "consider the use of risk-based approaches in the design and enforcement of regulatory compliance strategies." OECD, Recommendation of the Council on Regulatory Policy and Governance, March 22, 2012 (http://www .oecd.org/regreform/regulatory-policy/49990817.pdf). Greg Paoli and Anne Wiles

have noted that the label " 'risk-based' . . . has become a 'badge of legitimacy' for regulatory organizations." Greg Paoli and Anne Wiles, "Key Analytical Capabilities of a Best-in-Class Regulator," Best-in-Class Regulator Initiative Research Paper (University of Pennsylvania, Penn Program on Regulation, 2015) (https://www.law .upenn.edu/live/files/4710-paoliwiles-ppr-researchpaper062015pdf).

2. For more details on the tendency of consumers and insurers to exhibit systematic biases and the tendency to use simple decision rules with respect to low-probability, high-consequence events, see Howard Kunreuther, "The Role of Insurance in Reducing Losses from Extreme Events: The Need for Public-Private Partnerships," *The Geneva Papers* 40 (2015): 741–62.

3. For analyses of automobile risk regulation, see Robert W. Crandall and others, *Regulating the Automobile* (Brookings Institution Press, 1986); John D. Graham, *Auto Safety: Assessing America's Performance* (Dover, Mass.: Auburn House, 1989); Jerry L. Mashaw and David L. Harfst, *The Struggle for Auto Safety* (Harvard University Press, 1990).

4. For discussion of market failure and justifications for regulation, see generally Stephen Breyer, *Regulation and Its Reform* (Harvard University Press, 1984); Cass R. Sunstein, *After the Rights Revolution: Reconceiving the Regulatory State* (Harvard University Press, 1993); W. Kip Viscusi, John M. Vernon, and Joseph E. Harrington Jr., *Economics of Regulation and Antitrust*, 4th ed. (MIT Press, 2005).

5. For excellent treatments of these cognitive tendencies, see Erwann Michel-Kerjan and Paul Slovic, eds., *The Irrational Economist: Making Decisions in a Dangerous World* (New York: Public Affairs, 2010); Daniel Kahneman, *Thinking, Fast and Slow* (New York: Farrar, Straus and Giroux, 2013).

6. Howard Kunreuther, Robert Meyer, and Erwann Michel-Kerjan, "Overcoming Decision Biases to Reduce Losses from Natural Catastrophes," in *Behavioral Foundations of Policy,* edited by Eldar Shafir (Princeton University Press, 2013).

7. For various scholarly discussions of risk-based regulation, see, for example, Julia Black, "Risk-Based Regulation: Choices, Practices and Lessons Being Learnt," in *Risk and Regulatory Policy: Improving the Governance of Risk*, edited by Gregory Bounds (Paris: OECD, 2010); Julia Black, "The Emergence of Risk-Based Regulation and the New Public Risk Management in the United Kingdom," *Public Law* (2005): 512; Christopher Hood, Henry Rothstein, and Robert Baldwin, *The Government of Risk: Understanding Risk Regulation Regimes* (Oxford University Press, 2004); Cary Coglianese, *Listening, Learning, and Leading: A Framework for Regulatory Excellence* (University of Pennsylvania, Penn Program on Regulation, 2015), 44–46 (www.law.upenn.edu/live/files/4946-pprfinalconvenersreportpdf); Robert Baldwin, Martin Cave, and Martin Lodge, *Understanding Regulation: Theory, Strategy, and Practice* (Oxford University Press, 2012), pp. 281–95.

8. Claudio M. Radaelli and Fabrizio De Francesco, *Regulatory Quality in Europe: Concepts, Measures, and Policy Processes* (Manchester University Press, 2007); Jonathan B. Wiener, "Risk Regulation and Governance Institutions," in *Risk and*

*Regulatory Policy: Improving the Governance of Risk,* edited by Gregory Bounds (Paris: OECD, 2010).

9. Malcolm K. Sparrow, *The Regulatory Craft: Controlling Risks, Solving Problems, and Managing Compliance* (Brookings Institution Press, 2000).

10. Perhaps nowhere is the emphasis on "worst first" more evident than in environmental regulation. A former administrator of the U.S. Environmental Protection Agency, William Ruckelshaus, long ago stated that among the many risks regulators confront, they should be "aiming to get at the greatest first." William D. Ruckelshaus, "Risk in a Free Society," *Risk Analysis* 4 (1984): 161. The worst-first orientation has been supported by research findings that show highly varying estimates of the costs per life saved of various risk regulations in the United States. See, for example, Tammy Tengs and others, "Five-Hundred Life-Saving Interventions and Their Cost-Effectiveness," *Risk Analysis* 15 (1995): 369. Various policy recommendations explicitly endorse a worst-first orientation. See, for example, National Academy of Public Administration, *Setting Priorities, Getting Results: A New Direction for EPA* (Washington, 1995). For extended and varied views about a worst-first approach to risk regulation, see Adam M. Finkel and Dominic Golding, eds., *Worst Things First? The Debate over Risk-Based National Environmental Priorities* (Washington: Resources for the Future Press, 1994).

11. Richard Posner devotes considerable attention to asteroid collision risks and argues for increasing investments in space research to better address these risks. Richard A. Posner, *Catastrophe: Risk and Response* (Oxford University Press, 2004).

12. For more in-depth discussion, see Steven Shavell, "Liability for Harm versus Regulation of Safety," *Journal of Legal Studies* 13 (1984): 357; Kenneth R. Richards, "Framing Environmental Policy Instrument Choice," *Duke Environmental Law and Policy Forum* 10 (2000): 221; Adam D. K. Abelkop, "Tort Law as an Environmental Policy Instrument," *Oregon Law Review* 92 (2014): 381. For proposals that would expressly use insurance coupled with liability as a regulatory strategy, see Tom Baker, "Bonded Import Safety Warranties," in *Import Safety: Regulatory Governance in the Global Economy*, edited by Cary Coglianese, Adam M. Finkel, and David Zaring (University of Pennsylvania Press, 2009); Lori S. Bennear, "Beyond Belts and Suspenders: Promoting Private Risk Management in Offshore Drilling," in *Regulatory Breakdown: The Crisis of Confidence in U.S. Regulation,* edited by Cary Coglianese (University of Pennsylvania Press, 2012).

13. The loss corresponds to the risk producers' liability to compensate those who bear the untoward consequences of the risk. More details on the features of risk-based insurance discussed in this section can be found in Howard Kunreuther and Erwann Michel-Kerjan, "Economics of Natural Catastrophe Risk Insurance," in *Handbook of the Economics of Risk and Uncertainty,* edited by Mark J. Machina and W. Kip Viscusi (Amsterdam: Elsevier, 2013).

14. Georges Dionne, Neil A. Doherty, and Nathalie Fombaron, "Adverse Selection in Insurance Markets," in *Handbook of Insurance*, edited by Georges Dionne (Boston: Kluwer, 2000).

15. For discussion of the ambiguity in the concept of "risk-based regulation," see Coglianese, *Listening, Learning, and Leading*, 44–46.

16. Cary Coglianese, "Performance-Based Regulation: Concepts and Challenges," in *Comparative Law and Regulation: Understanding the Global Regulatory Process*, edited by Francesca Bignami and David Zaring (Edward Elgar, 2016); Cary Coglianese, Jennifer Nash, and Todd Olmstead, "Performance-Based Regulation: Prospects and Limitations in Health, Safety and Environmental Protection," *Administrative Law Review* 55 (2003): 705.

17. Cary Coglianese, "Moving Forward with Regulatory Lookback," *Yale Journal on Regulation* 30 (2013): 57–66; Coglianese, *Listening, Learning, and Leading*, 54–69.

18. Howard Kunreuther and Erwann Michel-Kerjan, "Policy Watch: Challenges for Terrorism Risk Insurance in the United States," *Journal of Economic Perspectives* 18 (2004): 201–14.

19. Howard Kunreuther, Mark Pauly, and Stacey McMorrow, *Insurance and Behavioral Economics: Improving Decisions in the Most Misunderstood Industry* (Cambridge University Press, 2013). To illustrate this point, prior to September 11, 2001, Chicago's O'Hare Airport had $750 million of terrorism insurance coverage at an annual premium of $125,000. After the terrorist attacks, insurers offered the airport only $150 million of coverage at an annual premium of $6.9 million. This new premium, if actuarially fair, implies the annual likelihood of a terrorist attack on O'Hare Airport to be approximately 1 in 22 (that is, $6.9 million divided by $150 million), an extremely high probability. The airport was forced to purchase this policy since it could not operate without it. Dwight Jaffee and Thomas Russell, "Markets under Stress: The Case of Extreme Event Insurance," in *Economics for an Imperfect World: Essays in Honor of Joseph E. Stiglitz*, edited by Richard Arnott and others (MIT Press, 2003).

20. For further discussion of this law and its history and structure, see Howard Kunreuther and others, *TRIA after 2014: Examining Risk Sharing under Current and Alternative Designs* (University of Pennsylvania, Wharton Risk Management and Decision Processes Center, 2014) (http://opim.wharton.upenn.edu/risk/library /TRIA-after-2014_full-report_WhartonRiskCenter.pdf).

21. Laure Cabantous and others, "Is Imprecise Knowledge Better Than Conflicting Expertise? Evidence from Insurers' Decisions in the United States," *Journal of Risk and Uncertainty* 42 (2011): 211–32.

22. For further details about this example, see Howard C. Kunreuther and Erwann O. Michel-Kerjan, *At War with the Weather* (MIT Press, 2009), on which this section draws.

23. This subsection of this chapter draws from Howard C. Kunreuther, Patrick J. McNulty, and Yong Kang, "Improving Environmental Safety Through Third Party Inspection Risk Analysis," *Risk Analysis* 22 (April 2002): 309–18.

24. Jweeping Er, "A Third Party Approach to Environmental Regulation: Possible Roles for Insurance Companies" (PhD diss., University of Pennsylvania, 1996).

25. Michael J. Moore and W. Kip Viscusi, *Compensation Mechanisms for Job Risks: Wages, Workers' Compensation, and Product Liability* (Princeton University Press, 1990).

26. W. Kip Viscusi, *Reforming Products Liability* (Harvard University Press, 1991).

27. Cary Coglianese, "Getting the Blend Right: Public-Private Partnerships in Risk Management," Discussion paper prepared for the Wharton Risk Management and Decision Processes Center's 30th Anniversary Symposium (University of Pennsylvania, Wharton School) (http://opim.wharton.upenn.edu/risk/conference/pprs/Coglianese_Getting-the-Blend-Right--Public-Private-Partnerships.pdf).

28. For further details on the NFIP, see Carolyn Kousky and Howard Kunreuther, "Addressing Affordability in the National Flood Insurance Program," *Journal of Extreme Events* 1 (2014): 1–28.

29. Dan R. Anderson, "The National Flood Insurance Program: Problems and Potential," *Journal of Risk and Insurance* 41 (1974): 579–99.

30. Thomas L. Hayes and D. Andrew Neal, *Actuarial Rate Review: In Support of the Recommended October 1, 2011, Rate and Rule Changes* (Washington: Federal Emergency Management Agency, 2011) (www.fema.gov/media-library-data/20130726-1809-25045-6893/actuarial_rate_review2011.pdf).

31. The path forward described in this paragraph is developed in Kousky and Kunreuther, "Addressing Affordability."

32. James E. McCarthy and others, "Clean Air Act: A Summary of the Act and Its Major Requirements" (Congressional Research Service, November 26, 2008), p. 3. Of course, if the alternative to extending air-quality compliance deadlines had been to eliminate entirely federal authority to regulate air quality, then the extended deadlines were the better outcome (assuming that the underlying air-quality standards reflected an optimal level of pollution reduction). For a related argument, see Richard Zeckhauser, "Preferred Policies When There Is a Concern for Probability of Adoption," *Journal of Environmental Economics and Management* 8, no. 3 (1981): 215.

33. Cary Coglianese and Christopher Carrigan, "The Jobs and Regulation Debate," in *Does Regulation Kill Jobs?*, edited by Cary Coglianese, Adam M. Finkel, and Christopher Carrigan (University of Pennsylvania Press, 2013).

34. Bruce A. Ackerman and William T. Hassler, *Clean Coal/Dirty Air: Or How the Clean Air Act Became a Multibillion-Dollar Bail-Out for High-Sulfur Coal Producers* (Yale University Press, 1981).

35. See, for example, Aanund Hylland and Richard Zeckhauser, "Distributional Objectives Should Affect Taxes but Not Program Choice or Design," *Scandinavian Journal of Economics* 81 (1979): 264–84.

# 16

# A Systems Approach to Regulatory Excellence

ANGUS CORBETT

**SYSTEMS ARE ALL AROUND** us. They make up the technology that we use in our daily lives: computers, cars, and cell phones, to name just a few. Not only are common technological devices themselves complex systems of interactive components such as gears, wiring, chips, software, and the like, but these devices interact within larger systems too: computers interact with the Internet; cars operate within a larger transportation system; cell phones tap into telecommunications systems; and so forth. Furthermore, the processes by which manufacturers produce technological devices and build the larger systems in which they operate depend vitally on a variety of systems, such as supply chains and other industrial systems. The uses to which modern technologies are put also become embedded in complex systems, something particularly evident for computer systems, which are used in everything from running hospitals to managing the electrical grid. But systems are much more than technology; they involve people interacting with each other, in teams, offices, firms, and sectors, and then interacting with technology and with the environment within which they are situated. Systems even comprise other systems, interacting and overlapping with each other.

A system can be formally defined as "a set of elements or parts that is coherently organized and interconnected in a pattern or structure that produces a characteristic set of behaviors, often classified as its 'function' or 'purpose.'"[1] How any system functions can only truly be known by observing its behavior or performance. Moreover, no single element or actor is in control of a system's performance; that is, it is possible for the function or purpose of the system to be at odds with the intentions of some or even all of the actors in that system. Systems do not always act in a linear fashion; often multiple factors interact with each other to produce results that can be hard to foresee. Actions taken at one part of a system can form feedback loops that affect other parts of the system. We inhabit a complex world today, and that complexity arises because of the many systems in which we are situated or with which we interact. These systems often help make the world a better place, but they also can sometimes create serious problems, affecting safety, reliability, sustainability, and other important values. As a result, systems need to be managed and regulated so as to promote positive outcomes and minimize negative ones. Yet systems create particular challenges for regulators because the different actors and components within them are interacting in hard-to-discern ways. The actors in any system are often seeking to achieve different goals simultaneously, and these goals can be at odds with the regulator's mission. Seldom will there exist any single, clear point of regulatory "control" that can determine the results of a system.

Excellent regulators understand these challenges and seek to influence events to enable systems to achieve regulatory goals. Whether in the fields of environmental protection, occupational health and safety, transportation safety, or health care delivery, among many others, the very best regulators will take a systems approach to their work. By a systems approach, I mean one that defines the regulatory problem as one of influencing the order that emerges in systems, often trying from the bottom up to guide those systems toward socially useful and productive goals. The best way regulators can influence the emergence of order in systems is to enable actors in those systems to find ways to integrate those socially useful and productive goals into their everyday processes and activities. In this way, excellent regulators work to ensure that all of the elements of a system work synchronously in pursuit of both private and public goals. The best regulatory leaders learn that, to succeed in influencing any complex system to promote public value, they must abandon the quest for a single, fixed point of control, such as by crafting the one "best" rule. Instead, they must learn that regulatory excellence has more to do with "strategically, profoundly, madly, letting go and dancing with the system."[2]

## WHY A SYSTEMS APPROACH IS VITAL FOR ACHIEVING REGULATORY EXCELLENCE

When regulators consider the patterns of interactions occurring within a system—whether across people, firms, technologies, or the environment—they create opportunities to identify problems, understand what causes them, and imagine new ways to solve them.[3]

In the United States, the publication in 2000 of a now well known Institute of Medicine report, *To Err Is Human: Building a Safer Health System,* brought to public attention the occurrence of as many as 98,000 deaths caused by health care errors.[4] This report is also significant because it shifted attention away from a conception of risk that treated errors as caused by negligence on the part of individual health professionals to a conception that considered harm to be a product of "preventable" system errors.[5] The report's authors relied on James Reason's distinction between "active errors" and "latent conditions," or system errors.[6] In this frame of analysis, an "active error" is the act or decision that contributes to harm, while a latent or system error increases the risk that operators will make such errors.[7] For example, although it is well known that the drug vincristine used in chemotherapy should be injected into patients only intravenously, a pattern of reported incidents has arisen across many different health care institutions in which doctors have mistakenly injected the drug into the spinal cavity of patients, causing their patients to die. Although in such cases it is true that active errors caused the death of patients, these incidents also occurred because of system errors in the organization of hospitals that created the conditions for the incorrect delivery of vincristine.[8] Examples of system errors include modifications to medicine protocols, improper labeling and packaging of vincristine, and other communications errors.[9]

The distinction between active failures and latent or system errors gave rise to Reason's "Swiss cheese model of accident causation."[10] This model is typically visualized by lining up several hunks of Swiss cheese, with the holes in the cheese representing gaps in the defenses protecting operators and patients from harm. An accident or active error results when the gaps in the defenses—the holes in the Swiss cheese—line up. This way of thinking about accidents has proven highly influential for regulators working in contexts where there is a public mandate to reduce accident risks, including aviation safety and workplace safety in addition to the regulation and management of health care delivery. A systems approach to assessing regulatory problems is, in most settings, essential for adopting a "risk-based" approach to regulation.[11]

Recognizing that problems as varied as medical errors and offshore oil spills arise not just from negligent individual behavior but also from larger system failures can lead to new types of solutions. Requiring the use of checklists, for example, has been shown to be highly effective for safely managing complex medical procedures, even though one might not expect truly competent individual practitioners to need such a simple tool.[12] In a similar vein, recognition of the system-like qualities of hazardous waste management has led U.S. environmental regulation to mandate that written documentation accompany every drum of hazardous waste from its point of generation through transporting and disposal, with information filled out at each step and a copy of the completed documentation returned to the generator once the waste has been disposed of.[13]

Identifying problems as system breakdowns, or unintended alignments in the gaps in a system's defenses, does not mean that all problems can readily be solved.[14] Merely naming a pattern of interactions between actors as a "system" is not always enough to identify discrete leverage points that regulators can use to influence those interactions. In a number of domains, regulators fully recognize the systemic nature of the underlying problems but also recognize that they, as regulators, lack the real-time, fine-grained information needed to know what interventions might be best. In realms as varied as environmental protection, occupational health and safety, food and drug regulation, and pipeline safety, regulators have used a regulatory strategy known as management-based regulation, through which regulators try to engage firms' managers in the analysis and management of their own systems with the attainment of regulatory goals in mind.[15] Although the precise requirements of management-based regulations vary, they generally require a firm's managers to engage in a planning process that includes identifying sources of potential problems, developing practices and procedures to solve them, and documenting their implementation of the plan and procedures. This form of regulation seeks to "'build in' regulatory considerations at every stage of the production process, to improve . . . social performance."[16] By requiring that managers consciously plan to reduce social harm, management-based regulation seeks to influence the interactions between managers and workers in ways that will change the outcomes of the system.

## WHY SYSTEMS ARE DIFFICULT TO REGULATE

Management-based regulation is premised on a belief that managers using bureaucratic planning can find ways to control the systems they oversee.[17] Usually this planning takes a reductive analytical form that tries to break a problem into its component parts and then attack each part separately. In food processing, for example, a process known as hazard analysis and critical control points (HACCP) planning calls on managers to identify discrete intervention points where cleaning should take place, temperatures should be controlled, or other concrete steps should be taken.[18] Nancy Leveson refers to this as a divide-and-conquer approach to problem solving:

> In the traditional scientific method, sometimes referred to as *divide and conquer*, systems are broken into distinct parts so that the parts can be examined separately: Physical aspects . . . are decomposed into separate

physical components, while behavior is decomposed into . . . events over time. [Such] decomposition (formally called *analytic reduction*) assumes that [such] separation is feasible: that is, each component or subsystem operates independently, and analysis results are not distorted when these components are considered separately.[19]

Unfortunately, especially with complex, fast-changing systems, management-based regulation may not work very effectively, especially if it calls for long cycles of planning and approval rather than near-constant cycles of monitoring and adaptation. A divide-and-conquer approach may not always be enough to influence interactions in systems to produce socially desirable outcomes—and producing socially desirable outcomes is what an excellent regulator strives to accomplish.

Influencing others so as to enable them to move a system toward multiple goals simultaneously—one goal being the regulator's—can be difficult because of at least five core characteristics of systems. Systems can be complex, dynamic, tightly linked, ordered both from the top and from the bottom, and hard to see due to unclear boundaries and inner workings. But these same characteristics also make it possible for excellent regulators to imagine new ways to achieve their goals.[20]

1. **Systems are complex.** The connections between patterns of interactions among actors in a system and the outcomes produced by that system are predictable but are not predictably regular. Systems cannot be fully described and mapped, but neither do they produce random outcomes.[21] Systems exhibit nonlinear responses to change. This means that a system can be both resistant to change and simultaneously hypersensitive to change when it reaches a tipping point.

Figure 16-1 provides a partial representation of the complex system surrounding the regulatory challenge of ensuring the viability of fisheries. It depicts the complex relationships between ocean ecosystems, commercial fishers, aquaculture and agriculture activities, government actors, and those who live near and make use of the ocean for recreation. This model shows the multiple pathways and feedback loops by which these actors are connected in the system. At the center of the model are stocks of fish—the key outcome of concern. The model shows how stocks are affected by the dynamic interactions among the system's components. Appreciating the complexity of the system can provide useful insights to fishery regulators. At first glance, a regulation imposing a quota on the fish catch might seem to be an effective way to restore fish stocks. But even if regulators could successfully enforce such limits, this intervention could have unintended consequences. It could reduce the incomes of fishers, leading them to pursue alternative forms of livelihood

**FIGURE 16-1.** The Complexity of Fisheries Systems

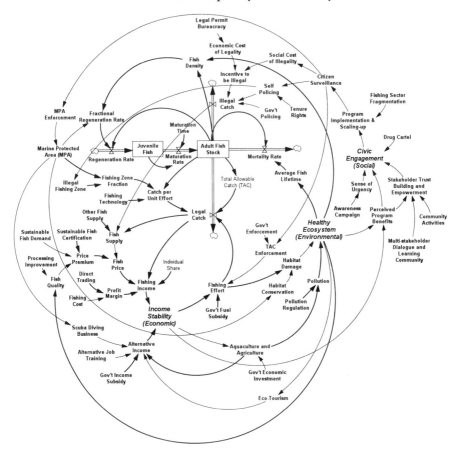

*Source*: Adapted from Joe Hsueh, "Fishery Causal Loop Diagram" (Academy for Systemic Change, 2011) (www.academyforchange.org/wp-content/uploads /2012/08/Fishery-Causal-Loop-Diagram-2011.9.pdf).

in agriculture and aquaculture, which in turn could do more damage to the ecosystem and cause further erosion of fish stocks. A fuller appreciation of the complexity of the system would open up the possibility of alternative governmental strategies, such as the promotion of civic engagement that might foster social-norms-promoting behavior that better maintains healthy fish ecosystems.[22]

2. Systems are dynamic. Many systems are constantly changing, and the distance between their current state and regulatory goals is often in constant

flux. Safety outcomes, for example, can be considered "dynamic nonevents" to indicate that the nonoccurrence of accidents is supported by many changing interactions between actors, groups, and organizations in a system.[23] Regulators are unable to influence systems very well if they overlook their dynamic properties, and yet this is a tendency that too many regulators succumb to, even if unintentionally. They put a rule in place to address a problem and then move on to something else. In this way, they may succeed in solving "yesterday's problem" but fail to keep pace with technological, economic, social, and environmental changes.[24] Even when organizations and systems seem to be meeting the regulatory goals, their performance can degrade over time. This can be the result of organizational processes that allow for the "normalization of deviance"[25] or that persistently "sacrifice" regulatory goals in favor of pressing production goals.[26]

3. **Systems are tightly linked.** Sometimes it may appear as if adding a public policy goal to an existing system is a simple arithmetic process, adding just another layer of planning to existing management structures and planning processes. Yet in complex systems, the tight linkages between actors can create unpredictable sequences of events and accidents that are difficult for regulators and managers to prevent.[27] Adding a regulatory intervention may generate a nonlinear result because it requires that patterns of interaction between actors change as those actors learn how to integrate the new public policy goal so that the system can simultaneously meet productive and safety goals. The nature and extent of the change required of actors is one reason many actors in systems adopt a ritualistic response to regulation designed to achieve a public policy goal. In Neil Gunningham and Duncan Sinclair's study of mine safety regulation, the mines with poor safety performance exhibited a lack of trust between management and workers, producing a ritualistic response to a required management system.[28] By contrast, in the mines with a good safety record, workers and managers used the management system as an opportunity to improve both productivity and safety goals.[29] Regulators should expect these kinds of interactive linkages and seek to ensure that actors in systems have spaces and time to experiment with new patterns of interactions to achieve new regulatory goals.[30]

4. **Systems can emphasize emergence of order from the bottom up.** In many complex systems, interactions between agents "lead to dynamic patterns created by iterative and mutual adaptation."[31] Order emerges from these interactions between agents. This property of emergence allows individual-level adaptation between agents to give rise to new or changing states of order at the macro or system level. For regulators, the emergence of order from interactions between actors or elements is perhaps the single most important characteristic of a system.[32]

Outcomes, such as safety, often emerge "bottom up" from a variety of interactions. The degree to which different organizations or parts of systems are affected by bottom-up emergence rather than top-down imposition can lead to different outcomes. Responses to the safety management systems in Gunningham and Sinclair's study varied across mine sites. In the low-ranked mines the culture of mistrust arose from a "long history of antagonism" between management and unions.[33] By contrast, in the highly ranked mines, "worker input and engagement (in short, ownership) was actively sought in the implementation of new safety systems and initiatives."[34] Excellent regulators will be attentive to these differences and will engage with the process of emergence in order to shape the direction that the system takes.

5. Systems are difficult to see. "Systems" do not follow organizational charts or institutional patterns. The complexity, dynamism, interactivity, and bottom-up quality of many systems make them inherently difficult to understand and map. Even the same organization can have other systems or subsystems within it; though not visible to the outside regulator, these subsystems could prove critical to overall system performance. Such internal tension presents a major challenge for regulators. Excellent regulators will recognize the challenge and attempt to gather the information needed to understand the system they seek to influence.[35] They will engage with actors in the system in order both to learn about the system and to influence interactions between actors within its subsystems and overlapping systems. Ultimately, changes in the outcomes of these interactions will prove more visible than the system itself; however, the excellent regulator is strategic and not just lucky, and therefore needs to peer into the system in order to connect the dots between the regulator's interventions and the outcomes that emerge.

## EXCELLENT REGULATORS *CAN* INFLUENCE SYSTEMS

Despite the difficulties, regulators do sometimes succeed at influencing systems in ways that deliver public value.[36] An instructive example is the experience of the U.S. Food and Drug Administration (FDA) during the latter half of the 1990s. As FDA commissioner at that time, David Kessler took the initiative to assert FDA authority to regulate tobacco for the first time, reversing a long-standing position the agency itself had taken. By 1995, when President Clinton announced that the FDA would formally propose a rule "to protect the young people of the United States from the awful dangers of tobacco,"[37] Kessler had succeeded in moving forward with a regulatory "initiative that most people outside the FDA would have thought unimaginable only months before."[38] The agency's proposal had sparked a political firestorm, with the tobacco industry mounting a major lobbying campaign against the agency and members of Congress from tobacco-producing districts berating Kessler and challenging him vociferously at legislative hearings. Nevertheless, Kessler moved the regulation forward, and in 1996 the agency made final its regulation limiting young people's access to cigarettes and restricting tobacco companies' ability to market their products to children, a historic regulatory step that prompted both the president and the vice president to praise the rule at a special press conference held in the White House Rose Garden.[39]

The FDA's regulatory saga turned out not to be entirely rosy. The tobacco industry challenged the rule in court, and several years later the U.S. Supreme Court declared the rule to be invalid, concluding that the FDA lacked statutory authority to regulate tobacco products.[40] Yet while that litigation was still pending, the larger political and legal system showed signs of shifting, no doubt in part because of the FDA's actions. In late 1998, tobacco companies reached a settlement with state governments over claims that the consequences of smoking had increased public health spending, a settlement that required tobacco companies to make payments of more than $200 billion over a twenty-five-year period and to accept some of the very restrictions included in the FDA's rule.[41] While the FDA's rule was ultimately found to be unlawful, it did help change the state of the larger system of smoking and the sale and marketing of tobacco products.[42] Steve Parrish, a vice president of Philip Morris, reportedly told David Kessler that for tobacco corporations "it was no longer a question of winning lawsuits"; it was, rather, "a question of obtaining permission from society to continue to exist."[43] By 2009, Congress did what had been completely unimaginable a little more than a decade earlier: it gave the FDA the express authority to regulate tobacco that the Supreme Court had held the agency lacked.[44] The congressional findings in the Family Smoking Prevention and Tobacco Control Act mirrored the findings that Commissioner Kessler and his team had made when issuing the FDA's original tobacco regulation. Under the authority of the new statute, the FDA reissued in 2010 the earlier restrictions that Kessler had pushed forward in the face of opposition.[45]

To initiate the FDA's original rulemaking in the late 1990s, Kessler navigated and bumped up against several important systems, economic, political, and legal, among others. But he also used systems thinking in the substantive policy approach his agency took in addressing the public health threat created by smoking. He was, in the end, normatively closed to the growing, manufacturing, marketing, and use of tobacco, but along the way he was cognitively open to and aware of the social as well as medical aspects of the systems that created addiction to smoking and contributed to more than 400,000 premature deaths per year in the United States.[46] David Kessler and many of those who worked with him at the FDA were relentlessly focused on the goal of improving public health, but disciplined in their approach to the practical but vital problem of learning what they needed to know to regulate the systems involved in growing, manufacturing, marketing, and consuming tobacco products.[47] Their disposition of openness enabled the FDA to learn about the "linkages, relationships, interactions, and behaviors" that made up the system for growing, manufacturing, marketing, and consuming tobacco.[48] In turn, the FDA was able to influence this system by focusing on the marketing and consumption of tobacco by young people.[49] They realized that a key leverage point in solving the public health problem created by the larger tobacco market system was at the point of entry into the market. Keeping children and teens from starting to smoke could help break a cycle of addiction and, with time, slow the rate of smoking and smoking-related diseases.

In relentlessly pursuing the goal of improving public health by reducing the consumption of tobacco, Kessler made use of the fundamental characteristics of systems. He did not just reflexively use the regulator's tool to remove a harm by banning the harmful activity.[50] Rather, Kessler and his team set out to learn about linkages and relationships between actors in the system and ultimately settled on a regulatory strategy that set in motion the process of changing patterns of consumption of tobacco by consumers. The use of this leverage point—namely, limiting the sale of tobacco to young people—also conformed to the structure of the legal system, which recognized special responsibilities for the protection of children. This strategy took advantage of the tight links between actors in systems. It recognized that *any* change in the system for marketing and consuming tobacco would change the interactions between *all* the actors in the system. It also took advantage of the property of emergence, as young people and their families responded to the regulation. It relied on this emergent order to put the system for growing, manufacturing, marketing, and consuming tobacco on the defensive, even should the FDA lose its initial battle in the courts over its regulation. By taking bold action, and winning the visible support of the president of the United States for the FDA's initiative, Kessler influenced more than just what the rule immediately affected: product marketing aimed at children. He also put the entire country, through its cultural, social, and even legal systems, on a path that would eventually yield significant positive outcomes for public health.[51]

## ADVICE FOR REGULATORS SEEKING TO INFLUENCE SYSTEMS

What are the lessons for regulatory leaders who seek excellence in their work? Excellent regulators must be committed, smart, nimble, vigilant, well resourced, trusted, and ever cognizant of the important role that systems play in causing regulatory problems and in solving them.

*Be committed.* Excellent regulators make it known to the industries and actors they seek to influence that they are singularly motivated by public policy goals.[52] By both word and deed, excellent regulators communicate a relentless will to achieve public policy goals. This does not mean pursuing those goals at any cost, or in ways that conflict with the interests, values, and commitments of the legal and political institutions that empower the regulator to act. But it does mean the regulator is clear about its mission to serve the public interest. All of the actors and organizations in the regulator's domain need to know that the regulator will amass knowledge with the aim of finding leverage points to achieve its stated policy goals.[53]

*Understand changing economic, social, technological, and political conditions.* An excellent regulator is smart. But rather than learning for the sake of learning, the excellent regulator should learn about the "linkages, relationships, interactions, and behaviors" in a system with the aim of finding effective leverage points to influence it. Learning about a system that affects the regulator's goals may seem to be a monumental task, but it is the only way a regulator can act strategically and effectively to influence a system.

*Remain nimble.* It is not enough for a regulator to learn how a system worked in the past or even how it works today. Adapting to change is difficult for any organization, especially legal ones, but the complex, dynamic nature of systems means that they will be in constant flux, changing as new actors enter the system and as background conditions change. Fortunately, there will (nearly) always be leverage points that excellent regulators can use to influence systems, but only if they find them.

*Stay vigilant.* Excellent regulators do not assume that just because they adopt a regulation the regulatory problem will be solved. Initial implementation of a regulation is just the start of learning how to change the dynamics of a system. Excellent regulators will be mindful of the potential for tight linkages in systems and of the emergence of bottom-up order to create unintended consequences as systems adapt to the implementation of the regulation. Regulators should also be vigilant in measuring changes in outcomes of systems as those systems respond to the implementation of the regulation.

*Build capacity.* Excellent regulators build the capacity to influence the interactions between actors in systems to achieve public policy goals. The dynamic nature of systems means that the capacity needed to influence interactions between actors in systems will change over time. Excellent regulators build capacity so that they are able to respond flexibly to new challenges as they arise. As David Levi-Faur argues in chapter 14 in this volume, building capacity might entail including different forms of experts, such as historians, criminologists, and political scientists. It decidedly means that they need the adequate funding that Shelley Metzenbaum and Gaurav Vasisht call for in chapter 10. The FDA's experience with tobacco revealed the importance of building the in-house team to investigate an industry and understand how it operates.

*Maintain public trust.* Excellent regulators generate the support needed to build the capacity they need to fulfill their mission. They earn the public's trust by using their authority wisely and in ways that conform to the values and commitments of the legal and political institutions that authorize and support them. They are entrusted more when they stay vigilant and committed to the task of achieving socially beneficial outcomes. David Vogel's account of the California Air Resources Board in chapter 13 illustrates how valuable it can be to a regulator to build and maintain a reputation for excellence.

*Remain systems-minded.* Above all, excellent regulators must remain "systems minded." They must find leverage points that simultaneously influence systems *and* conform to the interests, values, and commitments of the legal and political systems in which they operate. Doing so increases the likelihood that a particular regulatory initiative will succeed. But it also builds a relationship of trust with the political bodies that authorize and fund regulators to pursue their public policy goals. Ultimately, excellent regulators work synchronously with the systems that they are seeking to influence and with the political and legal systems that support them. Working synchronously with systems and their components gives the excellent regulator the essential ability to "dance with systems."[54]

## CONCLUSION

Given the inherent difficulties involved in regulating complex systems, an excellent regulator will never be a perfect regulator. It will, though, consistently seek and make use of leverage points. These leverage points must simultaneously put regulated systems on a path toward achieving public policy goals and conform to the interests, values, and commitments of legal, economic, and political institutions that support the regulator. The leaders of regulatory organizations who seek excellence must always seek to understand the bigger picture of what causes the problems they are tasked to solve, so they can then identify strategies to change the dynamics of the relevant systems and put them on a path toward achieving regulatory policy goals.

NOTES

1. Donella Meadows, *Thinking in Systems: A Primer* (White River Junction, Vt.: Chelsea Green, 2008), p. 188.

2. Ibid., p. 165.

3. Ruthanne Huising and Susan S. Silbey, "Governing the Gap: Forging Safe Science through Relational Regulation," *Regulation & Governance* 5 (2011): 35–37.

4. Institute of Medicine, *To Err Is Human: Building a Safer Health System* (Washington: National Academies Press, 2000). See also Robert M. Wachter and Kaveh G. Shojania, *Internal Bleeding: The Truth behind America's Terrifying Epidemic of Medical Mistakes* (New York: Rugged Land, 2004), pp. 55–64.

5. Institute of Medicine, *To Err Is Human,* pp. 1–5.

6. James Reason, *Human Error* (Cambridge University Press, 1990).

7. Institute of Medicine, *To Err Is Human,* pp. 65–66.

8. James Reason, "Beyond the Organisational Accident: The Need for 'Error Wisdom' on the Frontline," *Quality and Safety in Health Care* 13 (December 2004): Suppl. 2, ii28–ii33.

9. James Reason, *Organizational Accidents Revisited* (Boca Raton, Fla.: CRC Press, 2016), pp. 64–72.

10. James Reason, *Managing the Risks of Organizational Accidents* (Aldershot, England: Ashgate, 1997), pp. 1–12. For a critical analysis of the "Swiss cheese model of accident causation," see Erik Hollnagel and others, "Revisiting the 'Swiss Cheese' Model of Accidents," EEC Note 13/06, October 2006 (www.eurocontrol.int/revisiting -swiss-cheese-model-accidents).

11. For a discussion of a risk-based approach to regulation, see Bridget M. Hutter, "A Risk Regulation Perspective on Regulatory Excellence," chap. 7, this volume.

12. Atul Gawande, *The Checklist Manifesto: How to Get Things Right* (New York: Metropolitan, 2011). For a specific example of the use of checklists, see Mary Dixon Woods and others, "Explaining Michigan: Developing an Ex Post Theory of a Quality Improvement Program," *Milbank Quarterly* 89 (2011): 167–205.

13. U.S. Environmental Protection Agency, Hazardous Waste Manifest System (2016) (www.epa.gov/hwgenerators/hazardous-waste-manifest-system).

14. Unfortunately, medical errors remain a much too frequent cause of fatalities in the United States. Martin Makary and Michael Daniel, "Medical Error: The Third Leading Cause of Death in the U.S.," *British Medical Journal* 353 (2016): 2135.

15. Cary Coglianese and David Lazer, "Management-Based Regulation: Prescribing Private Management to Achieve Public Goals," *Law & Society Review* 37 (2003):

696–700. Management-based regulation is so-named because it "self-consciously seeks to affect the way that businesses manage" their affairs. Cary Coglianese, "The Managerial Turn in Environmental Policy," *N.Y.U. Environmental Law Journal* 17 (2008): 54. See also Cary Coglianese and Jennifer Nash, eds., *Leveraging the Private Sector: Management-Based Strategies for Improving Environmental Performance* (Washington: Resources for the Future Press, 2006).

16. Neil Gunningham and David Sinclair, "Organizational Trust and the Limits of Management-Based Regulation," *Law & Society Review* 43, no. 2 (2009): 867–68.

17. Coglianese, "The Managerial Turn," pp. 69–70.

18. See Coglianese and Lazer, "Management-Based Regulation"; Peter J. May, "Social Regulation," in *The Tools of Government: A Guide to the New Governance,* edited by Lester M. Salamon (Oxford University Press, 2002).

19. Nancy Leveson, *Engineering a Safer World: Systems Thinking Applied to Safety* (MIT Press, 2011), pp. 61–62.

20. Don de Savigny and Taghreed Adam, eds., *Systems Thinking for Health Systems Strengthening* (Geneva: Alliance for Health Policy and Systems Research and World Health Organization, 2009), pp. 40–52.

21. Leveson, *Engineering a Safer World*, p. 62.

22. Joe Hsueh, "Fishery Causal Loop Diagram" (Academy for Systemic Change, 2011), pp. 7, 8–12 (www.academyforchange.org/wp-content/uploads/2012/08/Fishery-Causal-Loop-Diagram-2011.9.pdf).

23. James Reason, *Managing the Risks of Organizational Accidents* (Aldershot, England: Ashgate, 1997), pp. 37, 107–24.

24. On the pacing problem more generally, see Gary E. Marchant, Braden R. Allenby, and Joseph R. Herkert, eds., *The Growing Gap Between Emerging Technologies and Legal-Ethical Oversight* (Heidelberg: Springer, 2011).

25. Diane Vaughan, *The Challenger Launch Decision: Risky Technology, Culture, and Deviance at NASA* (University of Chicago Press, 2009).

26. David D. Woods, "Essential Characteristics of Resilience," in *Resilience Engineering: Concepts and Precepts,* edited by Erik Hollnagel, David D. Woods, and Nancy Leveson (Aldershot, England: Ashgate, 2006), pp. 21–33.

27. Charles Perrow, *Normal Accidents: Living with High-Risk Technologies* (Princeton University Press, 1999). See also Woods, "Essential Characteristics of Resilience."

28. Gunningham and Sinclair, "Organizational Trust."

29. Ibid., pp. 891–94. See also Neil Gunningham, "'Culture Eats Systems for Breakfast': On the Limitations of Management-Based Regulation," Working Paper 83 (Canberra: Australian National University, National Research Centre for OHS Regulation, 2011).

30. See Katherine Kellogg, *Challenging Operations: Medical Reform and Resistance in Surgery* (University of Chicago Press, 2011), pp. 165–86, on the importance of "relational spaces" for learning how to integrate new regulatory requirements. See also Huising and Silbey, "Governing the Gap," pp. 33–37, on the significance of

macromanagement and "slack time" for compliance officers to engage in collaborative inquiry to support "relational regulation"; and Steven Spear, "Fixing Health Care from the Inside, Today," *Harvard Business Review* 83 (2005): 89, on the importance of mastering the learning process rather than problem-specific solutions.

31. Volker Schneider, "Governance and Complexity," in *Oxford Handbook of Governance,* edited by David Levi-Faur (Oxford University Press, 2012), p. 137.

32. Ibid., pp. 138, 134.

33. Gunningham, "Culture Eats Systems for Breakfast," p. 16.

34. Ibid., p. 13.

35. Cary Coglianese, Richard Zeckhauser, and Edward Parson, "Seeking Truth for Power: Informational Strategy and Regulatory Policymaking," *Minnesota Law Review* 89 (2004): 277–341.

36. On the concept of public value, see Mark H. Moore, *Recognizing Public Value* (Harvard University Press, 2013).

37. Esther Scott and Philip Heymann, "Taking on Big Tobacco: David Kessler and the Food and Drug Administration," Kennedy School of Government Case Program (Harvard University, 1996), p. 21.

38. David Kessler, *A Question of Intent: A Great American Battle with a Deadly Industry* (New York: Public Affairs, 2002), p. 333.

39. Scott and Heymann, "Taking on Big Tobacco," pp. 19–25.

40. Kessler, *A Question of Intent*, chap. 49.

41. Ibid., pp. 359–60.

42. *FDA* v. *Brown and Williamson Tobacco Corp.*, 120 S. Ct. 1291 (2000).

43. Kessler, *A Question of Intent*, p. 388.

44. Family Smoking Prevention and Tobacco Control Act, Public Law 111-31 (2009).

45. Food and Drug Administration, Regulations Restricting the Sale and Distribution of Cigarettes and Smokeless Tobacco to Protect Children and Adolescents, *Federal Register* 75 (March 19, 2010): 13,225.

46. Gunther Teubner, "Introduction to Autopoietic Law," in *Autopoietic Law: A New Approach to Law and Society,* edited by Gunther Teubner (New York: Walter de Gruyter, 1987), pp. 10–11. This systems perspective leads to a definition of regulation as one in which a regulator uses law "to trigger self-regulatory responses" in other systems. In order to be successful, a regulator must pursue a normative goal by using the properties of systems to explore ways of coordinating the interactions between legal, political, and economic systems that are also cognitively open and normatively closed. See Gunther Teubner, "Juridification—Concepts, Aspects, Limits, Solutions," in *Juridification of Social Spheres: A Comparative Analysis of the Areas of Labor, Corporate, Antitrust and Social Welfare Law,* edited by Gunther Teubner (New York: Walter de Gruyter, 1987), pp. 19–22.

47. Kessler, *A Question of Intent*, p. 12.

48. Savigny and Adam, *Systems Thinking,* p. 33.

49. Kessler, *A Question of Intent,* chaps. 35 and 36.

50. Kellogg, *Challenging Operations*, pp. 1–8. The use of regulation to limit work hours was an "intervention" that was difficult to implement, and it appears to have had little impact on improving patient safety.

51. In this way, Kessler and the FDA achieved what John Braithwaite describes as "transformative" regulatory excellence. See chap. 2, this volume.

52. Richard M. Locke, *The Promise and Limits of Private Power: Promoting Labor Standards in a Global Economy* (Cambridge University Press, 2013), pp. 174–82.

53. Ian Ayres and John Braithwaite, *Responsive Regulation: Transcending the Deregulation Debate* (Oxford University Press, 1992).

54. Meadows, *Thinking in Systems*, p. 165.

# PART III

# Assessing Regulatory Excellence

# 17

# Performance Principles for Regulators

## DONALD P. MOYNIHAN

**IN RECENT DECADES, GOVERNMENTS** have tried to instill a culture of excellence in public services by turning to performance management techniques. This turn to performance-based approaches extends to regulation. Regulators have been encouraged to use performance metrics to move from inflexible command-and-control approaches toward less adversarial relationships with regulated entities based on shared goals.[1] But there is little empirical evidence on the success of performance-based regulation. What lessons can we learn for regulatory excellence from the broader governmental experience with performance management?

Developing such lessons requires first understanding how the public setting affects the prospects for excellence. This terrain is characterized by task complexity and constraints, but it remains possible to seek performance improvements even under such conditions. Performance management can help, if applied with an understanding of its possibilities and limitations.

Regulators can use performance management to pursue excellence by applying three broad categories of lessons: *first principles:* understand the basic characteristics of performance management in the public sector before they are applied; *precautionary principles:* ensure that performance management does not do more harm than good; and *positive performance principles:* design lessons to get the most from performance management.

## EXCELLENCE AMID COMPLEXITY AND CONSTRAINTS: TWO VISIONS

At the broadest level, there are two alternative visions of how public organizations work, and both are relevant to the pursuit of regulatory excellence. The first describes public tasks as characterized by complexity and constraints, of which regulation is a prime example. The second emphasizes excellence but pays little heed to the practical difficulties that the public setting poses. Developing a vision of regulatory excellence is difficult enough, but the practical pursuit of regulatory excellence must also balance these competing visions.

In 1981, Herbert Kaufman, one of the preeminent social scientists of public organizations in the twentieth century, published the result of his efforts to understand what public leaders do. Kaufman had followed a handful of federal government leaders for a year, examining how they spent their time and what drove their agendas.[2] Public sector leaders, he determined, are defined by the constraints they must manage: hundreds or thousands of pages of written guidance, the habits and culture of employees, the agendas and needs of other actors, and surprising events, such as scandals or accidents. These constraints are not necessarily paralyzing, but must be considered in any effort to improve.

If anything, the context for public leadership has grown more demanding since Kaufman's time. The public expresses declining faith in governmental institutions and officials.[3] The news cycle has shortened, people can select into media that reinforce rather than challenge their beliefs, and social media form a new mechanism by which rumors abound and citizens express discontent. The array of tasks that government is asked to regulate has become more complex, and the failure to regulate well has arguably become more consequential, as evidenced by the imperfect regulatory oversight that contributed to the Great Recession of 2007–09. Some democracies have become markedly more sclerotic than others because of regulatory capture by private interests.[4]

The growing complexity of the broader political environment in which regulators work mirrors the inherent complexity of the task they work on. The claim that regulation is a complex function occurs consistently throughout this book. But if the job of the regulator is indeed complex, it may simply be an extreme reflection of a general condition of complexity in public functions. In most democracies, as a practical matter, the services we reserve for the public sector are those that reflect multiple and usually competing values that societies care about, and for which we cannot easily measure outcomes. Elected officials and society at large typically expect public organizations to perform on several dimensions, such as quantity, quality, efficiency, transparency, stakeholder satisfaction, and probity.[5]

Task complexity makes the pursuit and measurement of excellence more difficult for a variety of reasons.[6] First, tasks, or some aspects of tasks, may be difficult to measure well. As the esteemed management theorist Henry Mintzberg put it, "Many activities are in the public sector precisely because of measurement problems: If everything was so crystal clear and every benefit so easily attributable, those activities would have been in the private sector long ago."[7] The reality for public managers is that they oversee functions that are easily measured by one or a small number of performance items but are imperfectly measured by a great number of items, some of which imply inherent tradeoffs in the function (for example, serving an industry client well or avoiding regulatory capture).

The potential for multiple and conflicting goals is furthered in public settings where regulators must respond to more than one political master, and these masters may have differing views on what constitutes the appropriate cost, nature, and quality of a service. Although regulators enjoy greater autonomy from political involvement than most bureaucrats, they must still spend a great deal of time managing outward: networking with stakeholders, reassuring elected officials, explaining themselves to the media.

The vision of constraints and complexity is counterbalanced by another vision, one of aggressive pursuit of excellence. A year after the publication of Kaufman's study of public managers, management gurus Tom Peters and Robert Waterman wrote *In Pursuit of Excellence,* which gave life to a genre of management bestsellers, including public sector variations, most notably David Osborne and Ted Gaebler's *Reinventing Government.* The pursuit-of-excellence genre is characterized by heroic leaders performing inspirational feats of change and success. It serves as a breathless counterpoint to Kaufman's vision of the constraints of public sector leadership, which reflected the political realities of a system of government that was designed to limit power rather than maximize performance.

The public manager asked to take on the pursuit of excellence may be cautious, and perhaps cynical. Many have been in government long enough to have lived through wave after wave of reform efforts aimed at improving performance. Each takes employee time and attention but in the end may simply be removed and replaced by the newest method of the month.[8]

In such a context, a regulator might be forgiven for eschewing excellence and opting instead to pursue a more modest set of expectations. John Graham and Paul Noe make a compelling argument for the less ambitious approach by identifying the complexity and constraints of the regulatory task.[9] By contrast, Daniel Esty argues vigorously for regulatory excellence based on his experience in Connecticut and shares the *Pursuit of Excellence* vision.[10] The next section describes the primary mechanism that governments across the world have turned to in the pursuit of excellence, which is some sort of performance management system.[11] For such systems to be effective requires understanding and balancing these two visions of governance.


### PERFORMANCE MANAGEMENT: A PATH TO EXCELLENCE?

Performance management refers to "a system that generates performance information through strategic planning and performance measurement routines and that connects this information to decision venues, where, ideally, the information influences a range of possible decisions."[12] In the United States, for example, performance management systems have taken different forms. At the federal level alone, there is governmentwide legislation such as the Government Performance and Results Act (GPRA) of 1993 and the GPRA Modernization Act of 2010. Both require federal agencies and state and local recipients of federal funds to report and make use of performance data. Policy-specific changes, in areas such as welfare (the Personal Responsibility and Work Opportunity Act of 1996) and education (the No Child Left Behind Act of 2002 and the Race to the Top Initiative of 2009), further encourage the use of performance measures.

These broad policy changes overlay more specific practices, such as pay-for-performance, performance contracting, and the adoption of private sector approaches, such as Total Quality Management, Activity-Based Costing, Six Sigma, and Lean. These techniques hold in common the idea of paying close attention to processes, and reengineering these processes for greater efficiency and better outcomes.

The alphabet soup of jargon and acronyms can seem dizzying to the public manager. Each promises to revolutionize governance, but the collective evidence of success in the public sector is not strong. Best-practice case stories can be found, and are repeated, but systematic studies of the impact of these approaches give little reason for optimism. For example, a meta-analysis of forty-nine empirical studies of performance reforms between 2000 and 2014 concluded that most have only a small impact.[13] A study of U.S. federal managers concluded that those exposed to Clinton- and Bush-era performance reforms were no more likely to use performance data than managers who had not encountered these reforms.[14] Historical case-based studies are similarly discouraging.[15]

To be sure, performance management is attractive because it holds some symbolic value: politicians can tell citizens they are improving services by mandating performance techniques, and public organizations can burnish their reputation for competence by pointing to the use of such techniques.[16] But can they really make a difference?

**TABLE 17-1.** Principles of Performance Management

First principles *tell us about the nature of performance management.*

- Performance management can be a helpful tool but does not eliminate complexity or constraints.

- Performance data are socially constructed.

- Performance data are used in different ways.

- People approach performance data with a negativity bias.

Precautionary principles *stop bad things from happening.*

- Every performance measure should have a purpose.

- Don't attach high-powered incentives to goals you can only measure imperfectly.

- Don't let performance management prevent you from managing what you can't measure.

Positive principles *encourage purposeful use of performance data.*

- Communicating performance data is a form of storytelling.

- Build your performance regime around learning.

- Use data to engage in exploration and exploitation.

- Build learning forums.

- Encourage the use of performance information.

If performance management is a path to excellence, it is an uncertain one. It requires balancing the competing visions, understanding how the complexity and constraints of the public setting affect the implementation and efficacy of performance systems, and doggedly but realistically using performance management tools to provide value for citizens.

In the next sections, I lay out a series of principles for using performance management in a public setting. These principles, summarized in table 17-1, are not hard-and-fast rules that are self-enforcing, but instead rely on leadership craft that has a deep contextual knowledge of the policy areas. They are based on social science studies of public organizations that are pursuing excellence, but are tempered by the realities that this pursuit occurs in a complex setting.

### FIRST PRINCIPLES

These first principles are intended to convey basic insights about the nature and limits of performance management in a public setting.

Performance management can be a helpful tool, but it does not eliminate complexity or constraints. Performance techniques do not magically turn public organizations into private ones. Performance management can partially deal with some classic problems associated with public organizations; for example, they can help to reduce goal ambiguity by clarifying which goals are most important. But they cannot change the inherent nature of the public context itself.

Performance data are socially constructed. Part of the appeal of performance management is the promise of objectivity and clarity, offering a bottom line for the public sector. But for any moderately complex program, the creation and use of performance data reflects a series of choices. Regulators will have to make choices about what to define as a goal, what to measure, how to measure it, which measures to emphasize, and how to interpret the outcomes. Two reasonable people can look at a regulatory program and come to different conclusions about any of these choices. The choices will be affected by preferences (conscious or unconscious) and by the power of those making the choices, and will in turn shape how others respond to the performance management system.

Performance data are used in different ways. It is difficult to definitively prove that a performance management system is actually improving performance on any particular policy outcome. The empirical research on performance management therefore focuses a good deal on the behavioral impacts on public employees.[17] How employees use performance data can tell us something about how much attention they are paying to performance issues.

There are four broad ways to use performance data.[18] The goal of performance management is to encourage *purposeful* use, where public managers use the data to innovate and improve outcomes. But public employees may respond in a *passive* fashion, doing just enough to satisfy reporting requirements without actually using data to make decisions. They may also use performance data for *political* ends, incorporating performance data into external advocacy to stakeholders. Finally, if the stakes are high enough, performance management may encourage a *perverse* response, in which public employees use data in ways that are detrimental to the goals of the organization.

People approach performance data with a negativity bias. For most policy areas, members of the public care little about performance measures, and an agency that simply puts a great deal of data on a website that few will check does little to facilitate transparency. But one behavioral factor that does alter how people process performance data is negativity bias.

Individuals are more responsive to losses than to equivalent gains.[19] This has two implications. First, media coverage of negative performance, even if not representative, will attract more attention than evidence of generally positive performance. Second, when presented with performance data, the public, stakeholders, and elected officials will pay more attention to negative outcomes than to positive ones.[20] The reality of negativity bias means that, to maintain a reputation for regulatory excellence, preventing bad things from happening is more important than achieving marginal improvements on a performance metric.

### PRECAUTIONARY PRINCIPLES

Performance management systems intended to encourage excellence can sometimes make things worse. This occurs with enough frequency that performance perversity is not an unanticipated consequence, but a predictable, and therefore manageable, risk if some basic principles are observed.

Every performance measure should have a purpose. Performance management systems require the investment of administrative time and cognitive effort to capture and process performance data. A consistent pattern in public performance management is that more and more measures are added each year, and the transaction costs of maintaining the system increase. Governments must sometimes undertake "stock-takes" to prune the required measures to a manageable level. Each measure should serve a clear purpose and be of value to someone in the organization. Otherwise it is not worth the effort to collect it.

Do not attach high-powered incentives to goals you can only measure imperfectly. Governments that have pushed for greater performance in a variety of complex policy areas—most notably welfare services, education, and health services—have inadvertently encouraged performance perversity: organizational actors manipulate the performance regime through forms of gaming or outright cheating. For example, organizations may focus attention only on the subset of clients most likely to lead to reward, and ignore or systematically exclude others (creaming). A teacher might focus only on students likely to achieve a passing grade on a test and neglect the other students.[21] A job trainer might fail to provide adequate help to candidates deemed less likely to receive offers.[22] Organizations might simply invent performance data. In the area of education policy, for example, the link between performance measures and rewards has created an incentive for teachers to cheat.[23]

Both the corruption of data and the corrupt use of data become more likely as performance incentives increase, following a patterned observed in 1976 by Donald Campbell. Campbell's Law states: "The more any quantitative social indicator is used for social decision-making, the more subject it will be to corruption pressures and the more apt it will be to distort and corrupt the social processes it is intended to monitor."[24]

Many who come to public service are motivated by an intrinsic interest in the work itself or by a broader altruistic desire to help others.[25] Strong performance incentives have another negative effect for complex tasks, which is to "crowd out" such nonextrinsic forms of motivation, as employees become attuned only to targets that provide extrinsic reward. Research from psychology and behavioral economics demonstrates the crowding-out mechanism.[26] As intrinsic or altruistic motivations are eroded, so too are safeguards against performance perversity.

Do not let performance management prevent you from managing what you cannot measure. Another form of performance perversity is myopia or goal displacement. Following the old adage that what gets measured gets managed, the implication is that what is unmeasured is not managed.[27] This risk becomes greater when what matters is not easily measured. For regulators, in particular, managing poorly defined risks may be as important as, if not more important than, well-understood processes. Risk management means preventing bad things from happening; if all goes well, there is little to report. But negativity bias means that organizations face dramatic reputational costs when these risks are not attended to and things go wrong.

Some performance indicators can help to manage risk, identifying outliers, incidents, or questionable data that might predict problems to come, and regulators should look for such measures. A positive example is the way in which aviation regulators have used sophisticated incident management reporting systems to diagnose problems and improve air traffic safety.[28]

Another way performance data can help to manage risk is by tracking measures that reflect tradeoffs between complex goals—for example, between speed and quality of service. Performance systems that focus on only one of these values will likely maximize that value at the expense of the other.[29] In the context of regulation, one issue is customer service and satisfaction. Regulators still have a duty of care for the broader community, and in some cases this may come at the cost of making regulated parties unhappy. A balanced set of performance goals and metrics, which accounts for both an expectation of professional service to regulated organizations and responsiveness to broader public interest, forces regulators to consider how to make progress on both of these values.

Performance data may also serve to underestimate risk. For example, in 2014 the secretary of U.S. Veterans Affairs resigned after evidence revealed that military veterans' hospitals were misreporting wait times for treatment. There was no evidence that the secretary in question, Eric Shinseki, knew about or condoned the false reports. But auditors had warned for several years that the reported wait times were suspect, even as they were being used as a primary measure for evaluating regional health officials. In short, the signals were there, but no one responded to them.

Where measures are helpful in managing risk, they should be used. But the pursuit of excellence with formal tools such as performance management should not divert attention from risk or undercut the managerial qualities needed to manage it, such as imagination and tolerance for ambiguity.


## POSITIVE PRINCIPLES

This section considers principles that can facilitate the use of performance data to actively improve regulatory excellence.

Communicating performance data is a form of storytelling. Most of us are not natural consumers of numbers. Performance data have to be explained, not just as a list of numbers or a graph, but as a narrative, and this need is greater in contentious policy settings where stakeholders disagree on goals or question the impartiality of public actors.[30] Regulators operate in a political system, and using performance data is a legitimate means of communicating their independence and success in a contentious policy arena. It is not enough in a political environment to be an excellent regulator; excellence must be communicated.

Political uses of performance data can be part of an authentic account of the challenges regulators face and how well they are doing. In particular, performance data are useful for explaining what is at stake—the nature of the task or challenge, and progress toward it. When something unusual happens, data can also provide a reminder of what overall performance looks like. A reputation for high competence is a central element of building a broader reputation for excellence,[31] and performance data may provide evidence of competence. David Vogel's discussion in chapter 13 of the California Air Resources Board offers evidence of a regulator that was able to develop and use its organizational reputation effectively.

Some performance data are centered on internal management and are of little interest to the public. For communication purposes it is better to focus on salient data. For example, the U.S. government website Performance.gov focuses on a small number of key metrics that are explained in depth. It may also make sense for government to partner with stakeholders to share performance data, as the public views evidence of positive outcomes as more credible when it comes from sources other than the organization itself.[32]

Build your performance regime around learning. There are many potential goals of performance management. Some of them can coexist—for example, the use of some data for external communication and other data for internal management—but some goals may conflict with one another.

In particular, as performance management becomes geared toward accountability, and as accountability takes on a punitive dimension, it limits the potential for organizational learning.[33] When participants suspect that performance management will be used as a mechanism to belittle and punish them, they no longer treat it as a legitimate management tool worthy of their participation, but as something to be gamed and evaded.

Organizational learning should be the central management purpose of performance management for complex tasks, the means by which data are actually converted into intelligent action, and into excellence. Learning requires a willingness to observe and correct errors by engaging in frank discussions about what is working and not working.

Use data to engage in exploration and exploitation. Research points to two main ways organizations can learn: exploitation and exploration.[34] Exploitation involves taking accepted goals and identifying how to reengineer processes to increase their efficiency. Exploration means searching for novel challenges, goals, and risks, and requires a broad organizational dialogue and a long-term view. Regulatory excellence demands a balance between these two approaches.

Performance management techniques are most obviously useful for exploitation, since it involves identifying stable performance indicators and the processes that produce them, and gradually improving those processes over time. Exploitation is the type of learning that reengineering techniques such as Lean facilitate.

Exploitation may be more effective if organizations prioritize specific goals at different times. Given the range of processes and goals any moderately large and complex organization has, it is not possible to direct equal attention to all of them. Goals that are more important or have greater political salience will naturally demand attention. Another strategy for prioritizing attention is to look for performance gaps: In what organizational processes is the gap between reasonable expectations about performance and actual outcomes very large? If there are comparable units of government, identifying positive outliers facilitates the pursuit of "best-in-class" performance.

Exploration is the more contentious approach. Exploration walks the line between political and administrative authority, since it defines what the role of the organization is. For example, the move of the U.S. Food and Drug Administration into tobacco regulation, and the U.K. Food Standards Authority into food labeling, expanded the role of regulators. Those who worry about unaccountable bureaucracies might worry about crusading regulators exploring their way into new regulations. Regulators do, however, have some measure of independence because their task requires expertise and objectivity. These attributes include being able to identify appropriate levels of regulatory involvement given changes in risk to society.

Performance management can play a role in shaping exploration in a number of ways. A first step in a performance management system is to set goals. This is the point at which organizations calibrate their understanding of their mission, and adjust it, using evidence that includes data on new threats and opportunities. This is also an excellent stage to involve the public. For some public services, the public comprises customers who receive services directly; but for regulatory activities in particular, this is usually not the case. Those who receive regulatory services are a relatively specific group not broadly representative of the public. While measures of customer satisfaction with the services they receive are valuable for evaluating processes, they do not represent the public interest broadly. Similarly, asking the broader public to rate the quality of public services has limited utility if they have not directly experienced these services. However, focus groups and surveys provide a mechanism by which citizens can discuss the values they care about, express support for different goals, and respond to possible tradeoffs that are presented to them. Objective performance data on the values the public identifies as important can inform a regulatory agency's self-evaluation.

**Build "learning forums."** A classic error that governments make with performance management is establishing detailed and often burdensome routines to generate and disseminate performance data, but then paying little attention to developing uses for the data. Learning forums encourage actors to develop routines for closely examining information, considering its significance, and deciding how it will affect future action.

Taking time to discuss performance goals signals their importance to the organization. However, the meaning of performance data is not always straightforward; even the answer to such basic questions as whether performance is good or bad may be unclear. Learning forums are important because they provide a realm in which performance data are interpreted and given shared meaning. More complex questions, such as "why is performance at this level?" and "what should we do next?" cannot be answered by looking only at the data, but require deeper organizational insight and other types of knowledge that can be incorporated into learning forums.

Routines are more successful when they include ground rules for structuring dialogue, employ a nonconfrontational approach to avoid defensive reactions, feature collegiality and equality among participants, include diverse organizational actors responsible for producing the outcomes under review, and mix quantitative indicators of performance with experiential knowledge of process and work conditions that explain successes, failures, and the possibility of innovation.[35]

**TABLE 17-2.** Principles of a Well-Run Learning Forum

- Meetings take place regularly.

- Focus on important goals.

- Agency leaders are involved and seen as committed.

- Multiple levels of employees facilitate learning and problem solving.

- Need appropriate and timely information.

- Need staff and technological capacity to analyze data.

- Quality data (reliable, accurate, valid, disaggregated to the right level, comparative) facilitate analysis.

- Follow up on issues raised in prior meetings.

- Use positive reinforcement.

- Provide constructive feedback.

- Reviews establish a process of analysis.

*Source:* Adapted from Donald P. Moynihan and Alexander Kroll, "Performance Management Routines That Work: An Early Assessment of the GPRA Modernization Act," *Public Administration Review* 76, no. 2 (2016): 314–23.

Learning forums are called different things, such as data-driven reviews or "stat" meetings. When the United States updated its federal performance system in 2010, it required managers to talk about key organizational goals on a quarterly basis. Although prior studies had shown that exposure to federal performance reforms had little positive effect on whether managers used performance data, a survey of federal employees found that those who were involved in or aware of quarterly reviews about their programs were more likely to report using performance data. All learning forums are not created equal, however. Among those involved in quarterly reviews, those who rated their learning forum as well run, based on the attributes listed in table 17-2, were more likely to use performance data.[36]

Encourage the use of performance information. Learning forums are one technique for increasing the purposeful and advantageous uses of performance data. But learning forums depend on other organizational factors to be successful, and these factors are themselves important to performance.

Studies suggest that as managers have more *autonomy*, they become more likely to make use of data to improve performance.[37] Discretion allows them to exercise their expertise, and—especially relevant for regulators—shields them from client criticisms. Studies also show that policy contexts with *high stakeholder involvement* also increase the use of performance data.[38] How should one make sense of this apparent contradiction between discretion and stakeholder involvement? One easy explanation is that stakeholders primarily affect the use of performance data for communication purposes; that is, faced with a demanding audience, policymakers use performance data to tell their story. But more generally, highly engaged stakeholders serve to increase both the salience of goals and the expectations for achievement above what an organization would do for itself.

*Goal clarity* is also associated with greater use of performance data. Goal clarity occurs when employees understand their mission and purpose clearly. In contexts where goals are clear, it is easier to discuss and evaluate objectives, making performance data more meaningful.[39]

*Organizational culture* increases the use of performance information in two ways. First, if there is a perception that the organization is generally supportive of learning and the performance system, performance information use increases.[40] There is also evidence that other traits matter: cultures that value innovation, flexibility, adaptability, and growth (sometimes called developmental cultures) are associated with higher rates of performance information use.[41]

*Leadership* is one of the most consistent predictors of employee attention to performance. Leaders' ability to articulate and communicate a vision of organizational goals—sometimes called transformational leadership—increases the use of performance information, partly by improving other conditions, such as goal clarity and organizational culture.[42] Leadership commitment to the performance system itself also matters. Employees observe how leaders allocate their time and scarce organizational resources, which are credible signals of leadership commitment that encourage employees to overcome a passive response.[43]

There is some limited evidence on how *individual motivation* affects the use of performance data. Demographic factors appear to matter relatively little, but there are two factors that organizations can focus on to increase performance information use. First, employees appear to be more committed to performance management if they have participated in designing the system.[44] Participation increases the perceived salience and legitimacy of the system. The second factor is public service motivation.[45] As individuals develop a greater interest in using work to help others, they become more likely to use performance data.[46] In part, this reflects the fact that performance systems are costly for employees to implement, but the benefits are collective if they facilitate better public services. This insight returns us to the risks of high-powered incentives mentioned earlier: crowding-out effects can undercut one mechanism to improve organizational performance. Public organizations should look for opportunities to use performance goals that "crowd in" public service motivation by reminding employees what is at stake with public goals, and how achieving those goals positively affects important outcomes.

## CONCLUSION

This chapter draws lessons from the broad application of performance management in government for the purpose of better understanding how to evaluate regulatory bodies. There has been little research on the effectiveness of performance management as a tool for governmental regulation of the private sector, although Cary Coglianese has offered an excellent primer on this possibility.[47] Yet regardless of what types of regulatory instruments regulators decide to use, their own organizational performance is a matter of great public concern. Performance management of regulatory agencies has the appeal of simplicity: the promise that numbers can provide information that eases the fraught politics and difficulties of managing public organizations. But this appeal is more illusory than real: performance management may be useful, but the politics and complexities will remain.

One understandable temptation in the field of regulation is to believe that simply setting performance targets within an organization will set the wheels in motion for innovation and improvement. That sometimes happens, but the lessons described here reflect the need for performance management itself to be managed, both to sustain an impetus for improvement and to recognize risks associated with focusing on performance above all other values.

Although the application of performance management techniques to regulatory organizations offers promise, it does not eliminate the inherent political complexity that comes with the task of regulation. For regulators, stakeholders play multiple roles: they produce a good or service that must be regulated, or lobby government on the level and nature of regulation. For performance management as well, stakeholders help to determine reasonable goals and create and share innovations. For these reasons they should be included in performance management processes. But the socially constructed nature of performance also requires regulators to exercise due care to avoid capture in the setting of targets; and the degree to which performance metrics are actually achieved by regulated entities must be validated. To the extent that performance management of regulatory institutions implies the coproduction of goals (both the regulator and the regulated entities will be judged by the same measures), it erodes the distance between the two parties, even as the regulator remains ultimately responsible for outcomes for the public.

To admit that the public setting is complex and constrained is not to automatically accept that regulatory excellence is impossible, but to understand the demanding terrain in which public managers pursue excellence. Performance management techniques may help in achieving excellence, but only if applied astutely. The basic, precautionary, and positive principles identified in this chapter offer a useful starting point, alerting regulators to the nature of performance management, warning them of the risks that it may pose to good governance, and identifying steps they can take to facilitate better outcomes.

### NOTES

*Acknowledgments:* The author thanks Hank Spier, Robin Brown, Cary Coglianese, and Brent Fisse for helpful comments on aspects of this chapter.

1. Cary Coglianese, "Performance-Based Regulation: Concepts and Challenges," in *Handbook of Comparative Law and Regulation,* edited by Francesca Bignami and David Zaring (Cheltenham, U.K.: Edward Elgar, 2016); Cary Coglianese, Jennifer Nash, and Todd Olmstead, "Performance-Based Regulation: Prospects and Limitations in Health, Safety, and Environmental Regulation," *Administrative Law Review* 55 (2003): 705–29.

2. Herbert Kaufman, *The Administrative Behavior of Federal Bureau Chiefs* (Brookings Institution Press, 1981).

3. See Pew Research Center, "Public Trust in Government" (2014) (www.people -press.org/2014/11/13/public-trust-in-government/).

4. Francis Fukuyama, *Political Order and Political Decay: From the Industrial Revolution to the Globalization of Democracy* (New York: Farrar, Straus and Giroux, 2014).

5. George Boyne, "Concepts and Indicators of Local Authority Performance: An Evaluation of the Statutory Frameworks in England and Wales," *Public Money and Management* 22, no. 2 (2002): 17–24.

6. Simon Burgess and Marisa Ratto, "The Role of Incentives in the Public Sector: Issues and Evidence," *Oxford Review of Economic Policy* 19, no. 2 (2003): 285–300; Avinash Dixit, "Incentives and Organizations in the Public Sector: An Interpretative Review," *Journal of Human Resources* 37 (2002): 696–727; Carolyn J. Heinrich and Gerald Marschke, "Incentives and Their Dynamics in Public Sector Performance Management Systems," *Journal of Policy Analysis and Management* 29, no. 1 (2010): 183–208.

7. Henry Mintzberg, "Managing Government, Governing Management," *Harvard Business Review* 74, no. 3 (1996): 79.

8. Paul Charles Light, *The Tides of Reform: Making Government Work, 1945–1995* (Yale University Press, 1998).

9. John D. Graham and Paul R. Noe, "Beyond Process Excellence: Enhancing Societal Well-Being," chap. 5, this volume.

10. Daniel C. Esty, "Regulatory Excellence: Lessons from Theory and Practice," chap. 9, this volume.

11. Organization for Economic Cooperation and Development, *Government at a Glance* (Paris: OECD, 2013).

12. Donald P. Moynihan, *The Dynamics of Performance Management: Constructing Information and Reform* (Georgetown University Press, 2008), p. 5.

13. Ed Gerrish, "The Impact of Performance Management on Performance in Public Organizations: A Meta-Analysis," *Public Administration Review* 76, no. 1 (2016): 48–66.

14. Donald P. Moynihan and Stéphane Lavertu, "Does Involvement in Performance Management Routines Encourage Performance Information Use? Evaluating GPRA and PART," *Public Administration Review* 72, no. 4 (2012): 592–602.

15. Beryl A. Radin, *Federal Management Reform in a World of Contradictions* (Georgetown University Press, 2008).

16. Moynihan, *The Dynamics of Performance Management.*

17. Donald P. Moynihan and Sanjay Pandey, "The Big Question for Performance Management: Why Do Managers Use Performance Information?" *Journal of Public Administration Research and Theory* 20, no. 4 (2010): 849–66.

18. Donald P. Moynihan, "Through a Glass, Darkly," *Public Performance & Management Review* 32, no. 4 (2009): 592–603.

19. Amos Tversky and Daniel Kahneman, "The Framing of Decisions and the Psychology of Choice," *Science* 211, no. 4481 (1981): 453–58.

20. George A. Boyne and others, "Democracy and Government Performance: Holding Incumbents Accountable in English Local Governments," *Journal of Politics* 71, no. 4 (2009): 1273–84.

21. David N. Figlio and Cecilia Elena Rouse, "Do Accountability and Voucher Threats Improve Low-Performing Schools?" *Journal of Public Economics* 90, no. 1 (2006): 239–55.

22. Heinrich and Marschke, "Incentives and Their Dynamics."

23. Brian A. Jacob and Steven Levitt, "Rotten Apples: An Investigation of the Prevalence and Predictors of Teacher Cheating," *Quarterly Journal of Economics* 118, no. 3 (2003): 843–77.

24. Donald T. Campbell, "Assessing the Impact of Planned Social Change," Occasional Paper 8 (Dartmouth College, Public Affairs Center, December 1976), p. 49

25. James L. Perry, Debra Mesch, and Laurie Paarlberg, "Motivating Employees in a New Governance Era: The Performance Paradigm Revisited," *Public Administration Review* 66, no. 4 (2006): 505–14.

26. Edward L. Deci, Richard Koestner, and Richard M. Ryan, "A Meta-Analytic Review of Experiments Examining the Effects of Extrinsic Rewards on Intrinsic Motivation," *Psychological Bulletin* 125, no. 6 (1999): 627; Antoinette Weibel, Katja Rost, and Margit Osterloh, "Pay for Performance in the Public Sector—Benefits and (Hidden) Costs," *Journal of Public Administration Research and Theory* 20, no. 2 (2010): 387–412.

27. Dixit, "Incentives and Organizations."

28. Russell Mills, *Incident Reporting Systems: Lesson from the Federal Aviation Administration's Air Traffic Organization* (Washington: IBM Endowment for the Business of Government, 2013).

29. Dixit, "Incentives and Organizations"; Heinrich and Marschke, "Incentives and Their Dynamics."

30. Donald P. Moynihan and Daniel P. Hawes, "Responsiveness to Reform Values: The Influence of the Environment on Performance Information Use," *Public Administration Review* 72, no. s1 (2012): S95–S105.

31. Daniel P. Carpenter and George A. Krause, "Reputation and Public Administration," *Public Administration Review* 72, no. 1 (2012): 26–32.

32. Oliver James and Gregg G. Van Ryzin, "Incredibly Good Performance: An Experimental Study of Source and Level Effects on the Credibility of Government," *American Review of Public Administration* (April 2015), doi 10.1177/0275074015580390.

33. Lance DeHaven-Smith and Kenneth C. Jenne, "Management by Inquiry: A Discursive Accountability System for Large Organizations," *Public Administration Review* 66, no. 1 (2006): 64–76.

34. Barbara Levitt and James G. March, "Organizational Learning," *Annual Review of Sociology* 14 (1988): 319–40.

35. Moynihan, *The Dynamics of Performance Management*.

36. Donald P. Moynihan and Alexander Kroll, "Performance Management Routines That Work? An Early Assessment of the GPRA Modernization Act," *Public Administration Review* 76, no. 2 (2016): 314–23.

37. Moynihan and Lavertu, "Does Involvement in Performance Management Routines Encourage Performance Information Use?"; Poul Aaes Nielsen, "Learning from Performance Feedback: Performance Information, Aspiration Levels, and Managerial Priorities," *Public Administration* 92, no. 1 (2014): 142–60.

38. Jostein Askim, Åge Johnsen, and Knut-Andreas Christophersen, "Factors behind Organizational Learning from Benchmarking: Experiences from Norwegian Municipal Bench-marking Networks," *Journal of Public Administration Research and Theory* 18, no. 2 (2008): 297–320; Carolyn Bourdeaux and Grace Chikoto, "Legislative Influences on Performance Management Reform," *Public Administration Review* 68, no. 2 (2008): 253–65; Moynihan and Hawes, "Responsiveness to Reform Values," S95–S105.

39. Donald P. Moynihan and Noel Landuyt, "How Do Public Organizations Learn? Bridging Cultural and Structural Perspectives," *Public Administration Review*

69, no. 6 (2009): 1097–105; Donald P. Moynihan, Sanjay K. Pandey, and Bradley E. Wright, "Prosocial Values and Performance Management Theory: Linking Perceived Social Impact and Performance Information Use," *Governance* 25, no. 3 (2012): 463–83; Donald P. Moynihan, Sanjay K. Pandey, and Bradley E. Wright, "Setting the Table: How Transformational Leadership Fosters Performance Information Use," *Journal of Public Administration Research and Theory* 22, no. 1 (2012): 143–64.

40. Moynihan and Landuyt, "How Do Public Organizations Learn?"; Patria de Lancer Julnes and Marc Holzer, "Promoting the Utilization of Performance Measures in Public Organizations: An Empirical Study of Factors Affecting Adoption and Implementation," *Public Administration Review* 61, no. 6 (2001): 693–708.

41. David H. Folz, Reem Abdelrazek, and Yeonsoo Chung, "The Adoption, Use, and Impacts of Performance Measures in Medium-Size Cities," *Public Performance & Management Review* 33, no. 1 (2009): 63–87; Tobias Johansson and Sven Siverbo, "Explaining the Utilization of Relative Performance Evaluation in Local Government: A Multi-Theoretical Study Using Data from Sweden," *Financial Accountability & Management* 25, no. 2 (2009): 197–224; Moynihan and Pandey, "The Big Question for Performance Management."

42. Moynihan and Lavertu, "Does Involvement in Performance Management Routines Encourage Performance Information Use?"; Moynihan, Pandey, and Wright, "Prosocial Values and Performance Management Theory."

43. Matthew Dull, "Results-Model Reform Leadership: Questions of Credible Commitment," *Journal of Public Administration Research and Theory* 19, no. 2 (2009): 255–84.

44. George A. Boyne and others, "Toward the Self-Evaluating Organization? An Empirical Test of the Wildavsky Model," *Public Administration Review* 64, no. 4 (2004): 463–73; Folz, Abdelrazek, and Chung, "The Adoption, Use, and Impacts of Performance Measures in Medium-Size Cities"; Julia Melkers and Katherine Willoughby, "Models of Performance-Measurement Use in Local Governments: Understanding Budgeting, Communication, and Lasting Effects," *Public Administration Review* 65, no. 2 (2005): 180–90.

45. Perry, Mesch, and Paarlberg, "Motivating Employees in a New Governance Era."

46. Alexander Kroll and Dominik Vogel, "The PSM–Leadership Fit: A Model of Performance Information Use," *Public Administration* 92, no. 4 (2014): 974–91; Moynihan and Pandey, "The Big Question for Performance Management"; Moynihan, Pandey, and Wright, "Prosocial Values and Performance Management Theory."

47. Coglianese, "Performance-Based Regulation."

# 18

# Measuring Regulatory Excellence

## CARY COGLIANESE

**MEASUREMENT AND RATING SYSTEMS** abound in all aspects of contemporary life. The *Michelin Guide* books rate restaurants and hotels. *Consumer Reports* magazine provides scores on new washing machines, microwave ovens, and a host of other products. Movie reviewers summarize their assessments using symbols that range from stars to thumbs up to the ripeness of tomatoes. The weekly news magazine *U.S. News and World Report* publishes an annual ranking of American colleges and universities. Accreditation bodies rank hospitals, schools, and other institutions on different criteria. In some jurisdictions, restaurants must display a hygiene rating near their entrances, disclosing to potential customers information about the results of their most recent health code inspection.[1] Various systems for rating corporations exist to guide investors, from the Institutional Shareholder Services' Corporate Governance Quotient to the Dow Jones Sustainability Indices. Numerous popular magazines routinely rank the "best cities" for unmarried individuals, retired persons, outdoor enthusiasts, and so forth.

Rating systems also proliferate in the governmental sphere. Management consultants have applied to governmental organizations a range of assessment tools, such as the Balanced Scorecard and Six Sigma. The financial news site *24/7 Wall St.* issues an annual survey of the best- and worst-run states in America.[2] The U.S. federal government has formally institutionalized performance measurement systems, including the annual program performance reporting called for under the Government Performance and Results Act (GPRA) and a six-year experience with the Program Assessment Rating Tool

(PART) used during the George W. Bush administration.[3] The United Nations rates governments' use of information technology to connect with their citizens.[4] The World Bank and the Organization for Economic Cooperation and Development (OECD) have created rating systems that seek to capture the extent of government regulation as well as the ease of doing business in different countries.[5] The journal *Global Competition Review* has, since 2000, issued its own annual rating of antitrust regulators around the world, purporting "to gauge exactly how capably and efficiently they are policing their economies for anti-competitive activity."[6]

With the proliferation of rating systems for all aspects of life, including regulation, the question naturally arises: What exactly is the role that measurement should play in a regulator's quest for excellence? This chapter takes up this question. It explains why measurement is a vital tool for achieving regulatory excellence, namely because measurement is how a regulator learns how it is doing and what it must do to improve. In addition, this chapter considers how measurement can be used to gauge a regulator's overall level of excellence. Whether using measures *for* achieving excellence or measures *of* excellence to assess progress, regulators need to take a strategic approach to performance measurement and evaluation. They should not simply measure what is easy to measure, and not simply measure for measurement's sake. The aim of an excellent regulator should be to use measurement to improve its organizational traits, actions, and outcomes.

## WHY MEASUREMENT?

Measurement and ratings systems exist to help inform and guide choices. These systems articulate criteria or attributes of quality, and then in some fashion they aggregate the various attributes to achieve an overall rating or score. For example, *Consumer Reports* generates an overall rating for cell phones based on factors such as ease of use, battery life, voice quality, and so forth. The *Consumer Reports'* system works (at least its popularity would suggest it works) because its criteria reflect the types of things that many people care about when selecting a cell phone. Staff members at *Consumer Reports* have identified attributes that matter to people and then have selected a method of weighting and summing these attributes to achieve an overall score or ranking. All popular measurement systems like the one used by *Consumer Reports* succeed because the attributes being measured, and the way they are weighted and aggregated, reflect the needs of users.

When it comes to the measurement of regulators, who exactly are the users and what do they need? The senior leaders of a regulatory organization are obviously one type of user. They need measurements that tell them how well they and their organization are doing. Of course, even though a regulatory agency's leaders are a single type of user, each agency's need for performance measures will be highly varied. They will vary across different kinds of regulators, as well as within the same regulator at different times and for different purposes. Some of these purposes will be internal: measurements can help the leaders and others inside the organization make improvements. Other purposes will be external, such as to communicate with outside overseers, including elected officials, community members, the regulated industry, and perhaps even customers of the regulated industry. The specific internal and external purposes will vary with time as conditions change in the industry, new problems emerge, and changes in political leadership lead to new priorities.

Decisions about how to design measurement systems for regulators depend ultimately on the types of needs they are being used to fill. As public management scholar Bob Behn has observed, there is "no one magic performance measure that public managers can use for all . . . purposes."[7]

When he was commissioner of the Connecticut Department of Energy and Environmental Protection, Daniel Esty used different measures for internal and external purposes (see chapter 9). One of his main internal measures tracked how long permit applications were in "pending" status, as Esty wanted to improve the department's timeliness of decisions on permit applications. For external purposes, his department collected other measures, such as the levels of nitrogen loading in the Long Island Sound, so as to be able to communicate with the public.

## MEASUREMENT *FOR* EXCELLENCE VERSUS MEASUREMENT *OF* EXCELLENCE

A subtle but key distinction exists between measurement *for* excellence and measurement *of* excellence. Measurement *for* excellence refers to the kinds of measures and measurement practices that an excellent regulator would put in place in order to run its operations well. It encompasses measurement for the myriad of internal and external purposes that Behn and Esty have articulated. In chapter 17 of this volume, Don Moynihan lists essential principles that excellent regulators should follow in using measurement in their daily operations and to inform efforts to make continuous improvement.

Measurement *of* excellence is different, even if related. Measurement *of* excellence seeks to answer the question: Is this regulator *excellent*? As such, it seeks to determine how well a regulator's organizational traits, actions, and outcomes align with and satisfy specific standards for regulatory quality. In this way, measurement *of* excellence is comprehensive, providing an overall account of how well a regulator is doing. A regulator, after all, might be excellent at some aspects of its operations but not at others, although presumably the truly excellent regulators will be excellent, or at least exceedingly good, across the board.

The difference between measurement *for* and measurement *of* regulatory excellence can be illustrated with an example of measurement applied within a different domain: higher education. University professors routinely use exams to grade their students, and university administrators routinely conduct course evaluations to assess faculty teaching performance. Presumably all universities use both of these types of measures, so the mere existence of their use will not suffice as an indicator *of* excellence. They are instead an example of measurement used *for* excellence. For a university to be excellent, it is necessary, even though not sufficient, that it routinely ensure that its students are learning (hence, student exams) and that faculty are taking their teaching responsibilities seriously (hence, faculty evaluations). But neither student exams nor faculty teaching evaluations are the means one would use to evaluate how well a university is doing overall—that is, whether it has achieved some degree *of* excellence. Whatever stock one takes in the measures and methods used by the editors at *U.S. News and World Report*, it should be clear that those editors are seeking measurements *of* excellence. They are using altogether different measures than student grades and faculty evaluations to rank the overall excellence of universities: reputational surveys, data on institutional resources, student retention figures, metrics of admissions selectivity, and so forth.

Measurement *of* excellence may sometimes rely on some of the same measures that an institution uses *for* becoming excellent. Universities use individual standardized test scores of applicants when making admissions decisions, for example, while outside evaluators draw on averages of these same test scores as an indicator of universities' selectivity and one potential factor in assessing its overall excellence. Nevertheless, since measurements *of* excellence serve a purpose that is distinct from measurements *for* excellence, the former objective will often necessitate entirely different measures than what might be at hand and used on a day-to-day basis within an organization.

The comprehensive nature of any measurement *of* excellence means that a measurement system used for this purpose must either rely on a single magic-bullet metric of excellence or find ways to aggregate and weight a series of discrete metrics. No single magic-bullet metric exists for regulators. Determining whether they are excellent requires, in principle, tallying up performance measures or other criteria for different facets of their operations, ideally using a common unit of measure. In theory, it would then be possible to combine these measures and arrive at a single score which, if sufficiently high, would provide the basis for deeming the regulator to be "excellent." Measuring all of a regulator's goals with a common unit may well be impossible, but it is possible to weight scores and force them all into a predetermined regulatory excellence algorithm, much as *Consumer Reports* does for appliances and other consumer products, and as *U.S. News & World Report* does for colleges and universities.

The key question, of course, is how meaningful such an exercise would be. At times, regulators seek to maximize seemingly incommensurable, if not utterly conflicting, objectives. Consider, for example, a regulator charged with reducing risks from an industrial activity while also keeping compliance costs low, promoting distributional equity, and acting transparently, rigorously, and quickly. Some of these objectives are likely to be in tension with one another. Can they all be converted into a single unit of analysis? If all of the regulator's operations with respect to each of these objectives could be measured and then monetized accurately, the negative effects could be subtracted from the positive ones to yield a unified net-benefits estimate, which would provide, in principle, a meaningful measure of the regulator's overall excellence. But while compliance costs may be readily accessible in monetary terms, and while sophisticated (albeit sometimes criticized) techniques exist to estimate the monetary equivalent of risk reductions, it is rarely possible to obtain reliable monetized estimates of all of a regulation's costs and benefits. Furthermore, no well-accepted way exists to monetize the value of distributive equity or process values like transparency.

The measurement of overall regulatory excellence will unfortunately never be easy or tidy. For this reason, measurement *for* excellence should take precedence over any regulator's desire to pursue a measurement *of* excellence. In other words, regulatory leaders should not go about, as public management scholar Mark Moore puts it, "losing their minds in the quixotic pursuit of a single numeric value" that purports to reveal the regulator's overall level of excellence. Rather, the aim should be to use measurement, as Moore puts it, "to engage in 'value-oriented' management that puts the production of public value front and center but acknowledges the complexities of defining and recognizing value in the public sector."[8]

Despite the priority that measurement *for* excellence should receive, the leaders of a regulatory organization might believe that measurement *of* excellence could help motivate major transformations throughout their organization. Perhaps it could encourage their workforce to improve by measuring how the organization is progressing along the regulatory excellence path. Measurement for this purpose is analogous to a traditional community fundraiser sign that, often fashioned to look like a thermometer, indicates how close the fundraising campaign is to reaching its goal. A more contemporary example in today's digital era is GoFundMe.com's symbol, which looks like a cell phone's battery level.

Calling to mind the oft-repeated aphorism that "what gets measured gets managed," it is not unreasonable to think that performance measurement could play a key role in effectuating major cultural change at a regulatory organization. Yet as much as performance measurement should factor into any effort to transform and improve a regulatory organization, measurement can play only a circumscribed role in the process of organizational change. By itself, measurement will not facilitate major change, old aphorisms notwithstanding. As public management scholar Allen Schick has explained, "the great mistake of the performance measurement industry is the notion that an organization can be transformed by measuring its performance." He notes that such "optimism is not justified, for organizations—public and private alike—can assimilate or deflect data on performance without making significant changes in their behavior."[9]

Rather than performance measurement leading organizational change, organizational change needs to lead performance measurement. Managers and staff need to buy into the notion that both change and measurement are important. They need to want to use performance measurement and take it seriously, not merely to game the system. This is why, as Bob Behn has noted, "real performance management requires active leadership."[10]

## MASTERING MEASUREMENT CHALLENGES

For the leaders of regulatory institutions, measurement of regulatory performance is not, then, an abstract, academic exercise. It is a tool they must use actively and purposefully to get feedback, demonstrate progress, identify weaknesses that need shoring up, and fill other internal and external needs for information. Measurement helps leaders learn better what works (and what does not), identify and track regulatory problems, communicate progress, and ultimately manage for continuous improvement.

To make measurement matter, it not only must speak to and be integrated with regulatory managers' goals; it also must be based on meaningful and reliable measures. What makes measures meaningful will, of course, in large part be determined by how they speak to the purposes measurement aims to serve. But they also have to align with the values and priorities of their audience. In other contexts, as already noted, ratings and measures work when they speak to and support the choices that people wish to make. The attributes and weighting used by the raters need to match up with the preferences of an individual decisionmaker. *Consumer Reports* may prioritize "ease of use" in a smart phone, but a savvy young computer engineer and a senior citizen are likely to care about that attribute differently. Undoubtedly, parents of young children find movie rating systems that measure violence and sexual content more useful than do other adults.

The U.S. Centers for Medicare and Medicaid Services cautions about overreliance on its rating system for nursing homes precisely because of the potential for mismatch between ratings and the needs of individuals who might be affected by their use:

> No rating system can address all of the important considerations that go into a decision about which nursing home may be best for a particular person. Examples include the extent to which specialty care is provided (such as specialized rehabilitation or dementia care) or how easy it will be for family members to visit the nursing home resident. As such visits can improve both the resident's quality of life and quality of care, it may often be better to select a nursing home that is very close, compared to a higher rated nursing home that would be far away.[11]

Furthermore, even if a measurement system captures the "right" attributes, it still has to measure them accurately, which is not always guaranteed. For example, a restaurant's hygiene scores are typically based on the results of a single visit by a health inspector; they do not guarantee that kitchen countertops are wiped down cleanly on the day that you dine there.

It is also possible for a measurement system to miss the forest by focusing on the trees. Studies of corporate governance rating systems, for example, have found that the rankings these systems provide do not necessarily correlate well with firms' actual financial performance, presumably what investors care about most.[12] In the wake of the 2008 financial crisis, credit rating agencies have been subjected to intense criticism for favorable ratings given to Lehman Brothers and other firms heavily invested in risky mortgage-backed securities. Ultimately, the sum of the measured parts may not necessarily lead to an accurate "whole" assessment of quality.

Like their private sector counterparts, public sector performance measurement systems face a variety of measurement challenges. That is, they might not rely on the "right" attributes (key performance indicators), errors might arise in measuring the attributes, the weights given to different attributes by the rater might differ from the weights others think they should have, and the sum of the attributes might not lead to the resulting whole that users and decisionmakers care about most.

But public sector performance measurement can face some unique challenges too. One potentially distinctive challenge in the governmental sphere relates to the relative importance given to the "parts" versus the "whole." The specific attributes, or parts, of an electronic product like a cell phone do matter to people, so it makes a lot of sense to rate such products based on these attributes (for example, display quality and battery life). With respect to governmental programs or agencies, it is less clear whether the specific parts matter as much, at least to the general public. To many people, what matters most are the outcomes that a government program or organization achieves: the whole. Is the air getting cleaner? Is the economy prospering? Are highways safe?

To be sure, citizens do and should care about certain attributes or parts of a governmental entity, such as its fidelity to democratic principles, its transparency, and so forth. Indeed, what we know from social psychologists about procedural justice suggests that, in addition to substantive outcomes, people care about the nature of their interactions with government; they care about process and about how they are treated.[13] Nevertheless, on many attributes that might be used to measure governmental quality, perhaps few will care very much about the specific attributes of the program or agency, such as its organizational practices and its processes. As long as government "works," it undoubtedly matters little to many people how governmental entities organize their routines, what kind of human resources and computer systems they deploy, whether they use performance standards or means standards, or whether they rely on adversarial or cooperative enforcement strategies. One might well imagine that if Rome were burning (or if it were prospering beyond measure), few people would care whether their governmental entities checked all the boxes in a rating system of regulatory quality.

Performance measurement in the regulatory sphere will also be complicated by the fact that government's performance—especially the performance of government regulators—is dependent on the performance of others, namely those they regulate. Unlike the rating of a manufacturer's cell phone, which can be based on the individual phones that the company produced and that rest in the testers' own hands, a regulator's performance rests in the hands of someone else (the regulated entity).

Regulators' dependence on others not only creates some difficulties in accurately measuring their performance (especially when comparing different regulators), but the multilayered nature of regulatory performance has another important implication. A regulator could be ranked very highly on any number of metrics (for example, it could be highly transparent about its rules; it could treat its employees well and train them to meet high professional standards, etc.), and yet the industry it regulates might still experience a disaster that the regulator was supposed to prevent. In other words, because responsibility for risk control in the regulatory sphere is shared between the regulator and the regulated, a failure by the latter will inevitably be viewed as a failure on the part of the former, notwithstanding even a high ranking of the former on the metrics of a performance measurement system. The best measures of regulatory performance may therefore be those that are closely connected to, or capable of being connected to, the regulator and not susceptible to dilution or signaling noise by the actions of others.

In the end, we can say that the most meaningful regulatory performance measures will exhibit three main characteristics, each with two defining features. The best measures will be:

1. **Relevant**

   *Related.* Measures need to speak to the goals of the user. If they are not related, they cannot be useful.

   *Tight.* The more closely or tightly connected measures are to their purpose and to what they represent (for example, the regulator's performance), the better they will be.

2. **Reliable**

   *Accurate.* Measures need to be accurate. Garbage in, garbage out.

   *Resistant.* Measures that can be easily gamed or manipulated will not turn out to be very reliable.

3. **Realistic**

   *Available.* Measures should have data associated with them or such data should be able to be gathered with reasonable time and money.

   *Intelligible.* Measures should be understandable to their intended audience.

In developing performance measurement systems, regulators need to keep these key characteristics in mind, assessing their selection of each measure with care.

### METHODS OF MEASUREMENT

In addition to using relevant, reliable, and realistic measures, regulators must deploy appropriate *methods* of performance assessment. Some methods seek simply to track the actions of regulatory officials and document how they are carrying out their work. Others track conditions in the world, including changes in the behavior of regulated entities, to determine if conditions are getting better or worse. Still other methods try to do more than track actions or outcomes; they seek to link measures of the regulator's actions with measures of conditions in the world, with the aim of determining whether the regulator is indeed causing positive change in the world. In other words, the regulator can choose from one or more of the following three methods of measuring regulatory quality, but only the last of these can truly inform conclusions about whether the regulator is making a difference:

1. *Actions.* Learn about the regulator and what policies it is adopting and administrative actions it is taking.

2. *Outcomes.* Learn about the world outside the regulator (for example, measures of regulated entities' behavior or of perceptual or substantive outcomes or conditions).

3. *Causation* (Actions → Outcomes). Learn about the extent to which the regulator (#1) is causing any (positive) changes in the world (#2).

Only the last of these three—what can be called *causal attribution evaluation*—can definitively answer persistent questions about whether and how well regulation is working. Only evaluation can explain reliably *why* problems are getting better (or worse) and, more important, whether the work of the regulator has anything to do with whatever change has occurred.

To undertake noncausal measurement—that is, either of the first two measurement methods—a measurement team needs "only" relevant, reliable, and realistic measures on either actions or outcomes. To undertake evaluation, the third method, more than just relevant, reliable, and realistic measures are needed. Also needed is a method of evaluation that will support valid causal inferences, specifically either randomization or statistical techniques that essentially replicate randomization.[14] These latter techniques include multiple regression, propensity scoring, difference-in-differences, instrumental variables, and regression discontinuity.[15]

Causal attribution evaluation can be even more challenging and often more time-consuming than noncausal forms of performance measurement. As a result, an excellent regulator will not be able to subject everything to the most careful, ex post causal evaluation research. But the best regulators will dedicate some resources to rigorous causal evaluations on an ongoing basis because only these kinds of evaluations can definitively determine whether particular regulations, programs, or enforcement strategies are working.

## MEASUREMENT AND INCENTIVES

Measurement and evaluation offer practical insights to the leaders of a regulatory organization, but how they should respond to measurement findings raises another set of questions concerning whether or how to link measurement scores to organizational incentives. Before linking, regulatory managers should tread carefully. When performance measures are used to evaluate employees or to support other internal incentives, they may crowd out intrinsic motivations and lead to problems captured under the banner of "teaching to the test." Shelley Metzenbaum, who led the U.S. Office and Management and Budget's effort to implement performance management in the Obama administration, has cautioned about overreliance on government rating scores for management decisions in government:

> Perhaps the biggest problem is that [directly tying incentives to performance measures] mistakenly suggests that the true objective of performance management is hitting a target rather than improving performance and increasing public-value return on investment. Many of us working in and with government are trying hard to reset this mistaken mind-set, treating target attainment as the purpose rather than a means to an end. It is my hope that researchers, in choosing areas and methods of study, will redirect their inquiries to the real purpose of performance management: continually finding and applying government practices that work better.[16]

Of course, the potential for misuse of performance measurement systems exists in any setting where ratings are used to measure the performance of individuals, teams, or organizations, whether in the private or the public sector. But if rating systems in the public sector are primarily intended to be used for managerial decisions to shape organizational incentives, concerns about misuse or misaligned incentives may well take on heightened importance because the measures themselves are likely to be imperfect or incomplete due to the very measurement challenges discussed earlier in this chapter. Donald Moynihan correctly concluded in chapter 17 of this volume that public managers should avoid linking "high-powered incentives to goals you can only measure imperfectly."

## A STRATEGIC APPROACH TO MEASUREMENT

Developing a sound measurement strategy—that is, reaching clarity on the purposes of measurement, finding and using appropriate measures and methods, and avoiding dysfunctional incentive structures—will seldom be easy. But it can be done. Moynihan's twelve principles for performance management in chapter 17 offer valuable practical guidance to the regulatory leader seeking to use measurement to achieve excellence. What he terms "purposeful" measurement will make a good tool for learning, and learning, after all, should be a core part of the excellent regulator's culture. Of course, using performance measurement to learn does not mean the goal should be learning for learning's sake alone. Regulatory leaders need to be strategic about measurement. To use measurement well, regulatory managers need to know what they seek to learn, who will use that knowledge, and how that knowledge will contribute to decisionmaking.

Measurement can focus either narrowly or broadly on regulators' actions or conditions in the world, including industry behavior. Narrower measurements can be used to inform decisionmakers about specific conditions or problems (for example, automobile exhaust emissions) or about how specific policies, regulations, and programs are working (for example, an auto emissions regulation). At their narrowest, performance review measures can be applied to individual employees and their work.

Contrasted with such narrow and focused measures are broader ones that can serve other purposes. Broader measures can help policymakers understand general patterns and trends in conditions or problems, such as measures of overall ambient air quality that might be relevant to an environmental regulator, or service reliability scores that might be relevant to an electricity or telecommunications regulator. Broader measures can also help provide a wide-angle picture of what the regulatory organization as a whole is doing, such as measures of its total budget or the annual number of inspections. The broadest conceivable measurement would be an overall "excellence assessment"—at the extreme, that quixotic hope for a single number. Less extreme but still very broad measures can inform a regulator's top leadership as well as political overseers and the public about the performance of the regulator as a whole.

Regulators need a range of measures, narrow and broad. Narrower measures, focused on existing programs and ongoing problems, are the kind that regulators routinely track. They sometimes fall under an established performance measurement or performance management system. Examples of such systems include the Balanced Scorecard, Six Sigma, and Lean.[17] Whichever system is used, the key is for the regulator to obtain well-defined feedback that informs decisions about adjustments to existing programs and practices or about whether to start new ones. The excellent regulator needs that kind of performance information on a regular basis, even daily, in order to learn continuously how to allocate resources and design or modify specific rules, practices, and programs.[18] This is measurement *for* excellence.

But the regulator must also take pains to avoid what is known as the "lamp-post problem." This problem's name derives from an old joke about a drunk man who late at night looks for his lost keys under a streetlight outside a bar, even though he knows he dropped them in the parking lot, far away from the lamppost. The drunk says he is looking under the lamppost "because that's where the light is." The excellent regulator should obviously be more deliberate. Whether designing measurement *for* or *of* excellence, its leaders must start by determining what general attributes of excellence they aspire to improve—say, competence, engagement, or integrity—and then proceed to define more specific attributes, find indicators, obtain data sources, choose methods, and determine when third-party evaluators or peer review may be needed.[19]

More specific attributes of excellence will sometimes take the form of prox-ies for the more general attributes, and other times they will constitute build-ing blocks. For example, the presence (or absence) of a whistleblower policy might provide the basis for a measure of the regulator's overall integrity—a general attribute of regulatory excellence—even though the policy is a building block of integrity and not itself a direct measure of overall integrity. Indeed, perhaps no direct measure could exist for integrity qua integrity, in its most general form. Assessors may therefore need to rely entirely on building blocks and proxies for the attributes of excellence that they seek to measure. For in-tegrity, proxy measures could include surveys of people's perceptions of the integrity of a regulator. Or building blocks like transparency could be mea-sured. Since a highly transparent regulator will presumably have less ability to cover up poor or biased decisions, measures of transparency might provide good indicators for integrity.

The point is that even if direct measures are not available, attributes of ex-cellence can be meaningfully operationalized and indirectly measured. Of course, the specific ways of operationalizing core attributes like integrity, en-gagement, and competence will vary from regulator to regulator, and some of these ways will be clearly more relevant, reliable, and realistic than others. The best ways of operationalizing attributes of excellence will also likely need to change over time. Regulators' priorities change; as some old problems are solved, new ones take priority that then call for measurement. Industry changes too. Data on horse-and-buggy crashes are no longer needed, but the need for data on automobile drivers' distraction by cell phones certainly has become salient.

As industry and societal needs change and as the regulator learns more, prompting changes in measurement protocols, a tradeoff will emerge that the excellent regulator must seek to address: a tradeoff between measurement ad-aptation and continuity. The greater precision and relevance that derives from updating measures over time can come at the cost of comparability across time, sacrificing what is needed to discern trends and conduct causal attribution evaluation on a time-series basis. For an excellent regulator, some performance measurement data will need to stay the same to serve some purposes, while other measures will always change to serve other purposes.

## ON MAKING COMPARISONS

Regulators can always learn from other regulators, but can they also benefit from comparing their performance measures with those of other regulators? The appeal of benchmarking or ranking against other regulators is strong for much the same reason that people find appealing the rankings of colleges, football teams, and any number of other popular schemes for comparing different entities. Which regulator is best in its class? Despite the desire to answer questions like this, any effort at comparative performance measurement must overcome at least four hurdles.

First, not all regulators face the same problems, the same social and economic environments, or the same kinds of regulated firms. The U.S. Office of the Comptroller of the Currency and the Rhode Island Department of Business Regulation's Banking Division both regulate banks, but they are hardly comparable institutions, and they do not confront the same magnitude or types of regulatory problems. The Pennsylvania Department of Environmental Protection oversees a large and growing natural gas industry, but it does not have large oil sands operations to regulate like the Alberta Energy Regulator does.

Second, data are not always well aligned across jurisdictions. What counts as an oil "spill" in one jurisdiction, for example, might not be a spill elsewhere. In 2012, the Energy Resources Conservation Board in Alberta, Canada, a predecessor of the Alberta Energy Regulator, commissioned a pipeline safety review that sought to compare the efficacy of regulation in the province with regulation in other jurisdictions. The authors of the review report concluded that such a study could not be accomplished because "comparison of pipeline leak or failure statistics for Alberta with other Canadian and international jurisdictions is not possible, as each jurisdiction has unique requirements as to which incidents, and what detail[s, must be] reported."[20]

Comparability of data systems across jurisdictions is not, of course, inherently insurmountable. If jurisdictions can cooperate and coordinate, they may be able to harmonize their data systems to facilitate comparative measurement and assessment. The International Regulators' Forum on Global Offshore Safety has initiated a Performance Measures Project designed to develop a "common framework" for data collection by its members for incidents such as gas releases, collisions, and fires.[21]

Third, comparison raises the classic breadth-versus-depth tradeoff. Superficial comparisons may be possible using tractable data. Some studies, for example, try to compare the rules on the books.[22] But such comparisons are not particularly meaningful if the implementation and enforcement of rules are not also compared. The law on the books is almost never the same as the law in action. Moreover, laws on the books are not the same as outcomes or actual performance in solving the problems the regulator has been charged to solve.[23]

Finally, comparative assessments face another problem if a regulator seeks to use them to provide a measure *of* excellence: just because a regulator ranks well against other regulators does not necessarily mean it is an excellent regulator. It could simply be a regulator that is a little better than a lot of other regulators that happen to be rather mediocre.

Given these challenges, no regulatory leader should think it will be easy to declare its organization as having achieved excellence by reference to other regulators in the same field. Instead, as with performance measurement generally, learning should be the priority in making comparative assessments.[24] The value for a regulator in benchmarking lies less in finding out how it stacks up against peers in some kind of rating system than in learning potentially better ways of doing the hard work of regulating. The excellent regulator will be eager to exchange ideas with other regulators and be open to finding potentially superior means of regulating risks, conducting public engagement, and ensuring compliance.

## CONCLUSION

In the end, learning is the key to measurement, but it must be learning with a purpose. Learning objectives should motivate and guide all choices about regulatory performance measurement. How useful will a measurement system be to a regulator? That can only be answered by asking further: useful to whom and for what purposes?

Measurement not only needs to be useful but it must also be realistic. Not all performance measurement can take the form of causal evaluations, as sometimes these will take too long to generate useful results, or other times they will be practically impossible due to a lack of data or other constraints. That said, it is also not realistic for regulatory officials to ignore causality altogether. If they never seek to draw any causal inferences, they will never be sure that they are not investing large amounts of organizational resources to accomplish little or nothing, when those resources could be better spent somewhere else.

A key purpose of measurement is to find out if regulatory actions are effective, cost-effective, efficient, and equitable. If they are, they should be continued and even emulated. If they are not, they should presumably be discontinued or modified. Without measurement, and without at least some causal evaluation research, regulatory authorities and their leaders simply cannot learn very well. And without learning, they cannot expect to achieve regulatory excellence.

**NOTES**

1. Ginger Zhe Jin and Phillip Leslie, "The Effect of Information on Product Quality: Evidence from Restaurant Hygiene Grade Cards," *Quarterly Journal of Economics* 118 (2003): 409–51.

2. Thomas C. Frohlich and others, *The Best and Worst Run States in America: A Survey of All 50* (December 3, 2015) (http://247wallst.com/special-report/2015/12/03/the-best-and-worst-run-states-in-america-a-survey-of-all-50-4/).

3. See, for example, Donald P. Moynihan and Stéphane Lavertu, "Does Involvement in Performance Reforms Encourage Performance Information Use? Evaluating GPRA and PART," *Public Administration Review* 72 (2012): 592–602.

4. See, for example, United Nations E-Government Survey 2014: E-Government for the Future We Want (2014) (https://publicadministration.un.org/egovkb/Portals/egovkb/Documents/un/2014-Survey/E-Gov_Complete_Survey-2014.pdf).

5. The World Bank ranks countries based on the "ease" of doing business. World Bank, *Doing Business 2016: Measuring Regulatory Quality and Efficiency* (October 27, 2015) (www.doingbusiness.org/reports/global-reports/doing-business-2016). The OECD conducts a survey of its member countries in order to develop a series of indicators on regulation. See, for example, Isabell Koske and others, "The 2013 Update of the OECD's Database on Product Market Regulation: Policy Insights for OECD and Non-OECD Countries" (Paris: OECD Economics Department Working Papers, 2015).

6. "Rating Enforcement 2015," *Global Competition Review* (June 18, 2015).

7. Bob Behn, "Why Measure Performance? Different Purposes Require Different Measures," *Public Administration Review* 63 (2003): 586.

8. Mark H. Moore, *Recognizing Public Value* (Harvard University Press, 2013), p. 47.

9. Allen Schick, "Getting Performance Measures to Measure Up," in *Quicker, Better, Cheaper? Managing Performance in American Government,* edited by Dall W. Forsythe (SUNY Press, 2001), p. 43.

10. Robert D. Behn, "What Performance Management Is and Is Not," *Government Executive,* November 19, 2014 (www.govexec.com/excellence/promising-practices/2014/11/what-performancemanagement-and-not/99284/).

11. Centers for Medicare and Medicaid Services, "Five-Star Quality Rating System" (2015) (www.cms.gov/Medicare/Provider-Enrollment-and-Certification/CertificationandComplianc/FSQRS.html).

12. Roberta Romano, Sanjai Bhagat, and Brian Bolton, "The Promise and Peril of Corporate Governance Indices," *Columbia Law Review* 108 (2008): 1803.

13. See, for example, E. Allan Lind and Tom R. Tyler, *The Social Psychology of Procedural Justice* (New York: Plenum, 1988).

14. For a discussion of the advantages of randomization, see Michael Abramowicz, Ian Ayres, and Yair Listokin, "Randomizing Law," *University of Pennsylvania Law Review* 159 (2011): 929–1005.

15. For an overview of these techniques for the regulator, see Cary Coglianese, *Measuring Regulatory Performance: Evaluating the Impact of Regulation and Regulatory Policy* (Paris: OECD, 2012) (www.oecd.org/gov/regulatory-policy/1_coglianese%20web.pdf). For an in-depth treatment, see, for example, Joshua D. Angrist and Jörn-Steffen Pischke, *Mostly Harmless Econometrics: An Empiricist's Companion* (Princeton University Press, 2009).

16. Shelley H. Metzenbaum, "Performance Management: The Real Research Challenge," *Public Administration Review* 73 (2013): 857–58.

17. Managers in a number of governmental entities have found systems such as lean enterprise and Six Sigma to contribute positively to process improvements. See, for example, U.S. Environmental Protection Agency, "Lean Government" (2015) (www.epa.gov/lean/government/index.htm).

18. Jim Collins, *Good to Great and the Social Sectors* (New York: HarperCollins, 2005).

19. On the attributes of regulatory excellence, see Cary Coglianese, *Listening, Learning, and Leading: A Framework for Regulatory Excellence* (University of Pennsylvania, Penn Program on Regulation, 2015) (www.law.upenn.edu/live/files/4946-pprfinalconvenersreportpdf).

20. Group 10 Engineering, Alberta Pipeline Safety Review (December 7, 2012), p. 5 (www.energy.alberta.ca/Org/pdfs/PSRfinalReportNoApp.pdf).

21. International Regulators' Forum, *IRF Performance Measurement Project* (www.irfoffshoresafety.com/country/performance/scope.aspx).

22. WorleyParsons, *An International Comparison of Leading Oil and Gas Producing Regions: Environmental Regulation* (2014) (www.capp.ca/-/media/capp/customer-portal/documents/249637.pdf?la=en).

23. Brown and others caution, "The danger of limiting an evaluation to what is written in laws and decrees . . . is that it may give an inaccurate picture of how the regulatory system works in practice. Although such evaluations can be done quickly, they may also be very mistaken." Ashley C. Brown and others, *Handbook for Evaluating Infrastructure Regulatory Systems* (Washington: World Bank, 2006), p. 39 (http://siteresources.worldbank.org/EXTENERGY/Resources/336805-1156971270190/HandbookForEvaluatingInfrastructureRegulation062706.pdf).

24. Others have similarly cautioned against expecting more than this from comparative assessment. See ibid.; Martin Cole and Greg Parston, *Unlocking Public Value: A New Model for Achieving High Performance in Public Service Organizations* (Hoboken, N.J.: Wiley, 2006), p. 108.

# Contributors

**ROBERT BALDWIN** is Professor of Law at the London School of Economics and Political Science.

**JOHN BRAITHWAITE** is Distinguished Professor and founder of the Regulatory Institutions Network at the Australian National University.

**CARY COGLIANESE** is the Edward B. Shils Professor of Law, Professor of Political Science, and Director of the Penn Program on Regulation at the University of Pennsylvania.

**ANGUS CORBETT** is Research Fellow at the Penn Program on Regulation.

**DANIEL C. ESTY** is the Hillhouse Professor of Environmental Law and Policy at the Yale School of Forestry and Environmental Studies and the Yale Law School, and Director of the Yale Center for Environmental Law and Policy.

**ADAM M. FINKEL** is Senior Fellow at the Penn Program on Regulation and Clinical Professor of Environmental Health Sciences at the University of Michigan School of Public Health.

**TED GAYER** is Vice President and Director of the Economic Studies Program and the Joseph A. Pechman Senior Fellow at the Brookings Institution.

**JOHN D. GRAHAM** is Dean of the Indiana University School of Public and Environmental Affairs.

**NEIL GUNNINGHAM** is Professor at the Regulatory Institutions Network at Australian National University and Director of the National Research Centre for Occupational Health and Safety Regulation.

**KATHRYN HARRISON** is Professor of Political Science at the University of British Columbia.

**BRIDGET M. HUTTER** is Professor of Risk Regulation in the Department of Sociology at the London School of Economics and Political Science.

**HOWARD KUNREUTHER** is the James G. Dinan Professor at the Wharton School at the University of Pennsylvania and Co-director of the Wharton Risk Management and Decision Processes Center.

**DAVID LEVI-FAUR** is the Head of the Federmann School of Public Policy and a member of the faculty in the Department of Political Science at the Hebrew University of Jerusalem.

**SHELLEY H. METZENBAUM** is a consultant and Senior Fellow at the Volcker Alliance, where she was its founding President.

**DONALD P. MOYNIHAN** is Professor of Public Affairs at the Robert M. La Follette School of Public Affairs at the University of Wisconsin, Madison.

**PAUL R. NOE** is the Vice President for Public Policy at the American Forest and Paper Association.

**GAURAV VASISHT** is the Director of Financial Regulation at the Volcker Alliance.

**DAVID VOGEL** is Professor Emeritus at the Haas School of Business and the Department of Political Science at the University of California, Berkeley.

**WENDY WAGNER** is the Joe A. Worsham Centennial Professor at the University of Texas School of Law.

# Acknowledgments

**THIS BOOK GREW OUT** of an expert dialogue session held at the University of Pennsylvania Law School in March 2015. The two-day session was part of a larger "best-in-class" regulator initiative convened under the auspices of the Penn Program on Regulation (PPR) and initiated and sponsored by the Alberta Energy Regulator (AER). The AER, which serves as the single regulator of oil, natural gas, coal, and oil sands development within the Canadian province of Alberta, sought PPR's help in leading a process that would generate guideposts and strategies for improving regulatory performance. A relatively new organization at the time, the AER aspires "to do more than regulate well" but instead to "be recognized for regulatory excellence, innovation, and delivering measurable results at home and around the world."

PPR's best-in-class regulator initiative was designed to inform the AER's efforts to achieve its high aspirations. The initiative aimed both to convene deliberative processes and to develop a framework of regulatory excellence that could be applied by any regulator seeking to go beyond merely good, or even great, performance. With the AER's goal of becoming a "world leading regulatory organization," part of the initiative involved engaging with leading experts from around the world in the quest to understand what regulatory excellence means and what strategies can be used to achieve it. I brought together a group of global academic experts (several of whom also had high-level regulatory experience) and engaged with them in two days of intense dialogue with a diverse international group of experienced regulators, business leaders, and representatives from public interest advocacy groups. The chapters in this book resulted from that dialogue.

Needless to say, I give my thanks first to the authors of these chapters. They took on a unique but vital challenge to think holistically about what makes for an excellent regulator, and they met this challenge under demanding deadlines. I also want to express my heartfelt thanks to the other participants in the expert dialogue: Valerie Baron, Alan Barstow, Darryl Biggar, Rob Brightwell, Filippo Cavassini, Tim Church, Jim Ellis, Ted Enoch, Elise Harrington, Brad Herald, John Hollway, Deirdre Hutton, David Kessler, Eric Kimmel, Matt Lepore, David Mitchell, Eric Orts, Marcus Peacock, Adam Peltz, Susan Phillips, Wendell Pritchett, Chris Severson-Baker, Shari Shapiro, Michael Silverstein, Harris Sokoloff, Dan Walters, and Peter Watson. The outstanding staff at Penn Law played key roles in supporting the dialogue, including Anna Gavin, Norva Hall, and Debbie Rech. Several Penn students—Kaiya Arroyo, Chris Henry, Elise Harrington, Matt McCabe, Andrew Schlossberg, and Zach Sinemus—ensured that we came away from the dialogue with helpful notes, while Shari Shapiro worked with me to prepare a summary report of the ideas exchanged. Jennifer Evans, Chelsey Hanson, Alexandra Johnson, Jennifer Ko, Benjamin Meltzer, Melody Negron, Evan Silverstein, Yoko Takahashi, Timothy Von Dulm, and Janet Walker provided superb assistance with the various research and formatting tasks essential to putting this book's manuscript together. I cannot thank Bill Finan, the editorial director at the Brookings Institution Press, enough for his support and guidance.

In addition to the expert dialogue we held in Philadelphia, my PPR team and I convened two provincial dialogues in Alberta, conducted over sixty individual interviews, undertook a variety of complementary research projects, convened a Washington, D.C., dialogue with high-level U.S. regulatory leaders, and participated in discussions with the OECD's Network of Economic Regulators. Interested readers can learn more about PPR's full initiative at www.bestinclassregulator.org, where they can also download the initiative's final report. The acknowledgments and appendices of that final report list many other individuals whose efforts were crucial to the success of the entire project, and who therefore also helped to enrich this book. I renew here my expressions of appreciation to everyone I listed there. Angus Corbett, Adam Finkel, Shari Shapiro, Harris Sokoloff, and Dan Walters deserve special mention for being such invaluable—and dearly valued—collaborators on the overall initiative, and time and again Anna Gavin exemplified the essence of excellence through her stellar competence in overseeing all of the initiative's moving parts.

Without question, this book would simply not have been possible had it not been for the Alberta Energy Regulator and its leaders' vision in conceiving, initiating, and commissioning the larger project of which this book is a part. Not content just to do their jobs well, the AER's leaders have committed themselves publicly to a process of continual listening, learning, and leading, so as to deliver the highest possible level of public value. Not only do they seek to secure transformative value for all Albertans, they are also remarkably generous in sharing what they learn with others throughout Canada and around the world. I know they helped me and the others involved in this project learn a great deal, productively grounding much of our thinking in day-to-day regulatory struggles. I want especially to thank Jim Ellis for his public-spirited leadership and his engagement throughout this project. Kirk Bailey, Kim Blanchette, Tim Church, Richard Dixon, Deborah Eastlick, Tristan Goodman, Cal Hill, Diane Holloway, Eric Kimmel, Tiffany Novotny, Carey-Ann Ramsay, Jennifer Steber, and Zeeshan Syed are just a few of those who serve or have served with the AER who supported this project. Their dedication to regulatory excellence infuses the pages of this book.

My extraordinarily supportive family deserves, and has, my unending love and gratitude, most especially Debra, for sustaining my spirit and sharing her incredible wisdom and understanding; Anne, John, and Patrick, as well as Erin and now Bridget and Calvin, both for inspiring me and keeping me centered; and my mother and siblings, for always believing in me. Finally, this book is dedicated to the memory of my dear professor, mentor, and friend, Dr. Orville G. Cope, who taught by example what arête means.

# Index